INTERNATIONAL POLITICAL ECONOMY

The Struggle for Power and Wealth

INTERNATIONAL POLITICAL ECONOMY

The Struggle for Power and Wealth

Thomas D. Lairson
Rollins College

David Skidmore
Drake University

Harcourt Brace College Publishers

FORT WORTH PHILADELPHIA SAN DIEGO NEW YORK ORLANDO AUSTIN SAN ANTONIO
TORONTO MONTREAL LONDON SYDNEY TOKYO

Publisher: Ted Buchholz
Acquisitions Editor: David Tatom
Developmental Editor: Fritz Schanz
Project Editor: Deanna M. Johnson
Production Manager: Debra A. Jenkin
Book Designer: Carol Kincaid
Cover Designer: Candice Swanson

ISBN: 0-03-054589-7

Library of Congress Number: 92-81265

Address editorial correspondence to:
301 Commerce Street, Suite 3700
Fort Worth, TX 76102

Address orders to:
6277 Sea Harbor Drive
Orlando, FL 32887
1-800-782-4479 outside Florida
1-800-433-0001 inside Florida

PRINTED IN THE UNITED STATES OF AMERICA

3 4 5 6 7 8 9 0 1   016   9 8 7 6 5 4 3 2

PREFACE

T he writing of this textbook was motivated by the concern that students often find the study of international political economy a formidable task. Because the subject lies at the intersection of economics and political science, students face the daunting prospect of mastering and integrating two complex fields. Despite the merits of existing international political economy textbooks, we think they underestimate the challenges facing both students and instructors. Such textbooks do not explain basic economic concepts; do not provide a well-rounded integration of history, theory, and policy; and are not written in an accessible style.

We, therefore, set out to write a textbook that is clear and readable and that does not sacrifice sophistication and rigor. We also wanted to produce a book accessible enough to be used as a supplement in an introductory international relations course but challenging enough to be assigned as a main textbook for upper-level courses.

In addition to clarity and readability, we have included several features that set this book apart. Throughout the text, we depict the international political economy as a realm of both struggle and cooperation. We show how these contrary imperatives coexist and how the mix between the two varies over time, across countries, and with issues. In pursuing this theme, we weave together theory, concepts, and arguments throughout and tie these ideas closely to the topics under discussion.

Several chapters are particularly distinguishable in comparison with other texts. Chapter 2 clearly explains economic concepts and terms important to the field of international political economy. Chapter 3 traces the development of the world economy during the nineteenth and early twentieth centuries. This historical background allows students to appreciate the enormous swings that can take place in the economic fortunes of countries over time while also placing contemporary events in historical context. Chapter 6 examines the issue of national competitiveness in the contemporary world. The strategies and fortunes of the United States, Japan, and the European states receive special attention. Chapter 8 explores the sources of international economic inequality. It offers a critical evaluation of modernization and dependency theories, two competing perspectives on the development gap between North and South. Looking ahead, Chapter 12 compares alternative scenarios concerning the future balance between struggle and cooperation in the world economy.

We include a number of pedagogical aids, including illustrations and tables, anecdotes, an annotated bibliography at the end of each chapter, and a glossary of essential terms at the end of the textbook.

We thank the editors at Harcourt Brace Jovanovich, including David Tatom, Acquisitions Editor, who first took this project under his wing; Martin Lewis and Fritz Schanz, Developmental Editors, who provided help and guidance at different stages in the preparation of the manuscript; and Deanna Johnson, Project Editor, who guided the book through production. We also appreciate the advice offered by reviewers: Timothy Amen, University of Puget Sound; Steve Chan, University of Colorado; Robert Denemark, University of Delaware; Esmail Hosseinzadeh, Drake University; George Kieh, Illinois Wesleyan University; Howard Lehman, University of Utah; Michael Mastanduno, Dartmouth College; Sylvia Maxfield, Yale University; Karen Mingst, University of Kentucky; Dean Minix, University of Houston; George Modelski, University of Washington. Professor Lairson also thanks Joan Davison for her comments on Chapter 7 and Pam Martin for her help in preparing the graphics. Finally, we each thank our spouses, Sally Lairson and Charlene Skidmore, for their patience and support.

Thomas Lairson and David Skidmore

CONTENTS

CHAPTER 5

COOPERATION AMONG ADVANCED INDUSTRIAL STATES   95

CHAPTER 6

COMPETITION AND CONFLICT AMONG ADVANCED INDUSTRIAL STATES   125

CHAPTER 7

EASTERN EUROPE, THE FORMER SOVIET UNION, AND THE WORLD ECONOMY   157

CHAPTER 8

RICH AND POOR STATES IN THE WORLD ECONOMY   181

CHAPTER 9

Strategies of Southern Trade and Development   201

CHAPTER 10

Foreign Aid and Third World Development   223

CHAPTER 11

Multinational Corporations in the Third World   251

CHAPTER 12

The Politics of Third World Debt   275

CHAPTER 13

CHARTING THE FUTURE: ECONOMIC INTERDEPENDENCE AND NATIONAL COMPETITIVENESS 315

INTRODUCTION: THE POLITICS
OF INTERNATIONAL POLITICAL ECONOMY

U nderstanding international affairs is exceedingly difficult and perhaps impossible without a clear sense of how politics and economics are related. This assertion, very controversial even fifteen years ago, may still provoke dissent and perhaps confusion from students today. After all, political science is taught in one department and economics in another. One looks at power and the other at money and products. But consider the following set of anecdotes drawn from recent events and notice how power, money, and profits are entangled.

■ In a series of negotiations between Japan and the United States, known as the Strategic Impediments Initiatives Talks, each nation prepared a list of changes it believed were needed to make the other more competitive in international trade. The United States called on Japan to prosecute companies that fix prices; to change its preference for small retail outlets; to spend more on sewage plants, airports, and bridges instead of on foreign investment; and generally to make its markets more accessible. The Japanese, on the other hand, insisted that the United States reduce its large budget deficit, improve its poor educational system, and reduce its level of consumption and increase savings. They also criticized the high salaries paid to U.S. corporate executives who focus only on short term profits and fail to spend enough on research and development. This remarkable set of discussions, which produced agreement on many of these matters in April 1990, came about because of the massive trade

1

imbalances between the United States and Japan and the resulting purchase of U.S. assets by the Japanese.[1]

■ On at least two occasions, in 1989 and 1991, former Soviet President
Mikhail Gorbachev warned that his nation was close to economic collapse. He proposed making drastic changes in the Soviet political and
economic system, including a restructuring that would sweep away much
of communism and replace it with a more private, market-oriented system. In order to ease this transition and support the Soviet economy,
Gorbachev made several pleas for economic aid from the West. He even
attended an economic summit conference held annually for the leaders
of the seven most important capitalist nations. In July 1991, Gorbachev
came to London to renew his request for aid. The most important factor
prompting both the decline of communism and the Soviet leader's policies
was the immense and dynamic capitalist world economy and the military
complex sustained by it. The Soviet Union simply could not compete
with this system and its ability to generate rapid economic growth and
technological development.[2]

■ Related to events in the Soviet Union is the reunification of West and
East Germany in 1989–1990. Owing to the economic backwardness of the
East, this process will require a massive injection of aid from the West
to rebuild industries and infrastructure and support those who cannot
find employment. This process will place some pressure on German financial markets to supply perhaps the equivalent of $70 billion to $100
billion. Interest rates are likely to rise as a result. Less obvious is the
impact on the United States, where interest rates could also be forced
higher. Because the process of raising and providing capital has become
a global one and because interest rates fluctuate together, the reunification
of Germany could make it more expensive for an American to buy a
house or for an American business to borrow funds for expansion. This
process may become more intense when the incorporation of all of Eastern Europe and the former Soviet Union is contemplated.[3]

---

[1]For more detail on these discussions, see Clyde Farnsworth, "Japan Warned by U.S. Official
to Ease Imports," New York Times, October 28, 1989; Steven Weisman, "Japan, Weary of Barbs
on Trade, Tells Americans Why They Trail," New York Times, November 20, 1989; Clyde Farnsworth, "U.S., Japan Near Accord on Barriers," New York Times, April 5, 1990; Peter Truell, "U.S.,
Japan Reach Accord on Trade, Fiscal Policies," Wall Street Journal, April 6, 1990.

[2]Bill Keller, "Gorbachev Calls for a Strike Ban, Saying Economy is Near Collapse," New York
Times, October 3, 1989; Serge Schmemann, "Gorbachev Orders Republics To Halt Rebellious
Moves," New York Times, April 10, 1991; Steven Weisman, "Gorbachev Pleads For Japanese Aid
To Soviet Economy," New York Times, April 18, 1991; Francis Clines, "Gorbachev Pleads For
$100 Billion In Aid From West," New York Times, May 23, 1991; Steven Greenhouse, "Wealthy
Nations Wary Of Offering Quick Soviet Aid," New York Times, June 6, 1991.

[3]Alan Riding, "West Europeans Near A Consensus on East-Bloc Ties," New York Times, March
2, 1990; Ferdinand Protzmann, "Germans' Corporate Lag In East," New York Times, August 20,
1990; Madis Senner, "The Grim Shortage of Global Capital," New York Times, July 28, 1991.

■ Those who believe that private enterprise freed of governmental interference is the only source of dynamism in the world economy will find the close cooperation between business and government in Japan somewhat surprising. The U.S. version of this arrangement — though much less well-developed — is an obscure unit of the Defense Department known as the Defense Advanced Research Projects Agency (DARPA). Its bureaucratic location is a consequence of the willingness of Americans to tolerate close government-business ties in defense production and illustrates the strong connection between technology and national security. DARPA has played a key role in the development of several industries, especially computers and software. Today, it provides more than $250 million per year to such projects as superconductivity and high-definition television. But it also provokes strong criticism from those who fear any governmental role in defining industrial development and from others who support the principle underlying the agency but object to the role of the military. Perhaps the key question raised by DARPA is whether success in the world economy today demands a major role for government in subsidizing and even selecting where research and development funds for expensive and risky high technology should be spent.[4]

■ The politics of business and government relations is also a crucial element of the world aircraft industry. Recent gains in global market share by the European consortium Airbus have hurt U.S. companies which have historically dominated this market. And the fact that Airbus is partially state-owned has led to complaints of unfair subsidies and threats of a trade war. Between 1988 and 1990, Airbus increased its world market share of commercial jet aircraft from 15 percent to 34 percent, cutting Boeing's from 59 percent to 34 percent and McDonnell Douglas' from 22 percent to 15 percent. Government subsidies for development costs may have permitted Airbus which is owned by private companies from Germany and Great Britain and state-owned companies in France and Spain, to undercut the prices of the American firms. The Airbus case has helped prompt calls for similar actions by the U.S. government in order to preserve America's market share. Meanwhile, Boeing and McDonnell Douglas are independently scrambling to devise a plan to counter this new competitive environment.[5]

■ Our last vignette helps to point out the consequences of international economic interdependence and the role of government power and money

---

[4]Andrew Pollack, "America's Answer to Japan's MITI," *New York Times*, March 5, 1989; Bob Davis, "Favored Few: Pentagon Unit Steers Supercomputer Deals to Certain Companies," *Wall Street Journal*, August 6, 1991; William Broad, "Pentagon Wizards of Technology Eye Wider Civilian Role," *New York Times*, October 22, 1991.

[5]Steven Greenhouse, "There's No Stopping Europe's Airbus Now," *New York Times*, June 23, 1991; Artemis March, "The Future of the U.S. Aircraft Industry," *Technology Review*, January 1990, 26–36.

in supporting that system. During a serious recession in 1982, the U.S. government took steps to prevent a loan default by Mexico to U.S. and other foreign banks. We provided additional loans to Mexico, supported loans by the International Monetary Fund, and lowered interest rates, thereby reducing the annual payments of Mexico and other debtor states. These actions also served to protect the interests of those U.S. banks who had loaned Mexico and other Third World states nearly $100 billion. The U.S. Secretary of the Treasury, Donald Regan — a former Wall Street tycoon — defended this policy before Congress. He pointed out that a loan default would invariably lead to a contraction in U.S. bank lending at home and would probably force interest rates higher.

> . . . we are not talking here just about the big money-center banks and the multinational corporations. Well over 1,500 U.S. banks, or more than 10 percent of the total number of U.S. banks, have loaned money to Latin America alone. . . . Those loans, among other things, financed exports, exports that resulted in jobs, housing and investment being maintained or created throughout the United States.[6]

For Mr. Regan, an immensely practical man with a strong commitment to private enterprise and American interests, it was essential that the U.S. government spend considerable sums on protecting and preserving the international financial system.

This set of stories should make clear that the connections between politics and economics in international affairs are many and complex. We have seen how international political negotiations can lead to significant changes in the ways people live and work; how all nations are caught up in an immense world economy of production, technology, and competition that can shake the very foundations of their society; how systems of economic interdependence can have unexpected consequences for prices and profits as a result of political changes thousands of miles away; and how deeply involved governments are in helping private businesses succeed in the world economy.

These examples could be multiplied many times, but political scientists prefer to establish categories of relationships that can help us economize and organize our thinking. By way of introduction, we will focus on two broad categories: the political economy of relationships within a nation and of those among nations.

DOMESTIC POLITICAL ECONOMY

■ The nature and scope of a country's participation in the world economy is greatly affected by political decisions made within its borders. The politics

---

[6]As quoted in John C. Pool and Steve Stamos, *The ABC's of International Finance*, Lexington: Lexington Books, 1987, 80. For a detailed discussion of the debt crisis, see Chapter Eleven.

of this decision-making is often influenced by the fact that different groups are affected in different ways by involvement in the world economy: some groups win while others can be disadvantaged, which sets up a political struggle over what to do. Taxes, interest rates, decisions about tariffs, and economic negotiations with other nations are but a few of the choices involved in this process. The outcome is typically a result of both the power relationships and resources of the groups involved and the degree to which governmental leaders can act independently of those interests.

A more general version of this process is the long-standing question of how governments and private business interests are to be related in making economic decisions. Within Western capitalist states, the experience of depression and war from the 1930s to the 1950s worked to politicize economic choices and focus them on the national government. Political leaders became much more deeply involved in regulating the economy, and national prosperity became their responsibility. Presidents and prime ministers now regularly win and lose elections based on whether the economy is expanding or contracting. Further, the intensification of international economic competition has prompted many governments (like the Europeans supporting Airbus) to play a much more important role in supporting particular industries.

The increasing role of the state in economic affairs is a defining element in our study of international political economy. Even in the United States, with its long-standing and now mostly mythological notions of a sharp separation of government and business, political leaders are deeply involved in business decisions. Regulating banks and bailing out bank failures, subsidizing basic research, giving tax breaks for investors, spending on defense, maintaining incomes for the poor, imposing regulations on polluters, and managing the economy through fiscal and monetary policy are but a few of the many areas of government direction of the economy. At the same time, many other nations — especially those first moving toward industrialization in the twentieth century — have gone beyond the Western model toward an intimate business-government partnership in promoting economic growth. These governments mobilize national resources and energies, build up certain industrial sectors, and restrict access to their markets in the name of a national economic strategy. The result is to establish a competitive environment in which the capabilities of entire nations are being harnessed to succeed in the world economy.

INTERNATIONAL POLITICAL ECONOMY

■ The frequent and extensive economic interactions among nations define our second category. Perhaps the most general and least obvious point here is the relationship of the world economy to the power politics among nations. The organization of markets is made possible by the political agreements that nations reach. It is international power that defines legal relationships, creates and destroys economic opportunities, and raises and lowers profits. This comes about in many ways. The French conquest of Indochina in the nineteenth century opened that area to French entrepreneurs, many of whom made vast fortunes. The creation of the International Monetary Fund in the 1940s, made possible by the preponderance of U.S. power, eventually helped create legal rules that today permit the movement of money around the world. And raising or lowering tariffs, which affects whether and how much of a good is imported, is closely linked to simultaneous negotiations among more than 100 nations.

Similarly broad in its relevance to world affairs is the fact that the international military and political power of a nation rests largely on the dynamism of its economy. The ability to support a large military system depends on a nation's wealth, and its success in war depends on how this wealth and productive capability compares to other nations. Both the technological prowess of a nation and its ability to turn its new developments into profitable products and implements of war are central to gaining its objectives in the international arena. The extraordinary advantages enjoyed by the United States in the 1990–1991 war against Iraq and the temporary American monopoly of atomic weapons are but two of many examples of this fact. Over the past 150 years, international competition has been defined by an ever-tightening relationship among military, economic, technological, and political processes.

When we probe these links between power and economics, matters become more complex. Things are usually not quite as simple as "the strong always win and the weak lose," though this sometimes happens. One of the most important ways of thinking about the origins of a world economy examines the role of the most powerful state in establishing an open international economy, where goods and money move about with few hindrances. But this gets complicated very quickly. An especially powerful nation — what political scientists call a hegemon — wants other, weaker, nations to participate in the system voluntarily. This may require bribing them or winning the support of their political and economic leadership. At the same time, the hegemon must be careful not to let its economic advantages wipe out the economies of those states whose cooperation it needs. Much less clear is whether this process of spending money to support the system actually weakens the hegemon in the long run. Also uncertain are the consequences of hegemonic decline. Does that mean the international economic system will also decline?

Power relationships are also crucial when we shift attention to the interactions of nations of sharply different capabilities. Much of the Third World is at a considerable disadvantage in the world economy. Many of these nations were subjected to Western imperialism in the nineteenth and twentieth centuries and have poorly developed mechanisms for international competition. Their corporations are small and undercapitalized, their educational and technological systems are underfunded, and their political systems are fragmented and conflictual. It is unclear whether this state of affairs is primarily the result of the capitalist world economy and the power disadvantages of these countries or is the consequence of weaknesses in their societies. Equally uncertain is whether the small number of Third World states who have been able to accomplish strong economic growth are exceptions or are models that others need to emulate.

Also of interest is how nations of more equal power interact. The growth of the world economy in trade and money functions to connect nations together in webs of interdependence, and this forces them to work together in order to manage the consequences. Interdependence sets up a tension between the domestic politics of making decisions and the international politics of reaching agreements. When we remember that national decisions are related to domestic interests, making compromises and sacrifices so as to smooth out international problems may be difficult. Equally important, nations may try to manipulate the fact that they are less dependent than others on the world economy in order to gain advantages in negotiations; winning their support for an agreement may require that other more dependent nations make special concessions.

Thus cooperation among nations, even when there are important gains from such arrangements, may not be easy. This is also true because nations who are partners in cooperation are also engaged in competition. The examples of Airbus and DARPA show some of the ways governments can become involved in the process of economic competition. The politics of cooperation and competition in the world economy are never far apart. For example, many of the nations in Europe have agreed to cooperate much more extensively in creating a free market for goods, services, and people in 1992. Much of the reason for this action comes from the need to improve their ability to compete against the Japanese and the United States. Sometimes these efforts to promote competitiveness can have unexpected and even unwanted consequences. In the 1950s and 1960s, the United States promoted the efforts of its multinational corporations to set up operations in Europe and elsewhere. But over time, the logic of the global marketplace has turned these into truly transnational firms that produce and sell based upon attention to costs and markets around the world. In many ways, their identity as American firms may have declined, and their profit-based decisions may not further U.S. interests in competition with other countries. How does nation-based politics, intent on promoting national economic interests and supplemented by limited arenas of international cooperation, cope with the development of transnational firms that carry out a large proportion of world trade and innovation?

The shifting tides of world affairs have helped reveal the enormous importance of international political economy for understanding global politics. The processes of struggle, competition, and cooperation — always the main elements of international relations — have become increasingly focused on national capacities for generating wealth and technological innovation and for supporting institutions capable of adjusting rapidly to a changing environment. New and powerful interests in preserving and extending a global economy have been created. Nations and their leaders are involved as never before in each other's "domestic affairs." More and more, issues must be decided in international forums because behaviors and consequences spill across borders. And the collapse of Soviet power, the decline of communism, and the end of the Cold War have shifted even more of our attention toward the entanglements of international politics and economics.

APPROACHES TO INTERNATIONAL POLITICAL ECONOMY

■ What is the best way to learn about international political economy? Before answering that question, you should realize that economic and political interests are deeply engaged by how people think about this subject. Consequently, several strongly held ideologies have grown up around international political economy. Some persons — usually called liberals — promote the benefits of markets and their capacity to solve virtually all problems in the most efficient manner.[7] Others argue for policies framed around maximizing the power and interests of the nation: Mercantilists call on governments to manipulate markets so as to capture special benefits for their nation. Radicals, by contrast, believe the system of capitalism — national and international — biases economic outcomes to the benefit of certain social classes within the most powerful capitalist nations.

These three views sometimes have merit for understanding international political economy.[8] At several points in the text, we will consider these in detail. But they are more frequently abstract and general and fail to raise or adequately answer important questions. Reflective of this situation is the fact that much of the scholarly literature has moved beyond these categories. The focus in this book is less on the ideology of international political economy and much more on understanding the origins and sources of policies and outcomes.

Our purpose is to introduce the subject of international political economy by providing students with the necessary background in politics and economics and a broad overview of major topics. Although theoretical questions govern our selection of issues and problems, we believe these are much more meaningful when students have a detailed sense of the context from which

---

[7]The term "liberal" may surprise some. It refers to the philosophy of liberalism as developed in the nineteenth century.

[8]For a review and critique of these perspectives, see Robert Gilpin, *The Political Economy of International Relations*, Princeton: Princeton University Press, 1987, 25–54.

they are derived. Further, we will follow the lead of contemporary research in international political economy and focus on a set of overlapping and specific theoretical questions. The questions we address include:

■ How do governments and domestic interests affect foreign economic policy?

■ How do we understand the different ways political leaders and institutions are entangled in managing and conditioning market outcomes?

■ What is the role of political power and international institutions in shaping the terms of trade flows and capital transfers?

■ How does a nation's economic growth and technological prowess affect its international influence?

■ What are the sources of the development gap between the North and South?

■ How do domestic and international factors affect the choice of development strategies?

■ What are the sources of and barriers to international cooperation?

■ How has the character of international economic competition changed?

■ Why do different development strategies succeed and fail?

■ How do the political interests of rich and poor states affect the success of foreign aid?

■ How do we understand the relative bargaining power of North and South over the terms of foreign investment and borrowing?

These analytical themes are always wrapped into a context of background, events, stories, and anecdotes.

The purpose of this approach is to give students information they can use both to appreciate and evaluate these theoretical matters. Much attention is devoted to the history of the world economy before 1945. This period is rich in events that offer perspective on the main points of analysis: the political origins of free trade; industrialization by poor states; the shifting tides of competitive advantage; the effects of war on economic relationships; and examples of cooperation, conflict, and competition. These and many other topics are considered in the post-1945 era in terms of the rise and decline of U.S. power, the explosion of interdependence, and tenuous efforts at development in the Third World.

The plan of the book progresses the student toward a further understanding of the issues involved in international political economy. Chapters Two and Three are designed to serve as a further orientation to the subject. Chapter Two does this by offering a basic literacy in economics, developing those concepts indispensable to understanding international political economy, and Chapter Three gives some historical depth to the concept of a world economy, offering a sense of how we got to the present and some perspective on the outcome of past efforts at cooperation and struggles for international economic and political power. Chapter Four moves on to consider the special role of the United States in creating the political and economic basis for the new shape for the world economy and international interdependence after 1945. Chapters Five and Six expand the dramatic transformation of Eastern Europe and the former Soviet Union and examine at some length the major features of contemporary relations among advanced industrial states. Five considers cooperation in managing the global economy and in the formation of economic blocs. Six focuses on the problems of conflict and competition. We look at Japan and the implications for international competition along with the rise of a new protectionism as a response to an uncertain world economy. Chapter Seven considers the special case of communism and command economies in the world economy and the dramatic transformation of Eastern Europe and the former Soviet Union.

Chapter Eight begins a new section focusing on the Third World. It gives students a clear understanding of the different ways of thinking about the problems of development in the Third World and the relationship of North and South. Chapter Nine evaluates the role of foreign aid in promoting or inhibiting development. The topic for Chapter Ten is the bargaining power and distribution of benefits between multinational corporations and nations in the Third World. The political issues involved in the Third World debt crisis and the problems associated with suggested solutions is the focus of Chapter Eleven. Several strategies of economic development have been followed by nations in the Third World. Chapter Twelve evaluates these strategies in terms of case studies of success and failure. And Chapter Thirteen offers some general conclusions focusing on possible future directions for the world economy, in particular the balance between struggle and cooperation and the competitive positions of several nations.

International political economy is certainly not an easy subject. It takes two areas of intellectual inquiry and mixes them together in new and complicated ways, but we expect the following presentation will help you sort through these difficulties and emerge with a much clearer understanding of an immensely important area. With patience and some dedication on your part, this will be the case.

THE ECONOMICS OF
INTERNATIONAL POLITICAL ECONOMY

S tudying the intersection of politics and economics at the international level cannot proceed very far without a firm grasp of basic economic relationships. Reading this or any book on international political economy requires that you understand a somewhat diverse set of economic concepts. This chapter is designed to introduce these ideas in a straightforward and nontechnical manner. At each stage of the book we will mix economic and political matters, with the balance sometimes shifting in one direction or another. This is just such an occasion and its purpose is to provide a basic literacy in economics.

The most important task is to see how international and domestic economies are related, especially the ways the international environment constrains and directs national decisions. Governments strive to maintain control over their economies and at the same time reap the benefits of international trade. Increasing global interdependence makes this effort much more difficult and uncertain. Understanding how these spheres of economic activity affect each other requires a common language of concepts that summarizes the most elemental features of each.

Acquisition of a command of the language will involve a mastery of five basic tasks. First, it is necessary to have a clear sense of why trade takes place among nations in the first place. The prevailing understanding of this is the theory of free trade, and the basic elements of this theory and some alternative approaches will be considered. Second, we need to learn how to measure the movement of goods, services, and money across national boundaries — the balance of payments — and how to interpret this somewhat complex and daunting array of statistics. Third, we need to understand the tools of economic management by the central government that define the basic features of domestic political economy. The most important of these tools are fiscal and monetary policy, in which the government, by its spending, taxing, and banking policies, has a major impact on the economy. Fourth, the fact that international transactions require the exchange of one national currency for another creates a special set of problems that must be explored. Fluctuation in exchange rates not only influences the level of imports and exports but also creates an opportunity and need for political intervention. Finally, these concepts are brought together through an examination of the dynamics of monetary and fiscal policy, interest rates, exchange rates, financial markets, and the balance of payments.

These are complex matters, but they must be understood in order to deal with the rest of the material in this book. Consider reading this chapter at least twice and playing with the ideas and relationships so that you are quickly able to see causal linkages. Once these are clearly in mind, the rest is much easier.

FREE TRADE AND PROTECTIONISM

■ Why do nations enter into trade with each other? Economists have long argued — for over 200 years — that trade without restrictions between almost any two states would be of benefit to both. Standing behind this view is a concept of allocating resources to the production of goods in the most efficient way; that is, a division of labor operates among nations so that each concentrates on the set of goods to which it is best suited as compared with other nations and with all the kinds of goods it could produce. Since no country can make everything it needs, trade will take place to exchange specialized goods for those produced elsewhere.

The argument for international trade rests on the fact that countries differ in their ability to produce goods. Often any given nation will possess an absolute advantage in the cost of production of a particular good. This concept can be illustrated very easily with some simplifying assumptions: two countries, Great Britain and the United States; and two products, wheat and iron. Workers in each country are better at producing one good over the other; this can be seen from the per-worker production of each.

	WHEAT bushels	IRON tons
BRITAIN	100	250
UNITED STATES	200	150

Clearly, Britain has an absolute advantage in iron while the United States enjoys an absolute advantage in wheat.

Suppose each country has 200 workers. If both devote half their work force to each good and avoid trade, they obtain the following output:

	WHEAT *bushels*	IRON *tons*
BRITAIN	10,000	25,000
UNITED STATES	20,000	15,000
TOTAL OUTPUT	30,000	40,000

The benefits of specialization and trade should be apparent by inspecting the figures. The United States can produce 200 bushels of wheat per worker, and Britain can produce 250 tons of iron per worker. If each shifts all its workers into the production of the good at which it is best, the total output of both will increase. Britain will produce 50,000 tons of iron by itself, and the United States will produce 40,000 bushels of wheat. Then trade can take place at the rate of 4 bushels of wheat for each 5 tons of iron, and both countries will benefit.

The amount of trade depends on how much of each good is needed. But notice that Britain can trade 5 tons of iron for 4 bushels of wheat. If they produce wheat themselves, Britain will need to give up 10 tons of iron for every 4 bushels of wheat.[1] For simplicity's sake, assume Britain and the United States are happy trading 16,000 bushels of wheat for 20,000 tons of iron. The following is the amount of wheat and iron each can consume as a result of this specialization and trade:

	WHEAT *bushels*	IRON *tons*
BRITAIN	16,000	30,000
UNITED STATES	24,000	20,000
TOTAL OUTPUT	40,000	50,000

Both the United States and Great Britain end up with more wheat and iron in this scenario than if they try to produce each commodity by themselves.

The benefits of trade in instances of absolute advantage are intuitively plausible and can be measured by the increase in total output and in the additional consumption in both countries. But economists argue convincingly that trade can benefit both nations even if one is inferior in the production of both goods. As long as the inferior nation has a comparative advantage in one good over the other, trade can be beneficial. This can be illustrated by assuming the British-U.S. production ratios are now:

	WHEAT *bushels*	IRON *tons*
BRITAIN	300	1200
UNITED STATES	100	200

---

[1]Look above to remember that British workers can produce 2.5 times as much iron in tons as wheat in bushels. So to get 4 bushels of wheat from their own workers, they will need to give up 4 times 2.5, or 10 tons of iron.

This depicts a situation in which a British worker has an absolute advantage in the production of both wheat and iron. But because the United States is not equally inferior in both goods, the basis for trade is available. Notice that the trade-off in transferring resources from the production of iron to wheat is 4:1 for Britain while it is only 2:1 for the United States. It is this comparative advantage that can be used to make trade profitable.

The easiest way to depict this relationship is to examine the difference between the cost of producing the goods at home and the cost of buying them from the other country. If it costs less to buy it abroad, specialization and trade is the best path. If we assume that cost is measured in terms of the ratios of production capabilities, comparative advantage is somewhat obvious. Thus, for Britain the cost of producing the good in which it has a comparative *disadvantage* — wheat — is 4 units of iron. But the U.S. cost is only 2 units of iron and Britain should be able to buy the wheat at that price. For the United States, the domestic cost of each unit of iron is 2 units of wheat, but Britain should be willing to trade iron at its cost, which is one unit of iron per one-quarter unit of wheat. The United States is clearly better off paying the British price for iron, and Britain is better off paying the United States price for wheat. Thus, comparative advantage makes trade beneficial for both countries. Although the benefits of trade are less pronounced under a situation of comparative advantage, this is the most difficult and unlikely case. Most nations will possess an absolute advantage in the production of some goods. But, demonstrating benefits from trade under comparative advantage makes a very strong case for free trade.

And yet, those more sensitive to the political consequences of trade have raised several arguments against an unrestrained enthusiasm for free trade. Specialization may not produce the type and degree of economic development desired. If a country concentrates on food and raw materials, whose price relative to manufactured goods is falling over time, they will inevitably fall behind these industrial states in national income. Further, the great gains in income and social development to be had from advanced technological production will be denied to the state concentrating on low value and low tech production. The population of these countries will be condemned to a permanently inferior position in the international hierarchy. In addition, certain goods are often thought to be essential to national security — for example, those used to produce armaments. An infrastructure of technological capability may be critical for maintaining military parity with other states. Specialization can expose nations to dependence on external supplies of such goods and thereby compromise security and other international goals. Lastly, movement toward free trade and specialization would require shifting resources away from some goods and toward others. This entails political consequences as those affected are likely to resist the personal costs and disruption associated with change. Adopting free trade or protection is an intensely political process involving differences in who will receive the benefits and who will bear the costs. When we consider the added dimensions of development, security, and redistribution, the choice of free trade becomes somewhat less clear; it should not be surprising to learn that free trade is the exception and not the rule over the past 175 years.

THE BALANCE OF PAYMENTS

■ One of the most basic and essential concepts for understanding the international economy is the balance of payments, which focuses on a particular nation and its transactions with the rest of the world. This accounting technique records the movement of goods, services, and capital across national boundaries for some period of time (month, quarter, year). The notion of "balance" here is somewhat misleading, for although this statistic always balances (because of the requirements of double-entry bookkeeping), we are really interested in the imbalances that inevitably appear in its various components.

Given that the parts are more important than the whole, what are the main items in the balance of payments? First, note that we want to measure all transactions of resources and claims on resources that the citizens of one nation have with the rest of the world.[2] For the purposes of this book, we will focus on eight major categories:

1. **Merchandise Exports and Imports**
   This refers to tangible goods produced at home and sold abroad (exports) and tangible goods produced abroad and sold in the home country (imports). This is the most familiar item in the balance of payments and includes all goods from clothing to computers to auto parts.

2. **Exports and Imports of Services**
   This refers to more intangible items, such as the transportation costs for goods and people, insurance, information, satellite transmissions, and banking.

3. **Investment Income and Payments**
   When someone invests resources in another country, he/she expects a return in the form of interest or dividends. This item measures payments of investment income by foreigners to citizens of the home country and by the home country to foreigners.

4. **Government Exports/Imports and Foreign Aid**
   The government may be engaged in selling or buying goods internationally, such as weapons. Additionally, the government may give or receive foreign aid.

---

[2] There are many complications about who counts as a citizen. One important example is a company with units overseas; the branches or facilities abroad are treated as foreigners.

5. **Balance on Current Account**

   The Balance on Current Account is a summary measure of items 1–4, that is, Merchandise, Services, Investment Income, and Government. Along with the Merchandise Account taken alone, the Current Account balance is the most frequently used measure of a nation's international transactions.

6. **Capital Account**

   This measures the actual investment of resources abroad or in the home country by foreigners. Typically, a distinction is made between short term investments, which have a maturity of less than one year, and long term investments, which have a maturity beyond one year. For example, when a Japanese bank purchases a U.S. government security, such as a Treasury note, that matures in 180 days, this is recorded in the short term Capital Account. (When the government pays interest to the Japanese bank, this is recorded in the Investment Account, which is described in number three above.)

7. **Official Reserves**

   The central bank of a country holds reserves of foreign exchange and gold which it uses in transactions with the central banks of other nations and when it intervenes in foreign exchange markets to buy or sell currency. The effect of these actions is to balance the net differences of other items in this list.

8. **Statistical Discrepancy**

   The measurement of the balance of payments is an inexact process, owing to its complexity and to the fact that some transactions are concealed (for example, trade in illegal drugs). This item is a statistical device used to express the imprecision of measurement and bring the overall credits and debits into balance.

A handy way to think of the balance of payments is whether a transaction results in a payment to the country (credit) or a payment to a foreigner (debit). Or, as a famous student of politics once said, "Follow the money." Table 2.1 offers a hypothetical example.

The balancing in the balance of payments is due not only to the accounting technique but also to the fact that everyone must get paid in one form or another. For example, imbalances in the merchandise, services, and investment accounts tend to be offset by the capital account. A current account surplus permits investment abroad, or to put it another way, it allows the accumulation of foreign assets. The nation gets paid for its current account surplus with the assets of foreign countries. In Table 2.1, the $39.9 billion surplus on current account is partly offset by the outflow of funds recorded in the capital account. A trade deficit, on the other hand, encourages foreigners to invest in your country. This would mean that a deficit in the current account would be offset by an inflow of funds in the capital account.

TABLE 2.1

	CREDIT	DEBIT	BALANCE
	(IN BILLIONS OF DOLLARS)		
1. Merchandise			
Exports	164.3		
Imports		129.6	
2. Services			
Exports	21.1		
Imports		19.3	
Trade Balance	185.4	148.9	+36.5
3. Investment Income and Payments			
Income	14.6		
Payments		21.4	
4. Government			
Exports	13.5		
Imports		2.6	
Aid (net)		.7	
5. Balance on Current Account	213.5	173.6	+39.9
6. Capital Account			
Exports (long- and short-term)		58.4	
Imports (long- and short-term)	31.7		
Balance on Capital Account			−26.7
7. Official Reserves		−7.0	−7.0
8. Statistical Discrepancy		6.2	−6.2

To see how this process works and also gain some practice in understanding the balance of payments, look at Table 2.2. This is a comparison of our hypothetical nation's balance of payments over a four year period. Note that the figures for Table 2.1 are in year three.

What can we learn about the dynamics of the balance of payments from Table 2.2? Perhaps the simplest matter is comparison of each item across the four years. The hypothetical country experiences a growth in exports but imports grow even more rapidly. These different growth rates produce a shift from a current account deficit to surplus and then back to deficit. You can see this as the current account swings from a deficit of $21.4 billion to two years of surplus and then back to a deficit of $30.9 billion. The capital account tends to mirror these changes, with a net inflow of funds followed by two years of outflow and then a return to an inflow. In this hypothetical case, the country

TABLE 2.2				
			YEAR	
	1	2	3	4
Goods/Services				
Exports	102.2	156.7	185.4	191.4
Imports	119.9	140.1	148.9	227.5
Investments				
Income	3.2	3.7	14.6	20.2
Payments	8.4	11.9	21.4	23.1
Government	1.5	11.8	10.2	8.1
Current Account	−21.4	20.2	39.9	−30.9
Capital Account				
Exports	12.2	32.6	58.4	27.7
Imports	26.8	29.1	31.7	50.3
Reserve Account	3.2	−11.0	−7.0	4.1
Statistical Discrepancy	3.6	−5.7	−6.2	4.2

is able to invest more abroad and reap the benefits in income in the two intermediate years as a result of surpluses. The swing back to a deficit, however, sharply curtails this investment and, instead, pulls in foreign investment. This process can be followed in the sharp drop in capital exports and the rise in capital imports in year four.[3]

This may seem to be good since other countries are willing to make investments in our hypothetical country. Nevertheless, this situation has important and potentially costly consequences for the future. The increase in capital imports means you must pay income to foreign investors in the future, while future payments from abroad will diminish due to the decline in capital investments overseas. If the combination of a trade deficit and an increase in capital imports persists for a long period, it will set up some unpleasant choices for the future. One option is to reverse the current account deficit in

---

[3]The relation between the current and capital accounts is not a necessary one. A surplus in the current account means the country in question is accumulating foreign exchange. This permits it to use those resources to make investments abroad, but does not require this action. By contrast, a current account deficit results in foreigners accumulating the country's currency (or claims on its currency), and this allows them to purchase its assets (investments). What happens if these investments don't occur? The balancing factor then becomes the official reserve account, which entails transfers of liquid international assets among central banks. So a current account deficit not offset by investments from abroad will produce the transfer of official reserve assets to foreign countries.

order to pay income on investments to foreign investors, perhaps by curtailing imports. Alternatively, continuing the current account deficit will force the country to borrow more from abroad to pay income on past investments. But, the ability to use foreign debt to pay for a deficit depends on the willingness of those abroad to invest; they are not compelled to do so.[4] Thus, the need for everyone to get paid means that the nation must make adjustments for a current account deficit. The adjustments may come in market responses and/or in political action.

A related measurement is the nation's international standing as a creditor or debtor. This denominates the accumulated investment abroad by your citizens and by foreigners in your country, including governments and private actors. The position of our hypothetical state in year four might look something like this:

TABLE 2.3

Assets Abroad	
Official (Government Held)	$ 41.4
Private (Direct Investment and Securities)	219.6
Foreign Holdings of Country Assets	
Official (Government Held)	49.0
Private (Direct Investment and Securities)	238.0
Net Position (Debtor)	$−26.0

The table reveals that our hypothetical country is a debtor in the sense that foreigners own more of its assets than its citizens own of foreign assets. This is the result of the fact that deficits in the current account have, on a net basis over several years, been financed by investment from abroad. Worthy of note is the fact that a debtor state will likely pay out more in interest and dividends to foreigners than it receives (notice, in year four, the payments of $23.1 billion and $20.2 billion in receipts as shown in Table 2.2), a further negative item in the balance of payments. This will continue until the current account can be brought into surplus for several years.[5] Had the situation been the opposite, and the nation had more assets abroad than were held by foreigners, then it would be described as a creditor state. It then would likely receive a net income from abroad, a positive addition to its balance of payments.

---

[4] When this investment fails to happen, several things may occur. The country's exchange rate may fall, interest rates may rise to attract the investment, and the reserve account may be drawn upon to pay the bills for imports.

[5] In this case, the size of its debtor position is small and not terribly worrisome. However, the trends in its balance of payments toward a current account deficit create the possibility of continuing additions to its international debt. Should this debt become large, especially the proportion of interest payments in relation to exports, the potential for trouble would grow. Only when debt reaches these levels, such as with the United States and some Third World nations in recent years, does debtor or creditor status take on important consequences.

To repeat, the balance of payments is most important for what it reveals about imbalances, especially persistent ones in the current account. But how do deficits and surpluses affect a nation's prosperity and financial position? What options does a government have for correcting or ameliorating these problems? To answer these questions, we must clearly see the relationships between national and international economies, and this requires a discussion of some of the basics of macroeconomic management: interest rates, money supply, and monetary and fiscal policy.

MONETARY AND FISCAL POLICY

■ For much of the twentieth century, governments have expanded their role in influencing the overall level of national prosperity. The two most basic and well-established areas are fiscal and monetary policy. Fiscal policy refers to decisions about spending, taxes, and borrowing by the central government, while monetary policy involves efforts by the central bank to manage the money supply and interest rates. Of the two, monetary policy has the longest tradition, is the best institutionalized, and generally is the most effective. Fiscal policy, by contrast, tends to be much more politicized, for interest groups are easily able to identify its costs and benefits and act to influence decisions. The result is that efforts to use fiscal policy as a tool of macroeconomic management have a checkered legacy.

The decision to establish a central bank in the United States came early in 1913. The combination of financial panics and the management capabilities of other central banks pushed even conservative leaders to create the Federal Reserve.[6] The United States was much later in creating a central bank than other large and prosperous countries. Great Britain did so in the 1840s, Germany in the 1870s, and upstart Japan in the 1880s.[7] One important line of distinction among central banks is the degree to which they act independently or are subject to political control. On that score, the German central bank — the Bundesbank — is certainly the most independent, with the Bank of England and the Banque de France generally following the direction of the government. The Federal Reserve falls somewhere between the two extremes, able to act on its own but often responding to political pressure to expand the money supply or lower interest rates.[8]

---

[6]One of the recurring features of capitalism and free markets is a boom and bust cycle, often characterized in financial arenas by a panic. For an interesting history of financial crises, see Charles P. Kindleberger, *Manias, Panics, and Crashes,* New York: Basic Books, 1989.

[7]For detail on this process, see Charles Goodhart, *The Evolution of Central Banks,* Cambridge: MIT Press, 1988, 105–160. For establishment of the Federal Reserve, see Richard H. Timberlake, *The Origins of Central Banking in the United States,* Cambridge: Harvard University Press, 1978.

[8]For detail on the politics of Fed decision making, see John T. Woolley, *Monetary Politics: The Federal Reserve and the Politics of Monetary Policy,* Cambridge: Cambridge University Press, 1984. On the Bundesbank, see Ellen Kennedy, *The Bundesbank,* London: Pinter Publishers, 1991.

Monetary Policy

Today, the Fed, as it is commonly called, has two major tools for managing the economy: open market operations and the discount rate. The purpose of both is to affect the availability of credit — that is, the willingness of banks to make loans and of individuals and corporations to borrow.

Most of what we treat as money is intangible, found in checking accounts and not in bills and coins. Usually, we pay for goods and services by ordering a bank to transfer a computer entry from ourselves to someone else (writing a check). Moreover, increases and decreases in the money supply for a nation typically come much more from banks making loans than from printing money. The Fed manages the money supply by affecting this process. When banks loan money to their customers, whether to buy a boat, computer, or office building, this expands economic activity. The production of goods and services to meet this demand boosts employment, and these additional workers spend their incomes and perhaps borrow money for purchases. The process also works in reverse: when banks decrease the rate of lending, purchases of goods and services shrink, unemployment increases, and further decreases in spending result.

How do actions of the Federal Reserve affect this process? First, we need to know that the Fed is connected to member banks in several ways: it determines the proportion of bank assets that must be held as reserves; it has the right to inspect, without notice, bank records and force changes in lending policies; and it lends money to member banks. The most commonly used technique for management of the money supply is open market operations. Here the Fed is either pumping funds into or draining funds from the banking system by buying or selling U.S. government securities. When several billion dollars of securities are purchased, the selling institutions (usually banks and insurance companies) will receive a check from the Fed that will expand the money available for lending. In adding funds to the banking system, and thereby increasing the potential lending power of banks, the Fed is pursuing an expansionary monetary policy. By contrast, a policy designed to contract or tighten the money supply would involve selling government securities. In this case, the Fed receives payment and effectively drains resources from the banking system.[9]

---

[9]These actions also affect interest rates. Changes in the supply of money cause changes in the price of money, namely interest rates. Two key interest rates that often reflect open market operations are the Federal Funds and Treasury bills rates. When these rise, this may indicate the Fed is following a tight money path by selling government securities. When they fall, the Fed may be pursuing an expansionary policy through open market purchases. The same goals of open market operations can be achieved through changes in the reserve requirement. Increasing the proportion of its assets a bank must hold in reserve decreases its lending capacity, while reductions in the reserve requirement increase the ability to make loans. Because changing the reserve requirement is such a public act, it is an infrequently used tool.

The discount rate is also a powerful instrument for managing the money supply. This is the interest rate charged by the Fed to member banks when they borrow money from it. The discount rate also functions as an anchor interest rate, and changes in it tend to spark changes in other interest rates. If the discount rate is 7.5 percent, the prime rate (rate that banks charge their most credit-worthy customers) might be 9.5 percent, first mortgage loans at 10.5 percent, and credit cards at 18 percent. When the discount rate increases, other interest rates also rise, though not always in lock step. The reverse is also true: a fall in the discount rate will probably produce a drop in other interest rates.[10] Once again, the object is to expand or contract the money supply and thereby the economy as a whole. Raising the discount rate increases the price of money, discourages borrowing, and should slow down economic expansion. Lowering the rate encourages borrowing and should accelerate economic activity.

The role of the Federal Reserve in the United States is to provide stability to financial markets during times of crisis and to promote economic growth consistent with low inflation. The Fed was created in the early twentieth century largely to moderate the financial panics that had become increasingly severe. A panic is a time when frightened investors attempt to sell securities all at once or when depositors lose confidence in the banking system and try to remove their money. The Fed also serves as a lender of last resort to provide liquidity (meaning a money supply sufficient for the transactions people want to make) to the economy when fear paralyzes the actions of other lenders. An equally important role of the Fed is to control inflation while encouraging economic growth. Inflation is especially harmful to persons who lend money or who have their assets in fixed income instruments (such as government bonds). The fixed rates of future income are effectively reduced by inflation. Rising prices mean that interest received in the future has less purchasing power. In acting to control inflation, the Fed is protecting the interests of lenders and others who are hurt by rising prices.[11]

The decision makers at the Fed pay close attention to the capital and credit markets, as well as the indicators of economic expansion and contraction. If the evidence suggests that expansion is moving too fast and inflationary pressures are increasing, the Fed is likely to take action. The quiet and short-term method of attacking inflation would be open market sales of government securities, thereby reducing the money supply and pushing up interest rates. A more public declaration of policy would be an increase in the discount rate. Depending on the severity of the problem, some combination of these actions may continue for many months or even years. During

---

[10]Note that interest rates also rise and fall independent of Fed action, based on market driven changes in the supply and demand for funds.

[11]For a discussion of the contesting interests over inflation, see William Grieder, *Secrets of the Temple*, New York: Simon and Schuster, 1987, 11–47, 75–123.

much of the 1970s and 1980s, when inflationary pressures were strong, the Fed pursued a "tight money" policy, pushing interest rates to unprecedented levels.

Fiscal Policy

The other major instrument of economic management is fiscal policy — the use of taxing and spending by the national government to affect the economy. The basic ideas of fiscal policy can be traced to the thinking of John Maynard Keynes, an influential British economist. Keynes and others argued that fiscal policy need not, and should not, be tied to the rigid orthodoxy of a balanced budget, but instead could be used to manage the economy and smooth out the business cycle of expansion and recession (or depression).[12]

The notion of "pump priming" by the government to stimulate economic expansion involves deficit spending. Here, government spending exceeds tax revenue with the difference made up by having the Treasury Department sell government bonds. Before about 1960, the theory supporting deficit spending was that selling bonds and spending the funds on government projects stimulated the economy by returning unused savings into the spending and income stream. With the Kennedy-Johnson tax cut of 1964, the rationale changed. Rather than rely on increased government spending, economists promoted cutting taxes and maintaining spending to produce a stimulative deficit. Here recipients of lower taxes were expected to spend their increased income to accomplish the same result.[13]

The great weakness of fiscal policy as a means of macroeconomic management is that decisions about spending and taxes are rarely based on judgments about the "correct" size deficit or surplus to fine tune the economy. Not only do many groups — from the military to social security recipients — use political pressure to increase government spending, but politicians often use tax cuts to win votes, whether or not this is best for the economy. In 1966 and 1967, President Johnson chose not to increase taxes to pay for the Vietnam War because he felt this would undermine an already weakened bases of support for his policies. These extraneous factors may be rational as short-term political calculations, but they are harmful for economic management purposes. Often, the tendency to increase spending and decrease taxes has overstimulated the economy, resulting in inflation. This was clearly the consequence of Johnson's decisions in the 1960s. In the 1980s, budget proposals of the president became blatantly political documents in a struggle with

---

[12]There was great resistance to Keynes among conservatives, especially from the 1930s to the 1960s. An interesting discussion of the political struggles over Keynesianism is in Robert Collins, *The Business Response to Keynes*, New York: Columbia University Press, 1981.

[13]Some economists, known as "supply-siders," justified the Reagan tax cut of 1981 by predicting increased work and risk-taking as an additional economic stimulus.

Congress. Budgets served more as a way to score points with constituents than to manage the economy.[14]

Exchange Rates and
Trade Deficits

■ The one remaining set of concepts essential to understanding international political economy concerns the relationship between exchange rates and international trade. For trade to occur, money must change hands. But in international trade, one country's currency must be exchanged for another country's currency, and the rate of this exchange has significant consequences for the terms of trade and for the network of relationships linking domestic and international politics. This section explains how exchange rates can affect trade, explores the reasons for government intervention in foreign exchange markets, and examines the impact of interest rates on exchange rates.

The exchange rate for a currency refers simply to how much of another country's money can be purchased with a specified amount of your own country's money. At the end of 1991, one U.S. dollar would purchase 124.8 Japanese yen, .54 British pounds, and 1.52 German marks.[15] Or reciprocally, one Japanese yen would buy .0081 dollars (less than one cent); one British pound would purchase 1.87 dollars; and a German mark could be exchanged for .658 dollars (66 cents). These values are the result of daily trading in foreign exchange markets. Most of this trading is done by private individuals or corporations who are engaged in international trade or finance and need to buy or sell currencies. The price of a currency is determined by the demand for, and supply of, one currency in relation to another. Buying and selling currencies is partly the result of transactions recorded in the balance of payments between the two countries.[16] For example, trade between two countries generates a demand and a supply of both currencies as exporters return to their home currency. Exchange rates can be measured in terms of a single foreign currency or as an average of several currencies.

The following figures demonstrate the substantial volatility in exchange rates since 1971. Figure 2.1 shows the fall in the value of the dollar when priced in yen. (Notice that had we priced yen in dollars the curve would

---

[14]Another complicating factor is that fiscal and monetary policies are made in different political settings. The president and Congress are the chief actors in fiscal policy, while the Fed makes decisions about monetary policy. There is no guarantee of policy consistency, and actions at cross purposes are not uncommon.

[15]Most newspapers carry reports of daily transactions on foreign exchange markets, usually in the business pages.

[16]In addition, speculators hoping to profit from fluctuations in the price of a currency will affect demand and supply. The transactions of speculators may or may not be recorded in the balance of payments.

FIGURE 2.1

Japanese Exchange Rate

SOURCE: The data are taken from the Department of Commerce, *National Trade Data Bank*, October 1991.

have risen.) Essentially the same points are revealed by Figure 2.2, which shows the value of dollars in German deutsche marks and British pounds. But even within a long-term trend, there are important fluctuations. During the first half of the 1980s, the dollar rose in value against most currencies. Among the three currencies shown, this is most true for the deutsche mark; but against the pound, the dollar continued to fall.

An additional influence on exchange rates is that the central bank of a country (government-owned) sometimes intervenes in foreign exchange markets, buying or selling in hopes of influencing the price of their currency. But why would a central bank want to influence the value of its money? What effect does a particular exchange rate have on a nation's economic prosperity? Economists and government officials have long recognized that the value of a nation's currency affects the prices of its goods involved in foreign trade and the prices of foreign goods sold in its home market. By changing the value of its currency, these officials typically want to change the prices of imports and exports and thereby affect its overall balance of trade.

FIGURE 2.2

**Exchange Rates
Germany/United Kingdom**

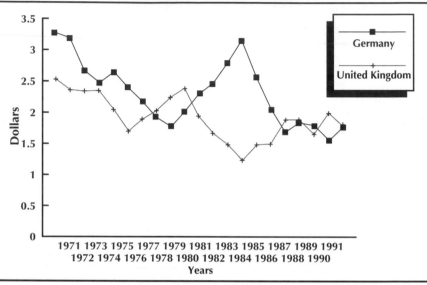

SOURCE: The data are taken from Department of Commerce, *National Trade Data Bank,*
October 1991.

How Exchange Rates Affect Trade

How is this supposed to work? First, remember that when someone engages
in foreign trade, they must price their goods in the currency of the selling
market, while they want to end up with their own currency. This means the
money received from selling goods must be exchanged for the home currency.
Thus, changes in the exchange rate directly influence the prices that can or
must be charged.

To see this in action, consider the following situation. A U.S. exporter is
selling computer disc drives in Great Britain. The exchange rate is £1 equals
$2 (or $1 equals one-half of a pound). The disc drives sell for $500.00 apiece
in the United States and the exporter is prepared to absorb the costs of
transportation in order to establish a position in Britain. Thus, he/she prices
the disc drives at £250 since this can be exchanged for the $500 he/she
actually wants. Now, suppose the exchange rate changes to £1 equals $3. The
pound has appreciated in value (it now brings $3 instead of only $2) while
the dollar has depreciated (since you need $3 to get £1 instead of only $2).
What effect does this have on our exporter? Remember, he/she wants to end

up with $500. To do this he/she need now charge only £166.67 in order to convert to $500.00 (166.67 X 3). A depreciating dollar *permits* (but does not require) U.S. exporters to lower their prices abroad.

The opposite result occurs when the dollar appreciates in value. Suppose the original exchange rate of £1 equals $2 becomes £1 equals $1. The pound has depreciated while the dollar has appreciated. Our exporter now has a big problem. In order to wind up with $500, he/she must increase the price to £500. Thus, an appreciating dollar virtually forces exporters to raise prices or see their profits fall. As an important aside, we should note that these effects also work, but in the opposite direction, for British exports to the United States.

This example gives us the basis for understanding how the government hopes to influence the nation's trade balance. We have a convenient example, namely the effort by the Reagan Administration, beginning in 1985, to first "talk down" and later push down the value of the dollar. This came in the face of an unprecedented deficit in the balance of trade. Why try to force the value of the dollar down? The purposes can be summarized in the following causal chain.

FIGURE 2.3

Verbally, this shows the expectation that a drop in the exchange rate of the dollar should lead to a drop in the prices of U.S. exports while the prices of imports rise. A decline in export prices should also lead to an increased demand for these goods, while rising import prices should lead U.S. citizens to purchase fewer imported goods. As a result, the amount of exports should rise while imports decline, and the trade deficit should improve.

But there are important limits on the ability of an exchange rate depreciation to eliminate a deeply entrenched deficit such as that of the United States. Look at Figure 2.4, which shows a trade weighted average of the value of the dollar and the U.S. merchandise trade balance.[17] It should be clear that the U.S. trade deficit has only been marginally affected by previous declines in the dollar. Although the dollar generally fell from 1971 to 1980, the trade balance worsened. Since 1985 the dollar has fallen by as much as 50 percent, while the trade deficit continued rising until 1987. The figures for 1988–1990 recovered only to about 1984 levels.

FIGURE 2.4

U.S. Merchandise Trade Balance
Compared To Dollar Exchange Rate

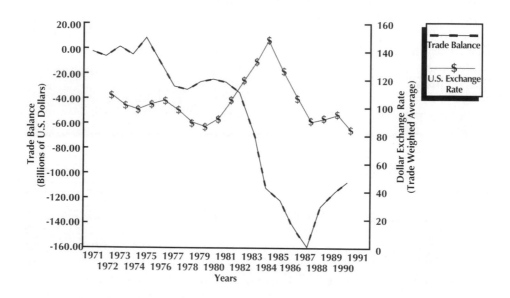

SOURCE: The data are taken from Department of Commerce, *National Trade Data Bank*, October 1991.

There are several fairly simple reasons why the desired reduction in the trade deficit has been limited. Perhaps the most important unrealized expectation is that, instead of falling, imports have continued to rise in spite of a falling dollar. Look at Figure 2.5, which shows an increasing trend line for imports after 1983. Two factors contribute to this problem. First, U.S. consumers believe that many foreign-made products are superior to those made in

---

[17]A trade weighted average means the value of the dollar is computed against an average value of several of its main trading partners. The average is weighted by the amount of trade conducted with the United States, with some countries' currencies counting more than others.

FIGURE 2.5

U.S. Exports and Imports 1980–1990

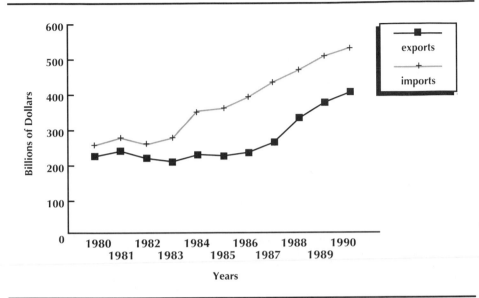

SOURCE: The data are taken from International Monetary Fund, *International Financial Statistics Yearbook*, 1991.

the United States, so even when the prices of imports rise, demand may not fall very much.[18] A second reason is that business persons who are selling goods in the United States may choose not to raise prices but instead absorb some of the effects of a declining dollar. They might take this step in order to remain competitive, retaining their market share in hopes of a rising dollar. Or they might decide to hold their money in dollars, investing in U.S. assets rather than reverting to a foreign currency. (Indeed, the growth of multi-national firms, with permanent operations abroad and less need to convert

---

[18]This relationship between the amount of change in demand produced by a change in price is referred to by economists as the elasticity of demand. Frequently, economists and others refer to this relationship between the volume of trade and the prices of goods traded as the "J curve." This term pays close attention to the effects of elasticity over time, in particular to the fact that the prices of imports and exports may rise or fall immediately following a change in exchange rates while the intended changes in demand may require some time. The J curve indicates that the immediate result of a fall in a currency's value may be a *worsening* of the trade balance. If export prices fall and import prices rise, with little initial change in demand, then exports (measured as volume times price) will fall and imports will rise. The deterioration in the trade balance, however, should be followed by improvement (thus the J curve) in the balance as elasticities in demand for exports and imports take over and swell the export volume beyond the fall in prices while lowering the volume of imports beyond the rise in prices.

to a "home" currency, increases the chances of this happening.) On the export side, those who sell abroad have options that would not necessarily help the trade deficit. Remember that a declining dollar permits, but does not require, the exporter to lower prices. But if they are already competitive in price, exporters may choose to keep prices about the same and reap the extra profits when the pounds (or whatever the currency of transaction) are exchanged for dollars. Once again, the presence of large, multinational firms, who are in a position to benefit from continuing exchange rate transactions, may nullify much of the anticipated impact of a declining dollar.[19]

EXCHANGE RATES, TRADE, AND MACROECONOMIC POLICY

■ We can now begin to see how the complexities of national and international economies work. Frequently, actions in one economic arena complicate the situation elsewhere. International economic interdependence creates important difficulties for economic management. This section is designed to discuss some of the ways this can happen.

First, we need to extend our earlier discussion of exchange rates to see how a purely economic or market-based analysis of this process might work. In a system where exchange rates are a result of only the forces of supply and demand for foreign exchange as generated by exports and imports, market processes can act to adjust trade balances automatically. For example, a trade deficit in country X adds to the supply of its currency in the hands of foreigners. (If you don't see why this is true, go back and review the sections on exchange rates and the balance of payments.) When foreigners exchange X's currency for their own, assuming other factors don't change, the price of X's currency should fall. This decline activates the process, discussed above, of falling export prices and rising demand for exports, accompanied by rising import prices resulting in lower demand. This fall in price should continue until the trade deficit has disappeared. A trade surplus brings the same arrangements into play, except in the opposite direction. But caution should be used in accepting this rather neat system. We have already considered how the connections among exchange rates, prices, and demand are subject to important qualifications. Equally significant are other complications that emerge when we consider the political and other economic dimensions of the relationship between domestic and international economic systems.

---

[19]A detailed discussion of the adjustment process is found in Paul R. Krugman, *Has the Adjustment Process Worked?* Washington: Institute for International Economics, 1991. Krugman answers this question in the affirmative. See Chapter 6 of this book for more discussion of this issue in relation to the question of competitiveness.

Allowing exchange rates to cure a trade deficit, or attempting to manipulate these rates toward the same end, can have unpleasant consequences. A fall in the dollar, if it works right, should force import prices up, thereby increasing inflationary pressures and even permitting domestic producers to raise their prices. Equally, export prices may fall abroad, leading to increased demand that spurs the domestic economy. But, the combination of rising import prices and accelerating economic growth also creates the specter of inflation. This brings on the Federal Reserve (or the central banks of most countries), who we know has a major commitment to fighting inflation.

As we have seen, one of the main weapons in the Fed's arsenal for combating inflation is interest rates. Specifically, the Fed may use the discount rate and open market operations to force interest rates to rise, in anticipation of the inflationary effects of a falling dollar, so as to reduce business investment and consumer spending. This, they hope, will reduce overall economic activity and hold down inflationary pressures. In other words, the Fed may try to induce a recession, or at least an economic slowdown, in order to counteract the inflationary consequences of a falling dollar. In addition to helping control inflation, a recession can also result in a declining demand for imported goods as the economy contracts.[20]

But this effort to counter the effects of the falling dollar can have negative consequences for the stock market, which is very sensitive to changes in interest rates. The individuals and institutions who own stocks pay close attention to the somewhat more certain returns from securities that pay a fixed return rather than in the more speculative form of dividends or price appreciation. When interest rates rise, especially if the expectation is for continuing increases, many investors may sell stocks and buy securities that offer the new (increased) interest rates. Rising interest rates frequently lead to a declining stock market. Often, the sequence works like this. The trade deficit for the month is announced, and it shows a larger than expected gap between imports and exports. People who own stock, anticipating actions by the Fed to cope with the expected inflation from a falling dollar, will sell stocks, sometimes creating frightening declines. This is part of what happened in October 1987, when the Dow Jones Industrial Average fell more than 1000 points, or more than one-third of its total value, over the space of a few days.

Thus, the effort to improve the trade deficit through a declining dollar can lead to inflation, higher interest rates, and even a recession. But matters do not stop here. Interest rates themselves also affect exchange rates. Remember, the value of a currency is a result of the demand and supply in foreign exchange markets. Interest rates affect the capital account portion of the balance of payments by influencing the level of investment in a country. To

---

[20]This is similar to the adjustment often imposed by the International Monetary Fund on countries having persistent trade deficits. The "belt tightening" usually means cutting government spending, raising taxes, and increasing interest rates.

see this, suppose you are a foreign banker with the choice of investing in the government bonds of five countries. The interest rates on these bonds are:

U.S.	JAPAN	FRANCE	BRITAIN	GERMANY
8.7%	3.6%	6.1%	9.2%	4.8%

If the Fed raises the discount rate and drives U.S. bond yields up to 10.0 percent, this will attract investors. In order to purchase U.S. bonds, the foreign banker must first buy dollars with his/her currency. If large numbers of investors do this, the increased demand for dollars will drive up the exchange rate.[21]

So what do we have? A declining dollar designed to improve the trade deficit ignites inflation. This prompts the Fed to raise interest rates, attracting foreign investors. And this pushes the value of the dollar higher, which we know could make the trade deficit expand. Economic interdependence makes policy choices much more complicated since the international and domestic consequences of actions may negate each other.

This happens in other ways as well. If one country chooses to pursue an expansionary economic policy, it must consider the international consequences. An expanding economy, especially if accompanied by inflation, pulls in imports. If this occurs when other nations' economies are not expanding, the consequence is likely to be a weakening of the current account balance. Because other countries are experiencing an economic slowdown, they are not likely to be very good markets for exports. A declining current account surplus or widening deficit acts as a drag on overall GNP and may even negate the expansionary stimulus. This was the situation confronting the French government in the early 1980s as it sought to stimulate its economy at a time when other western capitalist economies were in or entering a recession. The result was a serious worsening in the current account balance. As exports faltered and imports poured in, the value of the franc fell, and inflation rose.

Clearly, international economic interdependence means that domestic economic policies frequently must be coordinated with other states in order to be effective. Furthermore, it is too simple to say that market systems, left alone, can solve the problems created by a payments imbalance or that intervention by governments can always smooth out market imperfections. There are several markets at work, sometimes operating at cross-purposes, and always functioning both with some autonomy and with powerful linkages

---

[21]An additional consideration for foreign investors is the stability of the exchange rate, since this affects the net yield. A falling exchange rate reduces the net return, since you must have more foreign currency to get back to the home currency. Conversely, a rising exchange rate adds to the overall return; thus, the combination of high interest rates and a rising exchange rate tends to be self-reinforcing. But the key to the process is high interest rates relative to the rest of the world. Consequently, rates don't actually have to rise for the exchange rate to increase; they simply need to remain *relatively* high.

to each other. Exchange rates, interest rates, and the markets for exports and imports certainly share this interesting combination of contradictory effects, independent operation, and interdependence.

Beyond the economics, there is the politics of the problem of managing domestic and international economic relations. Two situations are worth emphasizing here. Manipulating exchange rates, either with active intervention or passive acceptance of market forces, is a politically cheap way of trying to solve a trade deficit. Since most persons do not understand the mechanisms involved, the costs of such a policy can be disguised or hidden. Assertions that a trade deficit results in transferring claims against a nation's resources to the rest of the world or that it means a nation is consuming more than it is producing have a limited political impact. Certainly, exchange rates are politically preferable to a strategy of economic restructuring or deflation and recession. But equally clear is the possibility that exchange rates may fail.

Also worthy of emphasis is the complex problem of international political cooperation to manage interdependent economic systems. Obviously, such cooperation is influenced by the status of political relationships on other matters. As we shall see in later chapters, success in cooperation is entangled in a web of conflicting and common interests and the ability of leaders to maneuver and build a set of acceptable compromises among internal and external constituencies. This game of complex interdependence is at the heart of the problems of cooperation and conflict. But before we can talk intelligently about the present, we need to understand the paths of the past in the historical origins of a world economy.

CONCLUSIONS

■ This chapter was designed to give you many of the concepts of economic analysis essential for understanding international political economy. At this point you should be comfortable with the following:

1. The concepts of free trade, absolute advantage, and comparative advantage are the key to understanding why trade occurs and how the benefits of free trade are spread to all who participate. But remember, the benefits are not equal, nor do nations seeking security always gain what they need.

2. The components of the balance of payments, including some of the summary measures such as the "current account" along with related terms like creditor and debtor nation, should be familiar concepts. Additionally, you need to understand the relationship of the current account and capital account.

3. The differences between fiscal and monetary policy and the basic mechanisms of their operation must be almost second nature. Pay special

attention to the use of monetary policy and interest rates to manage the domestic economy.

4. The lines of influence between exchange rates and the prices and demand for exports and imports is an especially important set of relationships. You need to be able to work through this process quickly and apply it to various policy options. Equally significant, however, is the plethora of factors that undermine and distort this process.

5. Finally, the most difficult but also most important matter is the interacting effects of the balance of payments, monetary and fiscal policy, and exchange rates. This is a major topic for treatment in subsequent chapters, and in a somewhat more complex form.

There are other important economic concepts left for consideration in subsequent chapters, including the gold standard, fixed exchange rate systems, key currency, and protectionism. But with the ideas of this chapter in mind, you are now prepared to begin thinking seriously about international political economy.

ANNOTATED BIBLIOGRAPHY

Richard Caves, *World Trade and Payments: An Introduction*, Glenview: Scott Foresman, 1990.
Provides an excellent introduction to the entire field of international economics.

Robert Heilbroner and Lester Thurow, *Economics Explained*, New York: Touchstone, 1982.
A very clear and basic introduction to economics.

Paul Krugman, *The Age of Diminished Expectations*, Cambridge: MIT Press, 1991.
Offers a series of clearly written essays relating to many of the central topics of economics and economic policy.

John C. Pool and Steve Stamos, *The ABC's of International Finance*, Lexington: Lexington Books, 1987.
A theoretically limited but very clear introduction to the basics of international economics.

Paul Samuelson, *Economics*, New York: McGraw Hill, 1990.
The standard textbook in the field of economics.

Leonard Silk, periodic columns in the Business Section of the *New York Times*.
Silk provides a consistently stimulating commentary on current issues in political economy.

CHAPTER 3

THE ORIGINS OF A WORLD ECONOMY

I n some respects a world economy is very much like other economic systems: goods are produced and services provided; wealth is accumulated and destroyed; investments are made on the basis of maximizing returns; and prices fluctuate according to supply and demand. And yet, because these things are taking place across national borders, we know that something different is happening. We are accustomed to thinking of economies as coextensive with the nation. Historically, nations have guarded their borders jealously; after all, this is one of the things that make them nations. Governments have always tried to place some controls on trade, immigration, and monetary transactions with the outside world. Consequently, the stupendous growth of a world economy over the past 150 to 175 years calls for understanding on its own terms.

The purpose of this chapter is to provide the student with the tools and information needed to begin thinking about the world economy as a special phenomena. The approach is largely historical so that the student can appreciate the long-term background to contemporary events and gain some perspective on the many different outcomes to international economic cooperation and conflict. Especially important is understanding how the transformation of the world economy is inextricably enmeshed with international political and military developments. The discussion will follow along two related lines. The first part deals with developments within nations, such as technology and production, special advantages in raw materials, labor skills, and entrepreneurial strategies and behaviors. The second part considers economic relations among nations, including the flow of goods, capital, information, and technology, and competitive advantages and their effects on political and military relations. The focus includes the beginnings of international trade in manufactured goods in the early nineteenth century, the formation of a world economy of expanding trade and interdependence from 1840 to 1875, and the breakdown and collapse of this system in World War I and the Great Depression.

INDUSTRIALIZATION AND INTERNATIONAL TRADE

■ We begin our story with the late eighteenth and early nineteenth centuries. This is when the industrial system spread from England across Europe and, in conjunction with the explosion of British trade in manufactures, began to create a world economy somewhat like our own. Of course, international economic relations of substantial proportions did exist before this time.[1] But what distinguishes our starting point from previous periods is the sense of potential economic gains for all from world trade, the growing importance of manufactured goods in foreign trade, and the enormous increase in the degree of interdependence among nations.[2] These factors combined to create new forms of production and thereby expanded dramatically the benefits from trade. The growth of world trade changed the willingness of nations to participate in this new system even as expanding profits encouraged overseas investments at unprecedented levels. This process extends over the years from 1780 to 1850 and results in a world economy with features resembling that of our time.[3]

British Industrialization

An enduring and exceedingly important characteristic of the world economy is its unevenness. Nations compete with each other on quite unequal terms based on distinct advantages in technology, economic organization, and

---

[1] Fernand Braudel believes a world economy of significant proportions has existed for a very long time. Fernand Braudel, *Civilization and Capitalism, 15th–18th Centuries, Vol. 3: The Perspective of the World*, trans. by Sian Reynolds, New York: Harper and Row, 1984.

[2] The ideas associated with free trade contrast sharply with those of mercantilism. Operating from a zero-sum concept of a world economy, mercantilism asserts that the gains made from trade by one nation must come at the expense of all others. Nations, under this thesis, try to protect their own markets while seeking to take export markets from others. See Jacob Viner, "Power Versus Plenty as Objectives of Trade in the Seventeenth and Eighteenth Centuries," *World Politics*, 1.1, October 1946.

[3] In the period from 1500 to 1750, localism and barter were still predominant, with international trade largely confined to luxury goods, including foodstuffs, silk, hides, copper, spices, metals, and timber. The slow and uneven growth of world trade probably contributed to a zero-sum attitude. See Kristof Glamann, "European Trade, 1500–1750," in Carlo Cipolla, ed., *The Fontana Economic History of Europe: The Sixteenth and Seventeenth Centuries*, Glasgow: Collins/Fontana Books, 1974, 427–526; and P. J. Cain, *Economic Foundations of British Overseas Expansion 1815–1914*, London: Macmillan, 1980.

resources. Such was the case with the industrial development of Britain in the late eighteenth century and the changes in the world economy that followed. The British enjoyed the benefits of being the leaders in new manufacturing processes because of a particular configuration of factors favoring this development.

In 1750, Britain was already a highly commercialized society with the largest market in Europe. Rising agricultural productivity over much of the eighteenth century supported a rapidly increasing population. A monetary economy (in contrast to one based on barter) was widely accepted, and the country had a long and successful tradition of international trade.[4] In terms of labor, Britain had few restrictions on movement from agriculture to manufacturing and also possessed a significant number of persons competent in the somewhat low-level technical skills needed for the manufacturing processes of the period. Additionally, sufficient capital was available for the scale of investment in manufacturing processes.[5] The focus of these activities initially was in the production of wool cloth and, by the late eighteenth century, in manufacturing cotton cloth. Buoyed by the opportunities in domestic and foreign markets, British entrepreneurs quickly adopted new techniques of production. The result was a dramatic decline in costs and prices and a consequent explosion in sales.[6]

It was the sale of cotton goods abroad that fueled a general rise in British exports from 1784 to 1814. "Exports became, for the first time, a powerful 'engine of growth' of national income."[7] Sales abroad accounted for 18 percent of national income in 1801, and the cotton industry alone represented 7 percent of all national product in the same year.[8] Of equal significance was the fact that markets and sources of supply increasingly came from areas outside the Empire and, consequently, not under British political control. Trade relationships with other sovereign states were eventually to take on quite a different color than those with colonial areas. Unfortunately, these tendencies were interrupted somewhat by the international conflicts of 1792–1814 (the wars between revolutionary and Napoleonic France and much of Europe). The combination of the British blockade of continental ports and

---

[4]Eric Hobsbawm, *Industry and Empire*, New York: Penguin, 1969, 53; E. L. Jones, "Agriculture, 1700–1800," in Roderick Floud and Donald McCloskey, eds., *The Economic History of Britain Since 1700*, Cambridge: Cambridge University Press, 66–86; P. K. O'Brien, "Agriculture and the Industrial Revolution," *Economic History Review*, 30.1, 1977, 166–181; David Landes, *The Unbound Prometheus*, Cambridge: Cambridge University Press, 1969, 52–54, 46–49. Landes reports that Britain had the highest per capita income in Europe, which meant Britain had the highest wage rates and a significant domestic market for consumer goods.

[5]Hobsbawm, *Industry*. . . , 39; Landes, *The Unbound*. . . , 61–66.

[6]D. N. McCloskey, "The Industrial Revolution 1780–1860: A Survey," in Floud and McCloskey, eds., *Economic History*. . . , 110–111.

[7]P. J. Cain and A. G. Hopkins, "The Political Economy of British Expansion Overseas, 1750–1914," *The Economic History Review*, 33.4, November 1980, 472.

[8]McCloskey, "The Industrial Revolution . . .", 112.

extreme protection by the French from British products retarded economic development in Europe and let Britain move into French overseas markets.

But we should not overestimate the impact of industrial production or international trade on Britain in this period. Industrialization, although rapid, did not transform Britain or the world economy all at once. For this to happen, British political and economic leaders had to develop an understanding of trading relationships based on something other than a mercantile effort at national aggrandizement. That is, we need to understand how developments in British political economy, the adoption of industrial systems and the growth of markets in Europe, and the unilateral British decision for freer trade produced a world economy with familiar features.

After 1815, many nations in Europe raised protectionist barriers to British goods, fearing competition and the political consequences of a flood of foreign goods.

> The cardinal fact for most French producers after 1815 was the existence of an overwhelmingly dominant and powerful industrial producer not only as their nearest neighbor but as a mighty force in all foreign markets and sometimes in their own heavily-protected domestic market.[9]

For several reasons, these same nations were unable to match British productivity quickly, often taking nearly fifty years to catch up in any meaningful sense. In some cases, it was technological backwardness (often rectified by industrial spies); in others, the growing scale of competitive enterprise had outpaced the capital capacities of family firms. Many European countries were disadvantaged by higher costs, by attitudes that undermined effective entrepreneurship, and most of all by their patchwork nature as countries and markets. The complex set of political and cultural divisions often carved markets up into areas too small to support the most efficiently sized production unit.[10] In some instances, patterns of industrialization can be linked to abundant coal reserves (Belgium), while others took advantage of human capital, awaited political efforts at national unity, depended on the agricultural sector, or simply failed in their efforts to make the transition.[11] In spite of the myriad paths and fitful efforts at industrialization, many European states had made a significant beginning by mid-century, and this process accelerated considerably thereafter.[12]

---

[9] Alan Milward and S. B. Saul, *The Economic Development of Continental Europe 1780–1870*, 2nd Edition, London: Allen and Unwin, 1979, 307–309.

[10] Landes, *The Unbound. . .* , 125, 127–132, 142, 145–150.

[11] Rondo Cameron, "A New View of European Industrialization," *Economic History Review*, 38.1, February 1985, 9–16. France, for example, was restrained by relatively high-cost coal. Behind a wall of protection it was able to develop a textile industry but could export only specialized and high-priced textiles. Milward and Saul, *Economic Development. . .* , 312–331.

[12] A helpful discussion of the various means for transmitting industrialization to Europe is in Sidney Pollard, *Peaceful Conquest: The Industrialization of Europe, 1760–1970*, Oxford: Oxford University Press, 1982, 142–190.

THE TURN TO FREER TRADE

Repeal of the Corn Laws

Meanwhile, several developments in the British and world economies contributed to a British-led effort to create a more open international economy. In Britain, agriculture remained an important but declining sector. Indeed, between 1815 to 1845, Britain lost the capacity to feed itself as population growth outstripped agricultural output. At the same time, exports failed to expand at a rate sufficient to provide employment to a growing population. Stagnation in exports was due mainly to falling prices and to successful efforts in mainland Europe and the United States at protection of their infant industries. The combination of greater dependence on imported food and slow economic growth fueled radical political challenges to the government and helped prompt a somewhat novel political and economic response.[13]

Traditionally, Britain had followed a policy, reflecting the political power of its landed interests, of protecting agriculture with tariffs and other restrictions — the Corn Laws. But these restraints on trade came increasingly to be seen by manufacturing and financial interests and by political leaders as a barrier to solving the problems of food and exports. Some hoped that a unilateral reduction in British tariffs would induce a freeing of trade elsewhere, and that this would lead to an international division of labor resting on British manufacturing with agricultural and raw material production elsewhere. (Not inconsequently, this arrangement would nip in the bud the growing industrial competition from Europe and the United States.) The 1840s produced repeal of the Corn Laws and of the Navigation Acts restricting transport to British ships and brought about the revival of British trade.[14]

The repeal of the Corn Laws is important for two reasons. First, this helps us see the role of domestic political alignments in producing foreign economic policy. "Economic theories prevail . . . only when they have mobilized

---

[13]Ralph Davis, *The Industrial Revolution and British Overseas Trade*, Leicester: Leicester University Press, 1979, 15.

[14]This paragraph is based on Cain and Hopkins, "The Political Economy. . . ," 474–481; and P. J. Cain, *Economic Foundations of British Overseas Expansion, 1814–1914*, London: Macmillan, 1980, 17–21. Accompanying the move toward free trade was an end to efforts designed to prevent other nations from obtaining British technology and manpower skills. In the 1820s, laws barring the export of machinery and the immigration of skilled artisans were relaxed and, by 1843, repealed. See Pollard, *Peaceful Conquest. . .* , 144. The Navigation Acts are discussed in R. P. Thomas and D. N. McCloskey, "Overseas Trade and Empire 1700–1860," in Floud and McCloskey, *Economic History. . .* , 94. For an interesting variant on the Corn Laws, see Scott James and David Lake, "The Second Face of Hegemony: Britain's Repeal of the Corn Laws and the American Walker Tariff of 1846," *International Organization*, 43.1, Winter 1989, 1–29. Below we shall raise questions about the appropriateness of the hegemonic thesis as applied to nineteenth century Britain.

political authority, that is, only if those who believe the theories get the resources that enable them to take authoritative action."[15] For decades before 1846, economists had promoted the benefits of free trade. But only when the coalition of political forces favoring free trade was able to convince government leaders and defeat protectionist agriculture could this become national policy.[16] Second, this unilateral move to free trade was of crucial importance in shaping the world economy. In 1860, Britain and France signed the Cobden-Chevalier Treaty, substantially reducing tariffs on trade between the two. This was followed by tariff reductions in eight other European countries and ushered in the first major period of relatively free trade.[17] Equally important, a system of multilateral trade and capital flows, centering largely on Britain, emerged to form a world economy of substantial proportions.

The Expansion of the World Economy

The movement toward freer and increased trade was influenced by and helped advance several related developments between 1850 and 1875. The political unification of Germany, pushed by the need for unified markets and the desire for greater international influence, changed the economic landscape in central Europe. Much of the process of economic change was centered on building railroads, an activity which required substantial amounts of capital and had the consequence of expanding dramatically the scope and scale of markets. Initially, much of the capital for railroads in Belgium and France came from Britain. Later, France became a capital exporter even as Germany was able to meet its own needs.

In the midst of these developments, industrial progress in Europe produced a widened scope of economic relationships. Expansion of textile production in France and Germany, along with continuing growth in Britain, resulted in sharp increases in wool and cotton imports from the United States, Australia, and New Zealand. The improvements in continental and oceanic transportation, beginning especially in the 1860s and 1870s, led to dramatic

---

[15]Peter Gourevitch, *Politics in Hard Times: Comparative Responses to International Economic Crises,* Ithaca: Cornell University Press, 54.

[16]An alternative view emphasizing the ideological power of the idea of free trade is in Charles Kindleberger, "The Rise of Free Trade in Western Europe, 1820–1875," in his *Economic Response: Comparative Studies in Trade, Finance, and Growth,* Cambridge: Harvard University Press, 53. Two other approaches to understanding the adoption of free trade are found in Paul E. Rohrlich, "Economic Culture and Foreign Policy: the Cognitive Analysis of Economic Policy Making," *International Organization,* 41.1, Winter 1987, 61–92; and Cherly Schonhardt-Bailey, "Specific Factors, Capital Markets, Portfolio Diversification, and Free Trade: Domestic Determinants of the Repeal of the Corn Laws," *World Politics,* 43.4, July 1991, 545–569.

[17]Kindleberger, "The Rise of . . . ," 54–56. For a view of French behavior emphasizing domestic political and economic interests, see Michael S. Smith, *Tariff Reform in France 1860–1900: The Politics of Economic Interest,* Ithaca: Cornell University Press, 1980.

increases in European imports of grain and meat. A multilateral division of labor based on the level of industrialization and geography developed within Europe. British goods, especially railroad equipment, machinery, coal, and textiles were sold in advanced sections of Europe while German industry, for example, was successful in central and eastern European markets. Ironically, British trade in machinery and railroads helped the newly industrializing areas of Germany and France utilize their own advantages (for example, German wages were lower than those in Britain) to close the gap with Britain and to adopt the role of leading other European states into the world economy.[18]

Equally telling, in addition to these general reservations about free trade, are the calculations made by countries who chose to participate in freer trade in the mid-nineteenth century. France used the 1860 treaty to deflect Britain from interfering in a conflict with Austria over Italy. The German free trade area — the Zollverin — recognized that its substantial sales of grain in Great Britain would be protected by lowering tariffs on British goods. In the United States, the new possibilities for trade with Britain created by lower tariffs helped solidify a political coalition supporting lower U.S. tariffs. These examples strongly reinforce the importance of understanding matters like free trade in terms of political economy, a perspective that acknowledges a relationship between economic and political influences.[19]

THE PERILS OF INTERDEPENDENCE: 1873–1914

Transformation of the World Economy

The period from 1873 to 1914 produced changes in the world economy equal in importance to those of the preceding 100 years. The pace of change accelerated, with an extraordinary shift in the distribution of relative international economic power resulting from the decline of Great Britain and the rise of the United States and Germany. Accompanying this were the first stirrings of industrialization in what we today call the Third World. This was true in India, China, and especially in Japan. The continuing expansion of international trade and finance led to a growing interdependence of national economies, as

---

[18]The discussion in this paragraph rests on Pollard, *Peaceful Conquest. . .* , 172–183; E. J. Hobsbawm, *The Age of Capital, 1848–1875*, New York: New American Library, 1975, 27–71; William Woodruff, "The Emergence of an International Economy 1700–1914," in Carlo M. Cipolla, ed., *The Fontana Economic History of Europe*, London: Fontana Press, 1973, 658–672; Hobsbawm, *Industry. . .* , 97–140; Landes, *The Unbound. . .* , 158–219; and Alan Milward and S.B. Saul, *The Economic Development of Continental Europe 1780–1870*, Second Edition, London: Allen & Unwin, 1979, 309–310, 352–353, 380–396, 404–414.

[19]See James Foreman-Peck, *A History of the World Economy: International Economic Relations since 1850*, Totowa: Barnes & Noble Books, 1983, 57–58; James and Lake, "The Second Face . . .", 13–14.

measured by price movements, common financial crises and economic fluctuations, increasing proportions of foreign trade and investment, and a more
coherently organized international monetary system centered on gold.

At the same time, the free trade system created after 1846 was largely
dismantled and reversed by widespread protectionist sentiments. Higher tariffs were a reflection of an intensification of competition for markets and of
the political and economic dislocations caused by dramatic increases in trade.
And finally, the very character of industrial life began to change in fundamental ways. New industrial systems such as chemicals, oil, electricity, and steel
emerged in the late nineteenth century not only as leading, but even dominant
sectors. In these and other industries a new type of enterprise developed, one
of much greater size and designed to take advantage of significant economies
of scale in production and national and international marketing and distribution networks.

The changes in the distribution of international economic and industrial
power can be seen in the following charts:

TABLE 3.1

Distribution of World Industrial Production, 1870–1913 (*in percentages*)

YEARS	UNITED STATES	GREAT BRITAIN	GERMANY	FRANCE	RUSSIA	JAPAN	INDIA	REST OF WORLD
1870	23	32	13	10	4	——	——	17
1881–1885	29	27	14	9	3	——	——	19
1896–1900	30	20	17	7	5	1	1	19
1906–1910	35	15	16	6	5	1	1	20
1913	36	14	16	6	6	1	1	20

SOURCE: Walt Rostow, *The World Economy*, Austin: University of Texas Press, 1978, 52–53.

The precipitous decline of Great Britain and France and the equally rapid
rise of the United States, and to a lesser extent Germany, are the most striking
features of Table 3.1. That Britain, in the space of two generations, could fall
relatively so far in spite of a growing economy over most of this period is
testimony to the tenuous position of all in the modern world economy.[20] The

---

[20]The effects of compound rates of growth can be seen in the statistics of economic expansion
spread out over forty years. The average annual growth rate from 1870 to 1913 for Britain was
1.6 percent, in the United States 5 percent, and Germany 4.7 percent. Seemingly small differences, extended over such a long period, produced the dramatic relative decline by Great
Britain. See Aaron Friedberg, *The Weary Titan: Britain and the Experience of Relative Decline*,
Princeton: Princeton University Press, 1988, 25.

United States and Germany, along with Russia, also experienced a rapid expansion in population, with growth from 1890 to 1913 of 55 percent, 36 percent, and 50 percent respectively. By contrast, British population growth for the same period was only 22 percent, while in France it amounted to less than 4 percent.[21] In selected areas, the shift toward a United States and German advantage was even more dramatic.

TABLE 3.2

Iron/Steel Production, 1890–1913
(*millions of tons*)

	1890	1900	1910	1913
United States	9.3	10.3	26.5	31.8
Great Britain	8.0	5.0	6.5	7.7
Germany	4.1	6.3	13.6	17.6

SOURCE: This table is adapted from Kennedy, *The Rise.* . . , 200.

TABLE 3.3

Energy Consumption, 1890–1913
(*in millions of metric tons of coal equivalent*)

	1890	1900	1910	1913
United States	147	248	403	541
Great Britain	145	171	185	195
Germany	71	112	158	187

SOURCE: This table is adapted from Kennedy, *The Rise.* . . , 201.

Clearly, by 1913 British dominance of world industrial capabilities had been swept away.

How are we to understand this remarkable transformation? Perhaps the best explanation lies in the simple but powerful fact that certain special advantages in the United States and Germany were well-suited to the industrial

---

[21]The data on population growth are computed from Paul Kennedy, *The Rise and Fall of the Great Powers*, New York: Random House, 1987, 199. Britain retained second position in per capita industrialization. See Kennedy, page 200, Table 14.

developments of the age. In Germany, an extensive and diversified system of scientific education produced large numbers of trained scientists and technical personnel who were able to take advantage of a cascade of theoretical innovations. This was especially true in the newly emerging chemical industry and in the production of complex machine tools. Further, Germany used its raw materials and industrial capabilities to press rapidly ahead in steel and coal production and in railroad construction (including central and eastern Europe).[22]

Similarly, the United States used its substantial raw material resources and very large and affluent domestic market as the base for creating the biggest economy in the world.

TABLE 3.4

Gross Domestic Product:
United States, Great Britain, and Germany
(*1970 United States Prices*)

COUNTRY	1870	1913
United States		
Gross Domestic Product (billions)	$3.050	$17.628
Gross Domestic Product — per capita	$764	$1,813
Great Britain		
Gross Domestic Product (billions)	$3.036	$6.808
Gross Domestic Product — per capita	$972	$1,491
Germany		
Gross Domestic Product (billions)	$2.099	$7.184
Gross Domestic Product — per capita	$535	$1,073

SOURCE: Albert Chandler, *Scale and Scope: The Dynamics of Industrial Capitalism*, Cambridge: Harvard University Press, 1990, 52.

The unification of markets produced by the introduction of the railroad and telegraph had its greatest impact in the United States. It was here that the system of modern managerial capitalism was born and developed furthest in the pre–World War I era. Over a wide array of products, U.S. firms launched into mass production, distribution, and marketing for the giant domestic market, thereby taking advantage of substantial returns to scale.[23] The organization

---

[22]Alan Milward and S.B. Saul, *The Development of the Economies of Continental Europe, 1850–1914*, Cambridge: Harvard University Press, 1977, 19–20, 27, 30, 33–38.

[23]The concept of economies of scale refers to a decline in the per unit cost of production as a result of increases in the volume of production. Typically, this is greatest for those firms with

and direction of these firms rapidly shifted to professional, hierarchically arranged, salaried managers and away from owner-managers. It was this structural innovation that permitted the coordination and direction of these vast enterprises.[24]

British Hegemony?

What about Great Britain during this period? One important point to recognize is that Britain remained the dominant force in international trade and finance. Even in 1913, Britain accounted for 31 percent of world trade in manufactured goods, with Germany at 27.5 percent, and the United States at 13 percent.[25] In 1914, the British share of international investments was clearly in a commanding position and perhaps still growing.

TABLE 3.5

Overseas Investments of the Major Economic Powers, 1870–1914
(*in millions of dollars*)

	1870	1900	1914	% OF WORLD IN 1914
Great Britain	4,900	12,000	20,000	44.0
France	2,500	5,800	9,050	19.9
Germany	_____	4,800	5,800	12.8
United States	100	500	3,500	7.8
Others	500	1,100	7,100	15.5

SOURCE: Sidney Pollard, "Capital Exports, 1870–1914: Harmful or Beneficial?" *The Economic History Review*, 38.4, November 1985, 492.

But this strong international investment position cannot disguise the serious relative decline in the British economy, from which it never really recovered.

One important source of difficulty was Britain's incomplete adaptation to the emerging world of capital-intensive, large-scale, scientifically based, and professionally managed firms. British businesses and investors were content with retaining a much more personal system of management, often resting with the founder's family. This meant smaller enterprises with

---

large fixed costs. Larger volume of production permits them to spread these costs over more units, thereby reducing the per unit cost.

[24]Chandler, *Scale and Scope*. . . , 52–89.

[25]Friedberg, *The Weary*. . . , 24.

relatively limited managerial hierarchies. The reasons for these developments are complex but lie mainly in the fact that British advantages contributing to their leading role in the first industrial revolution did not transfer into advantages for the second industrial revolution. The British domestic market, once the largest in Europe, was not only small in comparison with the United States and Germany but grew much more slowly. Large domestic markets were crucial in supporting U.S. and German industries in their move into new industrial areas and provided the justification for creating large and sophisticated enterprises. The domestic British market simply did not support the widespread adoption of this kind of business organization. Moreover, the areas of early British advantage — textiles, iron, and ships — did not lend themselves to economies of scale, nor were they greatly affected by the new systems of communication and transportation. Thus, British export markets remained in the older industries even as the United States and Germany, resting on the large base of a domestic market, pushed their exports in the new industries such as "refined oil, processed foodstuffs, mass-produced light machinery, and electrical equipment." In the emerging age of large-scale production, marketing, and distribution, British industry lacked the advantages that would push its entrepreneurs to take the lead in developing these areas.[26]

Almost certainly, the most important British roles during this period were to extend international capital markets, contribute to a loosely organized international monetary system based on gold, and maintain open markets in a time of increasing protectionism. Britain's dominance resulted from the importance of the City of London in short-term financing of international trade, from the role of sterling as virtually equivalent to an international currency, and from the vast sums of capital that flowed abroad into long-term foreign investments. These bases of power enabled the London banking system to affect interest rates around the world, to provide international liquidity during times of crisis, and to finance, over many years, the balance of payments deficits of a variety of countries without harsh adjustments.[27]

Central to this process was an international monetary system based on the gold standard and sterling. This developed in the 1870s when several countries in addition to Britain adopted a gold backing for their currencies and permitted the free movement of gold exports and imports. The effect was to fix the exchange rates of these currencies based on the ratio of gold backing. That is,

[26]This paragraph is based on the analysis found in Chandler, *Scale and Scope.* . . , 235–294; with quote at page 250. Also helpful in filling out the picture of the competitive system of the 1873–1914 era are Derek H. Aldcroft, *The Development of British Industry and Foreign Competition: 1875–1914,* Toronto: University of Toronto Press, 1968, especially pages 11–36; and Foreman-Peck, *A History.* . . , 94–110.

[27]Robert J. A. Skidelsky, "Retreat from Leadership: The Evolution of British Economic Foreign Policy, 1870–1939," in Benjamin Rowland, et al., eds. *Balance of Power of Hegemony: The Interwar Monetary System,* New York: New York University Press, 1976, 152–163; Foreman-Peck, *A History.* . . , 67–84; Milward and Saul, *The Development.* . . , 487–492.

the exchange rate between any two currencies was simply the ratio of the amount of gold backing their currencies. The result was a rudimentary but evolving international monetary system, built around British management and protection of its own position along with an almost constant outflow of British capital to cushion the adjustment problems created by its perpetual current account surplus.[28]

The combination of economic growth (especially in the United States and Germany), increasing world trade, and expanding capital flows generated both greater interdependence among nations and a reaction designed to reduce the costs of this connectedness. The links among nations and the importance of these links can be seen in the increasing tendency for simultaneous expansion and contraction in national economies, including both production and finance. By the late 1850s, the price of wheat in any given country was heavily influenced by world market conditions. In 1857, both an oversupply of wheat in the world and falling prices produced a financial panic in the United States that had serious effects in Great Britain and Germany. Throughout the 1860s, the American Civil War greatly affected financial conditions in Britain and land prices in India. By 1873, the French indemnity payment to Germany (following their 1870 war) produced such imbalances in the international financial system as to precipitate an international depression.[29]

This depression coincided with a growing supply of wheat, especially from the United States, made possible by improvements in land and sea transportation and in the technology of production. Price declines in many commodities were substantial, accelerating a trend common to much of the nineteenth century. This continued until an upturn began in the 1890s. The result was to rearrange the economic and political interests of several groups, especially with regard to tariff questions. Many agricultural and industrial producers were confronted with the possibility of being forced out of business, suffering major losses, or substantially changing their methods of production. Their demands for protection were not ignored, and several governments, led by Germany and France, began raising tariffs. By 1890, much of the system of freer trade had been reversed.[30]

---

[28]Barry Eichengreen, "Editor's Introduction," in Barry Eichengreen, ed. *The Gold Standard in Theory and History*, New York: Methuen, 1985, 5–19; Barry Eichengreen, "Conducting the International Orchestra: Bank of England Leadership under the Classical Gold Standard," *Journal of International Money and Finance*, 6, March 1987.

[29]Foreman-Peck, *A History*. . . , 84–88. Foreman-Peck also reports on the "fairly close synchronization of price movements. . ." among gold standard economies. See pages 161–163.

[30]Gourevitch, *Politics in* . . . , 71–123. What were the consequences of increasing protectionism? In political terms it was to solidify conservative regimes. Economically, the result was to redistribute the costs and benefits of production and trade. Tariffs almost always raise the prices paid by consumers for goods associated with international trade, increase government revenues, and provide protected domestic producers with greater profits. Moreover, they remove or reduce the competitive incentives to innovate and lower costs for those domestic industries receiving protection.

The major exception to these trends was Great Britain, which resisted domestic pressure for protection and refused to retaliate against other nations. And yet, any consideration of Britain's behavior during the late nineteenth century raises questions about the role and importance of the world's leading economic power in creating and sustaining a stable and orderly world economy. How important was British leadership for the nineteenth century world economy? Did British leaders see themselves as responsible for maintaining a system of free trade and international economic prosperity? Or rather, did they simply look to extend their position and engage in leadership only when it could be linked to narrow national interests?

This question has usually been framed in terms of whether or not Britain acted as a hegemonic state, that is, whether the British were willing to apply overwhelming economic, military, and political strength to the formation and preservation of an international economic order. The evidence for this is mixed. Clearly, British market power in the 1840–1860 period helped move several nations toward freer trade, while British financial power was key to the functioning of a world trading and monetary system for much of the century. Further, British policies, capital, and businessmen served to transmit technology and bring many peripheral areas into the world economy. Perhaps most important was the willingness of private financiers to supply credit during periods of financial distress.[31] But, on the whole, Britain acted as a passive hegemon, reflecting the laissez-faire political economy of the day. It led largely by example and not by organizing multilateral efforts to manage the system. The instruments and practices of domestic economic management were limited, thereby restricting similar efforts at the international level. The failure to punish those nations that increased tariffs after 1873 suggests a much more aloof Britain, rather than one seeing its role as responsible for keeping an open system in place.

If we think beyond economic relationships, British military power was certainly important for forcibly opening China and Japan to the world, controlling India, and preserving free movement on the world's oceans. But, Britain was equally important in the process of expanding imperialism and thereby closing off areas from the world economy (except as trade went through Britain itself). Britain certainly made no effort to oppose the principle of international aggrandizement in the non-Western world (again, except as it encroached on British interests). We can safely say that the link between British security, international security, and the world economy was a tenuous

---

[31]Charles Kindleberger, "International Public Goods Without International Government," *American Economic Review*, 76.1, March 1986, 1–13; and Charles Kindleberger, *Manias, Panics, and Crashes*, New York: Basic Books, 1989, 201–231. British power was also very important in promoting "a politically stable environment for trade and investment." Charles Lipson, *Standing Guard: Protecting Foreign Capital in the Nineteenth and Twentieth Centuries*, Berkeley: University of California Press, 1985, 42. The strongest and clearest statement of Britain as hegemon is in Skidelsky, "Retreat from. . . ," 151–163.

one. The effect of this was to remove a key element providing incentives for a stronger involvement in managing world affairs. Thus, when nations began raising trade barriers in the 1870s, Britain stuck to its policy of splendid isolation from the continent, accepted this outcome, and shifted much of its trade to the Empire.[32]

The first great test of the ability of Great Britain and other nations to manage the vicissitudes of economic interdependence and international competition resulted in failure. Economic and political nationalism reinforced military competition, and nations increasingly found themselves unable to find a secure basis for pursuing prosperity within an open international system. The growing tide of protectionism and destructive competition did not eliminate the web of interdependence in the world economy. At the same time, the level and nature of political and economic cooperation was stunted and, consequently, did not provide mechanisms for collective gain. The spiral of struggle, alliances, armaments, and planning for war overwhelmed the logic of comparative advantage and mutual benefits from trade.

JAPAN AND LATE ECONOMIC DEVELOPMENT

■ One of the most important and enduring questions of international political economy concerns the relationship between more developed and less developed states. Do advanced states, through trade and capital investments, serve to transmit the technology, money, and ideas for industrialization? Or, do these more powerful states use their leverage to exploit weaker states and perpetuate underdevelopment? We will reserve a more thorough treatment of these questions for Chapter Eight. For now, one very important part of the answer lies in determining whether any less developed and non-Western states have been able to break through from backwardness to industrialization. Japan, over the last third of the nineteenth century, surely presents the most remarkable example of just such a case.

It was Western determination to gain access to Japan that set this process into motion. Isolated for more than 200 years and beset by a feudal system and weak government, the Japanese were overwhelmed by Western military technology. In 1853–1854, and continuing over the next fifteen years, Japan was subjected to demands by the United States and Great Britain (among others) for special privileges and rights that compromised its sovereignty. The effort to cope with these demands without inviting war destroyed the legitimacy of the Japanese government. At the same time, the Western presence activated a virulent anti-foreign reaction among the samurai (a military

---

[32]In some ways, this acquiescence to tariffs is similar to acceptance of German unification in the 1864–1871 period.

caste that had declined over the preceding two centuries of peace). Additionally, access to and the ability to utilize Western military technology effectively
became the decisive factor in determining the outcome of the domestic political struggle that ensued. The result was a new Japanese government with the
political strength and unflinching determination to make Japan into a modern
nation capable of maintaining its independence.

Non-industrialized states entering the world economy at such a late date
are often said to face a special set of disadvantages in comparison with early
industrializers. Late arrivers encounter established competitors with more
complex systems of technology and education and a set of institutions experienced in adjusting to the demands of international competition. Those who
hope to succeed must adopt some way of compensating for their weaknesses.
Often, this has meant relying on the government to finance, or even establish,
enterprises, especially when the capital requirements for large industries such
as coal or steel are needed.[33] Equally important, the state has usually provided the means for creating the broad social infrastructure needed for a
modern society.

The pattern of Japanese development conforms in several respects to these
expectations, but in others it deviates in significant ways. In 1868, the year of
the Meiji Restoration, Japan had already developed a substantial market economy based largely on rural enterprises.[34] Over the next thirty years, much of
Japan's economic growth derived from agricultural improvements and from
rural industrial enterprises. These small-scale industries were primarily silk-
worm, silk reeling, and cotton textile operations, and most of the production
was for export.[35] Unlike the tendency toward large-scale, capital-intensive heavy
industries found in other late industrializers, the first wave of Japanese industrialization was concentrated in areas of comparative advantage.

This may have been the result of a convergence of two factors: Japan's
forced exposure to the world economy and changes in the competitive position of several more advanced states. One of the consequences of the unequal
treaties of the 1850s and 1860s was that Japan forfeited control over its tariff
policy. In addition, a decline in Britain's ability to dominate the cotton industry opened the door for Japan. The technology of production was readily
available and inexpensive (compared to heavy industry) and much easier to
adopt. The sensitivity to the world market, the presence of a disciplined,

---

[33]This argument is traditionally acknowledged to come from Alexander Gerschenkron, *Economic Backwardness in Historical Perspective*, Cambridge: Harvard University Press, 1962.

[34]Thomas C. Smith, *Native Sources of Japanese Industrialization, 1750–1920*, Berkeley: University
of California Press, 1988, 71–102, 133–147, 199–235.

[35]Sidney Crawcour, "Industrialization and Technical Change," in Marius Jansen, ed. *Cambridge
History of Modern Japan*, Cambridge: Cambridge University Press, 1989, 388, 407–414; W. G.
Beasley, *The Rise of Modern Japan*, New York: St. Martin's Press, 1990, 102–114; Osamu Saito,
"Commercial Agriculture, By-Employment, and Wage Work," in Marius Jansen and Gilbert
Rozman, eds. *Japan in Transition: From Tokugawa to Meiji*, Princeton: Princeton University Press,
1986, 400–420.

reliable labor force, and entrepreneurial experience in the countryside gave Japan enough of an advantage to enter the world market successfully.

The greatest similarity between Japan and other late industrializers is the role of the state. The new Meiji government acted rapidly to reshape the country based on the needs of centralized power and economic development. It abolished the regional authorities (the domains), enacted a centralized tax system, eliminated the special status of the samurai, started conscription, and created a national educational system all within seven years.[36] This extraordinary capacity for moving Japan so far so fast constitutes the distinctive quality of the Japanese state.[37] But like most European states in the 1820–1870 period, the Japanese government mobilized capital, invested in infrastructure, started demonstration enterprises, offered subsidies, promoted market unification, and regulated industries needing help in establishing common production standards.[38] And yet, the greatest part of the industrialization process came from private action, even when supported by the state. This is true not only of Japan but also of France and Germany in the mid-nineteenth century. What may have been most unusual about Japan was the extraordinary cooperation of private and public actors.

WORLD WAR I AND AFTERMATH

■ The world war that began in August 1914 was the culmination of the failure of nations to find security and prosperity within a context of tightening interdependence. Even more important was the extraordinary restructuring of the world economy caused by the war: it redistributed international economic power, disrupted the world economy, and destroyed trade and financial relations. The period from 1919 to 1939 is largely the story of limited, and somewhat unsuccessful, efforts to reorganize a functioning and prosperous world economic system.

There were three major impediments to international economic stability after World War I. First, most governments lacked the political strength and experience to design and carry out a managerial role in the domestic and

---

[36]Richard Rubinger, "Education From One Room to One System," in Jansen and Rozman, *Japan in. . .* , 191–230; and W. G. Beasley, *The Meiji Restoration*, Stanford: Stanford University Press, 1973.

[37]I am grateful to Albert Craig for clarifying this point for me.

[38]Barry Supple, "The State and the Industrial Revolution, 1700–1914," in C.M. Cippola, ed. *The Fontana Economic History of Europe: The Industrial Revolution*, Glasgow: Fontana/Collins, 1973, 301–357; William Lockwood, "The State and Economic Enterprise in Modern Japan, 1868–1938," in Simon Kutznets et al., eds. *Economic Growth in Brazil, India and Japan*, Durham: Duke University Press, 1955, 540–547, 563; Henry Rosovsky, *Capital Formation in Japan, 1868–1940*, New York: Free Press, 1961, 53–104; David Landes, "Japan and Europe: Contrasts in Industrialization," in Lockwood, ed. *The State and Economic Enterprise in Japan*, Princeton: Princeton University Press, 1965, 93–182.

international economies. As a result, the world economy lacked effective mechanisms for transferring capital from surplus to deficit countries, especially during times of economic distress. Second, the failure of the world's largest economic power, the United States, to accept a leadership role opened a major void. British weakness prevented a resumption of its nineteenth-century role, and the U.S. political system was too immature to support an assumption of this responsibility. Third, the ferocity of the downturn in the world economy after 1929 almost guaranteed a retreat into autarchy and protection as nations struggled to defend their domestic economies. But, in spite of these barriers, there were significant elements of reconstruction and cooperation. Private efforts frequently attempted to fill the vacuum created by government reticence. In the 1930s, the United States became less timid about organizing international cooperation. As it happened though, these actions almost never proved sufficient.

The Economic Consequences of World War I

The pattern of participation and fighting in the war helps explain many of its economic consequences. Great Britain and France, allied with Russia, fought Germany and Austria-Hungary for nearly three years before the United States joined the war. The United States acted as a neutral but emerged quickly as the chief supplier of war-related material to Britain and France. Before entering the war in April 1917, the allies paid for these goods by liquidating their overseas investments and by using credit provided by private U.S. banks. After U.S. involvement, credit was supplied by the U.S. government. By the war's end, Britain and France had accumulated more than $10 billion in debts, and the United States had become the largest creditor nation in the world.[39] Equally significant, European reliance on external suppliers and the disruption of export markets provided a major boost to production in several peripheral states, but especially the United States and Japan.[40] The latter experienced dramatic improvements in its industrial and technological development from expanded markets in Europe and Asia. For other states, the breakdown of trade patterns provided incentives to develop domestic industries that could substitute for European imports. Thus, the European focus of the war helped shift industrial production to outlying nations and created an immense international debt burden.

---

[39]Kathleen Burk, *Britain, America and the Sinews of War, 1014–1918*, Boston: Allen and Unwin, 1985; Ross Gregory, *The Origins of American Involvement in the First World War*, New York: Norton, 1971, 63. The inter-allied financing system was more complex than simply sending funds from the United States to Britain and France. Several states operated as both borrower and lender, creating a tangled web of debts. See Derek Aldcroft, *From Versailles to Wall Street, 1919–1929*, Berkeley: University of California Press, 1977, 93.

[40]Aldcroft, *From Versailles. . . ,* 37–41.

Added to these hardships were problems created by worn-down and destroyed production facilities in Europe and by the financial disruption from measures used to finance the war. Four years of maximum production and difficulties in replacing old equipment reduced European competitiveness in the world economy. The war also forced abandonment of the gold standard at home and abroad — currency could no longer be exchanged for gold — along with a rapid expansion of the money supply to support deficit spending by the government. The result was unparalleled inflation, further deterioration in Europe's competitive position, and a continuation of a large trade deficit into the postwar period.[41] On top of the imbalances experienced by the victors in the war were the problems faced by Germany. The political importance of vengeance and the economic need to recoup losses combined to prompt Britain and France to demand reparations (payments for war losses) from Germany.[42] But payment of reparations had to come from a German current account surplus or from capital supplied from abroad. The combination of trade imbalances and debt payments created a very unstable situation for the world economy.

A Failure of Political Vision

Effective solutions to these difficulties were hampered by the fact that political thinking failed to keep up with the real changes produced by the war. Statesmen and publics in many countries were eager to return to the world of 1914 and acted as though they expected few problems in doing this. This was reflected in the almost blind faith in the need to reestablish the gold standard, create monetary stability, and fix exchange rates. Wartime governmental controls were lifted quickly, and, at the same time, little thought was given at the peace conference to the importance of continuing intervention by governments in stabilizing the world economy.[43] Perhaps most short-sighted was the U.S. insistence on repayment of all war debts. This overlooked the payments deficit position of the Europeans and the negative impact repayment would place on recovery. The U.S. commitment to war debts made France especially determined to force Germany to make large reparation payments. But, lest we see war-debt forgiveness as an easy matter, to do anything other than exacting payment would have required raising taxes to absorb the debts into the U.S. budget. Although such a plan was highly rational in terms of world reconstruction and stability, the U.S. government did not have the political strength required for such an act. Conservatives

---

[41] Aldcroft, *From Versailles*. . . , 30–33, 63.
[42] The amount of reparations was never fixed in a permanent sense. But in 1921, the Reparations Commission determined the amount to be equal to $33 billion. See Aldcroft, *From Versailles*. . . , 81.
[43] Aldcroft, *From Versailles*. . . , 3–6.

and nationalists rejected any U.S. responsibility for these problems and demanded the debts be repaid.[44]

In spite of domestic pressures to ignore any international responsibilities and to insist on war-debt repayment, the leadership of the U.S. government and financial community could not ignore the difficulties created by such a policy, as they recognized the potential for great trouble created by the imbalances in the world economy. The current account deficits of European states obviously hampered the payment of reparations and war debts. But in 1922, the already protective U.S. tariff rose (even if only by a small amount), thereby undermining the ability of Europeans to sell in the United States, achieve a current account surplus, and make debt payments. Exchange rates, due to financial dislocations caused by the war, could not be fixed. These fluctuations undercut the ability of business persons to make calculations for investments. From the standpoint of American leaders, European stability was judged to be an important but not vital interest. The domestic economy took priority over U.S. efforts to promote European recovery.[45]

A more active U.S. policy had to await French military action in 1923 to collect German reparations and the virtual financial and economic collapse of Germany over the next year. A coalition of U.S. government officials and private financial interests took steps to deal with the situation. The Dawes Plan, negotiated in conjunction with Britain and France, called for reductions in annual reparation payments and provided for private American loans to Germany. Over the next five years, a large volume of foreign loans, mostly from the United States, provided Germany with the capital to make its reparations payments and achieve an uneven economic recovery.[46] But this was a fragile and precarious arrangement, dependent as it was on an unending supply of foreign capital, which itself was contingent on calculations of profit by private bankers. Any interruption in foreign loans would prompt a return to the chaos of 1923–1924.

A second, and equally problematic, effort at producing stability came from Britain's decision to restore the gold standard and fix the value of the

---

[44]Joan Hoff Wilson, *American Business and Foreign Policy, 1920–1933*, Boston: Beacon Press, 1971, 70–80, 105–112, 121–133.

[45]Melvyn Leffler, *The Elusive Quest: America's Pursuit of European Security and French Security, 1919–1933*, Chapel Hill: University of North Carolina Press, 1979, 79–81, and generally 40–81. Many U.S. officials believed economic expansion abroad was beneficial but did not think U.S. prosperity depended on it. At the same time, major figures in the New York financial community were committed to making New York the world's financial center, displacing London. See Leffler, *The Elusive. . .* , 147, 173; and Carl Parrini, *Heir to Empire: United States Economic Diplomacy, 1916–1923*, Pittsburgh: University of Pittsburgh Press, 1969, 101–137. For a good sense of U.S. domestic politics as reflected in presidential thinking, see Robert K. Murray, *The Politics of Normalcy*, New York: Norton, 1972.

[46]Aldcroft, *From Versailles. . .* , 84–86; William C. McNeil, *American Money and the Weimar Republic*, New York: Columbia University Press, 1986, 24–34, 97–235. A view giving more weight to the stability of this postwar system is in Charles Maier, *Recasting Bourgeois Europe*, Princeton: Princeton University Press, 1974.

pound at the prewar rate. Wartime inflation had exacerbated the problem of British competitiveness, which was evident well before 1914. Rather than use a postwar recession to drive prices down and recoup some of its competitive position, Britain chose to let the pound float. Its price initially fell but by 1925 had returned to near prewar exchange rates, at which point the pound was placed on the gold standard. The success of such a system depended on two crucial factors. London had to be able to meet the demand for gold, which was complicated by the emergence of New York and Paris as alternative international financial centers. The greater strength of the dollar and the franc put pressure on the weaker pound and produced a constant drain of gold from London. Equally important was the need to provide for capital flows from surplus to deficit countries (which was part of the Dawes Plan discussed above). But Britain's ability to fulfill this function was greatly damaged by the financial restructuring of the war and the U.S. ability to take its place was hampered by the domestic priorities of the government and private bankers. When U.S. lending and imports both contracted from 1928 to 1930, the strains on the world economy were simply too great, and the system collapsed.[47]

Collapse of the World Economy

Although the imbalances created by the First World War and the patchwork efforts to resolve these problems were not the precipitating cause of the Great Depression, they did serve to transform a downturn in the business cycle into a hurricane of deflation and unemployment. The Federal Reserve in the United States, worried about the boom and speculation in the American economy, moved to restrict credit in 1928. The result was the aforementioned decline in U.S. foreign lending, a drop in U.S. production, and a bursting of the stock market bubble in October 1929. U.S. foreign lending was cut in half from 1928 to 1929 and halved again by 1930. This led to a decline in investment and production in Europe, which, combined with the slowdown in the United States, meant a sharp fall in commodity prices and contributed to the break in stock prices.[48]

---

[47]Skidelsky, "Retreat from. . . ," 168–173; Alcroft, *From Versailles.* . . , 168–186. Because the American government could not appear to be intervening in European affairs, the task of managing the unavoidable U.S. involvement fell to the relatively invisible Federal Reserve Bank of New York and its governor, Benjamin Strong. Strong developed a close working relationship with Montagu Norman, governor of the Bank of England. These men understood the international financial system could not function on its own and acted to supply the leadership needed to keep an unbalanced system in place, at least until the late 1920s. See Stephen V. O. Clarke, *Central Bank Cooperation, 1924–31,* New York: Federal Reserve Bank of New York, 1967.

[48]Aldcroft, *From Versailles.* . . , 261–267, 280–284, 231–236.

The rush of world economic decline between 1930 and 1931 exposed the weaknesses in the system of trade, finance, and economic management. In the United States during 1930, manufacturing production declined by 20 percent and exports by 35 percent. During the same time, unemployment in Britain rose from 10 percent to 16 percent and in Germany from 13 percent to 22 percent.[49] Initial government reaction was largely to accept these events, based on the expectation that investment would revive when prices fell far enough. What finally prompted government action was the impending collapse in May and June of 1931 of the debt system built up around reparations, war debts, and U.S. loans. Fearing a "complete collapse of Germany's credit structure within a day or two . . ." and its effect on the American banking system, President Hoover granted a moratorium on reparation payments.[50]

When this proved insufficient to halt the German banking crisis, Hoover pulled back, preferring to shift any additional relief burden to private U.S. bankers. But this was impossible, and in mid-July, the German government closed German banks and placed severe restrictions on foreign exchange transactions. The effect was to freeze all foreign assets in Germany. The crisis then shifted to London, and the threat to international financial stability moved Hoover to reverse the ten-year-old U.S. policy of refusing official (direct and open) participation in European affairs. He agreed to send Secretary of State Henry Stimson to a conference in London to address the crisis. Notwithstanding this break with the past, the U.S. government remained hamstrung by a deep reluctance to expand its budget deficit and by political forces insisting on domestic solutions to the depression. Consequently, the London Conference failed to solve the problem.[51]

The crisis continued throughout August and September, as Britain was forced to exchange gold for pounds. When additional credits from private and central bankers were exhausted, the British left the gold standard in a dramatic decision on September 21, 1931. The next day, the United States suffered massive gold withdrawals and, by the end of October, the first of an unceasing wave of bank failures. The spiral of declining world trade and domestic production; falling prices, investments, and profits; and rising loan defaults and bank failures continued throughout 1931 and 1932. By early 1933, the banking system in the United States was perilously close to complete collapse. Only a decision to close the entire system and rebuild it from the ground up averted this outcome.[52]

---

[49]Leffler, *The Elusive*. . . , 231–232; Charles Kindleberger, *The World in Depression, 1929–1939*, Berkeley: University of California Press, 1973, 128–145.

[50]Leffler, *The Elusive*. . . , 238–239, 246. The crisis in Germany started in neighboring Austria where a major bank, Credit-Anstalt, failed due to its own weaknesses and panicky withdrawals by foreign depositors. The effect was to frighten depositors into similar withdrawals in Germany and elsewhere in Europe. See Kindleberger, *The World*. . . , 146–153.

[51]Leffler, *The Elusive*. . . , 248–256.

[52]Susan Kennedy, *The Banking Crisis of 1933*, Lexington: University Press of Kentucky, 1973, 152–223; Kindleberger, *The World*. . . , 167–177, 186–198; Leffler, *The Elusive*. . . , 256–272.

Autarchy and Cooperation

The disintegration of the international monetary and trading systems ushered in a period in which many countries tried to cope with the depression apart from the world economy.[53] Earlier, in 1930, Congress passed, and President Hoover signed, the Smoot-Hawley tariff legislation, which increased U.S. protection substantially. This triggered a round of tariff increases around the world.[54] In 1931, Japan invaded Manchuria in China hoping to secure markets and resources.[55] After Britain left the gold standard in 1931, the pound fell in value by more than 30 percent, producing a substantial boost to the competitiveness of British exports. Britain also tried, with limited success, to organize a trading bloc of nations tied closely to the use of sterling. Coupled with cheap money and a housing boom, Britain began to crawl out of the hole in 1932.[56] France also organized a trading bloc of states remaining on the gold standard, but with little effect on recovery.[57] Germany, under the Nazis, used a vicious form of national economic planning, deficit spending, conscription, and arms production to spark recovery.[58] And in 1933, President Roosevelt left the gold standard to foster depreciation of the dollar, rejected international cooperation, and concentrated on using government reorganization of the domestic economy to encourage recovery.[59]

Notwithstanding the retreat into autarchy and the recovery this sometimes produced, most nations could not ignore their relation to the broader world economy. In June 1934, only one year after launching a strongly nationalistic recovery program, the United States adopted the Reciprocal Trade Agreements Act (RTAA). This authorized the president to negotiate substantial tariff reductions on a reciprocal and bilateral basis with other nations. Although many agreements did result and tariffs fell on many items, the importance of RTAA is mostly symbolic in indicating a shift by the United States away from a nationalist-protectionist tariff policy.[60] Also important for its symbolic value was the Tripartite Monetary Agreement of 1936 among the

---

[53]Kindleberger, *The World.* . . , 172, reports that world trade shrank from an average of $2.9 billion per month in 1929 to $1.1 billion per month in 1933.

[54]Leffler, *The Elusive.* . . , 195–202.

[55]Michael Barnhart, *Japan Prepares for Total War: The Search for Economic Security*, Ithaca: Cornell University Press, 1987, 22–58.

[56]Kindleberger, *The World.* . . , 162–167; 179–181; Skidelsky, "Retreat from. . . ," 178–188.

[57]Kindleberger, *The World.* . . , 247–261.

[58]Gourevitch, *Politics in.* . . , 140–147.

[59]Albert Romasco, *The Politics of Recovery: Roosevelt's New Deal*, New York: Oxford University Press, 1983.

[60]Robert Pastor, *Congress and the Politics of U.S. Foreign Economic Policy*, Berkeley: University of California Press, 1980, 84–93; Stephan Haggard, "The Institutional Foundations of Hegemony: Explaining the Reciprocal Trade Agreements Act of 1934," *International Organization*, 42.1, Winter 1988, 91–119; Wilson, *American Business.* . . , 98–100.

United States, Great Britain, and France. This agreement was designed to stabilize currencies and end the process of competitive devaluation. The scope of the agreement was somewhat limited, and stabilization continued to be an elusive goal.[61] A more thoroughgoing and effective organization of the world economy awaited the restructuring of domestic and international politics produced by World War II.

CONCLUSIONS

■ This chapter has focused on the development of a world economy over the century from the Corn Laws to the Great Depression. Several key themes emerge that will help us understand later events, in particular the processes of competition, economic transformation, and the growing importance of international cooperation for managing the world economy. This new system of economic relations originates with the growing industrial power of Great Britain and its special needs for imports and ability to sell abroad. By 1870, tariffs had fallen substantially and a system of freer trade encompassing much of the globe had formed around Great Britain. The accumulated profits from British manufacturing began flowing into foreign investments, which helped finance sales abroad as well as transmit the technology of a modern economy. The availability of technology and improvements in infrastructure meant that many countries could begin competing with Britain on equal terms. But changes in technology, transportation, and communication — especially the ability to deliver goods and manage large and dispersed organizations — altered the nature of business firms and markets. This worked to Britain's disadvantage and benefitted the United States and Germany. By 1914, Great Britain had lost its position as the world's leading economy.

Understanding the world economy in these terms helps to underline its extraordinary dynamism. This dynamism can be seen in the tremendous growth in productive capacity, self-sustaining economic growth, and the rapid changes in technology. Competition among states meant that these economic changes produced substantial shifts in the balance of world power. The capacity for war and international influence was rearranged along with the world economy. Further, circumstances that provided advantages at one point in time did not last. Leading states, by selling, buying, and investing in other states, transferred their advantages. Moreover, the deep structural dynamism of the world economy transformed the very bases of advantage. What works to benefit a nation at one time is eroded, and new arrangements of competition emerge that privilege other nations at a later time.

---

[61]Skidelsky, "Retreat from. . . ," 186–188.

The management of the world economy, a necessarily political process, becomes both more problematic and more important over this century. British interests and power worked to provide leadership and organization in the early stages, and their financial predominance supported an international monetary system until 1914. But the move away from free trade and toward economic nationalism in the last quarter of the nineteenth century marked the limits of British power. The intensification of competition and conflict accompanying these trends suggests a general failure in coping with the new relationships of interdependence. The First World War itself generated massive changes in economic power, but these did not lead to corresponding procedures for effective international cooperation. This made the world economy especially vulnerable and contributed greatly to the catastrophic depression of the 1930s. Only the combination of war and depression would produce new forms of domestic and international political power committed to new arrangements of international management.

ANNOTATED BIBLIOGRAPHY

W. G. Beasley, *The Rise of Modern Japan*, New York: St. Martin's Press, 1990.
A detailed history of Japan from the 1850s to the present.

P. J. Cain, *Economic Foundations of British Overseas Expansion 1815–1914*, London: Macmillan, 1980.
Provides a political economy approach to understanding nineteenth century British foreign economic relations.

Albert D. Chandler, Jr., *Scale and Scope: The Dynamics of Industrial Capitalism*, Cambridge: Harvard University Press, 1990.
A masterful study of the competitive capacities of the largest firms in the United States, Germany, and Great Britain between 1890–1914.

James Foreman-Peck, *A History of the World Economy: International Economic Relations Since 1850*, Totowa: Barnes and Noble Books, 1983.
Perhaps the best general overview of the world economy for the nineteenth and twentieth centuries.

Aaron Friedberg, *The Weary Titan*, Princeton: Princeton University Press, 1988.
A very important study of the domestic politics, economics, and foreign policy related to British economic decline in the late nineteenth and early twentieth centuries.

E. J. Hobsbawm, *The Age of Capital, 1848–1875*, New York: Mentor, 1975.

E. J. Hobsbawm, *Industry and Empire*, New York: Penguin, 1969.
Two indispensable studies of the origins and development of nineteenth-century capitalism.

Paul Kennedy, *The Rise and Fall of the Great Powers*, New York: Random House, 1987.

An important comparative study of the relationship between economic and military power.

Charles Kindlebeger, *The World in Depression*, Berkeley: University of California Press, 1973.
The best single source for understanding the world economy during the Depression years of the 1930s.

David Landes, *The Unbound Prometheus*, Cambridge University Press: 1969.
The classic study of technological and economic change over the past two centuries.

Charles Maier, *Recasting Bourgeois Europe*, Princeton: Princeton University Press, 1974.
The most important examination of the interaction of European interest groups, domestic politics, and the world economy in the 1920s.

Alan Milward and S.B. Saul, *The Economic Development of Continental Europe 1780–1870*, London: Allen and Unwin, 1979.

Sidney Pollard, *Peaceful Conquest: The Industrialization of Europe, 1760–1970*, Oxford: Oxford University Press, 1982.
Two important studies of industrial change in Europe.

Walt Rostow, *The World Economy*, Austin: University of Texas Press, 1978.
A very rich source of data on the history of the world economy.

CHAPTER 4

THE POLITICAL ECONOMY OF AMERICAN HEGEMONY: 1938–1973

T he years following World War II produced dramatic, even epoch-making, changes in the world economy. Unprecedented prosperity, the development of new international economic institutions, an explosion in world trade, and an extraordinary expansion in international cooperation were the key elements in this new international economic order. This chapter will describe these developments and the political structures that supported them, along with providing a detailed examination of the reasons for these events. How and why did these changes in the world economy occur? A considerable portion of the answer to this question rests with the actions of the United States. We have seen that prior to 1940 the United States was unwilling to commit any substantial resources to stabilizing either the world economy or the international political system. The consequence was a catastrophic depression and, ultimately, war. But during and after the war, the United States moved assertively to reconstruct the world economy. Understanding the political sources of this change and the consequences of this activity occupies the greatest part of this chapter.

This thirty-five–year period offers a rich set of events for understanding international political economy. Several of the most important empirical issues and theoretical questions are linked to this era. The first part of the chapter provides a detailed discussion of the essential features of the postwar international economic order, in particular the patterns of economic growth and the basic institutions created to manage the system. These include the International Monetary Fund (IMF), the World Bank, and the General Agreement on Tariffs and Trade (GATT). The second part of the chapter examines the very important question of how political power affects economic outcomes. What was the nature and significance of U.S. leadership in producing

61

the postwar international economic order? What were the motives for U.S. actions? Could the United States design the system alone? Who benefitted from this system? The third part of the chapter considers several crucial developments that emerge from the era of U.S. hegemony: the growth of multinational corporations, the political economy of U.S. foreign policy, and the emergence of economic integration in Europe. Finally, the last part of the chapter examines the two events that marked a change in the world economy: the collapse of fixed exchange rates and the end of cheap oil, both of which took place between 1971 and 1973.

STRUCTURES AND TRENDS IN THE POSTWAR WORLD ECONOMY

Growth of the World Economy

International trade and investment grew more quickly between 1938 and 1973 than in any other period after 1815.

TABLE 4.1

World Exports — 1938–1974
(*Current Value in Billions of U.S. Dollars*)

YEAR	VALUE
1938	21.1
1948	53.9
1958	96.0
1960	107.8
1965	156.5
1970	265.7
1972	355.3
1974	729.2

SOURCE: Robert A. Pastor, *Congress and the Politics of U.S. Foreign Economic Policy*, Berkeley: University of California Press, 1980, 99.

Comparison of the rates of GNP change for the pre- and postwar eras show a substantial acceleration of growth after 1950. Most industrial countries experienced a near doubling of the rates of growth between 1950 and 1960 as compared with 1913–1950.[1] International trade was a key ingredient in this growth, with world trade in manufacturing expanding faster than world manufacturing output by a ratio of 1.4:1 between 1950 and 1970.[2]

The importance of the United States to this process is evident from Table 4.2:

TABLE 4.2

U.S. Trade and World Trade — 1949–1973
(*Exports at Current Value in Billions of U.S. Dollars*)

YEAR	U.S.	INDUSTRIAL NATIONS	WORLD EXPORTS	U.S. AS % OF INDUSTRIAL NATIONS	U.S. AS % OF WORLD
1949	12.1	33.8	55.2	35.8	21.9
1960	20.6	78.8	114.6	26.1	17.5
1970	43.2	208.3	283.7	20.7	15.2
1973	71.3	376.8	524.2	18.9	13.6

SOURCE: International Monetary Fund, *International Financial Statistics Yearbook, 1979*, 62–67.

The recovery of Western Europe and Japan was also a driving force in this economic growth. The surge in exports of industrial nations is a measure of this process. The expansion in world trade was in many ways generated by declining tariff levels, convertible currencies, and more openness. The near-elimination of U.S. tariffs shown in Table 4.3 is also found in tariff levels for other advanced capitalist states who participated equally in the general reductions.

Also contributing to this process of economic growth was the availability of oil at stable prices. Inexpensive imported oil became the primary energy source supporting the dramatic increases in economic output.

---

[1] W.M. Scammell, *The International Economy Since 1945*, Second Edition, New York: St. Martin's Press, 1983, 53.

[2] Scammell, *The International. . .* , 127. Scammell notes that between 1876 and 1913 the ratio of manufacturing trade and manufacturing output was less than one. Walt Rostow, *The World Economy*, Austin: University of Texas Press, 1978, 67, provides a comparison of growth rates in world trade and in manufacturing from 1720 to 1971. David Landes, *The Unbound Prometheus*, Cambridge: Cambridge University Press, 1969, 512, provides data on growth rates in world trade from 1890 to 1960.

TABLE 4.3

Average U.S. Tariffs

YEAR	AVERAGE TARIFF
1940	36%
1946	25%
1950	13%
1960	12%
1970	10%
1975	6%
1984	5%

SOURCE: *Statistical Abstract of the United States.* For comparative data on tariffs see United Nations, *World Economic Survey,* New York, 1991, 52.

TABLE 4.4

World Energy Consumption by Source — 1950–1972
(*Percentage Shares*)

SOURCE	1950	1960	1965	1970	1972
Coal	55.7	44.2	39.0	31.2	28.7
Oil	28.9	35.8	39.4	44.5	46.0
Natural Gas	8.9	13.5	15.5	17.8	18.4
Electricity	6.5	6.4	6.2	6.5	6.9

SOURCE: Joel Darmstadter and Hans H. Landsberg, "*The Crisis,*" in Raymond Vernon, ed. *The Oil Crisis,* New York: Norton, 1976, 19.

The shift from reliance on coal to imported oil occurred principally in Europe and Japan. Between 1950 and 1970, Western Europe increased its dependence on oil for total energy needs from 14.3 percent to 55.6 percent while Japan increased from 5 percent to 68.8 percent. From 1962 to 1972, combined West European and Japanese imports of oil rose from 6.17 to 18.84 million barrels per day.[3]

International Institutions

The growth of the world economy took place within a context created by several new international institutions conceived of and established near the

---

[3]Darmstadter and Landsberg, "The Crisis," 20–21.

end of World War II. These include the International Monetary Fund, the International Bank for Reconstruction and Development (commonly known as the World Bank), and the General Agreement on Tariffs and Trade (GATT). The IMF was designed to manage exchange rates and payments imbalances among nations, the World Bank to supplement private capital for international investment, and GATT to serve as a negotiating forum for the reduction of tariffs and other barriers to trade.

One of the most distinctive and important features of the post-1945 world economy was this set of formal and informal institutions for managing the economic relations among nations. During the 1920s, a significant array of mostly informal institutions had been created to deal with the new complexity of economic ties among nations.[4] Those designed and established between 1942 and 1948 were framed by certain principles of international economic relations. These included a preference for convertible currencies, a lowering of trade barriers, a system of fixed exchange rates, and generally the promotion of a multilateral system of trade and payments.

The desire for fixed exchange rates was the result of a deeply felt need for stability in international transactions, a sentiment reinforced by the negative experience of floating exchange rates in the 1930s and memories of the "golden age" of fixed rates under the nineteenth century gold standard. The United States possessed the vast majority of the world's gold in 1945, and this was used as the basis for establishing fixed rates.[5] The dollar was fixed in value to gold at $35 per ounce, while other governments fixed their currencies to the dollar and pledged to intervene in foreign exchange markets to keep values within a narrow band around the fixed rate. All this came within the basic rules of operation of the International Monetary Fund (IMF), which itself was established through payments of gold and national currencies from member states. The United States provided the lion's share of the IMF's resources, 31 percent, and consequently received the largest share of voting power.

The primary purpose of the IMF was to provide short-term loans to countries experiencing a current account deficit in their balance of payments. The loans would typically be used to support the fixed value of the country's currency and were usually contingent on adoption of a national policy designed to reverse the deficit. This often meant some combination of cutting government spending and restricting the money supply. This "belt tightening" would produce an economic downturn, higher unemployment, and

---

[4]See Michael Hogan, *Informal Entente, The Private Structure of Cooperation in Anglo-American Economic Diplomacy, 1918–1928*, Columbia: University of Missouri Press, 1977. The most formal institution and the predecessor to the IMF was the Bank for International Settlements, established in 1929. See Frank Costigliola, "The Other Side of Isolationism: The Establishment of the First World Bank, 1929–1930," *Journal of American History*, 59, December 1972, 602–620.

[5]Cohen reports the level at 75 percent while Calleo sets the figure at 60 percent. Benjamin Cohen, *Organizing the World's Money*, New York: Basic Books, 1977, 95; David Calleo, *Beyond American Hegemony*, New York: Basic Books, 1987, 227.

lower inflation, which was expected to lead to higher exports and lower imports.[6] The IMF became the enforcer of the views of a conservative U.S. financial community, where trade deficits were seen as an indicator of domestic profligacy, and adjustments were expected to come in the domestic economy so as to make it more competitive internationally.[7]

If the current account deficit were serious enough — that is, if it were structural and not just temporary — the IMF would permit an alteration of the exchange rate (called a devaluation when the rate falls against other currencies). The British devaluation of the pound from $2.80 to $2.40 in 1967 is an example of this process. Burdened by an uncompetitive manufacturing sector, Britain faced an expanding current account deficit whenever the economy expanded. Because of the importance of the pound to the world economy, the United States and the IMF were ready to provide financial aid to help support the currency. Eventually, the British government concluded that only a devaluation would produce a current account surplus and stay the need for additional borrowing. This decision was made in conjunction with the IMF.

The International Bank for Reconstruction and Development, or World Bank, was also established at Bretton Woods. Eventually, the Bank was allocated $10 billion in capital with the ability to borrow funds in capital markets. Over its first decade, the World Bank played only a marginal role in the actual postwar reconstruction process. But in the late 1950s and early 1960s, an increasing interest in the Third World prompted lending at the rate of well over $1 billion annually in new loans.[8] In Chapter Nine we will consider in more detail the role of the World Bank in providing aid to developing states.

The mechanisms for managing international trade had a somewhat more checkered history. Originally, the United States hoped to create an international organization for this purpose but found the goals of other states incompatible with its own. Concurrent negotiations in 1947 and 1948 produced first

---

[6]Remember, a recession should cause some decline (or at least a lower rate of increase) in the prices of domestically produced goods. This should make the country's goods more competitive abroad and also cause a fall in imports.

[7]This somewhat harsh policy applied more to Third World nations than to economically advanced nations. But the tension over the importance of domestic adjustment to international requirements presents a classic case of a conflict of interests between debtors and creditors. This was present in the negotiation of the Bretton Woods agreements, especially between the United States and Great Britain. See Alfred E. Eckes, *A Search for Solvency: Bretton Woods and the International Monetary System, 1941–1971,* Austin: University of Texas Press, 1975; and Fred Block, *The Origins of International Economic Disorder,* Berkeley: University of California Press, 1974. The discussion that follows, of the actual functioning of Bretton Woods, will emphasize the arrangements of "embedded liberalism," in which efforts were made to establish a working compromise between forcing domestic adjustment and permitting efforts to achieve high levels of economic growth. See John Gerard Ruggie, "International Regimes, Transactions, and Change: Embedded Liberalism in the Postwar Economic Order," *International Organization,* 36.2, Spring 1982, 379–415.

[8]A detailed discussion of the origins and development of the World Bank is found in Edward S. Mason and Robert Asher, *The World Bank Since Bretton Woods,* Washington, D.C.: The Brookings Institution, 1973.

a General Agreement on Tariffs and Trade and an International Trade Organization. But the U.S. government was dissatisfied with the ITO because it placed restrictions on the United States while creating exceptions for other nations, and the president refused to submit the treaty to the Senate for ratification.[9] GATT was acceptable and has served for over forty years as the chief international organization for trade. It has provided a forum for negotiating reductions in tariffs and some other barriers to trade. In a series of meetings beginning with the sessions in 1947 and continuing with various "rounds" through 1992, GATT has produced a substantial drop in world tariff levels.[10] In the period from 1890 to 1935, U.S. tariff levels fluctuated between 30 percent and 45 percent of dutiable imports. By 1955 these had been cut to 15 percent and by 1970 to 12 percent.[11] This helps illustrate a key fact about GATT and U.S. postwar trade objectives. American leaders were strongly in favor of lowering tariffs and other barriers to trade, that is, in freer trade; they were really not interested, in spite of much rhetoric to the contrary, in *free* trade. But GATT did embody a commitment by its members to establish a schedule of tariff rates and a set of trade principles designed to produce uniformity and predictability in international commercial relations. Although tariff barriers on manufactured goods fell substantially, trade in agriculture and services remained largely outside GATT (as did the Communist bloc and many Third World nations). Beginning with the Tokyo Round, negotiations moved on to tackle non-tariff barriers to trade, and the Uruguay Round took up these matters, along with the areas of agriculture and services.

The growth and dynamism of the world economy, along with the new set of international institutions, produced an epochal change in international economic relations. How this came about, in particular the role of the United States in it, is the subject of the next section.

U.S. HEGEMONY AND THE WORLD ECONOMY

■ A common characteristic of all the social sciences, especially one as new as international political economy, is disputation over the most basic of theoretical and empirical relationships. Perhaps the most important question for this emerging field, and the topic producing the greatest discussion, is the relationship of politics and power to the creation and management of the world economy. Scholars have sought to trace the emergence of a liberal

---

[9]Robert Pastor, *Congress and the Politics of Foreign Economic Policy*, Berkeley: University of California Press, 1980, 96–98.
[10]The GATT rounds include: 1947, Geneva; 1949, Annecy; 1950–1951, Torquay; 1955–1956, Geneva; 1959–1962, Geneva (Dillon Round); 1963–1967, Geneva (Kennedy Round); 1973–1979, Tokyo Round; 1986–1992, Uruguay Round.
[11]Pastor, *Congress. . . ,* 78.

international economic order to the presence of a single dominant power in the international system. The "hegemonic stability" theory holds that such a nation has the opportunity to construct an open and stable international economic system. Because it possesses a preponderance of military and economic power, this hegemonic state is in a position to convince other nations to enter into a system of relatively free trade and regular procedures for monetary relations. That is, the hegemon has the power and the reasons "to make and enforce the rules for the world political economy."12

Application of these ideas to understanding the period after World War II has produced a set of important insights but also several points of intellectual conflict. What follows is a consideration of these issues in terms of posing and answering five basic questions. First, what was the nature of U.S. leadership? Over what issues or problems was U.S. power the key element? Second, what were the aims of the United States? Was it primarily interested in acting for the benefit of all states in providing international peace and prosperity, or was it more concerned with designing a system to benefit itself even to the point of turning a profit? Third, what factors motivated the United States to assume the responsibilities of world leadership? What mixture of domestic interests and external political, military, and economic concerns provided the incentives for these actions? Fourth, how important was U.S. leadership to international cooperation and political and economic stability? What were the extent and limits to U.S. power in engineering and/or coercing these outcomes? Fifth, what were the consequences of U.S. hegemony, particularly the distribution of benefits? These are broad and complex questions, and the answers are sometimes not yet clear. But they point out the basic elements of international political economy for the postwar world.

Economic Consequences of World War II

Some historical background about the Second World War and its political and economic impact is helpful in providing a context for answering these questions. First and foremost was the importance of productivity in fighting and winning the war. World War II was essentially a contest of physical capabilities, with victory going to the side best able to amass the implements and manpower of war. Events from 1939 to 1945 both revealed and accentuated the productive advantages of the U.S. economy. Not only did the United

---

12Robert Keohane, *After Hegemony*, Princeton: Princeton University Press, 1984, 37. Other works promoting the hegemonic stability theory are Stephen Krasner, "State Power and the Structure of International Trade," *World Politics*, 27, April 1975, 314–347; Charles Kindleberger, *The World in Depression*, Berkeley: University of California Press, 1973; Robert Gilpin, *U.S. Power and the Multinational Corporation*, New York: Basic Books, 1975; Robert Gilpin, *War and Change in World Politics*, Cambridge: Cambridge University Press, 1981; and Robert Keohane, "The Theory of Hegemonic Stability and Changes in International Regimes, 1967–1977," in Ole Holsti et al., eds. *Change in the International System*, Boulder: Westview Press, 1980.

States possess the greatest concentration of productive resources, but its productivity — output per unit of input, usually labor — was far higher than
any other nation. By 1944, the United States was producing 40 percent of the
world's armaments, and its productivity was twice that of Germany and five
times that of Japan.13 The result was that U.S. Gross National Product increased, in real terms, from $88.6 billion in 1939 to $135.0 billion in 1944.14

The war had equally profound effects on patterns of international trade
and finance. The United States supplied vast quantities of Allied war material
and financed this through Lend Lease. In spite of this largess, Britain liquidated its foreign reserves and large portions of its overseas investments to
pay for imports from the United States. By the war's end, the pattern of
British trade deficits financed by U.S. capital was firmly established. In addition, the rupture created by military operations made reestablishing prewar
trade practices difficult. This was most evident in central and eastern Europe,
where Soviet control served to remove this area from its traditional role in
European trade. Added to this was the physical destruction of the war, which
represented approximately 13 percent of the prewar capital stock in Germany
and 8 percent in France.15 The result was a high demand for imports, significant barriers to exports, and a substantial payments imbalance between Europe
and the United States.

The war and depression of the 1930s also had psychological and political
consequences that influenced economic choices. The fear of recurrent depression helped reinforce affirmative government action in guaranteeing domestic
prosperity. The depression left a legacy of significant barriers to trade and a
memory of the dangers of economic warfare. More ominous were the German
and Japanese experiences of military and economic organization designed to
obtain secure access to the resources needed for autarchy. Finally, the military
outcome not only disrupted traditional European trade but brought a politically and economically alienated great power — the Soviet Union — into
the heart of Europe.

The United States and World Order

Now, what are the main issues in which U.S. power played the key role in
defining the postwar international order? We will emphasize four: trade and

---

13Alan Milward, *War, Economy and Society, 1939–1945*, Berkeley: University of California Press,
1977, 67. The sources of this advantage came from economies of scale, new capital investment,
and incentives in winning the war. Much of the new investment was financed by the government. U.S. productivity was so great, it was able to increase war production on a vast scale
without reducing civilian consumption below the levels of 1939. See Milward, *War. . . ,* 63–68.

14Milward, *War. . . ,* 63.

15Milward, *War. . . ,* 333. He reports that the gross value of U.S. Lend Lease aid to the British
was about $30 billion. See pages 351, and 345–352, 359–360. Also useful is Scammell, *The
International. . . ,* 24–25.

finance, international security, vital resources, and international and domestic politics.[16] First, the United States was consistently the central actor in establishing and managing a framework of rules for international trade and finance and also made the system work by providing financial support. We have seen earlier how the Bretton Woods institutions and GATT were created largely through political initiatives from the United States. At the same time, these institutions confronted striking imbalances in the world economy measurable in terms of the sizable current account deficits between Europe and the United States.[17] Continuing the policy established under Lend Lease, in 1946 the United States provided additional funds to Britain and France to make up the payments gap. When this proved insufficient, the leadership in the United States moved to supply even more funds so the recovery of Europe could continue. The Marshall Plan provided the financing needed to cover this imbalance. This can be seen in Table 4.5.

TABLE 4.5

World Payments Imbalances — 1946–1949
(Billions of U.S. Dollars)

	1946	1947	1948	1949
U.S. Current Account Balance	+7.8	+11.5	+6.8	+6.3
Financed by:				
U.S. Government	−4.9	−5.8	−5.1	−5.9
Private loans and gifts	−1.1	−1.5	−1.6	−1.1
IMF and World Bank	0.0	−0.8	−0.4	−0.1
Liquidating foreign assets	−1.9	−4.5	−0.8	0.0
Errors and omissions	+0.1	+1.1	+1.1	+0.9
Total	−7.8	−11.5	−6.8	−6.3

SOURCE: W.M. Scammell, *The International.* . . , 21.

Over the first four years after the war, the U.S. government and private sources supplied $28.0 billion to finance the payments imbalance with the rest of the world. This pattern continued with Marshall Plan aid in 1950–1951

---

[16]This list builds on and extends similar lists proposed by Robert Keohane, *After.* . . , 139, and Susan Strange, "The Persistent Myth of Lost Hegemony," *International Organization*, 41.4, Autumn 1987, 565.

[17]Remember, the main reason for the imbalance was the war itself. U.S. productivity, European destruction, disruption of traditional trading patterns, and the political importance of making a strong economic recovery all contributed to the difficulties in the 1945–1948 period.

and largely with military aid thereafter. The chief consequence of these actions was to ensure European recovery and to enshrine the dollar as the key international currency. That is, the dollar became the primary medium of international payment and the currency serving as the store of value for all others participating in the system.

Beyond these immediate economic issues lay a set of political and security matters that cried out for U.S. attention. Further, the ability to persuade the leadership of many nations to participate in the new liberal world order depended on their confidence in the United States and its willingness to ensure their security. The recent war had demonstrated the vulnerability of many parts of the world to a determined and aggressive state. Much of the leadership in Europe considering joining the U.S.-defined system was deeply worried about the political effects of Soviet military power in the heart of Europe. Thus, when events such as the Soviet-inspired coup in Czechoslovakia or the Soviet blockade of Berlin intensified these fears, the United States felt compelled to act. The result, by 1949, was the North Atlantic Treaty Organization (NATO), which represented a standing U.S. commitment to defend Western Europe. U.S. international leadership depended on the ability to use its superior power to reassure allies and contain the Soviet Union. Especially critical was preventing Soviet actions from undermining confidence in and encouraging challenges to the United States. Many in the U.S government concluded that the success of the postwar system rested on the image of U.S. power in Europe and on preventing the use or threat of force from affecting the shape of international politics.

A related set of political and security issues was defined by relations among states in the emerging western system. The United States played a crucial role in encouraging cooperation, including convincing some — like the French — that their security would be ensured even as the German economy was being revived. A U.S.-imposed requirement for receiving Marshall Plan aid was European cooperation in establishing the scope of their economic problems and in administration of the funds. Much of the impetus for European unity came from constant encouragement by the United States. The occupations of Germany (a collective enterprise with the British and French)[18] and Japan (entirely by the United States) produced substantial efforts to change the domestic politics of these nations.

A final and equally important element of U.S. hegemony was ensuring access to vital resources through the normal course of market relationships. Nations should not feel the need to use military force to gain a special position on these resources. Perhaps the most important of these was oil. The principal agents of control of this resource were the large American, British,

---

[18]The Soviet Union, of course, occupied the eastern third of Germany. But the failure of joint occupation in May 1947 moved the United States to reorganize its plans and press forward with the Marshall Plan and unification of the three western zones.

and Dutch multinational oil corporations, but U.S. political and military power in the Middle East was an equally important ingredient.[19] This was especially evident in the U.S. effort to force the Soviets out of Iran in 1946, in the intervention in Iran in 1953, and in the close relationship with Saudi Arabia. The consequence was to ensure plentiful supplies at relatively cheap and stable prices.

U.S. Purposes?

Although we can identify the main issues of international order in which U.S. hegemony played an essential role, scholars have disagreed about the basic aims of U.S. policy. Some have seen U.S. actions in trade, money, politics, security, and resources as an effort to provide many nations with the generalized benefits of peace and prosperity, sacrificing its short term interests for the good of the world community. In this case, the United States was involved in providing what are called collective or public goods. Thought of very precisely, collective goods refer to identifiable benefits that are available to all who participate in the system (even if they don't pay part of the cost), and consumption of the good by one does not diminish consumption by others. In one version of hegemonic stability theory, collective goods, such as security and prosperity, will emerge only if the most powerful nation accepts the costs of providing them and defers its benefits to the future. This country, in effect, must be willing to think in terms of benefits to a wide set of nations.[20]

A second perspective proposes that the collective benefits of international order will only be supplied if the dominant state can extract a disproportionate amount of the benefits. This view sees the United States able to use its leverage to gain special privileges or compel member states to make contributions to the costs of world order, so as to make providing international order a profitable venture.[21] A third approach rejects the collective goods concept of international order and suggests instead that hegemonic power produced a substantial array of private benefits to the United States.[22]

---

[19]Lawrence Frank, "The First Oil Regime," *World Politics*, 37.4, July 1985, 586; Keohane, *After.* . . , 150–181; John Blair, *The Control of Oil*, New York: Pantheon Books, 1976.

[20]Kindleberger, *The World.* . . , is a good example of this viewpoint.

[21]Gilpin, *U.S. Power.* . . , and Krasner, "State Power. . . ," promote this position.

[22]Bruce Russett, "The Mysterious Case of Vanishing Hegemony; or, Is Mark Twain Really Dead?" *International Organization*, 39.2, Spring 1985, 207–231 is the sole proponent of this position. Additional discussion of the importance of collective goods theory in understanding hegemony is found in Duncan Snidal, "The Limits of Hegemonic Stability Theory," *International Organization*, 39, Autumn 1985, 579–614; John Conybeare, "Public Goods, Prisoners' Dilemmas, and the International Political Economy," *International Studies Quarterly*, 28, March 1984, 5–22; and Fred Hirsch and Michael W. Doyle, *Alternatives to Monetary Disorder*, New York: McGraw-Hill, 1977, 11–64.

As is often the case, the actual situation contains a complex mixture of all three perspectives. In terms of bearing the costs of international order, the United States was clearly the only state capable of providing capital and guaranteeing the security of nations. The proportion of GNP spent on defense by the United States was much higher than for other states in the "free world," and U.S. troops did a disproportionate share of the fighting and dying in wars for international stability. At the same time, free trade can provide great benefits to the most productive and low-cost nations since their exports are likely to expand relative to others. Further, the nation with the world's key currency receives special benefits by avoiding the need to adjust its domestic economy to payments deficits. Because the dollar functioned as a key currency and other nations accepted it as payment for goods, the United States was able to force these nations to bear some of the costs of its international operations.[23] At the same time, peace and prosperity in the postwar period was general, at least for developed nations.[24]

But the real key to understanding U.S. motives in promoting international stability lies with the perceptions of U.S. leaders about the military and political costs that would come from dissolution of world order. The experience of depression and war convinced many key government officials that U.S. prosperity and security depended on prosperity abroad and on eliminating or blocking the acts of hostile and aggressive states. Should the United States not act to ensure these outcomes, international economic conflict would doom any chance for full employment and free enterprise in the United States, while control of the resources of Europe and Asia by a hostile power would certainly force a garrison state in the United States and another world war.[25] In an important sense, the benefits of a liberal world order derived from the unacceptable costs that could be foregone with its presence.

Power and Outcomes

Should we conclude from this discussion that U.S. power was so dominant it could get whatever it wanted? The answer is certainly no, but for reasons that may not be obvious. Two critical examples help illustrate the point. Throughout the war, in negotiations leading to Lend Lease, in the discussions

---

[23] Allies like Germany and France accepted dollars in payment for a U.S. current account deficit, resulting in expansion of their money supply and inflation rates. The matter of a key currency and its benefits and costs is the subject of more discussion later in this chapter.

[24] Because nations could be excluded from the GATT and IMF systems and from the benefits of U.S. aid, the system of liberal world order does not qualify precisely as a collective good.

[25] These arguments, linking politics and economics together in ways not always recognized by scholars in international political economy, can be found in Waldo Heinrichs, *Threshold of War: Franklin D. Roosevelt and American Entry into World War II*, New York: Oxford University Press, 1988; and John Gaddis, *Strategies of Containment*, New York: Oxford University Press, 1982; and Gaddis, *The Long Peace*, New York: Oxford University Press, 1987.

of the Bretton Woods institutions, and in the agreements for the British loan in 1945–1946, the United States pressed the British very hard to dismantle the Imperial Preference System. This was the trade and monetary bloc created by Britain among past and present colonial areas to cope with the depression and the war. The U.S. position was consistent with a multilateral and open world order and would have eliminated the various mechanisms used to protect British trade.[26] The British grudgingly gave verbal assurances and, as a first step in 1947, moved to make the pound fully convertible. The result was to expose the weaknesses in the British economic position as they were forced to use most of the $3.75 billion loan to support the pound. After a six week trial, the idea of convertibility was shelved.

The U.S. objective of European political unity, a key element of Marshall Plan aid, suffered a similar fate. The idea was to create a stronger and more prosperous Europe through political and economic integration, and the expectation was for rapid movement toward this goal. One important consequence would be to establish an offsetting system of power in Europe and thereby reduce U.S. responsibilities. The other would be to move more rapidly toward a multilateral trading system based on convertible currencies. This plan ran headlong into British resistance. They genuinely feared the economic and political effects of integration into Europe. British leaders worried about ties to Commonwealth nations, about the loss of political and economic independence, about the economic consequences of competition with the United States and the rapid swings in the U.S. business cycle, and about their status as a world power. Other countries also feared the consequences of a single integrated market in Europe.[27]

Despite its overwhelming power advantages and the apparent leverage created by the importance of Marshall Plan aid to Europe, the United States could not always obtain its objectives.[28] Three factors contributed to this result. First was the audacity of the proposal; bringing Europe — an area of intense political conflict for centuries — toward political and economic integration within a few years was probably unrealistic. Moving Britain and Europe toward a liberal system had to wait until their economies could compete with the United States. Second, and more interesting, was the effect of European and British weakness. The importance of bringing these nations

---

[26]Similar actions were taken against the French bloc as part of a U.S. effort to break down the structure of colonialism built up in the nineteenth century.

[27]Stafford Cripps, the British chancellor of the Exchequer, asserted in November 1949 that "trade liberalization had gone far enough," and that the American proposal for European integration "amounted to a 'fifty-year programme.' " This quote and information on the U.S.– British dispute on European union are from Michael Hogan, *The Marshall Plan*, Cambridge: Cambridge University Press, 1987, 291. For evidence that Cripps had the timetable about right, see the discussion of Europe and 1992 in Chapter Five.

[28]A very useful discussion of these questions along with a detailed historical analysis is found in G. John Ikenberry, "Rethinking the Origins of American Hegemony," *Political Science Quarterly*, 104.3, 1989, 375–400.

into a western political and economic bloc meant that overt intimidation and coercion was likely to prove counterproductive. At the very least, adopting the U.S. vision of an unbridled multilateral world would have proved devastating to the economies of Europe. Pushing too hard would have produced either collapse of U.S.-oriented political elites or cooperation without actual consent. Finally, the very nature of U.S. hegemony placed sharp limits on the ability to achieve U.S. demands. From the U.S. standpoint, world stability required a collective and collaborative effort to contain the Soviet Union and create a more liberal international system. Achieving a genuinely cooperative arrangement among western nations forced the United States to make many compromises. U.S. hegemony was based mostly on leadership and not on coercion.[29]

The Consequences of U.S. Hegemony

Understanding the overall effects of U.S. hegemony is a very difficult problem, and much of the rest of the book can be seen as an extended answer to such a question. One major consequence of this hegemony was an extraordinary level of peace and prosperity, certainly with disproportionate benefits accruing to developed states but also with some previously poor states gaining in economic strength. The rapid recovery of West Germany, most of Europe, and Japan owed much to U.S. aid, investment, and a favorable political and security climate. The Third World as a whole did not fare as well, losing in share of world trade and total output. Much of this came as a result of a relative decline in the importance of primary products and food and an increase in the importance of manufactured goods. After the mid-1960s, some Third World states were able to break into the world market for manufactures. (See Chapters Eight and Twelve for more discussion of this process.) For the United States, many special benefits flowed from hegemony — the foreign policy benefits from having the key currency and the advantages to its corporations operating on a world scale are two examples — but it too experienced a relative decline in world product and trade. After 1971, U.S. policy took on a much more unilateral cast in trying to manipulate the world economy to its advantage. The Vietnam War experience from 1961 to 1973 also prompted the United States to become much more resentful of the military costs of hegemony and led to pressures on allies to share more of the burdens.

---

[29]The last point relating to the nature of hegemony is not the same as the second point, relating to weakness. U.S. leadership needed to be based primarily on persuasion even, and perhaps especially, had Europe and Japan been strong. The United States needed a commitment of political, economic, and military resources from its allies that was based on a belief in the justice of their cause. Under these circumstances, neither weak nor strong states could be coerced into this position.

Unquestionably, U.S. economic, military and political power defined the shape of the post-1945 world economy. Examining in more detail the costs and benefits of that system for industrial states is the subject of the next section.

THE HEYDAY OF U.S. HEGEMONY: 1958–1970

■ Although the United States commanded great power resources after World War II, it was not until 1958–1959 that its vision of a multilateral and liberal world economy began to be realized. The ten years from 1948 to 1958 produced several new and significant features in the world economy, most importantly the development of new institutions for economic cooperation, dramatic economic growth in Europe, rising U.S. military spending, foreign aid in the Third World by the United States, and the emergence of U.S.-based multinational corporations. These factors helped to generate the stability and prosperity that gave nations the confidence to participate in this liberal system. But each also contributed to an outflow of dollars, and this ultimately brought the Bretton Woods system down. In this section we will briefly consider these developments and then turn to the problems they created.

The European Economic Community

Perhaps the most important event during these ten years came in March 1957 with the signing of the Treaty of Rome. This treaty, signed by France, the Federal Republic of Germany (West Germany), Belgium, Luxembourg, Italy, and the Netherlands, called for the creation of the European Economic Community (EEC) beginning on January 1, 1958.[30] Several steps had preceded this decision. Marshall Plan aid had been made contingent on European cooperation, and the United States pressed hard for much greater levels of economic and political unity.[31] But in Europe, leadership for integration was supplied by the French, who were initially motivated by the need to bring German industrial power under international supervision and later by a recognition of the importance of creating a European system capable of dealing with the United States and the Soviet Union on equal terms. Under the U.S.

---

[30]Continuing its reluctance to join in European economic integration, Great Britain was not a member of the EEC. Instead, the British helped organize the European Free Trade Area (EFTA) along with Norway, Switzerland, Austria, Sweden, Denmark, and Portugal in 1960. The main difference with the EEC was that the EFTA did not have a common external tariff.

[31]In response, the Organization for European Economic Cooperation (OEEC) was set up in 1948 to coordinate Marshall Plan aid and reconstruction efforts.

concept of world leadership, this notion of independent power centers was actually encouraged, and the tariff discrimination and political independence that almost inevitably followed was tolerated. Further, the United States wanted German power accommodated to its other European partners and available to deal with the Soviets. First, in 1948, Belgium, Luxembourg, and the Netherlands had established a customs union,[32] and in 1950 the European Coal and Steel Community was created to manage and control German industrial power.[33] In 1955, negotiations began for a broader customs union, which reached fruition in the 1957 Rome treaty.

The basic purpose of the agreement was to establish a schedule for reducing tariffs and quantitative restrictions on trade. On the whole, the timetable was met or exceeded, with tariffs slashed dramatically and quotas eliminated entirely.[34] Shortly after the inauguration of the EEC — late 1958 and early 1959 — fourteen European nations, including Great Britain, moved to accept full convertibility of their currencies.[35] The same economic growth in the 1950s that made the EEC possible also gave these and other nations the financial strength to close their payments gap and accumulate the reserves needed to support a currency at a fixed price against the dollar. This also coincided with expansion of the resources at the IMF and a more liberal lending policy, both of which facilitated convertibility.[36]

Military Keynesianism and Foreign Aid

The 1950s also witnessed important developments in U.S. political economy, in particular the increasing role of military spending, the rise of foreign aid, and a persistent balance of payments deficit. The combination of a Soviet atomic bomb in 1949 and the outbreak of the Korean War in 1950 produced a militarization of the Cold War and a consequent rise in U.S. military spending. Actual spending increased more than threefold by 1952 and stood at more than 10 percent of GNP by 1953. The legacy of Keynesianism of the 1930s, the postwar commitment to high levels of employment, and the need for high military spending merged to form a relatively coherent national policy. Keynes' idea was to use increases in government spending during periods of economic recession to stimulate the economy. From a political

---

[32]Basically, a customs union acts to reduce tariffs and other trade barriers within the particular set of nations and also works to establish a common trade policy with outside states.

[33]1950 also produced the European Payments Union, designed to manage payments imbalances within Europe.

[34]Scammell, *The International Economy*. . . , 137–138.

[35]Convertibility, in the 1958–1971 period, occurred when a currency could be freely traded for gold or for a foreign currency. The economic dislocations from the war led most countries to place substantial restrictions on convertibility until 1958. After 1971, gold was no longer an element of convertibility.

[36]Eckes, *A Search*. . . , 231–233; Scammell, *The International Economy*. . . , 109–116.

standpoint, the easiest way to raise spending was for the military requirements of the Cold War. By the early 1960s, the new Kennedy Administration
had added the notion of reducing taxes while increasing spending so as to
provide an extra boost to the economy.

A key element in U.S. postwar aims was dismantling the nineteenth
century colonial system established by the European powers. The late 1940s
and 1950s produced a wave of new nations as this process came to fruition.
However, the Soviet Union moved to take advantage of this development
and increased its political and economic activities in what emerged as the
Third World. The U.S. response was to utilize its military capabilities to
engage in selective intervention and increase its aid — economic and military — so as to reinforce its political and military position in the Third
World. Castro's victory in Cuba and his swing toward the Soviet Union in
1959–1960 gave strong incentives to accelerate this trend. The Third World
and its economic and military orientation in the Cold War became important
enough to warrant much more attention and resources.

Dollar Glut

The revival and integration of Western Europe and the growing demands of
the Cold War came against the backdrop of troubling trends in the U.S.
international economic situation. The 1950s, which began with a dollar shortage, ended with the United States wanting to reverse a persistent balance of
payments deficit. In the early part of the decade, a payments deficit was
created through military and economic aid; this was desirable since it helped
close the dollar gap with the still economically weak Europeans. By the late
1950s Europe had recovered, and the deficit presented new problems.
Although the United States enjoyed a substantial surplus in its goods and
services and investment income accounts, this was more than offset by foreign
aid, military expenditures abroad, and private overseas investment.[37] The
sudden shrinkage in the surplus accounts in 1958–1959 produced a much
wider payments deficit and instability in the dollar.

Remember that under the Bretton Woods system the dollar was fixed in
terms of gold at $35 an ounce. This meant the U.S. government was required
to redeem dollars held by foreigners at that price, a commitment that served
as the core of the fixed exchange rate system. The likelihood of exercising
this option was based on the ratio of dollars held by foreigners to the gold
held by the United States. If the amount of dollars abroad surpassed the
amount of U.S. gold, all claimants could not be paid unless the United States
changed the price of gold. Raising the price of gold in terms of dollars — in

---

[37]The late 1950s are discussed in Robert Pollard and Samuel F. Wells, Jr. "1945–1960: The Era
of American Economic Hegemony," in William H. Becker and Samuel F. Wells, Jr. *Economics
and World Power*, New York: Columbia University Press, 1984, 379–381.

effect devaluing the dollar — automatically increased the dollar quantity of gold. Speculators in foreign exchange and others who feared this possibility would anticipate such an action and convert their dollars for gold — producing a "run" on the dollar and contributing to the very outcome they wanted to avoid or profit from. Since confidence in the dollar was a key element of the Bretton Woods system, and this confidence meant persuading those holding dollars to continue doing so, the U.S. balance of payments became a prime indicator of the stability of the system. A larger payments deficit meant more dollars abroad and more potential claimants on U.S. gold.

Political Economy and Hegemony

It was this problem which dominated international monetary management in the 1960s and ultimately led to the demise of the Bretton Woods system. In a sense, the requirements of hegemony — as expressed in U.S. foreign and economic policies from 1961 to 1969 — undermined a major pillar of that system. Kennedy and Johnson are the clearest examples of presidents whose policies were not only guided by the political, military, and economic demands of hegemony but who also point out the costs and contradictions of such policies. President Kennedy was determined to marshal U.S. power in order to contain the Soviet Union and Communism on a global scale. Expansion of military power and foreign aid were the chief means to this end. Kennedy was also concerned about the economic performance of the United States at home and abroad. He expected rapid domestic economic growth — the result of a fiscal policy based on military Keynesianism — to ameliorate the costs of the military buildup. Coupled with accelerating the liberalization of world trade, the improved productivity from growth was also expected to solve the balance of payments problem.

Links between domestic and international economies were more tightly drawn in the 1960s. Expectations about economic growth were driven by the requirements of competition with the Soviet Union. Moreover, the U.S. position in the world economy, as measured by the balance of payments, became a serious concern of the new president and his successor. One important advisor warned that "[we] will not be able to sustain in the 1960s a world position without solving the balance of payments problem."[38] But the harder the United States tried to meet its global responsibilities, the more it damaged the balance of payments and undermined its ability to act as hegemon. This behavior also began to prompt a backlash from allies who came to resent the

---

[38]The quote by Walt Rostow, Special Assistant to the President for National Security, is from William S. Borden, "Defending Hegemony: American Foreign Economic Policy," in Thomas G. Paterson, ed. *Kennedy's Quest for Victory: American Foreign Policy, 1961–1963*, New York: Oxford University Press, 1989, 63.

privileges and consequences of the dollar as key currency. Their chief complaint was that the unrelenting U.S. payments deficit — a product of U.S. foreign operations — presented a major policy dilemma. They were forced either to hold dollars and expand their money supply and inflation or exchange the dollars for gold and undermine the value of the dollars remaining in foreign hands. The French were especially critical, arguing that they and others were being required to pay part of the costs of a mistaken U.S. policy in Southeast Asia.

Over the decade, the U.S. response was to reject the option of devaluation and instead devise a variety of mechanisms to cope with a hopefully short-run balance of payments problem. These included efforts to have Europeans use their gold and currencies to support the dollar, voluntary and mandatory measures to restrict the movement of U.S. private capital abroad, and defending the value of the pound as the first line in defense of the dollar. The most lasting result of the efforts to salvage the dollar-gold connection was the establishment of a new form of international money. The Special Drawing Rights (SDR) established in the International Monetary Fund was a checking account that central banks could use to supplement their international reserves. Nations in deficit could use this overdraft privilege to settle international accounts with other central banks. The hope was that the liquidity role of the dollar could be eased by SDRs. But the small size of SDR allocations and reluctance to rely on "fiat" money limited their usefulness.[39]

On a more fundamental level, the United States pushed for additional liberalization of world trade. Congress passed the Trade Expansion Act in 1962, giving the president broadened powers to negotiate lower tariffs. In large part, this act was a response to the challenges presented by the new European Economic Community. The EEC created a common external tariff on goods from outside the six members while reducing tariffs within the group. This threatened to hurt U.S. trade and further weaken the balance of payments. The resulting Kennedy Round of GATT lasted from 1963 to 1967 and produced significant tariff reductions over a broad range of goods.[40] But, as we shall see, the U.S. trade balance, and with it the balance of payments, did not improve.

The Emergence of
Multinational Corporations

The efforts to cope with the EEC and payments difficulties also affected another very important development in the U.S. and the world economy: the rise of the multinational corporation and new international capital markets.

---

[39]Moffitt, *The World's.* . . . , 33; Eckes, *A Search.* . . . , 256–257.
[40]Pastor, *Congress and.* . . . , 104–120; Borden, "Defending Hegemony. . . ," 69–80.

The combination of the EEC and convertibility helped spur U.S. corporations to invest in Europe after 1958. The fear of tariff walls around the EEC provided the incentive, and the ability to convert profits back into dollars offered large U.S. corporations the opportunity to establish production facilities in Europe.[41] Multinational corporations (MNCs) — those with production and/or marketing facilities in at least two countries — have given rise to a new language for the analysis of international relations. Scholars now speak of the internationalization of production, the integration of national economies, global calculations of market relations, and the power of transnational actors in relation to nations themselves. These are matters we will take up in subsequent chapters. For now, our concern is with understanding the political consequences of MNCs and the economic motivations behind their expansion abroad.

A key feature of multinational corporations is direct investment abroad designed to establish and control a production and/or distribution unit.[42] The levels of direct foreign investment and its geographic and business direction can be seen in Tables 4.6 and 4.7.

TABLE 4.6

U.S. Direct Foreign Investment: 1950–1970
(Book Value in Billions of U.S. Dollars)

	TOTAL	MANUFACTURING	PETROLEUM & MINING	TRADE & PUBLIC UTILITIES
1950	11.79	3.83	4.52	2.18
1960	31.82	11.05	13.76	4.95
1970	78.18	32.26	27.88	9.42

SOURCE: Adapted from Mira Wilkins, *The Maturing of Multinational Enterprise: American Business Abroad from 1914 to 1970*, Cambridge: Harvard University Press, 1974, 330.

Clearly, expansion abroad is substantial in all categories but especially in manufacturing. Table 4.7 shows the geographic distribution of foreign direct investment in manufacturing.

---

[41] Gilpin, *The Political Economy.* . . , 233. An additional factor in the growth of MNCs was transportation and communication innovations, in the form of regular jet travel and the telex.

[42] This process of direct foreign investment can be distinguished from portfolio investment, which seeks merely to provide a non-controlling form of equity or debt to a foreign firm in the hopes of receiving returns in the future. Portfolio investment was characteristic of the British foreign investment in the nineteenth century and is discussed in Chapter Three. See Robert Gilpin, *U.S. Power.* . . , 9–11.

TABLE 4.7

U.S. Direct Foreign Investment
in Manufacturing, 1955–1970
(*Book Value in Billions of U.S. Dollars*)

	EEC	U.K.	EUROPE OTHER	CANADA	LATIN AMERICA	OTHER	TOTAL
1955	0.6	0.9	0.1	2.8	1.4	0.5	6.3
1960	1.4	2.2	0.3	4.8	1.5	0.9	11.1
1965	3.7	3.3	0.6	6.9	2.9	1.9	19.3
1970	7.2	5.0	1.5	10.1	4.6	3.9	32.3

SOURCE: This is adapted from Wilkins, *The Maturing. . .* , 331.

Several areas of the world received U.S. direct investment but especially Canada, the EEC, and Asia.

The process of direct foreign investment was overwhelmingly an American phenomenon. By the early 1970s, the book value of U.S. investments was $86.0 billion, which represented 52 percent of all direct foreign investment for all market economies. Even more impressive is the fact that U.S. companies produced $172.0 billion worth of goods and services abroad. This is compared to $43.5 billion worth of goods produced within the United States for export. That is, production abroad by U.S. firms was almost four times as great as all U.S. exports.[43]

The growth of multinational corporations in the period from 1958 to 1970 was the consequence of a complex mixture of political and economic factors. In political terms, the interests of the United States and the Europeans were accommodated, and this created the climate within which U.S. MNCs in Europe could flourish. Specifically, this meant acceptance by the United States of the EEC and its discriminatory and competitive effects on American trade, and in return, the Europeans (especially the Germans) agreed to finance the U.S. balance of payments deficit by holding dollars. This would permit operations such as stationing U.S. troops in Europe to continue and helped make other major actions, such as in Vietnam, possible. As part of this process, the United States persuaded the Europeans to give U.S. MNCs access to the EEC and treat them as if they were a European company.[44]

---

[43]Gilpin, *U.S. Power. . .* , 15. The propensity of U.S. firms to invest and produce abroad is indicated by the fact that only two other countries — Great Britain and Switzerland — produced more abroad than at home for export. And neither country did so to the same degree.

[44]This argument is found in Gilpin, *U.S. Power. . .* , 107–108, 154–155. Gilpin (124–125) points out the importance of the dollar as key currency, especially as the balance of payments deficit

Thought of only in economic terms, multinational corporations had a somewhat cloudy set of benefits for the United States. In 1971, U.S. MNCs engaged in $4.8 billion in direct foreign investment (remember, this is a negative item in the balance of payments) while generating $9.0 billion in investment income (a positive item).[45] More difficult to measure is the loss of jobs in the United States to overseas production, the transfer of technology abroad, and the exports back to the United States (our imports) of goods produced elsewhere by U.S. MNCs. But in terms of the immediate political needs of generating a positive return in the balance of payments, multinational corporations represented a support system for U.S. international responsibilities.[46]

From the standpoint of the multinationals themselves, the political climate created by U.S. hegemony and the economic climate of stability and opportunity intersected with a set of more specifically economic motivations. Several somewhat complementary explanations have been offered for the expansion of multinationals, each of which begins with the fact that these are typically firms operating in an oligopolistic environment that are seeking to maintain or extend their competitive advantages.[47] Since market share is an important asset for oligopolistic companies, these firms may expand operations abroad simply to make certain they are positioned to participate in any new or expanding market. Or, a giant firm that enjoys some special competitive advantage may look to production in foreign markets to exploit this advantage. Finally, the firm may be at a particular point in the evolution of its products so that foreign production becomes an economic necessity. Initially, the combination of a large home market and technological advantages make production for export a profitable strategy. But as the technology of the product and its production processes become more commonplace and available, the company may be forced to move abroad to take advantage of lower costs and/or to compete with a foreign producer. This "product cycle" theory may be especially relevant to U.S. firms in the 1950s and 1960s who faced rising European firms moving into markets U.S. firms had pioneered in the preceding ten to fifteen years.[48]

---

persisted and made the dollar overvalued. U.S. firms could use an overvalued dollar to purchase European assets and establish European branches without having to earn this currency through a balance of payments surplus.

[45]United Nations, "Multinational Corporations in World Development," in George Modelski, ed. *Transnational Corporations and World Order*, San Francisco: W.H. Freeman, 1979, 25.

[46]See Gilpin, *U.S. Power*. . . , 156–157.

[47]An oligopoly means the number of firms in the industry is very small, with each controlling a significant portion of the market. The size of the firm in relation to the market and to the economy permits it to influence the price of the good. That is, the firm is powerful enough to affect, in some significant way, the competitive environment in which it operates.

[48]This discussion relies on Gilpin, *U.S. Power*. . . , 115–125; and Gilpin, *The Political Economy*. . . , 232–238. Also see Charles Kindleberger, "The Monopolistic Theory of Direct Foreign Investment," in Modelski, ed. *Transnational*. . . , 91–107; along with Raymond Vernon, "The Product Cycle Model," in Modelski, ed. *Transnational*. . . , 108–117.

Lagging somewhat behind multinational corporations were U.S. banks, who began in the mid-1960s to expand substantially their foreign operations. Once again, several factors were at work. The dollar as key currency, acceptable for most international transactions, and the U.S. payments imbalance must be judged as critical ingredients. The transition from a dollar shortage to a dollar surplus in 1957–1958 resulted in the accumulation of dollars in foreign banks. London bankers, an ingenious lot, decided to begin lending these dollars rather than returning them to the United States. Thus was born the Eurodollar or Eurocurrency (since some other currencies were also involved) market, essentially an unregulated international money supply. When the U.S. government acted in 1963 to stem the dollar outflow for loans through the Interest Equalization Tax, many U.S. banks established operations abroad to continue their foreign lending and thereby took advantage of the Eurodollar process. The rise of the Eurodollar market, the expansion of U.S. international banking, and the growth of U.S. multinational firms were linked together throughout the 1960s.

Beyond this relationship, the Eurocurrency system became a phenomenon in its own right. Because no single state could regulate it effectively and because of the unceasing U.S. payments deficits, a Euromarket system developed consisting of the dollar and other currencies, a system of bank credit, and a Eurobond market (bonds denominated in dollars but floated outside the United States). A massive volume of funds emerged that, without much restriction, could move across borders in search of the highest yields available on a global basis (discounting for risk). By 1970, this market approached $70 billion and would triple in size in the next three years.[49]

The 1958–1970 period produced an extraordinarily complex set of developments for the world economy. It was simultaneously a time of American dominance and decline. Bearing the burdens of military competition and Vietnam, the United States was acutely aware of the continued importance of preserving global security and stability. The United States also encouraged the establishment of the EEC and the economic revitalization of Japan, both to marshal its assets against the Soviets and to facilitate the multilateral economic order sought since the 1940s. U.S. resources flowed abroad to preserve a liberal world order even as allies improved their competetive position in the world economy. But neither planned nor entirely desired was the acceleration of U.S. private investment abroad. As we shall see, this combination of events led to the breakdown of the Bretton Woods system so important to the United States and contributed to dramatic changes in the control of oil.

---

[49]See Jeffry A. Frieden, *Banking on the World: The Politics of American International Finance*, New York: Harper and Row, 1987, 79–85; Benjamin J. Cohen, *In Whose Interest? International Banking and American Foreign Policy*, New Haven: Yale University Press, 1986, 19–33; Michael Moffitt, *The World's Money*, New York: Simon and Schuster, 1983, 43–55.

MONEY AND OIL, 1971–1973

■ Between 1970 and 1973, two of the pillars of U.S. hegemony — fixed exchange rates and control of oil — came under pressure and eventually disintegrated, only to be replaced by new relationships. Several basic weaknesses of the Bretton Woods system were exposed by the continuing U.S. payments deficit and growing international financial interdependence, and between 1971 and 1973 the system largely collapsed. The ability of the United States to guarantee ample oil supplies at low prices ran aground on imbalances of supply and demand and growing nationalism in those Third World nations where the oil was located. Notwithstanding the collapse of these arrangements, U.S. power remained sufficient to organize new mechanisms for money and oil. But these new regimes required even greater coordination, cooperation, and compromise and cast doubt on the future of the world economy.

The End of Bretton Woods

The economic growth of Western Europe and Japan, a weakening position in the U.S. balance of trade, and the growth of international capital markets spelled doom for the Bretton Woods system of fixed exchange rates based on a fixed dollar-gold exchange rate. As early as 1960, the liabilities created by foreign-held dollars exceeded the U.S. supply of gold. In that same year, the price of gold in private markets rose to $40 an ounce. Over the next decade and more, the situation deteriorated.[50]

TABLE 4.8

Proportion of World Exports
(Billions of U.S. Dollars with % of World Totals)

	1960	%	1965	%	1970	%	1971	%	1972	%
U. S.	20.6	18.0	27.5	16.5	43.2	15.2	44.1	13.9	49.8	13.2
Great Britain	10.6	9.3	13.8	8.2	19.6	6.9	22.6	7.1	24.7	6.6
W. Germany	11.4	9.9	17.9	10.7	34.2	12.1	39.1	12.3	46.7	12.4
France	6.9	6.0	10.2	6.1	18.1	6.4	20.8	6.6	26.5	7.0
Japan	4.1	3.6	8.5	5.1	19.3	6.8	24.1	7.6	29.1	7.7
World Exports	114.6		167.1		283.7		317.4		376.8	

SOURCE: The figures are calculated from International Monetary Fund, *International Financial Statistics Yearbook*, 1979, 62–63.

---

[50]John Odell, *U.S. International Monetary Policy*, Princeton: Princeton University Press, 1982, 85–87.

This can be seen in several ways but especially in the growing importance of several countries in world trade and in the U.S. balance of payments. Table 4.8 shows a steady decline in the world proportion of home-based exports by the United States. (Remember the jump in U.S. MNC production abroad.) The same was true for Great Britain. At the same time, West Germany, France, and especially Japan made steady relative gains. U.S. exports rose throughout the period but not as fast as those of the world or of its industrial competitors. By 1972 West Germany had nearly equalled the United States in dollar volume of exports.

A close examination of the U.S. balance of payments for this period reveals some important refinements for our understanding of the U.S. problem.[51]

TABLE 4.9

U.S. Balance of Payments, 1960–1972
(*Billions of Dollars*)

YEAR	EXPORTS	IMPORTS	NET MILITARY	INVEST INC.	CURRENT ACCOUNT BALANCE	CAPITAL ACCOUNT BALANCE	ERROR	NET LIQUIDITY BALANCE
1960	19.7	−14.8	4.9	−2.8	2.8	1.8	−3.0	−1.1	−3.7
1965	26.5	−21.5	5.0	−2.1	5.3	4.3	−6.1	−0.5	−2.5
1967	30.7	−26.9	3.8	−3.1	5.8	2.1	−5.5	−0.9	−4.7
1968	33.6	−33.0	0.6	−3.1	6.2	−0.4	−3.4	−0.4	−1.6
1969	36.4	−35.8	0.6	−3.3	6.0	−1.1	−2.0	−2.4	−6.1
1970	42.0	−39.8	2.2	−3.4	6.4	0.4	−3.4	−1.2	−3.9
1971	42.8	−45.5	−2.7	−2.9	8.9	−2.8	−6.8	−10.8	−22.0
1972	48.8	−55.7	−6.9	−3.6	9.8	−8.4	−1.5	−3.1	−13.9

Note: some items in the balance of payments have been omitted. The result is that only net exports/imports adds across.

Source: The table is reconstructed from data in Odell, *U.S. International.* . . , 203–205.

Several points stand out in the data shown in Table 4.9. Perhaps most important is the slow growth of exports relative to imports, especially after 1967, and the development of a trade deficit in 1971. Although investment income (remember MNC direct investments) grew steadily and the capital account and military spending abroad were mostly under control, the U.S deficit

---

[51]The use of different sources for trade and balance of payments produces a slight variation in the export totals.

persisted and grew much worse from the deteriorating trade balance.[52] Another perspective on this process is revealed from data on exports and imports of manufactured goods.

TABLE 4.10

U.S. Trade in Manufactured Goods, 1960–1971

	1960	1965	1970	1971
Low technology goods				
Exports	3.573	4.409	6.778	6.262
Imports	4.494	7.350	12.928	14.550
Balance	−.921	−2.941	−6.150	−8.288
High technology goods				
Exports	9.010	13.030	22.565	24.187
Imports	2.369	3.895	12.978	15.898
Balance	6.641	9.135	9.587	8.289

SOURCE: This data is taken from Gilpin, *U.S. Power.* . . , 193.

Two points are notable from this evidence. First, imports of both low and high technology manufactures were growing more rapidly than exports of these goods. Second, by 1971 the deficit in low-tech goods equalled the surplus in high-tech goods.

The difficulties in the U.S. trade and payments balances can be traced in substantial part to the interaction of domestic and foreign policy in the mid-1960s. The decision to escalate U.S. involvement in the Vietnam War in 1965 came in the context of substantial increases in domestic spending for new poverty and welfare programs and was followed by the decision not to raise taxes. In many ways this combination of choices was consistent with the Keynesian notions of fiscal policy except that they came at a time of near full employment and a booming economy. Over the period from 1965 to 1973, the inflation rate rose (as measured by the Consumer Price Index), and the budget deficit widened.

In simple terms, the budget deficit contributed greatly to the rise in inflation, both by overstimulating the economy and from increases in the money supply encouraged by the Federal Reserve to help finance the deficit. The rising price of U.S. goods encouraged imports and discouraged exports.

---

[52] The large "Error" item in 1971–72, Table 4.9, reflects the substantial volume of speculation against the dollar discussed below.

In 1968–69, policy changed with a tax increase and tighter money. The result of this "belt tightening" was a budget surplus, an improvement in the balance of trade, and a stronger dollar. But the economy also went into recession even as inflation remained high. Later, in 1970, economic policy shifted back to stimulation.[53]

TABLE 4.11

Budget Deficits and Inflation

	1965	1966	1967	1968	1969	1970	1971	1972	1973
CPI %	1.7	2.9	2.9	4.2	5.4	5.9	4.3	3.3	6.2
Budget Deficit $	−1.6	−3.8	−8.7	−25.2	+3.2	−2.8	−23.0	−23.4	−14.8

SOURCE: The data on the Consumer Price Index is taken from David Calleo, *The Imperious Economy*, Cambridge: Harvard University Press, 1982, 201. The data on the budget deficit is taken from Calleo, *Beyond. . .* , 243.

The overall trade deficit in 1971 represented the culmination of several years of deterioration and, combined with the deficit in military and capital accounts, produced a major international monetary crisis. With pressure mounting against the dollar, on August 15, 1971 President Nixon announced a new policy. The United States suspended indefinitely the commitment to redeem gold for dollars, imposed domestic wage and price controls, demanded depreciation of the dollar, and placed a 10 percent tariff surcharge on U.S. imports. These actions amounted to a unilateral rejection of the basic rules of international monetary behavior and a demand for adjustment by U.S. military and economic allies.

What followed was more than eighteen months of coercion and pressure, resistance, seemingly solid agreements, and continued market instability. At issue was the future of the dollar-gold link, fixed exchange rates, the rate of exchange, and which countries would be forced to make the adjustments and trade concessions. The United States wanted substantial revaluations of major currencies, elimination of "unfair" restrictions on trade, and greater sharing of the costs of keeping U.S. forces abroad. The French and the Japanese resisted the most strongly, with the French refusing to alter the franc-gold price and the Japanese arguing that the United States should change its domestic economic system. Only after National Security Adviser Henry Kissinger became concerned about the damage this was doing to the alliance system did the United States accept the need for concessions. In December 1971, at

---

[53]Discussions of the links between domestic and foreign economic policy are found in Calleo, *The Imperious. . .* , 25–61; and Odell, *U.S. International. . .* , 110–111.

the Smithsonian Institution in Washington, a compromise agreement was reached. The United States devalued the dollar in terms of gold (but made no commitment to redeem dollars for gold) and dropped the import surcharge. The other major capitalist states revalued their currencies against the dollar by an average of 8 percent (Japan's was 16.9 percent against the dollar) and adjusted their currencies against each other. Trade issues were postponed. The result was a temporary return to fixed rates.[54]

This system held together through 1972 in spite of continuing U.S. trade deficits. But in February 1973, renewed selling of the dollar produced another currency crisis and a U.S. decision to devalue the dollar 10 percent (without consultation) accompanied by the threat to devalue another 10 percent unless the Japanese and the West Europeans agreed to float their currencies against the dollar. Acceptance of this arrangement led not to stability but to further selling of the dollar and the complete collapse of fixed exchange rates in March 1973.[55]

Two main reasons can be identified for the decline and fall of the Bretton Woods system. First, the system was inherently unstable because the mechanisms for adjustment of exchange rates were so inflexible. This was especially true for the United States where the value of the dollar also became the measure of the stability of the world economy, especially in the minds of U.S. leaders. The economic relations that developed after 1948 were structured by these fixed values even as the shift from U.S. surplus to deficit increasingly demanded adjustment of exchanges rates. The world of 1971 was significantly different from the world of 1945–1950, but the Bretton Woods system made few accommodations to that reality.

Second, and perhaps most reflective of those changes, was the massive growth of the market power of international capital and its impact on fixed rates. This is reflected in the emergence of transnational actors — multinational corporations and international banks — and the vast Eurocurrency market over the years from 1958–1973. As late as 1966, the Eurocurrency market and U.S. international reserves were of approximately equal size. But by 1973 the Eurocurrency market was almost nine times bigger than U.S. reserves.[56] Such an immense collection of resources was capable of overwhelming even concerted government action. Between 1971 and 1973, these new transnational actors collectively lost confidence in the system of fixed exchange rates and the ability of governments to establish any viable system. Eventually, in March 1973, the governments of the capitalist world were

---

[54]The best detailed discussion of these events is in Odell, *U.S. International.* . . , 188–291.

[55]Odell, *U.S. International.* . . , 292–326.

[56]Calleo, *The Imperious.* . . , 208. Additional measures can be found in Robert Keohane and Joseph Nye, *Power and Interdependence*, Second Edition, Glenview: Scott Foresman, 1989, 81–82; Eckes, *A Search.* . . , 240–241.

forced to accept the immense market power of these actors and adopt a new system of floating exchange rates.[57]

Loss of Control Over Oil

Concurrent with these dramatic changes in the international monetary order was an equally significant structural transformation of the international oil market. Several basic forces converged in the early 1970s that led to an overturning of the control of oil. These included changes in the political and military relationship of the United States and Great Britain in the Middle East, shifts in supply and demand for oil, increasing political control over oil exercised by Third World countries, and the 1973 Yom Kippur War. U.S. domination of the international oil market, operating through large multinational oil companies, came to an end as the price for oil skyrocketed and an embargo created shortages in the United States.

Between 1968 and 1971, Great Britain withdrew from its military commitments in the Middle East, leaving a political and military vacuum that it had filled for more than a century. During this time the United States was mired in the Vietnam War, which greatly hampered its ability to use military force anywhere else in the world. These developments damaged the ability of the West to defend its interests in cheap and plentiful oil.[58]

The early 1970s also provided the culmination of the trends of the preceding fifteen years during which the world became increasingly dependent on oil from the Middle East. From 1957 to 1972, the proportion of world oil produced in the United States declined from 43.1 percent to 21.1 percent, while the Middle East raised its proportion from 19.4 percent to 41.0 percent. Over the same period, U.S. oil imports rose from 11 percent of consumption to 35.5 percent.[59] Rapid increases in world production were linked to even more rapid increases in demand for oil. However, by the early 1970s world supplies of oil failed to match increases in demand, primarily due to flat U.S. production growth. This combination created the potential for substantial prices increases.[60]

Accompanying these trends was a growing boldness by the countries where the oil was located to challenge control over production and pricing

---

[57]Once again, Odell has the best discussion of this matter. See Odell, *U.S. International.* . . , 299–305. The arrangement adopted was a managed or "dirty" float in which governments periodically intervened to keep rate fluctuations within some acceptable bounds.

[58]The story of the oil crisis of the early 1970s is ably told in Daniel Yergin, *The Prize: The Quest for Oil, Money and Power*, New York: Simon and Schuster, 1991, 563–652.

[59]Darmstadter and Landsberg, "The Economic. . . ," 31–33.

[60]Rostow, *The World.* . . , 257, reports that U.S. growth in oil consumption outstripped production throughout the postwar era. U.S. production peaked in 1970 and fell each year from 1971 to 1975.

decisions by the great oil multinationals. Beginning with Libya in 1970 and soon spreading to other states, governments used various forms of intimidation to increase their take, their level of participation in ownership of the oil, and even in the price charged. The tightening supply situation helped accelerate this process as countries began leapfrogging each other in terms of price and control. The devaluations of the dollar in 1971 and 1973 also prompted price increases since oil was denominated in dollars. When the United States was forced to lift import quotas for oil in April 1973, the signal was given for a new round of negotiations.[61]

It was in this context of growing dependence on Middle East oil that Anwar Sadat, President of Egypt, launched an attack on Israel to begin the Yom Kippur War. U.S. support of Israel led several members of the Organization of Petroleum Exporting Countries (OPEC) to push prices up dramatically (from $3.01 to $5.12 per barrel) and impose an embargo. This consisted of reductions in overall production and a ban on shipments to the United States (and the Netherlands). By January 1974, prices had risen to $11.65 a barrel, and the United States was confronted with a shift in power relations that, in the words of Henry Kissinger, "altered irrevocably the world as it had grown up in the postwar period."[62]

CONCLUSIONS

■ In 1941, Henry Luce, publisher of *Life* magazine, wrote effusively of "The American Century." In many ways he was right; the United States was the key player in determining the outcome of World War II and in the shape of the postwar world. American money and military might provided the base for projecting a vision of a liberal world order of peace and prosperity. Confrontation with the Soviet Union pushed the United States beyond its original plans and led to a major effort to organize the political and economic resources of the industrial world for containment. Out of this process came a new set of international institutions, new forms of cooperation, and an unprecedented expansion of international trade, capital transfer, and world economic growth. Seen against the record of the preceding century, the years after 1945 were truly epochal.

The economic relationships of the American Century did not last as long as the political and military relationships. The United States largely retained its ability to foster military security but in the process lost many of its economic advantages. The effort to rebuild Europe and Japan as economic

---

[61]For more detail, see Edith Penrose, "The Development of Crisis," in Vernon, *The Oil Crisis*, New York: Norton, 1976, 39–57; and Yergin, *The Prize.* . . . , 577–587.
[62]Quoted in Yergin, *The Prize.* . . . , 588.

powers capable of resisting Soviet pressure worked very well. In the mean-time, military spending, foreign aid, and direct investment — the *sine qua non* of U.S. hegemony — kept the balance of payments in deficit and under-mined the dollar-gold link that stabilized the international monetary system. When America's political and economic allies took advantage of the liberal system of international trade and greatly expanded their exports in the 1960s, the United States found itself unable to maintain a favorable trade balance. Further, when the growth of the world economy and demand for oil ex-panded in the 1960s and early 1970s, the United States was unable to prevent Western loss of control over oil production and pricing.

Nevertheless, the United States retained great strength; it was by far the largest economy in the world, the predominant source of capital, the biggest export market, and continued as the guarantor of Western security. But in important ways, the game of international political economy had changed. In the first decade or so after the war, the Europeans and Japanese gained their leverage in negotiating with the United States from weakness; and the United States accepted the necessity for sharply limiting any use of coercion to bring about actions it favored. Instead, providing aid and accepting and even promoting discriminatory arrangements such as the EEC were common fare. By the 1970s, increasing European and Japanese economic strength tilted the bargaining relationship. Now adjustments had to come from them, and the United States sometimes found it necessary to coerce these concessions. A much more complex system emerged in which the major capitalist states found that their economic interdependence created a new balance of opposing and conflicting interests. Even parts of the Third World, long simply an arena of military and economic struggle with the Soviets, gained the capacity for independent action. The trick to international order changed from one of U.S. dominance to one of bargaining over the terms for creating and recreat-ing a framework within which economic competition on a global scale could take place. This extraordinary process is the subject of the next two chapters.

ANNOTATED BIBLIOGRAPHY

William H. Becker and Samuel F. Wells, eds. *Economics and World Power*, New York: Columbia University Press, 1984.
Contains several insightful pieces on the history of U.S. foreign economic policy.

Fred Block, *The Origins of International Economic Disorder*, Berkeley: University of California Press, 1977.
Offers a penetrating analysis of U.S. international monetary policy for the postwar era.

Benjamin Cohen, *Organizing the World's Money*, New York: Basic Books, 1977.
Very helpful on the economics of international finance.

Jeffrey Frieden, *Banking on the World: The Politics of American International Finance*, New York: Harper and Row, 1987.
A very useful study of the internationalization of U.S. financial institutions and the international financial system.

Robert Gilpin, *U.S. Power and the Multinational Corporation*, New York: Basic Books, 1975.
Perhaps the best theoretically informed analysis of U.S. multinational corporations.

Robert Keohane and Joseph Nye, *Power and Interdependence*, Glenview: Scott Foresman, 1989.
The most important study of the politics of bargaining within a framework of economic interdependence.

Charles Maier, "The Politics of Productivity: Foundations of American International Economic Policy After World War II," *International Organization*, Autumn 1977, 607–633.
A very perceptive argument concerning the expression of domestic political economy in foreign policy.

Robert Pollard, *Economic Security and the Origins of the Cold War, 1945–1950*, New York: Columbia University Press, 1985.
The best single source for understanding the relationship of U.S. political economy and national security from 1945–1950.

John Odell, *U.S. International Monetary Policy*, Princeton: Princeton University Press, 1982.
The best study of the breakdown and collapse of the Bretton Woods system.

W.M. Scammell, *The International Economy Since 1945*, New York: St. Martin's Press, 1983.
An excellent overview.

Daniel Yergin, *The Prize: The Quest for Oil, Money and Power*, New York: Simon and Schuster, 1991.
A comprehensive survey of the role of oil in twentieth century international politics.

Studies of U.S. hegemony include:

Simon Bromley, *American Hegemony and World Oil*, University Park: Pennsylvania State University Press, 1991.

David Calleo, *The Imperious Economy*, Cambridge: Harvard University Press, 1982.
Defends the thesis that U.S spending on foreign commitments undermined the domestic economy.

David Calleo, *Beyond American Hegemony*, New York: Basic Books, 1987.
Relates the end of U.S. hegemony to Europe and NATO.

Stephen Gill, *American Hegemony and the Trilateral Commission*, Cambridge: Cambridge University Press, 1990.
A brilliant investigation of elite interests in hegemony.

Robert Gilpin, *War and Change in World Politics*, Cambridge: Cambridge University Press, 1981.
  A theoretical investigation of the relationship of international systems, hegemony, and economic decline.

Robert Keohane, *After Hegemony*, Princeton: Princeton University Press, 1984.
  A very important study of international cooperation in the period after U.S. hegemony.

Stephen Krasner, "State Power and the Structure of International Trade," *World Politics*, April 1975, 314–347.
  A key statement of the hegemonic stability thesis.

Joseph Nye, *Bound to Lead*, New York: Basic Books, 1990.
  Counters the thesis that U.S. hegemony has waned.

CHAPTER 5

Cooperation among Advanced Industrial States

W e have just seen how important the dollar and oil were to the world economy of the 1950s and 1960s. It might be reasonable to predict, based upon the collapse of Bretton Woods in 1971 and loss of Western control over oil production and prices by 1973, that a fatal blow had been struck to the world economy. But rather than a downward spiral of trade and finance in the years after 1973, we have experienced instead an even greater expansion and deepening of global economic relationships. The internationalization of finance, spurred by the oil crises and massive debt requirements of the 1970s and 1980s, has grown to immense proportions. The financial markets of individual nations — for equity, debt, and foreign exchange — have been linked together on a 24-hour basis and frequently move in conjunction with each other. Trade levels, even though punctuated by two significant world recessions, have also increased dramatically. Alongside these largely positive events has been the development of serious imbalances in the world economy. The shift of resources produced by price increases for oil contributed to global inflation and the growth of debt in the Third World. Large tax cuts and the resulting budget deficits in the United States helped spark high interest rates, substantial increases in the exchange rate for the dollar, a whopping trade deficit, and accumulating debt for the United States. The trade deficits and debt growth were mirrored by large Japanese and German trade surpluses and by investment in the United States by Japan.

The scale and intensity of trade and financial flows have produced new efforts at cooperation and coordination, along with an accentuation of international competition. Nations and corporations frequently have found their interests bound together by the need to manage the burgeoning system of interdependence and thereby continue to reap the mutual benefits of free

95

trade and capital movement. This process has given rise to many new and strengthened arrangements for cooperation. Perhaps the most important are recurring efforts to manage the newly floating exchange rates and coordinate macroeconomic policies. Heads of state, finance ministers and their staffs, and central bankers have become deeply involved in these matters. Less visible are the efforts of firms to share the costs of development and moderate competition in the area of high technology. Also interesting, for the mixture of cooperative and competitive features, is the growth of trading blocs in Europe, North America, and Asia.

Discussion of the role of cooperation must also include a keen appreciation of the impact of conflicting interests, for a capitalist world economy generates powerful competitive incentives for nations and firms alike. Those who are able to define the rules for exchange or bring the best or least expensive product to the marketplace win a disproportionate set of the gains. Similarly, those who consistently fail to meet these demands fall further and further behind, whether it be in market share, technological innovation, the ability to attract investment, standard of living, or military competition. Thus, the need for international cooperation is often tempered by a countervailing need for institutions and national strategies capable of adapting to and flourishing in an intensely competitive environment. In recent years, the level of world trade, the swiftness of change, the declining dominance of the United States, and the astonishing success of the Japanese have combined to raise significant concerns about competitiveness across much of the world.

This chapter is the first of two that will focus on the complex mixture of cooperation and conflict among advanced capitalist states. After a brief overview of the events in the world economy since 1973, we will begin with a detailed discussion of the concept of cooperation. This is an elusive term, and it requires some extended discussion in order to understand its several dimensions. Under what conditions can we expect cooperation to occur? What are the main obstacles to resolving problems through cooperation? We follow a discussion of the factors supporting, and the barriers to, cooperation with a consideration of three very important cases: macroeconomic coordination through economic summits, management of exchange rates, and the creation of economic blocs, especially the European Community (EC). These cases will offer some basis for reaching conclusions about the effectiveness of and prospects for cooperation among the largest and most prosperous states.

AN OVERVIEW: 1973–1991

■ The arrangements of cooperation and conflict developed within a context of dramatic events, policy shifts, and cascading consequences between 1973 and 1991. The unprecedented increase in oil prices in 1973–1974 forced several important adjustments on the world economy. Paying for higher oil prices had a major impact on the economies of the developed and developing world. Since oil was essential for the functioning of all these economic systems, demand can be described as highly inelastic. That is, the short-term and near-term demand for oil remained about the same in spite of the price increases. The consequence was a combination of reduced purchases of other goods and a substantial rise in inflation as monetary authorities increased the quantity of money in circulation in order to offset oil price increases. In 1974–1975, many countries in the developed world experienced a serious case of stagflation — declining economic activity and rising prices. Historically, these rarely went together since recessions were thought to be a cure for inflation and vise versa. Economic recovery and relatively stable oil prices (at the new level of eleven to thirteen dollars per barrel) came to an end with the revolution in Iran and the overthrow of the shah in 1979. Once again, a tight oil supply situation was narrowed by the loss of production in a key state, this time in Iran. Oil prices rose to about $35 per barrel, and by 1980 recession and inflation again descended on the world economy.

Within the United States, a strong commitment by the Federal Reserve, under Paul Volcker, to reducing inflation pushed interest rates to astronomical levels, and this brought on a deep recession in 1981–1982. These actions also contributed to a serious world recession. Largely in response to the economic difficulties of the 1970s and early 1980s, several strategies for economic revitalization emerged in the United States and elsewhere. Deregulation and large tax cuts were thought by many conservatives to be the mechanism for a return to strong economic growth and higher rates of savings and investment. Parallel to these ideas were worries about Soviet military power and risk-taking, which reached a peak with the Soviet invasion of Afghanistan in late 1979. The solution was seen in much higher defense spending. The election of Ronald Reagan in 1980 brought together, once again, the political economy of the early 1960s: tax cuts and sharply higher defense spending. The result was a series of the largest peacetime budget deficits in U.S. history.

Imbalances in the U.S. economy spilled over into the world economy. Indeed, it was this link to the rest of the world that permitted some success for Reaganomics. The large budget deficits, combined with a looser monetary policy, produced a significant stimulus to demand and economic growth in the United States after 1982, including a significant rise in consumer and business spending. But as proportions of Gross National Product (GNP), both savings and investment fell while consumption rose. The greatest beneficiaries of the Reagan years were those at the highest income levels.[1] Also accompanying the budget deficits were interest rates that were high relative to those in other countries. This served to attract funds into U.S. investments (these investments provided the funds that otherwise would need to be diverted from U.S.

---

[1] Kevin Phillips, *The Politics of Rich and Poor*, New York: Random House, 1989.

consumption to buy the government debt that closed the government spending gap), which produced large increases in the exchange rate of the dollar. The rising dollar tended to raise the prices of U.S. exports and lower the prices of imports. This led to massive increases in the trade deficit, especially with the Japanese. The effort at revitalization worked in the sense that world economic growth occurred. But this came at a price — large trade deficits, even larger budget deficits, massive increases in the national debt and U.S. foreign debt, and very large swings in exchange rates.

The mixed effects of trends in the world economy can be seen in the following figures. The imbalances in the world economy are shown in Figure 5.1, which details the current account balances of the three major trading states.

FIGURE 5.1

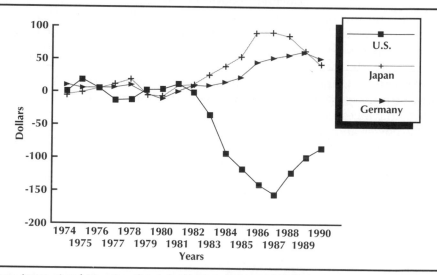

**Comparative Balance of Payments
Current Account Balance**

SOURCE: International Monetary Fund, *International Financial Statistics Yearbook*, 1991, 140.

The current account balances of the United States, Germany, and Japan hovered around zero until 1981 when the expansion of the U.S. deficit was mirrored in the large German and Japanese surpluses. Figures 5.2 and 5.3 indicate that at the same time there was substantial growth in world exports along with a sense of the distribution of trade around the world. Clearly, the greatest proportion of world trade occurs within the EC and between the EC and the world. When we add all this together, more than one-half of world trade operates through the European Community.

FIGURE 5.2

World Exports

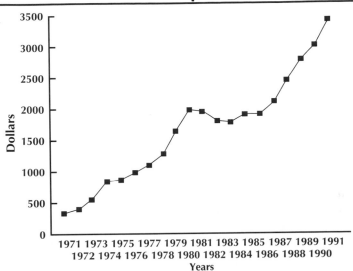

SOURCE: International Monetary Fund, *International Financial Statistics Yearbook*, 1991, 120–121.

FIGURE 5.3

Distribution of World Trade
(*Percent of Total World Trade*)

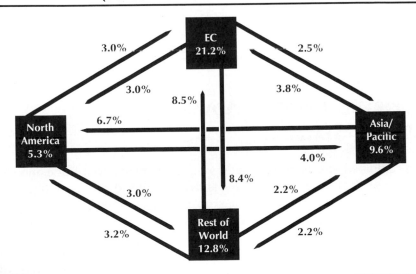

SOURCE: *The Economist*, September 22, 1990, special section on "World Trade," page 6.

Finally, one simple measure of interdependence is the common movement of interest rates. Figure 5.4 indicates the association of interest rates in the United States, Germany, and Japan along with a sense of the spread across nations.

FIGURE 5.4

Comparative Interest Rates
U.S./Germany/Japan

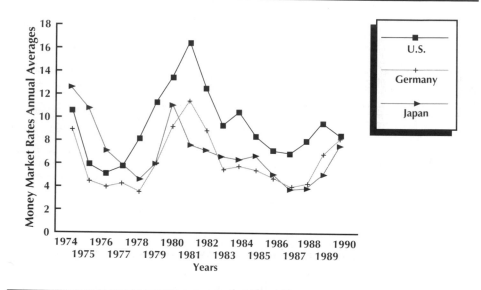

SOURCE: International Monetary Fund, *International Financial Statistics Yearbook*, 1991, 107.

COOPERATION AMONG ADVANCED CAPITALIST STATES

■ The combined effects of increasing interdependence from trade and capital flows and of floating exchange rates is that the world economy has a larger and larger impact on the economies of individual states. Since 1945, trade has grown relative to GNP, capital movement across national boundaries has become immense, and trading in foreign exchange (reflecting trade and capital) now dwarfs equity markets on the New York Stock Exchange. Further, exchange rates are also heavily affected by factors such as interest rates, which means that a fall or rise in a currency's value may not function to adjust a nation's current account deficit or surplus.

There are two major consequences of the forces of trade and capital. First, linking economies together puts more pressure on national leaders to coordinate their nations' fiscal and monetary policies. Going it alone can result in enlarged trade deficits or surpluses and/or undesired exchange rate fluctuations. Second, the emergence of several large and economically powerful states increases the competitive and even conflictual elements in the world economy. Failure to keep up can have immediate negative consequences for a nation and its firms. With more nations and firms capable of entering the fray in search of market share and profits, the world economy becomes much more dynamic. Relations of competition intensify, and failure produces stronger cries for help from those who lose.

This section examines the circumstances under which cooperation can occur. In particular, we will set out the factors that support cooperation and those barriers that stand in its way. This matter is a key element in the way scholars think about the basic nature of international politics. There is significant debate about whether we can expect any meaningful cooperation to take place in an international system based on sovereign states whose security depends on their own efforts. We will discuss the basics of this debate and follow it with two case studies of recent efforts at cooperation in the areas of macroeconomic policy and management of exchange rates. A separate section will take up the matter of cooperation and economic blocs.

Theories of Cooperation

Although the discussion to this point may seem to set cooperation and conflict apart as two distinct kinds of situations, the real world almost always consists of varying mixtures of the two. Harmony is both rare and uninteresting in analytical terms. Instances where the actions of one nation have no unwanted consequences for others are simply too unlikely to warrant our attention. Perhaps especially in world politics, cooperation is not a situation in which two nations simply recognize and act on a harmonious relationship. Rather, cooperation involves bargaining between two or more nations who modify their behavior and/or preferences in order to receive some reciprocal act from other nations. The aim is to arrive at a situation in which these nations coordinate their behavior so as to achieve some important purpose they cannot have by themselves.[2]

There are several important implications for this way of thinking about cooperation. First, cooperation does not require that the purposes of nations

[2]This definition and the discussion that follows relies on Robert Keohane, *After Hegemony*, Princeton: Princeton University Press, 1984, 12, 51–52; Joseph Grieco, *Cooperation Among Nations*, Ithaca: Cornell University Press, 1990, 22; and Robert Putnam and Nicholas Bayne, *Hanging Together: Cooperation and Conflict in the Seven-Power Summits*, Cambridge: Harvard University Press, 1987, 2–3.

be identical but rather that some degree of parallel or overlapping interests exist such that the actions of each make some contribution to the purposes of the other. Second, the most interesting forms of cooperation are those that persist over time. These are the cases most likely to have the greatest impact. Third, when cooperation reaches the point where some type of tacit or explicit rules and regularity occurs, scholars use the term *regime* to describe it. Finally, cooperation differs in terms of its scope — that is, broad or narrow issues — and in terms of the importance of the issue. Cooperation over issues of whaling can be distinguished from that involving nuclear weapons or the control of a nation's money supply.

Why should we expect cooperation to occur? What factors help bring it about? Perhaps the most obvious, but slippery, factor is the interests of the nations involved. Some degree of overlap of purpose is needed, but how much of what kinds? No clear answers exist at this point. But from the perspective of international interdependence, the interests most likely to be engaged are those affected by the benefits of coordination and/or the costs of not cooperating. National leaders must come to expect significant payoffs or the avoidance of major penalties from working together. However, this process becomes much more cloudy when we remember that nations are rarely unitary actors. Rather, governments are a collection of bureaucratic interests that see the issues relating to cooperation in quite different ways. Further, governments in the advanced capitalist world generally rest on coalitions of domestic interests that may be affected in very different ways by the proposed arrangements with other nations.

Also relevant to the potential for cooperation are the relationships among the nations involved. Certainly affecting a nation's calculations is the prior existence of regimes or institutions facilitating cooperation. Previous experience of cooperation, especially if successful and routinized in institutions, can pave the way for more in the future. Of equal or even greater importance is the power relationship among nations. The existence of a single powerful state, with significant economic resources and a strong commitment to international cooperation, can play a key role in whether nations are able to work together. The power advantages of this hegemon can be used to win, or even coerce, support from other states that otherwise might be reluctant to participate in cooperative ventures. There are two important corollaries to this argument. First, cooperation among states of relatively equal power is somewhat difficult because no country is in a position to bear the costs of promoting and encouraging cooperation. Second, when the power of the hegemon begins to wane, cooperation may also decline unless the institutions created have continuing value to the nations involved.[3]

What then are the main barriers to cooperation? Perhaps the greatest is the fact that nations operate as sovereign entities that must provide for their

---

[3]The ideas of this paragraph draw on Putnam and Bayne, *Hanging. . .* , 3–12.

own security within an environment of anarchy. The absence of any central political authority capable of making and enforcing peace among nations makes international politics quite different from politics within (most) nations. The result is that national leaders must be wary about the ultimate consequences of agreements with other nations. They must pay attention not only to whether the arrangement produces a gain or loss for themselves, but also whether it leads to a greater gain for other nations. The conditions of anarchy in the system mean that states must be concerned about whether the gains of another nation might be used to augment that nation's power and direct it toward some coercive or military purpose. One of the clearest patterns of the past 150 years is the tightening of connections among economic, technological, military, and political dimensions of national power. In a world where anarchy and self-help are the defining feature, the fear of relative gain by other states may block cooperation that otherwise would prove beneficial.[4]

A second impediment to cooperation results from the fact that a nation's interests are rarely unified, and any agreement may well help some groups while harming others. Understanding cooperation means that we need to inquire into the politics of interest representation in national decisions. For example, choosing to lower tariffs and join a free trading system will benefit those producers who are competitive within this new marketplace, probably damage those who are not competitive, and improve the choices for consumers. Whether the nation will drop its tariff protection depends in considerable part on the relative political strength of these three groups. If noncompetitive groups have control of the government or veto power over any policy change, cooperation that is in the interests of the nation as a whole will still not take place.

A further roadblock to cooperation lies in the structure of the incentives available to a nation. Using the example of participating in a free trade system again, each nation that joins can expect to receive some important benefit. But an even greater benefit, at least in political terms, may come from selling in the open markets of other states while maintaining protected markets at home. Thus, states may fail to reach agreement because they want to have their cake and eat it too, or because they fear others will try to accomplish this for themselves. But, even here we can turn this point around and see how cooperation can still take place. If all nations refuse to cooperate and protectionism becomes the norm, then the costs of this failure may press nations to agree to cooperate. If those who defect can be punished, then the

---

[4]For a debate about the effects of anarchy on cooperation in the newly emerging system in Europe, see John Mearsheimer, "Back to the Future: Instability in Europe After the Cold War," *International Security*, 15.1, Summer 1990, 5–56; and Jack Snyder, "Averting Anarchy in the New Europe," *International Security*, 14.4, Spring 1990, 5–41. An example of worries about the positional effects of cooperation is described in Charles Kupchan, *The Persian Gulf and the West: The Dilemmas of Security*, Boston: Allen and Unwin, 1987, 166–167. Also see Michael Mastanduno, "Do Relative Gains Matter?" *International Security*, 16.1, Summer 1991, 73–113.

expectation of a continuing need for cooperation to maintain free trade may be sufficient to make this happen.[5]

The question of the extent and degree of cooperation among nations depends on whether they focus more on the absolute gains they receive or on the relative gains, on whether the domestic politics of nations contribute to or detract from cooperation, and on whether the costs of not cooperating are sufficiently painful to overcome the inclination toward defection. To help illustrate these arrangements, we will now consider two cases of efforts at cooperation, one concerning macroeconomic policy coordination and the other involving attempts to manage flexible exchange rates. The former focuses on the economic summits beginning in 1975, and the other focuses on the agreements to bring down the value of the dollar in 1985 and afterward.

Macroeconomic Policy Cooperation

As we discussed earlier in Chapter Two, macroeconomic policy involves government efforts to manage the overall level of economic activity through fiscal and monetary policy. Traditionally, this means decisions regarding taxes and spending (usually made jointly by chief executives and legislatures) and decisions on expansion and/or contraction of the money supply and interest rates (usually made by central banks). Cooperation among nations on these decisions would include efforts to adjust and coordinate fiscal and monetary policy so as to produce some desired economic outcome that would otherwise prove elusive. In examining the economic summit process, we are interested in understanding the factors that promoted and inhibited cooperation and the outcomes of these efforts.

The fact that economic summits began in 1975 is not an accident.[6] Over the preceding four years, several events combined to produce incentives for cooperation at the level of heads of state. The collapse of the Bretton Woods system of fixed exchange rates, the expansion of the EEC to ten members, the oil crisis of 1973–74, and the world economic recession in 1974–1975 all created circumstances where cooperation could improve many nations' positions. Elections in advanced industrial economies had increasingly come to depend on the fate of the economy. When the prosperity of virtually all was swept by external events, this gave national leaders a very good reason to become directly involved in managing the trade-offs associated with the resulting discussions and agreements with other states. Finally, U.S. leadership,

---

[5]For a discussion of the varying sides of this issue, see Keohane, *After. . .* , and Grieco, *Cooperation. . . .*

[6]This discussion of economic summits draws heavily on Putnam and Bayne, *Hanging. . .* ; Richard N. Cooper et al., *Can Nations Agree? Issues in International Economic Cooperation*, Washington D.C.: Brookings, 1989; and Martin Feldstein, *International Economic Cooperation*, Chicago: University of Chicago Press, 1988.

traditionally the linchpin in coordinating the world economy, seemed to fail in the early 1970s as the United States tried to solve its problems through efforts that frequently forced adjustment on other nations.

Perhaps the two most important factors promoting cooperation were the manifest ties of interdependence and the shared experience of working together under the Bretton Woods system. The leadership of the Western world had developed a strong recognition and understanding of their common fate since at least 1945. The events of 1971–1975, even as they often produced conflicting policies, nonetheless acted to reinforce that understanding. Later events helped to bring home the consequences of not cooperating. In 1977, the United States pursued an expansionist macroeconomic policy but paid an important price when that policy resulted in a much larger current account deficit. This deficit came about when other nations failed to stimulate their economies, resulting in a poor showing for U.S. exports even as foreign goods were moving to the United States to take advantage of growth there. A similar fate befell France in 1981, when it too expanded alone. Eventually, this helped force a socialist government to devalue the franc twice and adopt a deflationary fiscal policy. Clearly, nations needed the export markets of each other in order to pursue policies of balanced growth.

The economic summits, which began at Ramboiullet, France, in 1975, can be divided into three groups. The first four summits, 1975–1978, were driven by the need to recover from the 1974–1975 recession. As such, they focused on the level and timing of economic stimulus and the management of demand, with secondary interests in protectionism and exchange rates. By 1978, after several years of discussion about coordinated fiscal stimulus, a genuine agreement was reached. It called for additional budget stimulus by Germany and Japan in return for a pledge by the United States to reduce its dependence on external oil. Although less than successful in the end, the 1978 Bonn agreement was perhaps the best example of nations adjusting their policies in ways that would not have happened in the absence of cooperation.[7]

The 1979 oil crisis and subsequent inflation and recession from 1980 to 1982 not only scuttled the Bonn agreement, but also shifted the tone and substance of the economic summits. The hammer blows produced by these events prompted many nations to search for ways to protect themselves, either by securing oil supplies or finding domestic economic solutions.[8] Between 1979 and 1983, several nations shifted their efforts toward attacking inflation through applying monetary brakes and raising interest rates and

---

[7]The best detailed discussion of the Bonn Summit is found in Robert Putnam and C. Randall Henning, "The Bonn Summit of 1978: A Study in Coordination" and Gerald Holtham, "German Macroeconomic Policy and the 1978 Bonn Economic Summit," both in Cooper et al., *Can Nations. . .* , 12–177.

[8]Somewhat contrary to this trend was the Tokyo Summit, which served to produce agreement on targets for controlling oil imports. However, these targets were inflated and were achieved mostly as result of the recession. See Putnam and Bayne, *Hanging. . .* , 110–118.

making structural changes that transferred economic responsibility to their private sectors. The most nationalist-oriented in its policies was the United States, which combined a very restrictive monetary policy with a strong fiscal stimulus. The result was a massive federal budget deficit, rising interest rates, and a rising dollar. Following the dollar's rise was a rapidly increasing deficit in the U.S. current account. The summits of this period, reflecting the situation created by U.S. policies, involved limited efforts at coordination coupled with criticism of the looming imbalances in the world economy.[9]

By 1985, the enormous size of the U.S. current account deficit forced the United States to acknowledge these imbalances, and the summits shifted back toward international cooperation. The primary focus was management of a realignment of exchange rates, with the dollar falling and other currencies rising. The major agreements (to be discussed below), were made outside the summits, but these arrangements were the core of the discussions there, along with increasing recognition of the need for a new round of trade negotiations under GATT. The Uruguay Round began in 1987 as a result of the endorsement of the 1986 Tokyo Summit.

Taken together, the summits have only a spotty record of accomplishment. Probably the greatest barrier to success lies in the domestic politics of each nation. Although all are tied together by interdependence, this has not yet created a politics that will produce decisions based on this interdependence. The formation of political power is based on interests that remain inward-looking. At most, about one-third of GNP of most nations is based on trade (the United States is closer to one-tenth), and the combination with internationalized capital has not yet formed a dominant political bloc in any nation. Political institutions represent national interests and their own bureaucratic interests, both of which reinforce the concept of sovereignty. Leaders of these groups will be very reluctant to surrender power to international institutions or systems of international cooperation. Further, the policy predispositions of nations reflect their domestic politics. Germany has consistently resisted inflationary policies, while the United States has frequently supported them. These differences have often prevented agreement on macroeconomic coordination.

At best, economic summits may work much like nuclear arms control negotiations in the 1970s: leaders exchange information about policy, build a sense of common purpose, and occasionally produce agreements with limited but desirable results. The key factors in such agreements over the 1975–1991 cycle have been the convergence of domestic political developments and the ability of the United States to assume the task of leading other nations to

---

[9]Criticism was somewhat muted after 1982, when the United States relaxed its monetary policy and experienced an economic boom produced by the stimulus of the budget deficit. This, in conjunction with the rising dollar, pulled in record levels of imports and helped to stimulate the economies of Europe and Japan.

cooperate. When these agreements take place, as in 1978 and 1985, cooperation of some significance is the result. Otherwise, much more limited results are the outcome.[10]

Exchange Rates

Does this somewhat gloomy conclusion bear out when we examine efforts to deal with the wild swings in currencies in the 1980s? Cooperation over exchange rates is much more substantial and continuous in some respects. At the same time, many of the same barriers to macroeconomic coordination can be found here. Perhaps the best conclusion is that the tension between cooperation and conflict may be more intense over exchange rates than for macroeconomic policy. Exchange rates engage internationally-minded domestic interests more clearly than macroeconomic policy, but the level and intensity of cooperation required is also much greater and more identifiable.

Exchange rates, whether under fixed or flexible systems, affect the interests of politically organized groups in a direct and intense manner. The prices which exporters charge are greatly influenced by a falling or rising currency, especially for those who operate using the nation as a home base to manufacture goods for sale abroad. A currency that rises by 10 percent confronts this exporter with the choice of absorbing the change and reducing profits by 10 percent, or raising prices and risking lower sales. (Review the discussion in Chapter Two if this does not make sense.) Meanwhile, importers must face the same choice when the currency falls in price. Banking interests engaged in overseas investments prefer a rising currency, since this reduces the price of assets abroad and increases their buying power. The impact of exchange rates on domestic interests is reflected in the choices of a government concerned about its international accounts and about the votes of those interests.

Cooperation among nations over exchange rates engages a common interest in stability, since this is the arrangement that strikes a balance between the different domestic interests involved. In a system of fixed exchange rates, this cooperation takes the form of establishing an initial price relationship of currencies and governmental intervention in foreign exchange markets to maintain the currency's value. Whenever a currency becomes out of line with the nation's balance of payments, cooperation is required to adjust the fixed rate of exchange.[11] The same circumstances in a flexible system may call for governmental intervention to move the exchange rate more into line with a current account balance. Flexible systems may also result in such rapid swings in a currency's rate that governmental intervention is needed.

Any significant effort to manage exchange rates under the flexible system since 1973 cannot hope to succeed unless the major economic powers cooperate.

---

[10]Putnam and Bayne, *Hanging*. . . .

[11]This was the major role of the IMF under the Bretton Woods system.

No nation acting alone can possibly control its currency. Without the combined resources and the overt and coordinated efforts of other nations, a single nation is essentially at the mercy of the market. Along with these powerful incentives for cooperation is the fact that exchange rates contain an inherent and substantial dimension of conflicting interests. A fall in one nation's currency and subsequent improvement in its current account is always matched by a general or more focused rise in the currencies of other nations, who then must suffer a worsened current account. At the same time, a failure to act invokes the immediate costs associated with price swings generated by the market. Indeed, one nation might coerce others into cooperation by acting to exacerbate market moves. These other nations will act to prevent an even worse outcome from inaction.

This interesting mixture of cooperative and conflictual dimensions associated with exchange rates is complicated further by several structural realities. Exchange rate markets are driven by many factors of supply and demand for currency in addition to those created by exports and imports. Differences in interest rates among nations can generate capital movements that move exchange rates up or down.[12] Thus, decisions about monetary or fiscal policy that affect interest rates can also influence the exchange rate. Markets are further affected by speculators trying to anticipate and profit from fluctuations in exchange rates. A currency's price sometimes changes as a result of perceptions of the nation's economic strength: stronger economies are expected to have stable or higher exchange rates and thereby attract those who want a stable store of value. What is clear is that exchange rates very often do not move in such a way as to adjust a nation's current account imbalances.

When intervention does take place, governments recognize that markets are simply too big for even coordinated action to control over extended periods of time. The hope from intervention is to move markets in the direction of fundamental forces and to stabilize movements that might prove damaging if left alone. In pursuing these goals, central banks can rely on a market tendency toward a herd instinct whereby traders play follow the leader. This makes it possible for small amounts of actual intervention, when coupled with clear signals of cooperation and resolve by major nations, to produce major moves in exchange rates. The risk, of course, is that the herd instinct will go too far and lead to precipitate changes or even panic selling.

A final and perhaps most crucial feature of government involvement in foreign exchange markets is the role of market confidence in government policies and leaders. Fiscal, monetary, and exchange rate policies must be made with an eye toward how they will be received in world markets for equities, bonds, and foreign exchange. A clear negative reaction to a nation's policies can act to veto those decisions before they have an opportunity to

---

[12]Generally, higher or rising interest rates cause a currency to rise, while lower or falling rates cause it to decline.

succeed or fail. Since money markets are the main suppliers of credit to governments, the latter cannot ignore how these entities respond collectively to their actions.[13]

Managing Exchange Rates: 1985–1987

The context for international cooperation on exchange rates in 1985 was more than a decade of floating rates following the collapse of the Bretton Woods system of fixed rates and severe imbalances in the world economy created by the U.S. budget and trade deficits. This meant that leaders needed to create a system for coordinating their behavior in the midst of serious economic difficulties.

Before 1981, U.S. international accounts were in equilibrium, while its fiscal accounts were at historically high deficit levels. The tax cuts of 1981, coupled with increases in government defense and welfare spending, produced massive increases in the budget deficit. Between 1983 and 1986, deficits hovered around the $200 billion level, nearly three times the level in 1980. A tight monetary policy pushed interest rates to record levels, and this served to attract foreign funds, driving up the exchange rate of the dollar. The dollar rose from about 200 yen in 1981 to 270 yen in 1983 and moved between 230 and 250 for the next two years. The dollar rose much more against other currencies. It moved up about 60 percent against a weighted average of currencies and rose steadily from 2 German marks to 3.3 from 1981 to 1985.[14] The consequence was to put great pressure on U.S. exporters to raise their prices, while importers enjoyed the luxury of keeping prices low. U.S. merchandise exports, which had been growing at the same pace as imports from 1976 to 1981, stagnated and even declined from 1981 to 1986. Merchandise imports rose from $260 billion in 1981 to more than $340 billion in 1986.[15]

The United States had two basic alternatives for dealing with this problem: the policies of the 1980s could have been reversed and efforts made to make the United States more competitive internationally, or price levels could have been readjusted through a lower dollar without altering basic policy. Adopting the first option would have meant a rejection of the basic premises of the Reagan Administration. Attacking the budget deficit through higher taxes would have permitted lower interest rates and thereby a lower dollar, but it also would have meant undermining both its political position with upper income groups and its image with others. Further, this policy almost

[13] An excellent discussion of this process is found in Jeffrey A. Frieden, *Banking on the World*, New York: Harper and Row, 1987, 112–122.

[14] I. M. Destler and C. Randall Henning, *Dollar Politics: Exchange Rate Policy making in the United States*, Washington: Institute for International Economics, 1989, 17, 23–25.

[15] John Pool and Steve Stamos, *The ABC's of International Finance*, Lexington: D.C. Heath, 1987, 77.

surely would have produced a serious recession.[16] A corollary policy would involve lowering costs and increasing savings, investment, and spending on research and development to improve U.S. competitiveness.

Rather than take on the political dynamite of this option, the Reagan Administration actually pursued two contradictory policies between 1981 and 1989.[17] For the first half of this period, they chose to ignore the international consequences of their policies (sometimes referred to as benign neglect) and concentrated instead on the domestic economic boom that resulted. Officials simply accepted the large deficits, the rising dollar, and the subsequent growth of U.S. debt that was needed to finance the boom. But after the 1984 election, a policy of reducing the dollar while preserving existing fiscal policy emerged. Exporters were provided with price incentives to attempt to regain lost overseas markets, and importers were forced to raise prices. Domestically, the costs of adjustment were born by consumers but were disguised by the intricacies of the connections between the dollar and imported goods.

Beginning in 1985, the new U.S. Secretary of the Treasury, James Baker, and his assistant, Richard Darman, moved to organize an international effort to lower the value of the dollar.[18] In a meeting at the Plaza Hotel in New York, the finance ministers and central bank heads of the G-5 (United States, Germany, Japan, France, and Great Britain) orchestrated a collective effort to increase the exchange value of the main nondollar currencies. This was to be accomplished by coordinated market intervention and other signals of determination to see this achieved.[19] Each country pledged a substantial sum of foreign exchange for this operation. Although initially scheduled for six weeks and a 10 to 12 percent drop, the dollar's fall actually extended until December 1987. Much of this period involved something other than smooth cooperation, as there was considerable disagreement over the wisdom of the continuing fall in the dollar.

Between the Plaza Accord in September 1985 and the Louvre Agreement in January 1987, the dollar fell from 240 to 140 yen and 2.8 to 1.8 deutsche marks.[20] The German government was ready to stop after a 7 percent mark

---

[16]Instead, the United States experienced a continued income recession for middle and lower wage groups, who have not had any significant growth in real income since 1973. Although jobs were being created at record levels, they were primarily at low wages. Households were often forced to maintain purchasing power by increasing the number employed. See Phillips, *The Politics.* . . .

[17]There is no evidence anyone in the Reagan Administration contemplated anything resembling this strategy, although Richard Darman indicated sympathy for some of its elements.

[18]The discussion of the events of this effort at cooperation draws heavily on Yoichi Funabashi, *Managing the Dollar: From the Plaza to the Louvre,* Washington: Institute for International Economics, 1989; and Destler and Henning, *Dollar.* . . .

[19]Market intervention means entering the foreign exchange markets to sell dollars and buy one or more of the other four main currencies: the pound, the deutsche mark, the yen, and the franc.

[20]Eventually the dollar fell to 120 yen and 1.6 deutsche marks in December 1987. See Destler and Henning, *Dollar.* . . , 23–24.

appreciation. The Japanese became concerned at 180 yen. At the Louvre in February 1987, the United States reversed its position and supported a stabilization of its currency. This proved ineffective until after the stock market crash in October of that year.

How can we understand this effort to manage exchange rates and the taut mixture of cooperation and conflict involved? In terms of interests, the Reagan Administration by 1985 was being subjected to a barrage of complaints about the high dollar from U.S. exporters, and sentiment in Congress, which also received these concerns, was increasingly protectionist. Some in the Administration who were most committed to letting markets set exchange rates were replaced by more pragmatic officials. From the U.S. perspective, the ideal arrangement would have been to engineer a coordinated effort to push dollar values down while preserving the levels of foreign investment needed to sustain the budget deficit.

For the Germans, concerns centered on the importance of removing the imbalances in the world economy produced by the U.S. deficits without generating a dollar collapse. Further, a rising deutsche mark would help hold down inflation in Germany, always a key element of policy choice in that country. But German leaders also thought the imbalances were largely a U.S.–Japanese problem and preferred that most of the exchange rate adjustment come between the dollar and yen. Perhaps most important, from the German perspective, was preservation of the European Monetary System (EMS). This was an arrangement among ten European states in the EEC to fix exchange rates for their currencies with each other and coordinate fiscal and monetary policies. The German central bank — the Bundesbank — played the key role in this system, setting the standard for conservative policies and using its resources to maintain currency parities. German leaders feared that a precipitous decline of the dollar would put intense pressure on the EMS for realignment and might even force its breakup.[21]

By contrast, the Japanese were more receptive to dollar depreciation. They worried about the consequences of rising protectionist sentiments in Congress much more than the Germans. Japanese financial sectors hoped to benefit from a higher yen, while some political figures saw exchange rate adjustment as preferable to structural changes in terms of openness to the world. Even so, the massive appreciation of the yen eventually led to the disintegration of the domestic political coalition favoring this policy. Small and medium-sized exporters were battered, and even large firms found themselves pressed to deal with the trade-off between raising prices and accepting lower profits. But the United States seemed determined to let or to push the dollar lower and used noncooperation to prevent stabilization.

---

[21]The Germans often repeated to the Americans what they saw as the basic structural difference between themselves and the Japanese. Germany was much more closely tied to Europe, with over half its foreign trade there compared to 10 percent with the United States and 3 percent with Japan. Funabashi, *Managing*. . . , 120–121.

We should remember that the strategy of a lower dollar had the effect of rescuing the Reagan Administration from acknowledging the costs of its economic policies. Japan and Germany were being forced to bear most of the politically difficult costs of adjustment. These countries (especially Japan) had simply taken advantage of a situation created by the United States. But as the dollar continued to fall, the United States refused to participate in a stabilization effort. Instead, it attempted to hold out the possibility of sanctioning additional decline unless these countries agreed to stimulate their economies and/or make structural changes. The United States pressed this position because of the very slow improvement in the U.S. current account deficit. Only when fears of an end to foreign investment in the United States became intense did the United States reverse its position.

The study of international political economy has not developed a clear understanding of the sources of cooperation, nor can we predict its future direction. However, much concern has been expressed about recent indications of fragmentation, protectionism, and conflict in the world economy. This brief review points out both the weakness of cooperation in macroeconomic coordination and the coercive elements of cooperation in managing exchange rates. From the early 1970s and the breakup of the Bretton Woods system, the incentives for cooperation have increased, but its incidence is only sporadic and temporary. Although a calamity has not happened and stability has eventually occurred, no real institutions for macroeconomic or exchange rate cooperation have developed. The interests that produce stability seem ad hoc and uncertain. Perhaps most disturbing is the role of the United States, which has taken on an increasingly nationalistic and even bullying posture in its international economic negotiations. The United States retains the power to force adjustments on other states while avoiding making difficult adjustments itself. This behavior may have undermined the ability of the major economic powers to work together effectively and may account in part for the movement toward economic blocs.[22]

At the same time, institutional manifestations of, and efforts at, cooperation are much more substantial than at any previous time. A massive array

---

[22]For evidence that interests remained opposed, see Leonard Silk, "Bonn's Contrasts with Washington," *New York Times*, May 17, 1991; Jonathan Fuerbringer, "Weak Effort to Aid Yen," *New York Times*, March 10, 1990; and Clyde Farnsworth, "U.S. Resists Japan Plea to Aid Yen," *New York Times*, March 24, 1990. The most interesting and important theoretical question raised by the exchange rate case concerns the behavior of the United States as hegemon. For much of the postwar period, the United States accepted the burdens of world leadership. Providing grants and loans, maintaining open markets for foreign goods, and supplying military security are but a few of many examples. The United States behaved as a liberal, somewhat benevolent, hegemon. The exchange rate case of the 1980s continues a trend beginning in 1971 to emphasize a much more narrow and nationalistic definition of U.S. interests. The United States has been willing to use its continuing power to force adjustments onto other, often allied, states. The implications of this pattern for multilateral cooperation may turn out to be very negative and support the view that cooperation diminishes in the wake of a declining hegemon.

of cooperative activities sustains the world economy every day.[23] Undoubtedly, the most important and far-reaching effort at international cooperation is the European Community. Less-developed, but also significant, are other economic blocs, including that between the United States and Canada and the potential one between the United States and Mexico.

Economic Blocs

The European Community

An economic bloc is simply a political and economic organization designed to promote high levels of internal economic cooperation, but typically it is also expected to enhance competitiveness. The European Community is by far the most important of the economic blocs. Established in the 1950s, the European Economic Community (EEC) successfully promoted the reduction of tariffs and quotas among its members, but after the early 1970s, it made little additional progress toward economic integration. This changed in December 1985 when the twelve EC members signed the Single European Act.[24]

There are three main fronts along which cooperation has moved since then. First is the Single Regional Market, which calls for the free movement of trade, people, and money among the twelve member states by December 31, 1992. This will bring to fruition the original goals of the EEC. The consequence will be more uniform standards throughout the EC, free banking across all EC nations, and lower costs of doing business. A single market of 380 million persons will permit many companies to lower costs by expanding production to sell to many more consumers. All indications are that the Single Regional Market will come about on schedule. In October 1991, the EC reached agreement with the seven members of the European Free Trade Area (EFTA) to bring them into the new trading system after 1992. EFTA nations will initially participate only as associated states, with their markets for goods, services, and money open to the entire EC, but they will be unable to take part in the full range of political and economic decisions. Each country will be able to apply for membership, as Austria and Sweden have already.[25]

---

[23]See Stephen Krasner, ed. "International Regimes," *International Organization*, 36.2, Spring 1982.

[24]A useful compendium of events and arrangements for 1992 is found in Nicholas Colchester and David Buchan, *Europower*, New York: Times Books, 1990.

[25]In addition to Austria and Sweden, members of EFTA are Finland, Norway, Switzerland, Iceland, and Liechtenstein. For details, see Alan Riding, "Europeans in Accord to Create Vastly Expanded Trading Bloc," *New York Times*, October 23, 1991. A potentially serious obstacle to the EC–EFTA relationship was created by a decision of the European Court of Justice declaring the agreement contrary to EC treaties. See "Jealous Judges," *The Economist*, December 21, 1991, 58–59. Several non–EFTA nations, such as Turkey, Malta, and Cyprus, also hope to join the EC.

FIGURE 5.5

Expansion of the European Community

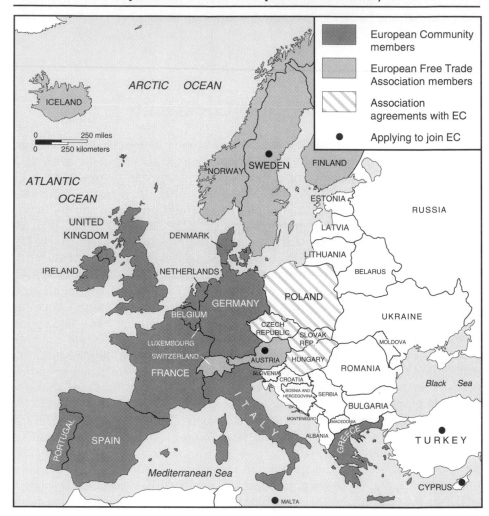

Comparison of the Economic Superpowers

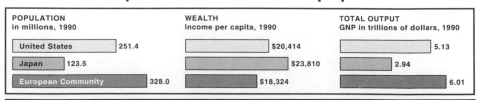

POPULATION in millions, 1990	WEALTH Income per capita, 1990	TOTAL OUTPUT GNP in trillions of dollars, 1990
United States 251.4	$20,414	5.13
Japan 123.5	$23,810	2.94
European Community 328.0	$18,324	6.01

SOURCE: Organization for Economic Cooperation and Development.

A second major front for transformation of the EC is the creation of a European central bank — known as the European Monetary Institute — and a single European currency as the end product of Economic and Monetary Union (EMU). Agreement was reached in October 1990 to set 1994 as the target date for establishment of the central bank. Before that time, all EC nations will join the European Monetary System and will work to bring their monetary policies and inflation rates into line with each other. In December 1991, agreement was reached to adopt a single European currency and to bring the European Monetary Institute up to full status as a central bank between 1997 and 1999. The third area of new cooperation is a political federation leading to common foreign and defense policies and a strengthening of the role of the European Commission in Brussels and the European Parliament in Strasbourg.[26]

Organization of the EC

The governing structure of the European Community, especially after passage of the Single European Act (SEA), is a complex system of overlapping responsibility, decision making, and representation. There are four main units to the EC, one executive, two legislative, and one judicial. These include:

European Commission — The Commission holds the executive power, vested in a President of the Commission (currently Jacques Delors).[27] The Commission, composed of the President and sixteen other commissioners appointed by the twelve heads of government (two commissioners each from the four largest states) of the EC nations and supported by a staff of 15,000, is located in a part of Brussels known as Berlaymont. The Commissioners, though appointed by member governments, are pledged to act in the interest of the EC. The Commission has the responsibility for initiating legislation and legal action against member nations.

Council of Ministers — The Council is composed of representatives of member states. The Council has final legislative authority. The Single European Act of 1985 broadened the scope of majority-rule decisions in the Council to include all actions required for creation of a single market. This enhances the ability of the Council to act, as

---

[26]William Miller, "Europe's Quest for Monetary Harmony," *Boston Globe*, July 8, 1990; Steven Greenhouse, "Europe's Bank: Dream vs. Reality," *New York Times*, October 30, 1990; Steve Prokesch, "Britain Is on the Spot As Monetary Holdout," *New York Times*, November 4, 1990; Alan Riding, "European Leaders Give Their Backing To Monetary Plan, *New York Times*, December 9, 1990; Clyde Haberman, "12 Europe Nations Formally Initiate Closer Federation," *New York Times*, December 16, 1990; Bruce Stokes, "Continental Shift," *National Journal*, August 18, 1990.

[27]See John Ardagh, "Will the New Europe Please Sit Down," *New York Times Magazine*, November 10, 1991, 42–46.

compared with a single state veto system.[28] Voting is weighted by national population, which creates a complex system of coalition-building.[29]

European Parliament — The Parliament is composed of 518 members elected by the populations of individual states for five year terms. Traditionally limited to a restricted power over the budget, the Parliament could well gain wider authority over the budget, the right to initiate legislation, and the ability to approve the Commission.

European Court of Justice — The Court is composed of thirteen justices nominated by member states. Its responsibility is to render final decisions on disputes among EC institutions, member states, or on suits against EC institutions.[30]

The process of political decision-making in the EC is very complex but mainly involves the initiation of legislation by the Commission, its modification by Parliament, and final decision by the Commission.[31]

But for our purposes, the most interesting aspect of the EC lies in understanding the origins of these new and dramatic efforts at international cooperation. The decisions of 1985 should be seen as a response by elements of the European political and economic elite to changes in the world economy of the 1980s. Most important were the decline of the United States as the primary source of cutting-edge technologies and the most innovative production techniques and the U.S. abdication of responsibility for the international monetary system. Wide elements of the political and economic elites of Europe concluded they could no longer rely on a U.S.–based system for economic organization. Reliance on the Japanese for technological developments — much as the Europeans had done with the United States for thirty years — was not seen as a viable option. The Europeans did not share common security or cultural interests with Japan, a country many saw as an economic predator. Contributing to these conclusions was the failure of individual national economic strategies of the 1975–1985 period. The decision was to establish a system that could be much more self-sufficient. A single large market would justify bigger research and development expenditures and would promote cost savings from economies of scale. A single monetary

---

[28]There are still areas where the veto system (or unanimity) prevails, primarily in taxes and decisions on social policy.

[29]The weighting in 1991 was as follows:

    10 votes (each) — Great Britain, Italy, Germany, France
     8 votes — Spain
     5 votes — Netherlands, Belgium, Greece, Portugal
     3 votes — Ireland, Denmark
     2 votes — Luxembourg

[30]See Colchester and Buchan, *Europower*, 131–143.

[31]The best description is in Colchester and Buchan, *Europower*, 40–41.

system could also help protect from the vagaries of U.S. exchange rate policies, and the newly competitive European firms could defend Europe from the Japanese.[32]

European Monetary Union

The incentives for cooperation can be understood even better by considering in detail the process leading toward EMU. Here again we draw on the earlier discussion of cooperation, especially the role of interests defined by the benefits and costs of cooperation, the costs of not cooperating, and the impact of existing institutions on the calculations of member states.

In important ways, an economic and monetary union can be traced to the breakup of the Bretton Woods system of fixed exchange rates in the early 1970s. The chief result of that event was a realignment of currencies, with the dollar falling against all others. Many in Europe (in and outside the EEC) attempted to set up a system of fixed exchange rates with each other so as to offer some protection against the falling dollar. This ultimately proved impossible because of the growth of private transactions, especially for purposes of speculation. Another round of dollar depreciation in the late 1970s helped rekindle the idea of a European system for managing exchange rates.[33] In 1978, most of the EEC (Great Britain was the main exception) joined in creating the European Monetary System (EMS). Its main feature was a system of linked exchange rates. Against a backdrop of fears of lost sovereignty and higher inflation, an Exchange Rate Mechanism (ERM) was created. The ERM defined a small band of fluctuation for each currency in the system. The benchmark was a weighted average of currencies called the European Currency Unit (ECU). Each currency had a fixed rate against the ECU, plus or minus 2.25 percent, and as a nation's currency approached this limit, its central bank was obligated to intervene to preserve the parity.[34]

The EMS contributed to the movement toward monetary union through a conditioning of the interests of the major states. In other words, the EMS

---

[32]This paragraph relies on Wayne Sandholtz and John Zysman, "1992: Recasting the European Bargain," *World Politics*, 62.1, October 1989, 95–128. For another view of the politics of the negotiation process that established SEA, see Andrew Moravcsik, "Negotiating the Single European Act: National Interests and Conventional Statecraft in the European Community," *International Organization*, 45.1, Winter 1991, 19–56.

[33]This was the period of 1977–1979, when the United States, in several Economic Summits, tried to move West Germany to adopt an expansionary economic policy to pull the United States out of its recession and trade deficit.

[34]Several states with weaker currencies were permitted a wider band. The weighting for establishing the value of the ECU is mainly based on five currencies — those of Germany, France, Great Britain, Italy, and the Netherlands — which together represent 80 percent of the value of the ECU. The German deutsche mark alone accounts for more than 30 percent. For more detail on the process, including the computation of the ECU, see John Pinder, *European Community*, Oxford: Oxford University Press, 1991, 119–130; Colchester and Buchan, *Europower*, 162–165.

demonstrated both the possibility of monetary cooperation and also its benefits. Fluctuations in exchange rates narrowed considerably in the 1980s because of the EMS and the efforts to foster a greater coordination of monetary and fiscal policies. Over time, the ECU gained in credibility as an important denominator of EC transactions. By the late 1980s, several defectors from the EMS were moved by its successes to join.[35] They found the costs of not cooperating were substantial and the benefits of participating in the system significant enough to warrant joining.

The key to the success of the EMS was the role played by Germany and its central bank, the Bundesbank. With Europe's strongest economy and the most intense commitment to monetary stability and low inflation, Germany offered the deutsche mark as a de facto key currency for the EMS. This role meant that participant nations used the deutsche mark for intervention in currency markets and, consequently, used German inflation rates and monetary policy as a benchmark for their decisions on these matters. The operation of this system resulted in a convergence of macroeconomic policies and inflation rates over the decade of the 1980s and opened the door for closer monetary cooperation.[36]

The decision to move toward an open market for goods in the European Community created a powerful momentum for a closer monetary union. Free trade also required the free movement of money. Permitting money to move freely, allowing banks to establish branches across the EC, and promoting the development of an integrated market for financial services contained a set of robust incentives for political cooperation designed to extend the EMS.

Also important as a conditioning factor was the further internationalization of finance during the 1980s. Prompted by the massive U.S. trade and budget deficits, this process accelerated with the computer and telecommunications advances that made global financial markets possible.[37] European firms engaged in global trade demanded new financial services, and financiers saw new profit opportunities. The Single European Act of 1985 established as a goal for 1992 free capital movement and an integrated market for financial services throughout the EC. This tapped into the interests of these firms and provided an enormous boost for monetary union.

The Maastricht Agreement

The broad outlines of how the new system might operate were worked out in a meeting in Maastricht, the Netherlands, in December 1991. Already in

---

[35] In particular, Great Britain, Greece, and Portugal joined EMS. Pinder, *European.* . . , 130.

[36] For more detail on the Bundesbank and its role in the EMS, see Ellen Kennedy, *The Bundesbank*, London: Pinter, 1991, 79–103.

[37] See "Ebb Tide," *The Economist*, April 21, 1991, 7.

place was the elimination of exchange controls and closer consultation on monetary policy. Next to come — probably in 1994 — will be the creation of an independent European central bank. The bank will be governed by a twelve-person board, with members nominated by, but not recallable by, each country. The European Council, after consulting the Parliament, would pick the chairman. The responsibilities of the European Monetary Institute will likely include a shared control with the Bundesbank over interest rates, broad direction for monetary policy, and a narrowing of the bands for exchange rate fluctuations. Movement toward a single currency and a genuine central bank (the current name for which is Eurofed) is dependent on success in achieving convergence in macroeconomic policy. For a nation to participate in the last stage of this process, its inflation rate, interest rates, public debt, currency stability, and budget deficit must conform to certain standards. But the Maastricht agreement commits those who meet these standards to establish a common central bank on January 1, 1998 and to lock exchange rates and establish a single currency on January 1, 1999.[38] Those who initially do not qualify may join later once they meet the requirements.[39]

The outcome at Maastricht, as with previous agreements, is the result of powerful common interests in the success of the EC venture, a complex mixture of complementary and conflicting interests that sometimes move countries toward opposing views on the shape of future cooperation, and a process of negotiation where nations modify their preferences in order to gain an agreement. Germany — now the key player in the EMS and the strongest advocate of financial stability — pressed for a rapid transition to a system modeled on the Bundesbank. This means a bank largely independent of control by politicians and capable of acting effectively to manage inflation. Ironically, many other EC states also prefer an independent bank because that would reduce German influence as compared to the EMS. Decisions on interest rates would no longer be set by the Bundesbank. The Maastricht agreement means that the Germans will ultimately give up the deutsche mark itself in return for a powerful European central bank. Other EC states likewise surrender an important element of their sovereignty, gain some additional role in policymaking, and also must lower their inflation rates and budget deficits.

Beyond this, interests begin to diverge and reform in interesting ways. The French, in particular President Francois Mitterand, see much closer

---

[38] The criteria for inflation is that a country must not exceed the average inflation rate of the three lowest EC nations by more than 1.5 percentage points, and its interest rates must be within 2 percentage points. A country's budget deficit cannot exceed 3.0 percent of its gross domestic product (GDP), nor can its public debt exceed 60 percent of GDP. Its currency must not have been devalued within the previous two years and may not have exceeded the normal 2.25 percent margin. In late 1991, only two states — France and Luxembourg — actually met these requirements. See "The Deal is Done," *The Economist*, December 14, 1991, 52.

[39] Great Britain won the option of deciding later whether it will participate, known as "opting out."

cooperation in Europe as an essential element in establishing a new political and economic entity capable of dealing effectively with the United States and Japan. French influence within a strengthened EC would be important, while dealing alone with the United States and Japan puts France in a position of weakness. Others in France take a more traditional view and see a renewed EC as the best means for containing German power.[40] Many British, especially among the Conservatives, fear the implications for national sovereignty of moves toward common monetary, economic, foreign, and social policies. British Prime Minister John Major urged delay in the timetable and less power for a central bank.[41] Several EC countries with a tradition of an easy monetary policy, large budget deficits, and high inflation have expressed concern over the deflationary implications of a central bank. Some, including Spain, Greece, Portugal and Ireland, have pressed for more economic aid from the wealthier EC states as the price for entering the new system.[42] Although some of these states may not make it into the late 1990s monetary union, they have nonetheless accepted the responsibility to work toward these goals.[43]

Developments in the EC after 1985 are certainly the most far-reaching efforts in international cooperation. Given the history of conflict in Europe in the twentieth century, the possibility of a politically and economically united Europe is an extraordinary accomplishment. The driving forces behind these recent moves are powerful structural changes in the world economy, including the decline in U.S. economic leadership, the explosion of economic interdependence, and the new competitive climate in the 1980s and 1990s. In some ways, the competitive potential from the EC may have helped spawn economic groupings elsewhere.

A North American Trade Bloc?

Two other areas where trade blocs appear to be forming are between the United States, Canada, and Mexico and around Japan, in East and Southeast Asia.[44] In the former, this involves establishing bilateral free trade agreements (FTA) with Canada and the initiation of negotiations with Mexico for a similar arrangement. An FTA can be distinguished from the cooperation in the EC in terms of the scale and scope of the system. The FTA generally does not

---

[40] Alan Riding, "France Pins Hopes on European Unity," *New York Times*, December 1, 1991.

[41] "A Dangerous Passage," *The Economist*, November 2, 1991, 49–50.

[42] Alan Riding, "The 'Poor Four' of Europe are Demanding More Aid," *New York Times*, December 5, 1991.

[43] For discussion of some of the additional problems associated with negotiation of the Maastricht agreement, see Alan Riding, "With No Thatcher to Assail, Europe's Unity Stalls," *New York Times*, March 17, 1991; Alan Riding, "The New Europe of 1992 Is Closer in Economics Than in Politics," *New York Times*, June 16, 1991.

[44] Lawrence B. Krause, "Regionalism in World Trade: The Limits of Economic Interdependence," *Harvard International Review*, 13.4, Summer 1991, 4–6.

have a common external tariff and, aside from arrangements for settling trade disputes among the parties, does not have significant institutions for further economic or political cooperation. For example, a North American Free Trade Agreement (NAFTA) is unlikely to produce anything resembling the linked currencies and moves toward monetary union in the EC.[45]

FIGURE 5.6

North American Trade: 1990
(*Billions of U.S. Dollars*)

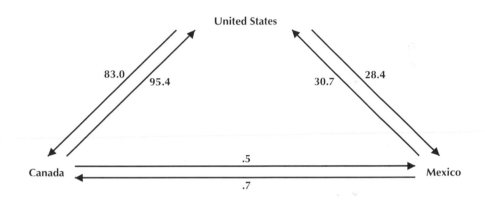

SOURCE: International Monetary Fund, *Direction of Trade Statistics*, 1991.

The free trade agreement with Canada took effect in January 1989. The objective is to eliminate virtually all tariffs and duties between the United States and Canada by 1999.[46] The arrangement with Mexico is still under negotiation and will presumably take the same shape. However, there is significant resistance within the United States to the deal with Mexico, due mostly to the substantial differences between the two economies. Labor unions object strongly, as do many environmentalists, producers in low-tech, low-skills industries, and some agricultural interests — such as citrus growers. Each of these groups is bound together by fears of a loss of sales and jobs to imports from Mexico or from the transfer of production to what they see as a low-wage, environmentally lax Mexico. Those supporting the

[45]Sylvia Nasar, "North American Currency Links?" *New York Times*, December 18, 1991; and "Free-Market Mexico," *The Economist*, December 14, 1991, 19–21.

[46]For an analysis of free trade agreements in general, see Jeffrey J. Schott, ed. *Free Trade Areas and U.S. Trade Policy*, Washington: Institute For International Economics, 1989. A more specific discussion of the U.S.–Canadian agreement is in Jeffrey J. Schott, *United States–Canada Free Trade: An Evaluation of the Agreement*, Washington: Institute of International Economics, 1988.

agreement anticipate easier access to Mexican energy resources and to the Mexican market.[47]

The motivations for the United States in pursuing these agreements stem primarily from difficulties in multilateral trade negotiations in GATT and from the competitive pressures generated by the movement toward 1992 in the EC.[48] Urged on by its own trade problems — the need to expand markets for exports and close a yawning trade deficit — the United States pushed for a new round in GATT to reduce barriers to trade even more. For much of the decade this was a slow and frustrating process. Negotiating FTAs proved to be a quicker way of establishing trade relationships more to the liking of the U.S. political leadership. These same officials also hoped bilateral agreements involving preferential access to the large U.S. market would spur negotiations in GATT. For Canadians, preserving access to the U.S. market and developing a clear set of mechanisms for settling trade disputes constituted the main considerations.[49]

Mexico's decisions relating to an FTA with the United States are conditioned by the size of its trade with the United States and similar fears of U.S. protectionism and are a radical departure in its foreign economic policy. In 1985, Mexico adopted a strongly liberal policy in trade, thereby casting aside a long tradition of protectionism. Reacting to an enormous foreign debt, a collapse in oil prices, and years of low increases in productivity, the Mexican government moved toward opening its markets to foreign competition and stimulating exports of manufactured goods. By 1987, tariff rates had been cut in half, quantitative restrictions drastically reduced, and price controls virtually eliminated.[50] This strategy accentuated the importance of access to the U.S. market.

As with other forms of political and economic cooperation in international affairs, the FTA contains important elements of conflict. We have alluded to some of these above, recognizing that substantial shifts in production and jobs will inevitably come with a NAFTA. Industries in the United States able to benefit from low wages in Mexico will move there, and U.S. consumers will presumably benefit from lower-priced goods. The logic of FTAs is that free trade and comparative advantage produce more gains than losses, but some groups will suffer painful adjustments. In more global terms, FTAs can both encourage multilateral trade negotiations and undermine them. And they may represent an effective competitiveness strategy if firms are able to

---

[47]Richard Stevenson, "Selling a Free-Trade Pact With Mexico," *New York Times*, November 11, 1990; Louis Uchitelle, "Mexico's Plan for Industrial Might," *New York Times*, September 25, 1990; Kirk Victor, "Trading Away Jobs," *National Journal*, April 27, 1991; Bruce Stokes, "Greens Talk Trade," *National Journal*, April 13, 1991.

[48]More detail on GATT can be found in Chapters Four and Six.

[49]See Jeffrey J. Schott, "More Free Trade Areas?" in Schott, ed. *Free Trade. . . ,* 1–58.

[50]Ignacio Trigueros, "A Free Trade Agreement Between Mexico and the United States?" in Schott, ed. *Free Trade. . . ,* 255–267.

reap the cost benefits of producing for larger markets. But the potential for FTAs to encourage exclusionary trade blocs is also present.

CONCLUSIONS

■ Cooperation among advanced industrial states has become both more essential and more problematic over the past two decades. The ability of these nations to bargain over concessions and thereby produce a mutually beneficial coordination of behaviors is much more important now because of the intensity of interdependence. Failure to coordinate macroeconomic policies can have sudden and rude consequences; ignoring exchange rate effects can result in enormous and persistent international imbalances. Nonetheless, the political relationships needed for cooperation to succeed are in turmoil.

Much of this can be traced to the decline of U.S. hegemony. The United States can no longer create the cooperative structures of the world economy and gain acceptance for them. For perhaps twenty years, U.S. officials have been much more conscious of the costs of leadership, especially a growing current account deficit and the burdens of defense spending. The considerable power remaining to the United States has sometimes been used to push other states to accept some of these costs. But weaknesses, measured by the relative decline in its weight in the world economy and by large budget and trade deficits, undermine the capacity for creating order. U.S. power is big enough to be an essential element of any multilateral system and big enough that other states will sometimes have to cooperate (exchange rate cooperation in the 1980s is a good example). And yet, the ability to fashion a multilateral system of cooperation has largely vanished. The era of U.S. hegemony has been replaced by a system of U.S. dominance in which a genuine bargaining and meshing of interests are prerequisites for cooperation. Frequently, cooperation has required disproportionate concessions by the Japanese and Europeans.

Recent developments in the EC and the stirrings of an infant bloc in Asia may be seen as a response to the breakdown of U.S. hegemony. The EC is certainly the best example of an effective system of cooperation responding to the ties of interdependence. This is a result of efforts to cope with the rush of connectedness in the 1980s and the need to protect themselves from some of the unfavorable consequences of U.S. decline and the rise of Japan. Circumstances favor the establishment of a federal system in Europe by the end of the century.

The record of cooperation in the EC has not extended to multilateral arrangements among the EC, United States, and Japan. Interdependence here has advanced enough to matter significantly in national political life, but not enough to generate effective cooperation. Powerful incentives for cooperation exist, but very strong barriers frequently prevent this from taking place.

When we remember that interdependence also has uncomfortable consequences — competition, involvement of other nations in what once were domestic political choices, and constant adjustment to external demands — we are reminded that conflict is often a partner in efforts at cooperation.

ANNOTATED BIBLIOGRAPHY

Nicholas Colchester and David Buchan, *Europower*, New York: Times Books, 1990.
A detailed and excellent description of the European Community.

Richard N. Cooper et al. *Can Nations Agree? Issues in International Economic Cooperation*, Washington: Brookings, 1989.
A series of excellent case studies in international macroeconomic coordination.

I.M. Destler and Randall Henning, *Dollar Politics: Exchange Rate Policy making in the United States*, Washington: Institute for International Economics, 1989.
A very useful case study of the domestic politics of efforts to manage the value of the dollar in the 1980s.

Wendy Dobson, *Economic Policy Coordination: Requiem or Prologue?*, Washington: Institute for International Economics, 1991.
A broad assessment of international economic cooperation.

Yoichi Funabashi, *Managing the Dollar: From the Plaza to the Louvre*, Washington: Institute for International Economics, 1989.
A detailed description of the process of cooperation in the operation of the international financial system in the 1980s.

Joseph M. Grieco, *Cooperation Among Nations*, Ithaca: Cornell University Press, 1990.
A theoretically informed study of cooperation in international trade.

John Pinder, *European Community*, Oxford: Oxford University Press, 1991.
The best study of the European Community.

Robert Putnam and Nicholas Bayne, *Hanging Together: Cooperation and Conflict in the Seven Power Summits*, Cambridge: Harvard University Press, 1987.
The best study of cooperation relating to macroeconomic coordination.

Jeffrey Schott, ed. *Free Trade Areas and U.S. Trade Policy*, Washington: Institute for International Economics, 1989.
A series of detailed studies of free trade areas.

Arthur A. Stein, *Why Nations Cooperate*, Ithaca: Cornell University Press, 1990.
A game-theoretic analysis of international cooperation.

CHAPTER 6

COMPETITION AND CONFLICT AMONG ADVANCED INDUSTRIAL STATES

One of the main themes of the preceding chapter is worth repeating, namely that discussions of conflict and competition cannot be far removed from an analysis of cooperation. The world economy simply could not function without the manifold layers of international cooperation. The notion of a global marketplace existing outside a framework of cooperative political relations among nations is as mythological as the bloodless world of perfect competition. Thus, we need to remember that competition among firms or nations is only possible in a context where the rules for trade, investment, and profit-making have been created and are maintained through international cooperation.

Having said this, competition and conflict are inherent elements of capitalism. Productive power, and the military power linked to it, generates an enormous prize to be won by sovereign states. Domestic political power frequently rests on economic growth and dynamism. International rivalry over at least the past two centuries has been caught up in the efforts of capitalist firms to secure markets and resources. The two great wars of the twentieth century began as conflicts among capitalist states. Late in the century, fears abound about the ability to compete in the world economy.

The ebb and flow in the balance between cooperation and conflict has led some to express concern about a tilt toward the latter. Chapter Six offers some perspective on this possibility. We begin with a detailed look at Japan as a nation that may have established a new competitive standard for others to match. Characterizations of Japan as a predator state that engages in unfair competition are common. This section will examine the postwar rise of Japan and the special business-government relationship often cited as the source of its extraordinary growth. A somewhat broader look at the political

125

economy of competitiveness follows. Key theoretical questions are the possibility of creating comparative advantage through government actions and the potential for state intervention to bolster certain industries. More concrete are considerations of what constitutes competitiveness for the United States and some of the policies followed by the Europeans.

The traditional reaction to increased competition is protectionism, whereby the government attempts to help a nation's firms by shielding them from the outside world. We will examine the nature of contemporary protectionism. In the wake of a general decline in tariffs, nontariff barriers (NTBs) have assumed a much greater role. This "new" protectionism, along with a consideration of the political economy of decisions to adopt such a policy, receive our attention. Finally, we will look at the Uruguay Round of GATT as the main international forum for debating and deciding about protection or free trade.

THE RISE OF JAPAN

■ At the end of World War II Japan was devastated, with 40 percent of its industrial system in ruins and occupied by the United States. For the next two to three years, U.S. officials used their special powers to make important economic and political changes. Japan's immense economic conglomerates, *zaibatsu*, were broken up; many persons associated with the war were purged from positions of responsibility; the military establishment was dismantled; and the economic system was liberalized. The harshest policies began to change in 1947. As the Cold War between the United States and the Soviets intensified, pressure on Japan was relaxed and replaced by a policy emphasizing economic recovery. Concern over the Soviet ability to exploit instability around the world prompted a shift of U.S. policy in Europe and Asia. The revival of the Japanese economy and its integration into the rest of East Asia became the primary means for establishing an economic and political bulwark against Soviet expansion there. Perhaps the most important by-product of this was the 1951 U.S. commitment to Japanese security and Japan's complete dependence on the United States for military protection. From the U.S. perspective, this arrangement bound Japan to a U.S.–based definition of international order. For the Japanese, this opened the door to economic recovery and security by using to its advantage this U.S. economic and security umbrella.[1]

---

[1]The best discussion of the occupation period is Michael Schaller, *The American Occupation of Japan*, New York: Oxford University Press, 1985. Also helpful is Bruce Cumings, "Power and Plenty in Northeast Asia: The Evolution of U.S. Policy," *World Policy Journal*, 5.1, Winter 1987– 88, 79–106.

The political system that emerged from the U.S. occupation represented a complex mixture of new democratic institutions and traditional oligarchical practices. In 1947, the United States imposed a constitution establishing a representative democracy elected by universal adult suffrage and requiring, through Article 9, that Japan renounce the right to use military force for national ends. By the mid–1950s, a dominant political coalition had been formed composed of the bureaucracy; big business and finance; and a conservative political organization, the Liberal Democratic Party. Business interests provided the money, and the bureaucracy supplied much of the political leadership. Genuinely liberal or radical political interests were systematically excluded from political power.[2] This coalition was able to establish a very strong state based on its institutional resources and a consensus on the need for economic growth.

The Strategy of Growth

In the 1950s and 1960s, Japan faced a situation not unlike that of the nineteenth and early twentieth centuries: catch-up. Almost from the beginning of the postwar era, Japan's political and economic leaders were determined to move into the ranks of the major industrial nations. They were unwilling to rely on the obvious comparative advantage of low wages and instead aimed to make Japan a nation of capital-intensive and high-technology production. This came in spite of capital deficiencies and poor resources and the great advantages of Western nations. The government acted to move the economy in these directions by establishing economic priorities, organizing large and economically powerful cartels, protecting certain industries, managing the foreign trade process, and providing guidance for investment. This industrial policy was designed to direct economic development and compensate for Japanese backwardness and economic weakness.[3]

The Japanese were extremely successful in promoting economic growth, as demonstrated in Figure 6.1. Throughout the postwar era, Japan's growth rate in GDP (remember, this excludes exports) consistently exceeded that of the United States and Germany by a wide margin. Over time, the gap has narrowed along with an overall decline in the rate of increase. Especially during the 1980s, Japan's advantage came from greater consistency of growth.

---

[2]A detailed analysis of the postwar Japanese political system is found in T. J. Pempel, "Japanese Foreign Economic Policy: The Domestic Bases for International Behavior," *International Organization*, 31.4, Autumn 1977, 723–774. Also important is Chalmers Johnson, *MITI and the Japanese Miracle*, Stanford: Stanford University Press, 1982, 50–51. Between 1956 and 1986, seven of ten prime ministers had also served as Minister of International Trade and Industry. See W. G. Beasley, *The Rise of Modern Japan*, New York: St. Martin's Press, 1990, 246. Additional detail on the Japanese political system can be found in Gerald Curtis, *The Japanese Way of Politics*, New York: Columbia University Press, 1988.

[3]Daniel Okimoto, *Between MITI and the Market*, Stanford: Stanford University Press, 1989, 23.

The German and the U.S. pattern was subject to greater fluctuation, with much sharper swings in the business cycle than in Japan.

FIGURE 6.1

Comparative GDP Growth: 1961–1990
U.S./Germany/Japan

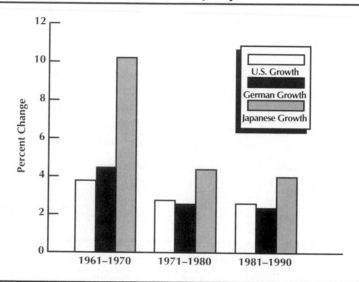

SOURCE: The calculations are in constant prices and come from International Monetary Fund, *International Financial Statistics Yearbook*, 1991, 159–160.

The initial strategy of development in the 1950s was to reestablish the textile industry, but this moved quickly into building infrastructure and the allocation of scarce resources. In terms of industrial production, Japan was helped by a large and protected domestic market and by relatively open access to large foreign markets.[4] This permitted Japanese industries to reap the cost advantages of high-volume production. During the 1955–1970 period, Japan was able to move beyond production of low-wage, technologically limited goods into much more advanced areas of steel production and shipbuilding.[5]

In the 1960s, the emphasis on exports resulted in a current account surplus and the beginnings of significant foreign direct investment by the

---

[4]Access to foreign markets was made possible by U.S. pressure on its western allies to admit Japan to full status in GATT. Several countries had resisted this. Ryutaro Komiya and Motoshige Itoh, "Japan's International Trade and Trade Policy, 1955–1984," in Takashi Inoguchi and Daniel Okimoto, eds. *The Political Economy of Japan, Volume 2: The Changing International Context*, Stanford: Stanford University Press, 179.

[5]Komiya and Itoh, "Japan's International Trade . . . , 174–177.

Japanese. Initially, this investment was concentrated in raw materials and in low-tech manufacturing facilities located in developing countries, and it had the effect of providing some input that would result in Japanese exports to third countries. The great boom in Japanese foreign direct investment came after 1980, in conjunction with large Japanese international surpluses and corresponding U.S. deficits. Accumulating foreign resources permitted Japan to invest abroad. Foreign direct investment rose from $36.0 billion in 1980 to $186.4 billion in 1988. This was increasingly focused in advanced countries and in industries where Japan was exporting. Protecting export markets, only a modest motive in the 1960s, became a much more important factor in the 1980s.[6]

The role of international trade in Japanese economic growth is sometimes misunderstood. The recent rise in U.S. imports from Japan and concern over this would suggest that Japan lives and dies from this relationship. Although quite important, foreign trade has a more limited impact on the Japanese economy. Table 6.1 provides a comparison of the role of international trade in the economies of four major industrial nations.

TABLE 6.1

Ratio of Exports and Imports to GNP

COUNTRY	1955	1965	1971	1983
Japan				
Exports	11.5%	11.1%	12.3%	15.8%
Imports	10.6	9.9	9.7	13.9
United States				
Exports	5.0	5.8	6.4	10.2
Imports	4.5	4.7	6.0	10.4
United Kingdom				
Exports	26.1	23.3	25.1	30.5
Imports	26.8	22.9	22.8	28.8
West Germany				
Exports	20.3	19.0	22.6	32.3
Imports	18.0	19.0	20.6	30.0

Source: The source of the table is Komiya and Itoh, "Japan's International Trade. . . ," 187.

[6]Note the similarity of motivation with U.S. MNCs in the 1958–1975 period discussed in Chapter Four. For the material in this paragraph, see Young-Kwan Yoon, "The Political Economy of Transition: Japanese Foreign Direct Investments in the 1980s," *World Politics*, 43, October 1990, 1–27.

Clearly, Japan's dependence on foreign trade is much less than that of the United Kingdom or West Germany and is approximately the same as that of the United States in the 1980s.

But this obscures some important elements in Japanese international trade policy. Japan, more than most other countries in the U.S.–organized world economy, has rejected the notion of mutual gains from free trade. Although Japan joined GATT in 1955, it was slow in removing restrictions on imports because of fears of backwardness and the dependence on external resources. The Kennedy Round of tariff negotiations in the mid–1960s represented an important shift in viewpoint, with Japan accepting the need for lower tariffs. This was due to the increasing competitiveness of Japanese exports and the expectation that lower world tariffs would spur these exports. By the early 1980s, Japanese tariff rates were generally as low as those of the EEC and somewhat lower than those of the United States.[7] At the same time, many countries continue to charge that substantial nontariff barriers to imports still exist. These include restrictions based on fear of disease, special regulations, and cultural resistance to foreign products.

Perhaps the greatest test of the Japanese economy came in the 1970s with the collapse of Bretton Woods and the oil shocks. The combination of a rising yen and a massive jump in oil imports put pressure on Japan's international accounts and on its domestic inflation rates. Oil imports rose from 20 percent of total imports in 1970 to more than 50 percent by 1981. Wholesale prices rose by 35 percent in 1974, which also saw a large current account deficit that recurred in 1980.[8]

Explanations for Japanese Growth

Although growth rates for the Japanese economy have declined over time, they have consistently remained higher than those for other industrialized countries. Japan clearly has produced a miraculous feat of economic recovery and growth. Efforts to explain this record have emphasized a wide variety of factors. Not surprisingly, economists have traced Japan's success to market relationships. Here, the generally accepted ability of the market to sort out the most efficient producers suggests that Japanese entrepreneurs were adept at responding to market incentives. But this approach fails to explain why the Japanese possessed this special market sensitivity.[9] Others have pointed

[7]For data comparing these countries and the ratio of tariff revenue to imports, see Komiya and Itoh, "Japan's International Trade. . . ," 193.

[8]Komiya and Itoh, "Japan's International Trade. . . ," 198–200; and M. Stephen Weatherford and Haruhiro Fukui, " Domestic Adjustment to International Shocks in Japan and the United States," *International Organization*, 43.4, Autumn 1989, 600, 613–617.

[9]David Friedman, *The Misunderstood Miracle: Industrial Development and Political Change in Japan,* Ithaca: Cornell University Press, 1988, 4–6.

to unusual features of the Japanese economy and culture, such as the harmony of labor and management, the high savings rate, or to the benefits of riding on the open world economy and security system provided by the United States.[10]

Perhaps the strongest argument, at least for many students of international and political affairs, is to trace the Japanese market perspicacity to the role of the government and its relationship to the economy. From the beginning of the modern era in 1868, the state has played a special role in rearranging Japanese society and politics so that it could compete effectively with the West. The focus of that effort in the post–World War II era has been the Ministry of International Trade and Industry (MITI). This and other importance bureaucracies, such as the Ministry of Finance (MOF), helped provide "domestic producers with the support and guidance they needed to achieve competitive advantages in global markets."[11] This "developmental state" sought to create or at least shape the incentives — market and otherwise — that directed the actions of Japanese firms.[12] Sometimes this took the form of subsidies to young or ailing industries, which is also somewhat common in the West. More important were efforts at organizing industries to achieve lower costs, defining national priorities in technological development, and developing national plans to reduce the risks associated with corporate decisions.

The texture of the relationship of MITI to the Japanese economy is not constant over time. Rather, it is affected in important ways by the nature of the external environment and the level of development of the business system. Shifts in the world economy and increasing strength of Japanese business have forced MITI bureaucrats to change their style and strategies for national economic management. Moreover, close analysis reveals that structural characteristics of the Japanese enterprise not only make it an effective partner for government but also offer numerous points of access for MITI influence.

The role of MITI reflects a long-standing judgment in the Japanese government about the proper role of the market in directing the economy. Although respecting the power of market forces, MITI officials have rejected the view that a policy of laissez-faire would necessarily produce the best possible use of Japanese economic resources. Left alone to follow the signals from the market, investors could easily direct resources toward areas such as real estate that would do little for the nation's international competitive position. Acutely conscious of Japan's backward status and fearful of the effects of weakness on the country's security and independence, MITI designed a strategy for making Japan an industrial power. It sought to identify specific industries where Japan might make major gains, anticipate changes

---

[10]Johnson, *MITI.* . . , 11–17.

[11]David Friedman, *The Misunderstood Miracle*, Ithaca: Cornell University Press, 1988, 3.

[12]Chalmers Johnson has used the term "developmental state" in *MITI and.* . . .

in the world economy, and organize the Japanese economy to make it competitive in areas that market forces, left alone, would likely avoid.[13]

After 1954, MITI used control over foreign exchange, technology imports, financial support, and tax breaks to target certain industries for development. In steel, shipbuilding, machine tools, plastics, petrochemicals, and automobiles, traditionally the province of countries with large natural resources or a big domestic market, MITI moved to establish a Japanese presence. The basic objectives were to drive down costs, improve productivity, protect the domestic market from foreign competition, and expand market share abroad. The long production runs permitted by a large market share would take advantage of economies of scale which would further reduce costs. Two aspects of the Japanese industrial structure assisted in this process. First, MITI was able to reconstitute the large business conglomerates of the prewar period, *zaibatsu*, into similar systems (now known as *keiretsu*) whereby banks, industrial firms, and trading companies functioned much like a cartel. Second, the reliance on debt rather than equity as the chief source of capital helped focus the business on MITI–style goals. Firms tended to look to the longer-term and to growth of market share rather than to short-term profits. Supporting this was the Japanese central bank, which acted to guarantee the debt of preferred industries. The result of these arrangements was to cushion the downside risks for certain businesses and thereby direct them toward national goals.[14]

Changes in these arrangements began in the early 1960s with external pressure for liberalization of trade and, later in the decade, for loosening controls on Japanese capital markets. Both efforts were prompted by the spectacular success enjoyed by the Japanese economy and the seemingly free ride created by the strict policy of protection. These events had several important consequences. The pressures for liberalization eventually produced results, with trade and capital barriers gradually falling between 1960 and 1980. Largely in response to these changes, MITI was forced to adopt a new strategy for internal economic management. It surrendered direct control over allocating scarce resources and began to rely more on persuasion and the adaptive skills of the *keiretsu* themselves.[15]

Perhaps the most significant recent developments came as a result of the two great changes in the world economy in the early 1970s, the collapse of the Bretton Woods system of fixed exchange rates and the price revolution in oil. Also significant were growing domestic political concerns over pollution and the increasing independence of Japan's very successful and powerful

---

[13]Okimoto, *Between MITI.* . . , 11–12, 23–24, 29–36; Johnson, *MITI and.* . . , 81.

[14]Johnson, *MITI and.* . . , 199–212. Of special significance in this process was access to the U.S. market, which offered an enormous opportunity to utilize economies of scale, cut costs, and raise productivity.

[15]Johnson, *MITI and.* . . , 249–272.

business empires. The result was a lengthy debate within MITI that brought a new bureaucratic faction into power, one more cosmopolitan and international in outlook. This led to a major policy shift toward energy conservation, reduction of pollution and overcrowding, and a drive to develop knowledge-intensive, high-technology industries.[16]

Japan's move into the realm of high-tech has been immensely successful and has produced a dramatic shift in the competitive environment around the world. The once comfortable lead enjoyed by the United States has evaporated in many areas, and other nations have been both encouraged and threatened by Japan's achievements. The primary impetus behind these developments has been a combination of government and private industry efforts. MITI contributed research subsidies, and Japanese firms devoted a much larger proportion of company resources to research and development and capital investment than similar U.S. firms. During the 1970s, Japan worked to develop and adapt its production capabilities to certain areas, but especially in semiconductors, computers, and consumer electronics. In the 1980s, Japan caught up in computers, surged ahead in semiconductors, consumer electronics, and robotics, and redirected research and development toward supercomputers, optoelectronics, and next-generation fighter planes.[17] At the beginning of the 1990s, Japan had established itself as a powerful international force in high technology. A 1990 report by the Defense Department acknowledges a Japanese lead in five high-technology industries crucial to U.S. national security, including semiconductors, superconductivity, robotics, supercomputers, and photonics.[18]

But MITI's role in this process has continued to evolve as its control over the Japanese economy has waned. This is due, in large part, to the size and economic strength of Japan's private business enterprises. The largest corporations now have the resources to support high levels of research and development and absorb investment risks. Further, the most intense competition for many of these companies is other Japanese firms, thereby undermining their interest in cooperation sponsored by MITI. Funds for research and development continue to flow from MITI, and it still provides an important sanction for investment decisions and supports businesses involved in strategically vital technologies. But its capacity to command has loosened with the maturing of the Japanese economy.[19]

---

[16]Johnson, *MITI and.* . . , 275–301.

[17]Okimoto, *Between MITI.* . . , 55–85.

[18]Martin Tolchin, "Pentagon Says It Lags in Some Technologies," *New York Times*, March 22, 1990.

[19]David Sanger, "Mighty MITI Loses its Grip," *New York Times*, July 9, 1989. For a discussion of the role of MITI in the early stages of Japanese entry into the computer market, see Marie Anchordoguy, "Mastering the Market: Japanese Government Targeting of the Computer Industry," *International Organization*, 42.3, Summer 1988, 509–543.

Future Prospects

In thinking about the future, we should keep in mind some of the important differences between Japan and Western nations that may act to temper a continuing pattern of spectacular economic success. Many Japanese pay a high price for their economic prosperity, as much of it does not filter down to the average consumer. High savings rates are the positive side of much lower rates of consumption. This is another way of saying that the forebearence of Japanese consumers allows the nation to devote more resources to investment. Moreover, the price of many consumer goods is at a large premium in terms of prices in other countries. Prices for many goods may be as much as one-third higher in Japan.[20] Housing in Japanese urban areas is extremely expensive, and the country tolerates major inefficiencies in food production and processing. Much of the competitive advantage of some Japanese industries derives from the economic subjugation of a large portion of the female work force. The rationale of weakness or national poverty can no longer serve as a justification for many of these practices. A stronger consumer orientation may well undercut future national investment priorities and trade surpluses.

But having said this, the rise of Japan to the world's second largest economic power in less than forty years is a stunning accomplishment with many important consequences. Perhaps the most important is that U.S. efforts in the 1980s to revitalize its economy have led to budget deficits, trade deficits, and (after 1985) a falling U.S. dollar, all of which have acted to transfer massive financial power to Japan. Between 1981 and 1988, the cumulative U.S. trade deficit with Japan totaled more than $300 billion.[21] In conjunction with the 50 percent appreciation of the yen after 1985, this has given the Japanese an immense financial surplus for investment abroad. The result has been a rapid movement into direct and portfolio investment that mirrors the pattern of financial outreach of Great Britain in the nineteenth century and the United States between 1948 and 1980.[22] By 1990, Japanese direct foreign investment totaled $311 billion, and when combined with its portfolio investment, made it the largest creditor nation in the world.[23]

---

[20]Richard J. Samuels, "Consuming for Production: Japanese National Security, Nuclear Fuel Procurement, and the Domestic Economy," *International Organization*, 43.4, Autumn 1989, 625–626. Much of this is due to high raw materials costs, an antiquated distribution system, and to protectionist barriers to imports of lower priced foreign goods.

[21]Robert Pear, "Confusion is Operative Word In U.S. Policy Toward Japan," *New York Times*, March 20, 1989; and Susan Chira, "U.S. Currency Policy Speeds Japan in Vast Economic Role," *New York Times*, November 28, 1988.

[22]Direct investment refers to the purchase of productive assets abroad, and portfolio investment refers to the purchase of financial instruments, such as stocks and bonds.

[23]"America and Japan," *The Economist*, November 30, 1991, 23.

The effects of Japanese financial power are many and range from the purchase of 30 percent of U.S. Treasury bond offerings and buying Rockefeller Center in New York to a growing role in foreign aid and investment in the Third World. Japanese financial power is both large enough and concentrated enough to affect global markets in substantial ways. Financial decisions in Japan are blamed for the collapse of world bond and stock prices in 1987 and also credited for their subsequent recovery.[24] Long an important presence in Asia, Japan has lately begun to assume the role of economic hegemon, especially in East and Southeast Asia. Japanese money, technology, and business strategy have started to play a key role in economic development in Thailand, Indonesia, Malaysia, Singapore, and mainland China. More than 10 percent of the Thai work force is employed by Japanese firms, and the figure is rising. Japanese companies have moved beyond a traditional interest in low-tech/low-wage manufacturing toward production of sophisticated equipment for local markets and for export. The result is a growing trend toward the organization of Asian markets and production by the Japanese.[25]

Beyond the strictly financial realm, Japan has begun to assume a much larger political role in the world. Even as late as the 1970s, Japan maintained a foreign posture that was "hesitant and withdrawn." This reflected the fact that for the period after 1945 Japan was dependent on the United States for its security, access to world markets, and technology. By the mid–1980s, however, the Japanese government had developed a much greater consciousness of its power and a willingness to apply that power to Japanese-defined goals.[26] Events of that decade have rearranged the power relationship between the United States and Japan. The collapse of Soviet power greatly alters the question of Japanese security, even as the United States has become dependent on Japan for financial assistance, borrowing to support its consumptive lifestyle, and increasingly for high technology. In important respects, the tables have been turned. The result shows up in a more independent, and even assertive, foreign policy, greater international thinking in such areas as foreign aid, and growing defense capabilities. Even so, Japan is still searching

---

[24]R. Taggert Murphy, "Power Without Purpose: The Crisis of Japan's Global Financial Dominance," *Harvard Business Review*, March-April 1989, 73–74.

[25]David Sanger, "Behind Thai Boom: The Japanese, *New York Times*, May 10, 1990; James Sterngold, "Japan Builds East Asia Link, Gaining Labor and Markets," *New York Times*, May 8, 1990; James Sterngold, "Japan Stakes Out Nearby Markets," *New York Times*, January 24, 1990; and Nicholas D. Kristof, "Japan Winning Race in China," *New York Times*, April 29, 1987.

[26]Bruce Stokes, "Who's Standing Tall?" *National Journal*, October 21, 1989, 2568–2573; Susan Chira, "Newly Assertive Tokyo," *New York Times*, September 6, 1989; Lawrence Summer, "What To Do When Japan Says No," *New York Times*, December 3, 1989; Clyde Farnsworth, "Japan's Maneuvering For A Big Global Voice," *New York Times*, October 24, 1989; Steven Weisman, "Japan Takes a Leading Role in the Third-World Debt Crisis," *New York Times*, April 17, 1989.

for a clear international role, as witnessed by its difficulty in responding to the war against Iraq in 1990–1991.27

Japan is the most spectacular example of postwar economic growth fueled by the extraordinary development of the ties of international economic interdependence. But most other advanced capitalist states have also experienced dramatic economic growth and are likewise caught up in the expanding web of international interchange. Such an environment contributes to deepening relations of cooperation, competition, and even conflict among nations. We turn now to a consideration of the capabilities of the United States and Western Europe to compete effectively in the world economy.

COMPETITIVENESS

■ From the beginning of the industrial era, the ability of specific industries in certain nations to achieve advantages over those in other nations has defined competitiveness and has distinguished countries from one another. Further, these same economic capabilities have been closely related to the capacity for producing military and political power. Whether in terms of generating wealth that facilitated a large military establishment or the technological infrastructure to support building railroads, dreadnoughts, or ICBMs, economic competitiveness has been linked with national power. Today the military, political, economic, and technological dimensions of international competition are bound together very tightly. World influence demands accomplishment in all four areas, while each increasingly depends on the other three.

For our purposes, competitiveness can be defined as the ability of a nation to achieve economic growth and a rising standard of living, even while exposed to international trade and capital flows.28 Understanding this process calls for an analysis of the broad characteristics of nations along with a consideration of specific industries, since it is here where actual competition takes place. Our interest lies in identifying those attributes of a nation that help or hurt an industry or industry segment in global competition. But additionally, examining competitiveness makes the economic performance of a business system a political issue along with the general relationship of the political system to business activity.

27A more theoretical treatment of Japan's position in the international system is found in Richard Rosecrance, "Japan and the Theory of International Leadership," *World Politics*, 42.2, January 1990, 184–209; and Henrik Schmiegelow and Michele Schmiegelow, "How Japan Affects the International System," *International Organization*, 44.4, Autumn 1990, 553–588. For a discussion of Japan's response to the war against Iraq in 1990–1991, see Steven R. Weisman, "Japan Counts the Costs of Gulf Action — Or Inaction," *New York Times*, January 27, 1991.

28The ability to produce rising standards of living in autarchy or without selling in world markets is an interesting but empirically limited experience. We are concerned here only with those involved in the world economy.

Not surprisingly, discussion in the United States of this question has expanded dramatically in the 1980s, and several perspectives have developed. It is important to keep in mind when considering competitiveness that it is a politically-charged issue, and information and argument are frequently skewed toward the interests of the source. Three broad schools of thought have emerged which can be simplified as: (1) the U.S. economic system has serious problems requiring major national efforts; (2) the United States is basically healthy, with perhaps the need for some adjustments around the edges; (3) the real problems are located in Japan, which unfairly blocks U.S. exports.[29] Our viewpoint is closer to the first group, but we will give you information drawn from all sides of the argument. We will consider competitiveness from the standpoint of economic theories of comparative advantage and free trade and examine evidence relating to the functioning of the economy as a whole and evidence involving specific industries.

Theoretical Issues

The competitiveness debate raises questions about the type of international trading system that is most desirable. The notions of free trade and comparative advantage — now nearly two centuries old — define the most desirable system as one in which each nation should specialize in a world of open trade, based on the existing factor endowments of the nation. In this system, no nation is better off defecting and engaging in autarchy or mercantilism. Those who pursue these paths will eventually produce and consume fewer goods at higher prices (less for more). One of the key issues of competitiveness is whether important gains can be had for one nation by taking steps to boost its proportion of high-profit and knowledge-intensive industries. Although this corresponds to historical experience, such an option does not fit well with the theory of comparative advantage.

A theoretical grounding for competitiveness as a political issue depends on showing how the actions of governments can make industries grow faster or even make industries develop that otherwise would not evolve. One version of this analysis, known as strategic trade, argues that government intervention can work if one of two situations holds. First, government action targets a high-profit industry, and this action helps to dissuade foreign firms from entering the market or compels them to leave. The object is to be the nation with the firms that capture a proportion of the global market large

---

[29]The political orientation of different industries may be generally related to these schools. Those industries which are less competitive may be more inclined to seek government help and support a major national effort. Those industries that are competitive or have the alternative of moving operations abroad or are unaffected by international competition may be indifferent to or oppose such efforts, especially if they require higher taxes and/or a more intrusive role for government.

enough to reap the greatest economies of scale. This serves to drive out other competitors, and international specialization is then based on lowering costs through expanding production. A second element of strategic trade theory focuses on actions that help establish industries with important economic spin-offs or externalities. Here the purpose is to make sure that your nation contains its share of industries whose operations generate benefits for other industries. The best examples are those knowledge-intensive industries that generate demand for other advanced businesses. The relationship between the computer industry and the computer software industry is an obvious case. The nation containing the greatest proportion of high-externalities industries will likely produce the highest rates of economic growth.[30]

Another approach to thinking about political efforts to improve international competitiveness relates to the concept of comparative advantage (discussed in Chapter Two). Research today rejects the standard view that factor endowments controlling comparative advantage are fixed, especially in certain high-growth fields. Rather, the factors that most influence production may be created in part through government action. Again, the proportion of knowledge-intensive industries, those characterized by high research and development costs, high risk and payoff, and rapid change, in a society can be a consequence of government decisions. A combination of policies designed to develop the infrastructure for knowledge generation and application may be a necessary ingredient for the establishment of these industries. Thus, education policies, efforts to enhance knowledge and technical skills in the population, and actions to assume some of the risks and costs of product development can have a major impact on where knowledge-intensive firms locate. Nations thereby compete in terms of creating comparative advantage that affects which ones will capture the largest proportion of these companies. The presence of high-tech industries makes a major contribution to wage rates, growth rates, and the nation's standard of living.[31]

Does the United States Have a Competitiveness Problem?

The main object of the competitiveness discussion is Japan. For it is this country, through its policies and performance, that appears to have

---

[30]Paul R. Krugman, "Is Free Trade Passe?" in Phillip King, *International Economics and International Economic Policy: A Reader*, New York: McGraw-Hill, 1990, 91–107; Paul R. Krugman, *Rethinking International Trade*, Cambridge: MIT Press, 1990. For a critique of strategic trade theory, see J. David Richardson, "The Political Economy of Strategic Trade Policy," *International Organization*, 44.1, Winter 1990, 107–135. Another critique of managed trade is "World Trade," *The Economist*, September 22, 1990, 19–25.

[31]Bruce Scott, "Creating Comparative Advantage," in Phillip King, *International Economics. . . ,* 78–90; Michael Porter, *The Competitive Advantage of Nations*, New York: Free Press, 1990.

established a new global competitive standard in the same way that Britain did in the early nineteenth century and the United States did throughout most of the twentieth century. But much of the 1980s was spent trying to respond to the economic malaise of the 1970s. We need to consider some of the evidence on this period to decide whether the United States actually has a competitiveness problem.

The standard measure of a nation's competitiveness in world markets is its balance of trade. We have described earlier the dramatic collapse in the U.S. position during the first half of the 1980s and the effort to reverse this slide through a policy of dollar depreciation. Did it work? The trade deficit has fallen, but certainly not enough.

TABLE 6.2

U.S. Manufacturing Trade Balance 1983–1990
(*Billions of Dollars*)

YEAR	1983	1984	1985	1986	1987	1988	1989	1990
Balance	−20.0	−63.0	−84.0	−107.0	−121.0	−100.0	−91.0	−64.0

SOURCE: U.S. Department of Commerce, 1991.

When the measure is expanded to include all merchandise, the 1990 figure remains near $100 billion. In 1991, the deficit improved somewhat more, falling to a level of about $5.0 billion per month. But the United States continued a deficit with every industrial country except Britain and the Soviet Union.[32] In some ways, this bad news obscures the fact that U.S. export growth has been substantial. From 1987 to 1990 exports have grown more than 60 percent. Imports have continued to grow, but at a slower rate, thereby blunting improvement in the trade balance.[33]

A clearer picture of the competitiveness issue can be had by comparing the U.S. economy's response to the rising dollar in 1981–1985 with the Japanese economy's response to the rising yen from 1985 to 1990. For the United States, the 60 percent rise in the dollar produced a flat line for exports from 1981 to 1986 and an explosion of imports, resulting in an enormous trade deficit. The Japanese, on the other hand, have adjusted to the high yen with

---

[32]Clyde Farnsworth, "Trade Gap Narrowed in November," *New York Times*, January 19, 1991; Robert D. Hershey, Jr., "Trade Gap Widened in April," *New York Times*, June 20, 1991.

[33]"The Bright Side of the Trade Gap," *New York Times*, September 9, 1990, F–13. From October 1990 to April 1991, imports began the longest period of decline since the effort to lower the dollar started in September 1985. Most analysts attributed this to the U.S. recession and not to the dollar decline. This suggests that economic recovery in the United States is likely to produce a return to a widened trade gap.

remarkable speed. The higher yen prompted efforts to cut costs, increase efficiency, accept more imports, and increase domestic consumption. Although the trade surplus has shrunk, it remains quite high. Japanese exports have been boosted by consumer perception of high-quality goods and the dominance of certain markets by Japanese products. Even though the yen rose by almost 100 percent against the dollar between 1985 and 1990, the Japanese trade surplus with the United States only declined from about $56 billion to $41 billion.[34] The remarkable contrast between the weakness of the U.S. response to shifts in the dollar exchange rate and the strength of the Japanese response to the rising yen suggest that we need to look deeper into the competitiveness question.

Perhaps the most important broad economic measures of a nation's competitiveness involve its productivity, savings, and capital investment. These represent the ability to withhold resources from present consumption and devote them to investments that permit production of more and better goods in the future. It is this capacity for improving and innovating that makes an economy competitive and makes it possible for incomes and living standards to rise.

The evidence on U.S. savings, investment, and wage growth is uniformly negative, while that on productivity is more mixed. Savings levels by U.S. business are decent, but personal and government savings levels are very bad. The effect is to place sharp limits on investment in the future.

TABLE 6.3

Net Personal Savings As a Percent of Disposable Income
(*Average for 1980–1988*)

U.S.	BRITAIN	W. GERMANY	SPAIN	FRANCE	JAPAN	CANADA
5.5	0.1	12.2	8.4	14.9	16.4	13.4

SOURCE: Nathaniel Nash, "Persuading Americans To Save," *New York Times*, December 17, 1989. The level of personal savings has fallen almost uninterrupted since the economic problems of the 1970s worsened in 1973. It was then at about 10 percent.

Net national savings for the United States, which includes business and government, fell from an anemic 3.2 percent over 1981–1985 to less than 1.9 percent for 1986–1987.[35]

---

[34]David Sanger, "How Japan Does What It's Doing To Keep Its Economy in Top Gear," *New York Times*, November 27, 1988; James Sterngold, "Japan Poised for Postwar Boom," *New York Times*, January 28, 1991; Clyde Farnsworth, "U.S. Is Asked To Review Japanese Trade," *New York Times*, March 25, 1991.

[35]George N. Hatsopoulos, Paul Krugman, and Lawrence Summers, "U.S. Competitiveness: Beyond the Trade Deficit," *Science*, 241, July 15, 1988, 305.

Investment figures reflect this disparity in savings. There are several ways to measure this process. The broadest calculations of investment indicate a relatively consistent and substantial advantage for Japan. Figure 6.2 shows this quite clearly.

FIGURE 6.2

Investment As a Percent of GDP

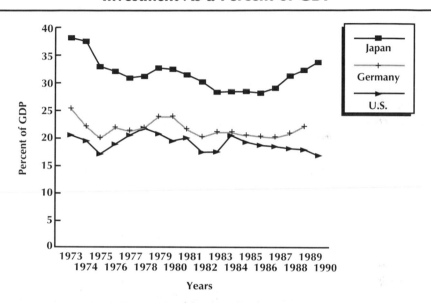

SOURCE: International Monetary Fund, *International Financial Statistics Yearbook*, 1991, 168–169.

More refined measures indicate much the same thing. Between 1981 and 1985, the Japanese spent 10.6 percent of their GNP (note the difference in comparison to GNP rather than GDP) to add to their stock of productive assets while the United States spent only 4.5 percent.[36] When we look at gross spending (which includes replacing worn-out plants and equipment) trends, the evidence is even bleaker for the United States. The proportion of U.S. GNP going to gross investment has been slowly falling for more than a decade from about 11 percent to 9 percent, while in Japan it has risen from about the same percentage level to 24 percent of GNP. Astonishingly, with an economy less than two-thirds the size of the United States, Japan actually spent $750 billion for gross investment in 1989 compared to $500 billion for the United States. Between 1985 and 1989, the gap between the spending rates of the two nations expanded from 15 percent to 10 percent to the present level of

---

[36]Hatsopoulos, et al. "U.S. Competitiveness. . . , 304.

24 percent to 9 percent. One economist, commenting on these figures, re-marked: "It's a bit scary. . . . What we are seeing is Japan becoming the new product laboratory for the world."[37]

In spite of the poor showing in savings and investment, productivity measures have given rise to encouragement. The 1980s led to a turnaround in productivity growth. This measures the quantity of output per worker, and its growth is usually tied closely to growth in income. During the 1970s, U.S. manufacturing productivity grew at only 1.4 percent, while that of other industrial nations grew at nearly 4.0 percent. But from 1979 to 1989, the United States matched these same nations at 3.6 percent. Much of this gain came from downsizing U.S. plants, laying off workers, and increasing the productivity of those who remained.[38] Less clear is whether these gains can be sustained in the face of low savings and investment levels. Even more telling is the fact that productivity growth for manufacturing did not extend to other employees. The result was that real wages have fallen throughout the period from 1973 to 1990. Even in manufacturing, real wages have been dropping since 1977, making some analysts skeptical about the genuineness of the productivity growth.[39]

But perhaps the aggregate measures have disguised more favorable trends in specific industries.[40] Unfortunately, the evidence here gives little room for optimism. Surely the most spectacular and far-reaching shift of the 1980s was the decline of U.S. preeminence in high technology. Nothing demonstrates this decline more clearly than the rapid erosion of U.S. dominance of the global semiconductor market and its replacement by Japan.

This story reflects our earlier discussion of government-business ties in Japan, with MITI supporting a crash effort to catch up and then surpass the United States in product development. Although semiconductors had long been considered an industry where the United States possessed overwhelm-ing advantages, MITI realized their importance to high-technology produc-tion and innovation. MITI's support, plus closing the Japanese market for a time to foreign-made semiconductors, gave Japanese producers the opportu-nity to develop production experience and an assured market. Japanese

---

[37]David Sanger, "Japan Keeps Up The Big Spending To Maintain Its Industrial Might," *New York Times*, April 11, 1990.

[38]Sylvia Nasar, "American Revival In Manufacturing Seen in U.S. Report," *New York Times*, February 5, 1991; Lawrence Klein, "Components of Competitiveness," *Science*, 241, July 15, 1988, 308–313. For a detailed and generally favorable picture of U.S. productivity, see William J. Baumol, et al. *Productivity and American Leadership: The Long View*, Cambridge: MIT Press, 1991.

[39]Louis Uchitelle, "Not Getting Ahead? Better Get Used to It," *New York Times*, December 16, 1990.

[40]Three good overviews of competitiveness issues at the level of industries are: Michael L Dertouzos, et al., eds. *Made in America*, Cambridge: MIT Press, 1989; Jean Claude Derian, *America's Struggle for Leadership in Technology*, Cambridge: MIT Press, 1990; and Martin Starr, ed. *Global Competitiveness*, New York: Norton, 1988. An older but still useful volume is Bruce Scott and George Lodge, eds. *U.S. Competitiveness in the World Economy*, Boston: Harvard Busi-ness School Press, 1985.

production wizardry soon enabled them to surpass U.S. producers in quality. These same Japanese firms took large losses by selling below cost in order to capture a large segment of the U.S. market. The combination of quality and cost led to rapid sales growth and to falling costs of production, as Japanese firms benefitted from economies of scale. The results were catastrophic for U.S. firms. From 1980 to 1986, the U.S. share of the global semiconductor market fell from 75 percent to below 30 percent, and Japanese companies share rose from 25 percent to 65 percent.[41]

Since this pattern seems to replicate much of the experience with the steel, automobile, and consumer electronics industries, many fear the Japanese can and will take over any industry they want. Perhaps the area of greatest immediate concern is the computer industry. The Japanese have recently made striking inroads at several levels here. In the portable, laptop, and palmtop market segment, which many believe to be the growth area in computer hardware, the Japanese have established a very strong position.[42] In supercomputers, the Japanese have moved from far behind to essentially even with the United States. Although the U.S. government appears to have discouraged sales in the United States, Japanese firms are likely to overtake the lone American firm in product development. The major Japanese firm, NEC, currently spends almost ten times as much for supercomputer research and development as the sole U.S. firm, Cray Research.[43]

Competitiveness Strategies

Perhaps the sharpest contrast in competitiveness styles can be seen in the different approaches to business-government relations in support of new or critical industries. The Japanese exemplify the prototypical case of close government-business relations and a have strong consensus on the need to organize the nation's resources for international economic competition. The U.S. preference for interfirm competition and a loose and distant role for government creates some difficulties. The United States must rely on private

---

[41]This paragraph relies on Clyde Prestowitz, *Trading Places*, New York: Basic Books, 1988, 120–178.

[42]Andrew Pollack, "Japanese Portables Threaten American Lead in Computers," *New York Times*, November 24, 1990. Meanwhile, the American computer giant, IBM, has suffered in the Japanese and world markets because it misjudged the direction of consumer tastes. David Sanger, "I.B.M. Losing Ground In Japan," *New York Times*, June 3, 1991.

[43]David Sanger, "A Tough Sell for 'Made in Japan,' " *New York Times*, November 30, 1990. Much the same could be said for another crucial technology, superconductivity. David Sanger, "Japanese Busy Seeking Superconductive Products," *New York Times*, January 29, 1989. An area where some think the Japanese may have taken a wrong turn, while others think it will position them to dominate future computer markets, is massively parallel processing. David Sanger, "Japan Sets Sights on Winning Lead In New Computers," *New York Times*, April 30, 1990. An example of a U.S. company winning the competitive race with the Japanese is Motorola. Keith Bradsher, "Beating Japan at Its Own Game," *New York Times*, July 13, 1990.

corporations to provide the capital for key industries. But, as with an important production facility for manufacturing computer chips, considerations of short-term profit can lead to a takeover by foreign firms. Another more common example is the reluctance of some firms to spend research and development funds on uncertain but promising products. They prefer the safer strategy of boosting stock prices by purchasing their own shares. "The attitude [of corporate management] is to throw up their hands. They figure, 'If I cannot compete, at least I can boost my stock price.' " Of course, this fixation on the short-term bottom line for stockholders may hinder the ability of the nation to compete with foreign firms willing to take risks and invest funds.[44]

Some of the most important U.S. efforts at business and business-government cooperation have a mixed record. Sematech, an attempt by private firms to establish a joint venture to manufacture computer chips, has been plagued by problems of raising capital.[45] More ambitious efforts at business-government cooperation have been plagued by ideological opposition from the Bush Administration and the lack of experience in these matters. The Defense Advanced Research Projects Agency (DARPA) has provided crucial support for U.S. industry in the past. But it has come under fire for trying to pick out certain firms and industries to support and from those who object to locating this activity in the Defense Department. Sematech has likewise been criticized for its ineffectiveness.[46]

One important bottom line in this matter of competitiveness is the ability of a nation to engage in innovation at the level of basic research and in products themselves. For much of the period after World War II, the United States held a commanding and seemingly insurmountable lead in this area. But recent indicators suggest this too is changing. In the area of patents issued

---

[44]John Holusha, "Are We Eating Our Seed Corn?" *New York Times*, May 13, 1990; and letters responding, *New York Times*, May 27, 1990; David Sanger, "Key Technology Might Be Sold To the Japanese," *New York Times*, November 27, 1989; Andrew Pollack, "The Challenge of Keeping U.S. Technology At Home," *New York Times*, December 10, 1989.

[45]Andrew Pollack, "Computer Makers Decide to Abandon Joint U.S. Venture," *New York Times*, January 13, 1990; Andrew Pollack, "New Drive By Sematech For Funding," *New York Times*, December 20, 1991. For a comparison of how Japanese firms cooperated at the research and development and start-up phases in the computer industry and competed in commercializing the product, see Anchordoguy, "Mastering the Market. . . ."

[46]John Markoff, "Making Industrial Policy at the Pentagon," *New York Times*, November 19, 1989; Andrew Pollack, "Sematech Starts to Make Progress," *New York Times*, April 19, 1991. For a good overview of these activities, see B.R. Inman, and Daniel F. Burton, Jr., "Technology and Competitiveness: The New Policy Frontier," *Foreign Affairs*, Spring 1990, 116–134. The U.S. Congress is considering a plan to provide funds to develop improvements in supercomputers. John Markoff, "U.S. Supercomputer Plan to Spur G.N.P., Study Says," *New York Times*, April 11, 1991. A theoretically informed discussion of these matters, including the debate over DARPA, is Michael Mastanduno, "Do Relative Gains Matter?" *International Security*, 16.1, Summer 1991, 73–113. Also useful is William J. Broad, "Pentagon Wizards of Technology Eye Wider Civilian Role," *New York Times*, October 22, 1991.

and the importance of those patents, the evidence shows a rapid loss of U.S. advantage to the Japanese. One analyst commented, "It's scary. The Japanese are continuing to expand in virtually every area of technology. . . . Their performance is impressive across the board, in virtually every field."[47]

The trends of the past ten to fifteen years are not promising for the United States. Although U.S. strengths are plentiful and there is no cause for panic, the ability of U.S.-based firms to compete in world markets against all comers has declined in significant ways.

> American firms have a diminished competitive advantage in a wide range of industries. The fundamental problem is a lack of dynamism. American industry, in too many fields, has fallen behind the rate, character, and extent of improvement and innovation. . . . American industry is on the defensive, preoccupied with clinging to what it has instead of advancing.[48]

To the extent this conclusion is accurate, and we believe it is on the mark, the behavior of U.S. industries has become a critical political question since this affects every U.S. citizen's ability to hope for a prosperous future.

European Approaches

The Europeans have not been unmindful of the new competitive environment. As we noted in Chapter Five, both the decision to move toward a single market in the EC and the incorporation of EFTA into the EC have been designed to increase the competitiveness of European firms. The removal of nontariff barriers to trade is being advanced through the development of 282 measures drafted by the European Commission, passed by the European Parliament, and sent on to national governments for enactment into law. The effect is to create a single set of rules across the EC for commercial transactions. There are mainly two impacts on competitiveness: the reduction of costs made unnecessary by the elimination of various trade barriers and the encouragement of the creation of EC-wide firms capable of operations in all of these markets. This will lead to additional cost savings from economies of scale and firms large enough to afford the investments needed to compete in world markets.

The free-market approach, embedded in the new single market in Europe, contrasts sharply with more traditional industrial and competitiveness policies in the countries of the EC. All of these countries have made extensive use of subsidies and other state aid in agriculture and manufacturing, have substantial experience in state-owned firms, and many have supported

---

[47]William J. Broad, "In the Realm of Technology, Japan Looms Ever Larger," *New York Times*, May 28, 1991.
[48]Porter, *The Competitive.* . . , 532.

development of cartels for industries in distress.[49] The movement toward the Single European Act and deregulation has prompted the European Commission to press for an end to subsidies, cartels, and other forms of market distortions.[50] The clash between these competing perspectives has not been sorted out. In the electronics and computer industries, an area of major importance to advanced industrial economies, EC states have acted to support private firms. And pressure from these same firms — especially in computers and semiconductors — to do more is increasing.[51] Nonetheless, the countries in the EC are sufficiently different to make a common competitiveness policy unlikely for the moment. Some, like France and Italy, are much more interventionist than Germany and Great Britain. Equally relevant is the fact that industries are not always in the same position in every country; some are competitive and some are not. This makes it difficult for the EC to opt for anything other than freeing up the market to improve competitiveness.

The terms of international competition have changed, making obsolete the advantages that once propelled Europe, and then the United States, to world economic preeminence. There is good reason to question whether either can respond effectively to the new competitive standard being set by Japan. The call for policies designed to create comparative advantage through investments in an infrastructure supporting knowledge-intensive industries, higher levels of national savings, and actions to cushion or even assume risks for certain key industries needs to be given a much wider hearing.[52] But beyond these proposals lies the traditional strategy for responding to the new climate of international competition: protectionism.

PROTECTIONISM

■ Ironically, the acceleration of the world economy toward freer trade and even greater interdependence since the early 1970s has also led to a revival of pressures for protectionism. This should not come as too much of a surprise since more interdependence means that the most competitive and innovative foreign producers have more opportunities to sell their goods. Those who cannot meet this competition invariably begin to call for government help. But in an international climate where GATT has led to very low tariffs, protectionism has become somewhat more sophisticated.[53]

---

[49]See Colchester and Buchan, *Europower.* . . , 147–148; Richard E. Foglesong and Joel D. Wolfe, eds. *The Politics of Economic Adjustment*, New York: Greenwood Press, 1989, contains several excellent articles on industrial policy in France, Germany, and Great Britain.

[50]See Colchester and Buchan, *Europower.* . . , 144–158.

[51]Steven Greenhouse, "Europe's Electronics Rescue Plan," *New York Times*, September 5, 1991.

[52]An example is Robert Reich, "The Real Economy," *The Atlantic Monthly*, February 1991, 35–52.

[53]For a useful, but now somewhat dated, overview of protectionism, see David Greenaway, *Trade Policy and the New Protectionism*, New York: St. Martin's, 1983.

Protectionism Without Tariffs

These "new" protectionist measures are typically designed to help a particular industry. They include efforts to use the threat of legally mandated restrictions to compel importers to restrict the sale of their goods "voluntarily." Known as Voluntary Export Restrictions (VERs) and Orderly Marketing Agreements (OMAs), these have been used to establish quotas for the sale of goods in the United States.[54] In 1981, the Japanese government acted "voluntarily" to mandate the number of automobiles sold in the United States so as to reduce pressure in the U.S. Congress for much more restrictive protectionism.[55] The arrangement has remained in place for more than ten years with several interesting consequences. Japanese penetration of the U.S. auto market has been slowed but not stopped. Japan's share of the U.S. auto market has risen from less than one-fifth in 1980 to more than one-fourth in 1991. Auto makers in Japan have modified the mix of cars sold in the United States toward more expensive models, and auto prices have risen much more rapidly than for other goods. In 1991, despite years of a VER and substantial improvements in quality and production efficiency, U.S. producers continue to have severe competitive problems.[56]

From the perspective of U.S. auto workers and executives, the VER was insufficient. Much more needed to be done to restrain the competitive pressure generated by Japan. From the position of U.S. consumers, qualitative improvements (and some jobs) were purchased at a very high cost.[57] In effect, U.S. consumers, through higher prices, subsidized both the U.S. and Japanese auto industries. From the position of a political leader, the VER can be a relatively quiet way to provide relief to a threatened industry without challenging the concept of free trade either at home or abroad. Of course, this works only so long as the exporting country cooperates.

Perhaps the most important and longstanding VER is the Multi-Fibre Arrangement (MFA), which can be traced back to the early 1960s. The textile

---

[54]Others include Countervailing Duties (CVD) and Anti-Dumping arrangements, which result from what are thought to be unfair trading practices. When foreign firms sell below "fair value" or receive a state subsidy, these methods are used to raise prices to establish a "level playing field." A useful overview of protectionist trends in the United States is found in I.M. Destler, *American Trade Politics: System Under Stress*, Washington: Institute for International Economics, 1986. Also helpful for its detailed examination of multiple case studies is Gary C. Hufbauer, et al. *Trade Protection in the United States*, Washington: Institute for International Economics, 1986.

[55]A similar agreement exists between the EC and Japan.

[56]The machine tools industry is another area where VERs have been used with very mixed results. Those producers whose resources make them uncompetitive, even in the near-term, support this policy. Those who are better able to remain competitive tend to oppose the VERs. See Steve Lohr, "A Split Over Machine Tool Imports," *New York Times*, October 7, 1991.

[57]One estimate is each job saved cost consumers $110,000 to $145,000. See Charles Collyns and Steve Dunaway, "The Cost of Trade Restraints: The Case of Japanese Automobile Exports to the United States," in King, *International Economics. . . ,* 13–21.

and apparel industry — where the industrial revolution began 200 years ago — is a good example of a labor-intensive, low capital investment, low-technology industry where comparative advantage comes largely from relative wage levels. High-wage nations have typically been unable to compete with low-wage nations in the absence of some form of protectionism. The MFA is a multilateral agreement designed to place quantitative limits on imports of textiles and apparel into high-wage countries. Associated with it is a series of bilateral agreements designed to serve the same purpose. Well over one-half of all world trade in this industry is subject to one of these agreements.[58]

Important variations from protectionism in the West can be found in Japan, which has increasingly become the target of those who are harmed by its exports. Many have argued that Japan continues to operate as a free rider — benefiting from free trade while blocking the import of many goods. Documenting this charge is difficult, owing to the fact that overt barriers to trade in Japan — tariffs and quotas — are generally lower than in most other advanced capitalist countries.[59] Rather, Japan retains a number of cultural and structural arrangements that effectively stand in the way of many imports. The result is a skewing of Japanese imports toward raw materials and semi-processed manufactures and away from high value-added and high-tech goods, as compared with other advanced capitalist states.

In general, barriers in Japan fall into one of several categories. They include:

(1) product standards (more important before 1980 than today), which indirectly or directly discriminate against foreign products;

(2) a distribution system, with many small retailers linked through exclusive arrangements with manufactures and protected by price fixing, that blocks foreign firms;[60]

(3) government favoritism toward Japanese firms in its purchases;

(4) a predominant form of business organization — *keiretsu* — which effectively creates a closed system of intrafirm purchases and suppliers that blocks entry by foreign firms;

(5) cultural and business structural barriers to direct foreign investment, especially the foreign purchase of Japanese firms;

---

[58]William R. Cline, "The Evolution of Protection in Textiles and Apparel," in King, ed. *International Economics. . . ,* 34–40.

[59]But it is true that in the recent past Japan has had much higher barriers and has also raised tariffs in an industry targeted by MITI for special development.

[60]This situation may be in for a change. See "Japan's Next Retail Revolution," *The Economist,* December 21, 1991, 79–80. The distribution system for automobiles is less subject to criticism. It involves an extraordinary system of individual selling in which each adult in Japan is personally contacted by a dealer to learn their car needs for the next year. This makes any effort to set up a distribution system for foreign cars very expensive.

(6) a strong cultural preference for Japanese goods and a bias against foreign goods that makes Japan a difficult market requiring a substantial investment of time and resources;

(7) substantial overt protection of Japanese agriculture that is tied to political support for the predominant party, the Liberal Democratic Party.[61]

The large Japanese trade surplus, the special Japanese government-business system, and the large Japanese consumer market help draw attention to these trade barriers. Some in the U.S. Congress have called for trade retaliation unless Japan opens its markets and reduces the trade surplus by a specified amount. This may make good politics, but it fails to deal with the fact that many of these same practices exist in the United States and most other nations.[62]

The Common Agricultural Policy (CAP) in the European Community also represents one of the most formidable systems of protection. As with many other things in the history of the EEC and EC, the Common Agricultural Policy was originally part of a compromise between France and Germany. French farmers were permitted to sell in Germany, while German farmers were protected from world prices. CAP established a free internal market for food within the EEC, a system of price supports through purchases of foodstuffs when prices fall below world levels, and a tariff and internal tax to pay for the program. Further, surplus food was often exported at subsidized prices. Because European farmers have consistently been inefficient relative to the rest of the industrialized world, and plans for modernization of agricultural production have been blocked, the gap between world prices and community support prices have widened over time. This meant the budget for support payments also had to grow, and by 1991 totaled $135 billion. The political basis for this system was the close relationship between farmers' organizations and the agricultural ministry in each state, which maintained effective control over CAP. Additionally, CAP is woven into the many political compromises and agreements that sustain the EC. This makes it a difficult arrangement to change.[63] Even so, the distortion of world trade from CAP is substantial, since the EC should be a major importer and instead is an important exporter of food. Prices inside the EC are much higher and world prices lower because of the oversupply of food.[64]

---

[61]For the link between the Liberal Democratic Party and farmers, see Gerald L. Curtis, *The Japanese Way of Politics*, New York: Columbia University Press, 1988, 49–61. A more general review of trade barriers is in Dorothy Christelow, "Japan's Intangible Barriers to Trade in Manufactures," in King, ed. *International Economics. . .* , 41–56.

[62]Keith Bradsher, "Mosbacher Joins Critics of Japan," *New York Times*, December 20, 1991.

[63]To date, only modest reforms designed to establish limits on the overall level of support payments have been adopted. There is great resistance to more dramatic reform, including slashing these payments and opening EC markets. We should note that the United States also subsidizes some exports of food, ostensibly only to offset the advantages gained by the EC.

[64]For more detail on CAP, see Pinder, *European. . .* , 77–93; and Colchester and Buchan, *Europower*, 106–117.

Why Do Nations Choose Protection?

Why should we expect protectionism to take place? The politics of the decision to place barriers on imports in any particular industry or as a general national policy is linked to a maze of interests, power relationships, and institutions. Political economists at this point can provide only a list of the main forces at work and cannot specify the circumstances under which protectionism will succeed or fail.[65]

(1) Since the benefits of protection are concentrated in a small number of owners and workers in the affected industry while the costs of protection are spread across many consumers, political organization for protection is easier than for free trade.[66]

(2) A nation's position in the world economy affects its foreign economic policy. That is, its relative proportion of world trade and the competitiveness of its products generate incentives and opportunities that largely define whether it pursues free trade or protection or some combination. Very large and competitive states — hegemons — will prefer a multilateral free trade system. Middle-ranking states will mix desire for free trade in the system with preference for some level of domestic protection, but they also realize that too much free riding on their part can lead to a collapse of the system. Small and/or uncompetitive states are likely to prefer protectionism at home and hope for free trade in the system.[67]

(3) The fate of the world economy — depression or prosperity — intersects with the structure of a nation's domestic interests — the relative power of protectionist versus free trade groups — to affect national decisions on foreign economic policy.[68]

(4) As a variation of #3, the growth of global interdependence and extensive participation of a nation in the world economy leads to more and more firms with interests in promoting free trade. As these firms

---

[65]For an overview of some the approaches discussed below and two case studies, see Richard Friman, "Rocks, Hard Places, and the New Protectionism: Textile Trade Policy Choices in the United States and Japan," *International Organization*, 42.4, Autumn 1988, 689–723. Another overview is Benjamin J. Cohen, "The Political Economy of International Trade," *International Organization*, 44.2, Spring 1990, 261–281.

[66]Real P. Lavergne, *The Political Economy of U.S. Tariffs*, New York: Academic Press, 1983.

[67]The best statement of this approach is found in David Lake, *Power, Protection, and Free Trade*, Ithaca: Cornell University Press, 1988, 1–65. I have omitted two of Lake's categories, the large and uncompetitive state that probably pursues imperialism and protectionism and the small but competitive state that pursues free trade.

[68]Peter Gourevitch, *Politics in Hard Times: Comparative Responses to International Economic Crises*, Ithaca: Cornell University Press, 1986; and Ronald Rogowski, *Commerce and Coalitions: How Trade Affects Political Alignments*, Princeton: Princeton University Press, 1989.

depend on global markets, they actively oppose efforts to increase protection for other industries because of fear of retaliation.[69]

(5) Choices about free trade and protection are constrained by ideas and institutions framed during particular historical periods. Once ideas come to permeate elite thinking and institutions are established, they create rules for the evaluation of policy.[70]

(6) Likewise, when a particular set of ideas and institutions achieve predominance at the international level, they also structure choices in bilateral and multilateral negotiations. The extension of free trade ideas and institutions after 1945 conditions the nature and extent of protectionist policies.

(7) Finally, protectionist or free trade proposals or policies may be used as part of a bargaining strategy designed to alter the preferences of other states.

The new protectionism described above is often an effort to strike a political balance between a general commitment to freer trade and the genuine economic damage such a policy can have on inefficient domestic producers and their workers.[71] The leadership of advanced industrial nations understand that withdrawal from the world economy would have disastrous economic and political consequences. The incentives to keep an open system functioning are simply too great to permit its demise.[72] At the same time, this viewpoint is politically viable only as long as the system produces a rising standard of living, and this requires that nations continually adjust to its inherent dynamism. Prolonged recession would surely unravel the political supports that make such a system possible. The recent growth of protectionism, the difficulties in GATT, and the rise of economic blocs do not clearly portend the end of an open system. But in a stagnant or shrinking world economy, these developments certainly could serve as a basis for fragmentation and even disintegration.

---

[69]Helen Milner, *Resisting Protectionism*, Princeton: Princeton University Press, 1988; Helen Milner, "Resisting the Protectionist Temptation: Industry and the Making of Trade Policy in France and the United States," *International Organization*, 41.4, Autumn 1987, 639–665; Helen Milner, "Trading Places: Industries for Free Trade," *World Politics*, 50.3, April 1988, 350–376; I.M. Destler and John Odell, *Anti-Protection: Changing Political Forces in United States Trade Politics*, Washington: Institute for International Economics, 1987.

[70]Judith Goldstein, "The Political Economy of Trade: Institutions of Protection," *American Political Science Review*, 80.1, March 1986, 161–184; Judith Goldstein, "The Impact of Ideas on Trade Policy: The Origins of U.S. Agricultural and Manufacturing Policies," *International Organization*, 43.1, Winter 1989, 31–71.

[71]Jagdish Bhagwati, *Protectionism*, Cambridge: MIT Press, 1988, 47–59. In this and a subsequent book, *The World Trading System at Risk*, Princeton: Princeton University Press, 1991, Bhagwati offers a spirited attack on the new protectionism. A response is in Paul Krugman, *The Age of Diminished Expectations*, Cambridge: MIT Press, 1990, 101–113.

[72]For the view that the structures and interests of interdependence are simply too powerful to permit any significant shift toward protectionism, see Susan Strange, "Protectionism and World Politics," *International Organization*, 30, Spring 1985, 233–259.

The Uruguay Round

In important ways the future of the free-trade order erected after World War II has focused on success of the latest negotiating session of GATT, the Uruguay Round. Throughout the postwar era, the United States has served as the chief instigator and supporter of GATT, and the substantial decline in tariff levels can be attributed to its leadership. But the Uruguay Round has been beset by problems from the outset in 1982. Its purpose was to move GATT regulations into new areas and deal with long-standing trade barriers and problems. These include tariffs and issues of trade in financial services, tourism and construction, trade involving copyrights and patents, and regulations restricting direct foreign investment.

The greatest stumbling block to an agreement came over agricultural trade, an area of U.S. strength and European and Japanese weakness. The United States has pressed Europe (with its CAP) for thirty years and Japan for more than ten to lower subsidies and tariff barriers on food products. Because of the political power of farmers in these countries and the likelihood that freer trade would put many out of business, governments in Europe and Japan have resisted liberalization. The price of these actions is a high cost of agricultural products for consumers there and lost markets for U.S. producers. The United States appeared ready to open its markets (and thereby damage its producers) in textiles, sugar, and dairy products. But the talks collapsed when the United States and Europeans could not agree on the level of tariff reductions in agriculture.[73]

The Uruguay Round has also taken up the Multi-Fibre Arrangement and its restrictions on textiles and apparel. Proposed changes involve replacing the MFA and the manifold bilateral agreements with a global quota. Less clear is whether this will actually result in a real dismantling of MFA protection. More certain is that any genuine movement here would be a boon for many Third World states. In return, developed states are looking to gain better protection in the Third World for intellectual property, especially patents and brand names. Another arena for expanding GATT is trade in services like shipping, banking, tourism, and investment. Proposals involve removing various restrictions such as requirements for local content in production facilities owned by foreigners and shipping that must take place only in containers owned by the host nation.[74]

---

[73]Steven Greenhouse, "Industrial Nations Agree to Push for Trade Accord," *New York Times*, June 5, 1991; Peter Passell, "Adding Up the World Trade Talks: Fail Now, Pay Later," *New York Times*, December 16, 1990; Bruce Stokes, "*Apres GATT, le Deluge?*" *National Journal*, January 12, 1991.

[74]H.B. Junz and Clemens Boonekamp, "What is at Stake in the Uruguay Round?" *Finance and Development*, June 1991, 10–15; Sylvia Ostry, "The Uruguay Round: An Unfinished Symphony," *Finance and Development*, June 1991, 16–17; "World Trade," *The Economist*, September 22, 1990.

From the beginning, the Uruguay Round faced the problem of confronting the most difficult and entrenched trade barriers. Furthermore, the threat of a U.S. pullout unless its terms were met has also hung over negotiations. The deadline of December 1990 failed to produce an agreement, and the talks moved into overtime. The main obstacle was the difficulty over CAP. The United States and other agricultural exporters wanted a dismantling of the CAP subsidies, while the Europeans resisted making anything but minor changes. The talks continued throughout 1991 with an oscillating mood of optimism and pessimism about their ultimate success. In December, after another breakdown, the director general of GATT moved to break the impasse by confronting the parties with a "take it or leave it" set of compromises. But even this was met with much hostility in both Europe and the United States. In April 1992, further efforts to reach agreement failed, leading to the possibility of a delay in serious negotiations until after the 1992 elections.[75]

The difficulties in achieving a GATT agreement can be seen better if we think of this process as a complex and multilayered bargaining game. This is a game with a set of domestic winners and losers in each nation. Among the most powerful and advanced states, the national executive and other political leaders have a varying commitment to the postwar institutions of free trade and international cooperation. Further, this game is taking place without a hegemon with the ability to make concessions, dispense rewards, and punish defectors across the system. The trick to a successful outcome is to gain international terms through agreement among many nations (adjustment and compromise) that will provide domestic winners with strong enough incentives to back the agreement and overcome the resistance of losers. This becomes a series of simultaneous bargaining games — at the international and domestic levels — which national political leaders try to manage toward a favorable conclusion. They are subject to pressure at home from a shifting balance of winners and losers based on the terms of the international agreement. And these leaders are also subject to pressure from abroad owing to the need to make concessions and adjustments in order to reach an agreement. We should not be surprised when such negotiations frequently seem to reach an impasse, especially when a hegemon is absent. But also constraining choices is the importance of preserving the global economic order itself and fear of the consequences of a decline in cooperation.[76]

---

[75]Keith Bradsher, "Bush and Europe Fail to Bridge Gap on Trade Barriers," *New York Times*, April 23, 1992; Steve Greenhouse, "A Move to Break the World Trade Deadlock," *New York Times*, December 21, 1991; Keith Bradsher, "Trade Plan Criticized, Stalling World Talks, *New York Times*, December 24, 1991. The talks can be followed in: "Rocking a Lifeboat Can Be Dangerous," *The Economist*, December 8, 1990, 69–70; "GATT Reprieved?" *The Economist*, October 19, 1991, 15.

[76]The best statement of the intersection of international and domestic politics is by Robert Putnam, "Diplomacy and Domestic Politics: The Logic of Two-level Games," *International Organization*, 42.3, Summer 1988, 427–460.

The United States has played the major leadership role in GATT since the 1940s. Should the Uruguay Round ultimately fail, this would be another indication of relative U.S. weakness in ordering the world economy. The outcome could also shift the forum for world trade negotiations from the multilateral GATT to bilateral FTAs. At the very least, many of these negotiations will not include the United States. If these emerging FTAs begin to establish a common external tariff — as the EC always has — then trade blocs may contribute to a fragmentation of the world economy. But this is a hypothetical result that is blocked by the tremendous web of global trade and financial interdependence and the domestic political interests tied to this connectedness. The balance of power still remains with this political bloc and, except in the case of a prolonged global downturn, protectionism will not win the day.

Conclusions

■ What is the future direction for competition and protection? First, there is some limited merit in the criticisms leveled at Japan, primarily in the areas of barriers to trade and investment. The Japanese retain a legacy from 250 years of isolation. Their leadership has never accepted the Western rationale for free trade, and their trading practices still retain some elements of a warlike posture. But Japan's success comes from marshaling its national resources to compete in global markets. It is as silly to condemn them for this achievement as it would be to charge the United States and Germany with unfair competition for their successes in the late nineteenth century. Attacking Japan for subsidizing industries or selling below cost to win market share is little more than sour grapes directed toward a nation that succeeds in these strategies where others have failed. The greatest part of the rhetoric attacking Japan comes from those who cannot, or will not, adjust to the new competitive environment.

Protectionist responses in this climate should come as no surprise. This is a classic case of spreading the costs of a policy across an entire society and concentrating the benefits with a few owners and workers. When these groups are privileged, they will usually obtain this special favor. Standing alongside the movement for additional trade barriers is the latent potential in economic blocs to become protectionist devices. The interesting aspect of the economic bloc is its position as a kind of halfway house between free trade and protection. In one sense, an economic bloc breaks down barriers to trade — at least among nations with acceptable competitive capabilities. At the same time, there may be a strong temptation to exclude the goods of "unfair" traders.

Can the multilateral world trading system survive the new climate of competition and protection? More specifically, can an acceptable compromise be found to keep the GATT-generated momentum for free trade alive? Even if it can, has the political capacity for cooperation in opening trade throughout the world dissipated? Many of the answers to these questions depend on whether states see their interests better served in economic blocs or in a broad multilateral system. The basic structures of the world economy — massive interbloc movement of trade and capital and robust global institutions such as the IMF — serve as an important barrier to a breakup of the postwar order. But this is a major arena for political struggle within and among nations, and the outcome remains in doubt.

Perhaps the purest example of protectionism in the twentieth century is the Communist system fostered by the Soviet Union. We turn to that topic next.

ANNOTATED BIBLIOGRAPHY

Bela Balassa, *Japan in the World Economy*, Washington: Institute for International Economics, 1988.
An overview with considerable data.

William J. Baumol, *Productivity and American Leadership: The Long View*, Cambridge: MIT Press, 1991.
Provides a detailed study of U.S. productivity.

Jagdish Bhagwati, *Protectionism*, Cambridge: MIT Press, 1988.

Jagdish Bhagwati, *The World Trading System at Risk*, Princeton: Princeton University Press, 1991.
Both books offer a spirited and convincing case against the new protectionism.

Jean Claude Derian, *America's Struggle for Leadership in Technology*, Cambridge: MIT Press, 1990.
A very useful examination of competitiveness in technology looking at several industries.

I.M. Destler, *American Trade Politics*, Washington: Institute for International Economics, 1986.
A detailed study of the political economy of trade during the early- to mid-1980s.

I.M. Destler and John Odell, *Anti-Protection: Changing Political Forces in the United States*, Washington: Institute for International Economics, 1987.
A rich set of analytical case studies.

David Friedman, *The Misunderstood Miracle*, Ithaca: Cornell University Press, 1988.
Counters the MITI thesis and focuses on the impact of small- and medium-sized manufacturing in Japan.

Takashi Inoguchi and Daniel Okimoto, eds. *The Political Economy of Japan, Volume 2, The Changing International Context*, Stanford: Stanford University Press, 1988.
A very insightful collection of essays.

Chalmers Johnson, *MITI and the Japanese Miracle*, Stanford: Stanford University Press, 1982.
An essential book on the evolution of Japan's business-government system.

Paul Krugman, *Rethinking International Trade*, Cambridge: MIT Press, 1990.
A very important critique of free trade.

Helen Milner, *Resisting Protectionism*, Princeton: Princeton University Press, 1988.
An essential source for understanding the political economy of support for free trade.

Michael Porter, *The Competitive Advantage of Nations*, New York: Free Press, 1990.
An essential study of the competitiveness of firms as they operate in a national context.

Daniel Okimoto, *Between MITI and Market*, Stanford: Stanford University Press, 1989.
Brings the analysis of changes in MITI into the 1980s.

Gilbert Winham, *International Trade and the Tokyo Round Negotiations*, Princeton: Princeton University Press, 1986.
A very detailed study of the negotiations.

Karel van Wolferen, *The Enigma of Japanese Power*, New York: Vintage Books, 1990.
Presents a very critical view of Japanese government and politics.

John Zysman and Laura Tyson, eds. *American Industry in International Competition*, Ithaca: Cornell University Press, 1983.
A dated but very helpful study of the political economy of firm competitiveness.

CHAPTER 7

Eastern Europe, the Former Soviet Union, and the World Economy

On November 8, 1917, Vladimir Ilyich Lenin appeared before the All-Russian Congress of Soviets. The previous day, Bolshevik forces had seized power from the Provisional Government in a coup. Proclaiming the goal of the revolution, Lenin concluded his speech with "We shall now proceed to construct the socialist order."[1]

Less than 74 years later, on August 19, 1991, the former communist Boris Yeltsin — the first elected president of the Russian republic — stood on a tank outside the Russian Parliament to beseech his followers and all people in the Soviet Union to resist a coup launched by members of the Communist Party against the President of the Soviet Union, Mikhail Gorbachev. Yeltsin's pleas helped to rally elements of the military to resist the coup, which was defeated shortly. Within days, the Communist Party had its activities suspended. Within four months, the Soviet Union had disintegrated, and Gorbachev himself had resigned. In January 1992, the newly independent states of the former Soviet Union adopted a policy of rapidly shifting toward free markets and something resembling capitalism. Lenin's "socialist order" was in tatters.

How are we to understand the broad trajectory of development in the Soviet Union and other Communist states and the eventual demise of this system of political, military, and social organization? One approach might emphasize the moral and political crisis of communism, another the limitations of the system, yet another its aggressive foreign policy and consequent overextension.

---

[1]Merle Fainsod, *How Russia is Ruled*, Cambridge: Harvard University Press, 1963, 84.

This chapter will sketch out an analysis consistent with the perspective offered by political economy. It will examine the problems generated by external competitive pressure on a system of political economy poorly equipped to compete. We will consider the basic characteristics of a command economy, focusing particular attention on its inherent flaws. Especially important are the problems faced by a command economy in developing institutions capable of adjustment, innovation, and dynamism in competing with the market-based system in the West. The discussion moves on to a consideration of the efforts at reform, particularly those after 1985, and the reasons for their failure. Finally, we will look at the process and problems of a transition to a market economy in postcommunist countries. The revolutionary nature of this process, the near-term and long-term economic prognosis, the likely political difficulties, and the role of Western aid are the main topics.

THE POLITICAL ECONOMY OF CHANGE IN COMMUNIST STATES

■ Any effort to conceptualize the dramatic changes in Communist states after 1985 is subject to important qualifications. The easiest qualification is that we certainly have not witnessed the end of this process, and so we must be careful not to produce an argument that can be rendered moot by a sharp turn of events. More important, any such analysis can provide only a partial understanding of a multidimensional process. The insights from political economy can give us a sense of some of the broad forces at work, but since we omit the role of such factors as ideology, leadership, and political struggle, an approach from political economy should not be taken as the final word.[2]

A central theme of this book is the importance of the competitive international environment, which we have understood as a complex process involving economic, technological, political, and military struggle. For much of its history, Russia has found itself hard-pressed to keep up with the nations of Europe in many areas of this competition. The sixty years before the Revolution in 1917 was a time of dramatic change. Russia's leaders sought to catch up with other states in Europe where industrialization was proceeding apace. The elimination of serfdom and substantial industrialization did lead to significant change. But wars with Japan in 1904–1905 and Germany from 1914 to 1917 exposed serious weaknesses. At a basic level, the capacity to produce and distribute the implements of large-scale warfare was grossly lacking. This became especially evident during the First World War when Russian

---

[2]For an effort that offers a somewhat comprehensive approach to change in communist systems, see Andrew C. Janos, "Social Science, Communism, and the Dynamics of Political Change," *World Politics*, October 1991, 81–112.

military failures, brought on by ill-equipped troops, helped spark a revolutionary movement that swept first the Czar and then a more democratic government from power. Between the two World Wars, this competition continued but in a context of economic uncertainty and depression and poorly developed institutions for managing the world economy.

During this very difficult era, several nations at somewhat different levels of industrial development embarked on a path of near-autarchy to insure their security in a hostile setting. Germany and Japan, rocked by the world depression, moved toward military aggression and closing themselves off from economic reliance on the rest of the world. Even earlier, a radical version of this strategy was adopted by Josef Stalin for the Soviet Union. Beginning in 1928–1929, Stalin dropped a more market-oriented posture and wrenched the Soviet Union toward "collectivization" and "socialism in one country." Stalin's decisions had the effect of creating a new model of political economy. After 1945, this system was imperfectly extended to the nations in Eastern Europe under Soviet military control and later to China, North Korea, Vietnam, and Cuba. This command economy became the main alternative to the world capitalist economy and was a centerpiece of the ideological struggle in the Cold War.

The development of a command economy in the Soviet Union during the 1920s and 1930s was mostly a result of the political needs of the Communist party. In 1921, a New Economic Policy had experimented with private ownership and free markets as a strategy of economic growth. Although growth occurred, it was modest and concentrated in agriculture. Peasant producers of grain were willing to accelerate production only when more consumer goods were available. Further, expansion of the private economy led to the creation of a larger class of wealthy entrepreneurs in urban and rural areas whose interests were in conflict with those of the Communist party. Stalin's victory in a power struggle with Leon Trotsky led to adoption of the policy of collectivization. This involved seizing control of all the means of production in the country. Resistance was met with military force, leading to millions of deaths. From Stalin's perspective, this eliminated those who might have resisted Communist political domination and opened the door to a development strategy designed to correct Soviet industrial backwardness.[3]

Stalinism combined political authoritarianism, control of virtually all the means of production by the state, and exclusion of external economic relations, except through a government trading company. Totalitarianism became an approximation of reality with the combination of a terroristic secret police, Communist party control of all meaningful organizations, and state allocation

---

[3]Especially useful for understanding the era are: Merle Fainsod and Jerry Hough, *How the Soviet Union is Governed*, Cambridge: Harvard University Press, 1979; Stephen F. Cohen, *Bukharin and the Bolshevik Revolution*, New York: Vintage, 1971; Alec Nove, *An Economic History of the U.S.S.R.*, New York: Penguin, 1989.

of economic resources. The essence of the system was the creation of a "garrison state" in which the process of industrialization was harnessed to the military requirements of international competition.[4] Much of the motivation for this crash program of industrialization came from fear of the West, especially Germany. Stalin was very conscious of his nation's weaknesses in military capabilities.

Thought of purely in economic terms, and ignoring the horrendous human cost, collectivization initially produced a rapid growth of industrial output. By taking control of agriculture, forcibly removing peasants from the country to the city and putting them to work in heavy industry, the state was able to achieve enormous increases in the production of steel, machinery, and raw materials. At the same time, the basic elements of a command economy were put into place. Agriculture was turned into a state enterprise on large collective farms, while heavy industry was largely created through governmental effort. In addition, a large bureaucracy designed to carry out centrally designed economic plans was established. The decade after 1928 achieved some measure of success, at least in areas related to the production of war goods. Spurred by reconstruction after World War II, growth resumed and provoked the continuing shift of peasants and workers to more productive and skilled activities. But this came at an economic cost on top of the human cost: the economic system became increasingly bureaucratic and rigid and less capable of adaptation and innovation.

Difficulties began to emerge in the late 1950s. The command economy that had proven its effectiveness in moving unused and poorly used resources toward more productive activities was much less able to organize and coordinate the multifaceted processes of input and output in an increasingly complex system. Central planning simply could not issue enough orders to the many interdependent layers of production to allow them to work together smoothly. Instead, the planners in Gosplan — the mammoth bureaucracy that designed and implemented the Five Year Plans — issued gross targets for production units. These often made little sense in terms of the needs of other economic units that required particular types of goods to reach their own targets. The result was an incoherent and even irrational economic system producing the wrong quantity of frequently low-quality goods.[5]

But the crisis of the command economy went even deeper, to the very fiber of political, economic, and social relations. The system was based on the political need for nearly total control of society and economy by the Communist party. At the same time, competition with the West and the link between expanding consumer goods and the preservation and extension of regime legitimacy created great pressure for rapid but qualitatively sophisticated economic growth. This kind of growth, which requires substantial flexibility

---

[4]This is a version of Janos, "Social Science. . . ," 97.
[5]Nove, *An Economic History.* . . , 357–359.

and dynamism in economic decisions, stood in sharp contradiction to the Party's need for control. Occasional efforts at reform designed to introduce more flexibility into the system came up against fears of loss of Party control.

After Khrushchev's ouster in 1964, his successors placed even greater reliance on bureaucratic modes of planning. The result was to entrench the position of groups whose interests lay with stability and routine. The bureaucratic system under Brezhnev gained such strength that central political leaders lost control of the economy. Information flows from bottom to top became corrupted when bureaucratic layers concealed massive failures. "A pervasive campaign of lies kept both the leaders and the populace misinformed."[6] The ability of the system to produce economic growth and goods of reasonable quality and to compete with the West ceased almost completely.

The source of this systemic crisis was the destruction of politics and economics in the fusion of state and society under Stalin and his successors.[7] The collapse of normal political and economic affairs into a realm dominated by the needs of the Communist party severely undermined the capacity of the institutions of the nation for effective adjustment and adaptation. The institutional vibrancy of nations operating in the capitalist world economy — from multinational corporations to state bureaucracies — was almost entirely absent from the communist system of state socialism.

Missing were a decentralization and autonomy of decision-making and responsibility, some meaningful criteria for measuring the success and failure of economic units, a realistic chance that these institutions could be eliminated by failure and prosper through success, and a market system capable of transmitting effective price signals to those persons responsible for production decisions. Such arrangements — approximately those of a modern market economy — create strong incentives to respond rapidly and effectively to the forces of supply and demand. When managers of business units have effective decision-making power and when those units survive and prosper only if they produce goods or services that succeed in an open market with other competing units, flexibility and dynamism will emerge.

The communist command economy, because of the centralization of decisions about production and the absence of prices based on supply and demand, was incapable of solving its own problems. Throughout the economy, goods of low quality were typical; quantities produced bore no relation to actual demand; distribution was hampered by poor delivery systems; and incentives for effective change simply did not exist. The sclerosis of Soviet society and economy became so severe that even elements of the Communist party concluded that radical reform was needed. Ironically, these efforts at change played a key role in the collapse of the system.

---

[6]Seweryn Bialer, "Gorbachev's Move," *Foreign Policy*, 68, Fall 1987, 67.

[7]This argument is made by Bartlomeij Kaminski, *The Collapse of State Socialism: The Case of Poland*, Princeton: Princeton University Press, 1991, 3–8.

Gorbachev and the Failure of Reform

The Nature of Reform

Even before Gorbachev's assumption of the position of General Secretary in 1985, some limited efforts at reform had been introduced. Half-hearted efforts at decentralization, but without meaningful price adjustments, were followed by efforts to create giant cartel-like organizations. Investment binges in areas like agriculture and attempts to plan innovation in technology had little effect on actual growth rates. Especially after Brezhnev's death in 1982, the problems of the Soviet economy and unfavorable comparisons with the West provoked a more fundamental questioning of the merits of a command economy.[8]

Over the next three years, a broad consensus on the need for significant change emerged within the Party elite. The main question for this group was whether the Soviet Union could continue as a great power.[9] Underlying this uncertainty was a recognition that the communist command economy had failed to make the transition from the development of heavy industry to high levels of mass consumption and then to the high-technology and information-based economy of the late twentieth century world. Much less clear to Communist officials was what to do about this failure. Behind virtually all proposals for change lay the potential for a serious diminution and even destruction of Communist power in the Soviet Union.

During his first three to four years, Gorbachev's strategy was based on loosening political controls and encouraging greater freedom of expression, combined with much discussion but little concrete action concerning economic restructuring. The main effect of *glasnost* was to help win public support, create a forward-looking coalition, and improve information about the real state of the Soviet economy. Only limited efforts at decentralization of decision-making were attempted, while the problem of the poor quality of goods was attacked by another bureaucracy for inspection. Although some autonomy was extended to local managers, nothing resembling a real price system was permitted.[10]

Aside from the threat that change posed to the Party bureaucracy, Gorbachev's desire for reform confronted a price system that had become a form of bribery for continued support of the system. The cost of basic commodities

---

[8]For efforts at reform in the period between Brezhnev and Gorbachev, see Timothy J. Colton, *The Dilemma of Reform in the Soviet Union*, New York: Council on Foreign Relations, 1986, 70–82.

[9]George W. Breslauer, "Linking Gorbachev's Domestic and Foreign Policies," *Journal of International Affairs*, 42.2, Spring 1989, 267.

[10]Marshall J. Goldman, *Gorbachev's Challenge: Economic Reform in the Age of High Technology*, New York: Norton, 1987, 77–78.

was maintained by massive subsidies, which permitted prices to remain exceedingly low. Any move toward genuine market-based prices would inevitably result in massive inflation and substantial economic hardship for many Soviet citizens. The resulting political backlash — in spite of the likely increase in the availability of goods as supplies rise to take advantage of higher prices — served as a major impediment to such radical reforms.

Domestic and International Politics

The combination of open political debate and persistent economic weakness produced a crisis atmosphere of increasing proportions. Issues and questions that previously were taboo — the empty shelves in stores, the proper role of the Party and the KGB, elections for local and national office, nationalities, and political independence — now became topics of fierce discussion. In this climate, support for the Communist party declined precipitously among its own membership and in the general public. The explosion of nationalism in many of the republics and the spreading demands for independence raised the specter of a disintegration of the state.

The creation of a meaningful political life after decades of domination by the Party has not yet led to a normal process of coalition formation. Not only is the tradition of open political links and trade-offs among groups missing, but the structure of interests makes the process more difficult. Old coalitions among the great power centers of Soviet society — the KGB, the Party, the bureaucracies, and the military — frayed because of turmoil and sharp differences within these groups. Republican nationalism produced a situation in which many who supported economic transformation also wanted a form of political change unacceptable to the central government. At the same time, Gorbachev's personal political standing declined due to his identification with the Communist party, economic failure, and his refusal to seek a popular mandate.

Accompanying this unraveling of the domestic system were equally dramatic shifts in foreign policy. Gorbachev engaged in important negotiations in arms control, articulated the policy of a nonthreatening defense posture, withdrew from Afghanistan, and recognized the overextension of Soviet interests abroad.[11] But domestic policy and foreign policy dovetailed most dramatically in 1988–1989 over Eastern Europe. Here weaknesses at home and long-standing difficulties in maintaining domination of Eastern Europe combined to produce a sudden and complete collapse of Soviet power in this area. Further, the disintegrating Soviet position in this great prize from World War II merged with the political and economic crisis at home to destabilize the system even more.

---

[11]Breslauer, "Linking Gorbachev's. . . "; and Seweryn Bialer, "The Domestic and International Sources of Gorbachev's Reforms," *Journal of International Affairs*, 42.2, Spring 1989, 283–297.

The events in Eastern Europe are also important in their own right, especially as an indication of the pathways from communist autarchy to participation in the world economy. Stalinism here was a result of Soviet occupation in World War II and the determination to retain control after 1945. Intensification of the Cold War in 1947 produced an even more heavy-handed domination with direct extension of the Soviet system westward. The result was a vicious version of nineteenth century imperialism, with the resources of Eastern Europe used on a massive scale to help rebuild the Soviet Union.[12] Stalin's death in 1953 ushered in a two-decade period of revolts against Soviet rule and some greater flexibility in techniques of control. Various forms of demonstration, riot, and revolution occurred in East Germany in 1953, Poland and Hungary in 1956, Czechoslovakia in 1968, and Poland in 1970. In 1956 and 1968, Soviet military force was used to crush independence movements in Hungary and Czechoslovakia. But alongside this intervention came an increasing recognition of the international political costs of such actions and a growing tolerance for limited economic experimentation. The Soviet hope was that economic growth would help stabilize these regimes. Restricted mainly to Hungary and Poland, this reform went beyond anything in the Soviet Union, but it did little to reshape their economic systems. In Hungary, the replacement of political criteria for planning with economic criteria did produce an initial jump in output but eventually resulted in a dead end for economic growth. During the 1970s and 1980s, borrowing from the West and energy subsidies from the Soviets helped close the gap between economic performance and expectations. Neither of these efforts made any real contribution to economic reform. Instead, Eastern Europe was caught in a sullen acceptance of Communist rule and a growing recognition of the vast differences in living standards between themselves and the West.[13]

The first real crack in the system occurred in Poland in 1980–1981. The labor union Solidarity, created to protest rising prices and a poor economy, succeeded in carving out a significant measure of political independence. Solidarity began to operate as a public interest group — claiming to represent all of the Polish people — in negotiations with the government over prices, wages, and political rights. Eventually, the Polish government and military, along with the Soviet government, found they could not accept the political demands made by such a powerful and independent organization. In December 1981, martial law was declared, Solidarity outlawed, and its leaders arrested. What followed was a period of several years in which the government was forced to adopt aspects of the Solidarity program (even with Solidarity officially repressed) as it tried unsuccessfully to deal with a national political paralysis and economic crisis.

---

[12]Charles Gati, *The Bloc That Failed: Soviet–East European Relations in Transition*, Bloomington: Indiana University Press, 1990, 24.
[13]Gati, *The Bloc. . .* , 29–62.

The continuing stagnation and deterioration in the economy drained the government of legitimacy. The spark for political change was provided by Gorbachev's announcement in 1988 of the unilateral withdrawal of some Soviet troops from Eastern Europe. This signaled the end of Soviet military protection for Communist regimes in this region. Motivated partly by the deepening crisis in the Soviet Union and partly by the adamant rejection of reform by much of the Communist leadership in Eastern Europe, this announcement had major repercussions. It was followed quickly by the reinstatement of Solidarity and the creation of what amounted to a coalition government in Poland consisting of the Communist party, the military, and Solidarity.[14]

These events opened the door to the political revolutions of 1989. The fragility of all Communist regimes in Eastern Europe was demonstrated by the cascading political crisis that ensued. Stunning electoral losses by the Polish Communist party and rapid political liberalization in Hungary were amplified in importance by another statement from Gorbachev foreswearing military intervention.[15] The Hungarian Party, sensing the tenuousness of its position, decided to curry favor with its people by permitting East German citizens to travel to West Germany where they could expect to be welcomed. The ensuing flood of refugees from East to West was symptomatic of the pathetic illegitimacy of the East German regime. But mass demonstrations and pressure by Gorbachev on Communist parties in other states also led to the disintegration of communism throughout Eastern Europe between October and December 1989.[16]

The Collapse of Communism in the Soviet Union

The biggest domino — the Communist party of the Soviet Union — survived another twenty months but likewise met its end in a dramatic fashion. Although some efforts at political reform continued, the dominant feature of Soviet life during 1990–1991 was an increasing political paralysis. Three special aspects of the Soviet situation worked against greater innovation. The continuing economic crisis, the political instability caused by independence movements in many of the republics (including Russia), and the trauma produced by the loss of Eastern Europe and Moscow's standing as a superpower all undercut efforts to forge a coherent program of change.

---

[14]Gati, *The Bloc. . .* , 61–66.

[15]With this statement, Gorbachev renounced the Brezhnev Doctrine, enunciated in 1968 to justify the Soviet military intervention in Czechoslovakia. Brezhnev announced that the Soviet Union had the right to use military force to protect socialist regimes in Eastern Europe.

[16]Gati, *The Bloc. . .* , 161–190.

Economic deterioration accelerated in 1990–1991, with the Soviet economy moving into a steep recession. Several plans for radical reform via a quick shift to a market economy were floated as a trial balloon only to die from the absence of a supporting consensus. Criticism from conservative circles prompted Gorbachev to backtrack and attempt to find a compromise solution.[17] The loss of superpower status cut into the position of the KGB and military, institutions benefitting from this status. And the unremitting pressure for independence by various republics placed the economic and political viability of the state itself in doubt.

These events came to a head in late August 1991, when conservative elements of the Communist party attempted to seize power from President Gorbachev and restore order. The rapid collapse of this effort not only revealed internal divisions within even groups like the KGB and military but also ushered in a popular attack on the Communist party itself.[18] In a stunning set of actions, Gorbachev quit as head of the Communist party, and the Party itself was suspended from political activity.[19] Perhaps most astounding was the decision to eliminate the central government and replace it with a government controlled by fully independent republics.[20] What did not follow, at least initially, was adoption of a plan for dismantling the existing economic system and its replacement by free markets. Instead, only fragile and uncertain efforts toward reestablishing economic union among the republics came in the wake of the failed coup.[21] The effect of the failed coup was to drain power from the central government and increase the significance of the individual republics. Gorbachev's fate hinged on support from Boris Yeltsin, the elected president of the Russian republic, and defeat of the coup enhanced Yeltsin's stature. The weakness of the central government shifted political initiative to the republics. The two most important — Russia and Ukraine — were determined to pursue their own agendas. For Russia and Yeltsin, it was a rapid transition to market reforms; for Ukraine, it was altering the political and economic terms of its relationship with other republics. These two republics withdrew their support from the Soviet government, which meant Russia

---

[17]For a sampling of the many stories of these events, see Bill Keller, "Gorbachev Turns to the Forces of Law and Order," *New York Times*, December 16, 1990; Serge Schmemann, "Gorbachev to Mix Plans on Economy of Left and Right," *New York Times*, June 22, 1991; Francis X. Clines, "Moscow Planning Tries to Sell New Plan," *New York Times*, August 12, 1991; "Beyond Perestroika," *The Economist*, June 9, 1990.

[18]Predictions of a coup from reformers can be seen in Francis X. Clines, "An Ex-Gorbachev Ally Warns of a Coup," *New York Times*, August 17, 1991. For the aftermath, see Bill Keller, "Soviets' Rush Toward Disunion Spreads," *New York Times*, August 26, 1991.

[19]Serge Schmemann, "Soviets Bar Communist Party Activities," *New York Times*, August 30, 1991; Serge Schmemann, "Gorbachev Quits as Party Head," *New York Times*, August 25, 1991.

[20]Serge Schmemann, "Soviet Congress Yields Rule to Republics to Avoid Political and Economic Collapse," *New York Times*, September 6, 1991.

[21]Francis X. Clines, "Soviet Republics Agree to Create an Economic Union," *New York Times*, October 12, 1991.

withholding tax revenues and Ukraine refusing to sign a new union treaty. These actions effectively sealed the fate of the central government. Change came rapidly in December 1991 as eleven of the fifteen republics created the Commonwealth of Independent States (CIS), thereby eliminating the Soviet Union and Gorbachev's position as president.

The situation at the beginning of 1992 is depicted in Figure 7.1 and Table 7.1.

FIGURE 7.1

Map of Commonwealth of Independent States
Showing the Various States

TABLE 7.1

Former Soviet Republics GNP and Poplulation

	% Former Soviet GNP	Population in Millions	% of Former Soviet Population	% Nationalities
RUSSIA	61.1	147.4	51.4	83 Russian
BALTIC STATES				
Estonia	0.6	1.5	0.6	68 Estonian
Latvia	1.1	2.7	1.0	54 Latvian
				33 Russian
Lithuania	1.4	3.7	1.3	80 Lithuanian
				9 Russian
				8 Polish
SLAVIC STATES				
Ukraine	16.2	51.7	18.0	74 Ukrainian
				21 Russian
Moldova	1.2	4.3	1.5	64 Moldavian
				14 Ukrainian
				13 Russian
Belarus	4.2	10.2	3.5	79 Belarussian
				12 Russian
				4 Polish
CAUCASUS				
Georgia	1.6	5.5	1.9	69 Georgian
				9 Armenian
				9 Russian
Armenia	0.9	3.3	1.2	90 Armenian
				5 Azeri
Azerbaijan	1.7	7.1	2.4	78 Azeri
				8 Russian
				8 Armenian
CENTRAL ASIA				
Kazakhstan	4.3	16.5	5.7	36 Kazakhs
				41 Russian
				6 Ukrainian
Uzbekistan	3.3	19.9	6.9	69 Uzbeks
				13 Russian
Turkmenistan	0.7	3.6	1.3	68 Turkmeni
				13 Russian
				9 Uzbeks
Tajikistan	0.8	5.1	1.8	59 Tadzhiks
				23 Uzbek
				10 Russian
Kyrgyzstan	0.8	4.4	1.5	52 Kirghiz
				22 Russian
				13 Uzbeks

SOURCE: This data is from the *New York Times*, September 1, 1991, E-2.

Among the newly independent states in the CIS, certainly Russia and Ukraine are the best situated to succeed in the long run.[22] Both possess large populations, large industrial complexes, and substantial natural resources. Belarus also enjoys some of the same capabilities. The Baltic states — Latvia, Lithuania, and Estonia — have not joined the CIS but might change their minds. Each of the Baltic states is heavily industrialized but may find access to the markets of the CIS more appealing (and more open) than those of the EC. Moldova was traditionally part of Romania and might move toward reintegration. Three small southern states — Georgia, Armenia, and Azerbaijan — have been the scene of heavy fighting and intense political conflict. The five Asian states — Kazakhstan, Uzbekistan, Turkmenistan, Kyrgyzstan, and Tajikistan — have large Muslim populations and are generally poorer than the rest. But Kazakhstan and Uzbekistan are certainly big enough and have sufficient natural resources to support economic growth.

The collapse of the Soviet Union and the creation of the CIS were quickly followed by dramatic economic moves. On January 2, 1992, Russia moved toward free markets and prices for most goods, thereby taking the decisive step to eliminate a command economy. This come about two years after a similar action by Poland and somewhat less drastic reform policies in other East European states. We now turn to a more detailed examination of the nature of this transformation from communism to a more market-based system.

POST-COMMUNIST STATES
AND THE WORLD ECONOMY

■ There is no better measure of the influence of the world economy than its impact on those communist states who excluded themselves from it for more than half a century. The dazzle of high incomes, technological innovation, and rapid economic growth played a key role in drawing these nations away from autarchy. The acceleration of growth in the 1980s, the dynamism of the European Community, the economic surge of Japan, and the threat of advancing military technology helped spur efforts at economic reform. The collapse of reform communism and the Soviet withdrawal from the field of competition appears to open a new era for the world economy — one of great promise but also new threats.

The integration into the capitalist world economy of more than 400 million persons, located in a dozen or more states and even more ethnic groups, all with low levels of income and serious weaknesses in competitiveness, is

---

[22]The Commonwealth that was created in December has not taken shape. The arrangements for economic cooperation, separate currencies, disposition of Soviet military capabilities, and political coordinating bodies remain unclear.

a daunting task. It is fraught with danger from the likelihood that economic transformation will be accompanied by even lower incomes, much higher inflation and unemployment, and the retraining and displacement of a large proportion of the population. This will also place great demands on the political and economic systems in the West.

We have seen how private and public capital flows have expanded technology, markets, and prosperity. The significant complementarity of interests between post-communist states and the West should not obscure the competitive and conflictual dimensions of this process. Integration also means opening world markets to the goods produced by former communist societies. This will surely play havoc with labor-intensive manufacturers and agricultural producers in Europe and elsewhere. Like much of our previous analysis of international political economy, this situation contains a complex balance of complementary and conflicting interests.

During the Tet Offensive in South Vietnam in 1968, a U.S. commander issued a famous justification for an especially brutal and destructive bombardment: "We had to destroy the town in order to save it." In many ways, this epigram of another time and place is more appropriate for Eastern Europe and the Soviet Union, for in order to save this area, much of its existing economic system must be destroyed. This will be very painful and dangerous.

Components of Economic Change

What are the main features of the economic transformation of post-communist states? Before answering this question, it is important to keep three things in mind. First, change of this sort will take a long time, perhaps two or three decades. Second, in many ways the changes have an organic quality in that developments in several areas depend on each other. Failure in any one area can therefore derail the whole process. Third, although the countries of the former Soviet bloc share the experience of command economies, there are substantial differences in history, politics, geography, and culture that will affect their development.

There is significant agreement among Western thinkers about what must be done to bring post-communist states into the capitalist world economy. Disagreement centers mainly on whether the pace of change needs to be moderate or rapid. The main lines of agreement are found in Table 7.2.

The basic and most important consequence of macroeconomic stabilization and restructuring is to create an effective market system in which prices act to transmit meaningful signals to producers about what to produce. Control of monetary and fiscal policy is needed to make sure that government actions in spending, taxation, and printing money do not distort prices through inflation. As we have seen, large budget deficits financed through an expanding money supply lead to inflation. The greatest part of government outlay in the former Soviet Union has been military spending, subsidies to firms, and price subsidies for basic commodities. Assuming a balanced set of government accounts (which also means an enormous cut in subsidies), opening the door to foreign goods and establishing a convertible currency will serve to "import world prices," and this will help ensure that production will reflect a nation's position of comparative advantage in the world economy.[23]

TABLE 7.2

Components of Transformation to Market Economy

I. MACROECONOMIC STABILIZATION AND RESTRUCTURING
    A. End fiscal deficits and establish monetary stability
    B. Eliminate controlled prices and state subsidies
    C. Base exchange rate on real prices
    D. Create a convertible currency
    E. Eliminate tariffs, quotas, and other trade barriers

II. INSTITUTIONAL REFORMS
    A. Transfer control of state firms to private hands
    B. Establish financial system with private banks
    C. Ensure legal protection of private property and eliminate restrictions on entrepreneurial activity
    D. Create legal guarantees for foreign investment and repatriation of profits
    E. Create new tax system
    F. Protect severely disadvantaged groups

SOURCE: This table is based in part on Susan M. Collins and Dani Rodrik, *Eastern Europe and the Soviet Union in the World Economy*, Washington: Institute for International Economics, 1991, 11; and "Business in Eastern Europe," *The Economist*, September 21, 1991, 6.

But even in the best of circumstances, instituting free markets and prices based on supply and demand will certainly lead to substantial inflation. This is because prices set under the old command economy, especially for basic commodities, contained no meaningful relationship to actual supply and demand. Free markets will result in large price increases to reflect actual scarcity and thereby produce substantial inflation.

Economic Change in the Soviet Union

The problems associated with establishing free markets were especially acute in the former Soviet Union. The command economy was the strongest here,

---

[23]Collins and Rodrik, *Eastern Europe. . . ,* 12; and John Williamson, *The Economic Opening of Eastern Europe,* Washington: Institute for International Economics, 1991, 22.

and the least progress had been made toward actual reform. Establishing free markets confronted more than sixty years of a command economy where the culture of markets, prices, and profits had been deeply suppressed. Several years of delay led to a near collapse of the old system, some development of market prices in an underground economy, and a frightening decline in actual production. Partially responsible for this state of affairs was a debilitating imbalance in government accounts and mismanagement of the money supply. The root of the crisis was the breakdown in the system of spending and taxation. The combined budget deficits of the central government and the republics totaled as much as 25 percent of GNP. Inflation reached as high as 365 percent per year in 1991, approaching the level of hyperinflation that can destroy entire economic systems. Growth in the money supply was completely out of control, limited only to the production capacity of printing presses.[24]

The beginning of the Russian "big bang" came on January 2, 1992 when prices were freed for all commodities except basic food and fuel. For these "essentials" a slower process of decontrol was used. Other former republics joined this process very reluctantly and only after it became clear that Russia planned to go ahead with it. An explosion of prices followed, with many rising as much as tenfold. The price system remains very primitive, with information and supply networks frequently nonexistent and commodity exchanges often little more than "flea markets." As these arrangements develop, prices may fall back a bit. The government has announced plans for massive cuts in military spending and subsidies so as to balance the budget. If successful, this should help hold down inflationary pressures and contribute to stabilizing the value of the ruble. The sorting out process that comes from creating the infrastructure of markets, importing world prices with a convertible currency, and developing production units capable of responding to price incentives will inevitably take some time. Unclear is just how much time is available.

Early reaction to the "big bang" was generally one of resigned acceptance, but scattered demonstrations and acts of violence indicated a potential backlash. Markets systems and rising prices typically exacerbate class differences. Those with low incomes and little savings are forced to make very unpleasant choices on what to buy. These circumstances generate intense pressure for increasing wages. The central bank, acting at cross purposes with the government, continued a very expansionary monetary policy. This made granting wage demands much easier. Yeltsin received passionate criticism, even from former supporters of his programs. Some demonstrations were led by military

---

[24]"Free Fall," *The Economist*, September 28, 1991, 73. These estimates in the Fall of 1991 may have been too optimistic. In January 1992, inflation was estimated at 700 percent and the decline of GDP at 40 percent. G. Bruce Knecht, "From Soviet Minister to Corporate Chief," *New York Times Magazine*, January 26, 1992, 25.

officers, and the danger remains that former communists will use their continuing institutional positions to organize a political opposition that capitalizes on the pain of economic reform. The substantial differences in resources and productive capabilities among the former republics led them to embargo the transportation of some goods across their borders, and they began the process of establishing separate currencies. The great difficulties associated with the change from communism to capitalism present an extraordinary challenge to the fragile political order in many of the newly independent states of the former Soviet Union.[25]

Economic Change in Eastern Europe

A somewhat more favorable, but still difficult, situation can be found in Poland, which carried out even more of these same macroeconomic reforms in early 1990. Faced with inflation rates worse than in the CIS, the Polish government, under Solidarity, freed prices, gained control of fiscal and monetary policies by cutting subsidies, established currency convertibility at a market rate, placed a ceiling on wage increases, and liberalized trade. This version of the "big bang" created most of the elements of a market system in one bold stroke. Given the inherent difficulties in this transition, the result (at the end of 1991) has been mixed but mostly positive in economic terms. Politically, the Solidarity coalition has fallen apart. Initially, the budget deficit was eliminated and inflation fell, but more recently these problems have returned. Inflation for 1991 is estimated at 80 percent, down from 600 percent in 1990 and 250 percent in 1989. Foreign trade is in balance, goods are plentiful, and the private sector has expanded considerably.

But overall, the decline in state-owned firms has more than offset this growth. Industrial output fell by more than 28 percent in 1990 and is expected to decline by another 10 percent in 1991. Unemployment has risen to more than 10 percent, and real income has fallen by as much as one-quarter.[26] Feeding off these problems is an increasingly fragmented political situation. The broad coalition established by Solidarity has come unglued, as shown by the splintered voting in the first post-communist election. Thirteen parties divided almost 90 percent of the vote, with the ex-communists taking one-fifth of the parliamentary seats in an election that appeared to reject the strategy of a rapid move to free markets. The election resulted in a government headed

---

[25]Reaction to economic reform is found in the following reports from the *New York Times*: Francis X. Clines, "Ex-Ally of Yeltsin Demands Cabinet's Ouster Over Prices," January 14, 1992; Serge Schmemann, "5,000 Angry Military Men Gather With Complaints in the Kremlin," and "Uzbek Students Riot in Worst Violence on Prices," both in January 18, 1992; Celestine Bohlen, "New Russian Budget Is Strong Medicine," January 25, 1992; and "Ruble-Rich Ukrainians Looking for Bargains," January 29, 1992.

[26]"Business in Eastern Europe," *The Economist*, September 21, 1991, 5; Collins and Rodrik, *Eastern. . . .* , 15–17.

by an avowed critic of free markets and financial discipline. This leaves the political viability of the "big bang" in doubt.[27]

Hungary and Yugoslavia offer some interesting variations on the Polish model. Before 1989, both countries had pursued substantial market reforms. Since then, Hungary has adopted a limited version of Poland's "big bang" with some controls remaining on foreign exchange and trade. The effects have been more moderate than in Poland with a balanced foreign trade, inflation at 36 percent, rising unemployment, and falling industrial output. Yugoslavia, by contrast, has been torn by a civil war partly related to efforts to control inflation. Prior to 1989, Yugoslavia lacked any central monetary authority with several units having the power to issue money. The effort to create a central bank located in Serbia clashed with the independent authorities in the economically advanced areas of Slovenia and Croatia. Policies similar to those in Poland, regarding prices and convertibility, also broke down over regional differences. This resulted in efforts to win independence by Croatia and Slovenia and a move by a militarily superior Serbia to gain the upper hand through force. The Yugoslav economy is in tatters, and any solution seems very distant.[28]

Czechoslovakia, Romania, and Bulgaria also present variations on the Polish model. Czechoslovakia is the most economically advanced nation in the region and has adopted a slower transition to a market system. The results include very favorable international balances and a less brutal economic decline. Even so, the shift toward free markets threatens many in the less developed sections of Slovakia, and this has fueled an independence movement. Bulgaria followed a similar path, but its lower level of development and lack of political consensus have hindered real progress. Perhaps the greatest difficulty is the persistent large budget deficit that undermines efforts to shift to market prices. Romania has taken the fewest steps toward a market economy. There, successors to the Communists remain in control and have hesitated to launch a policy that will almost surely sweep them from power. The result is much like that in the former Soviet Union, with output dropping and inflation rising.[29]

Ironically, what formerly was East Germany is in both the best and the worst of situations. It has the advantage of becoming part of a booming and strong capitalist economy in Germany and has reaped the benefits of aid and

---

[27]"How Many Polish Parties Does It Take to Make a Cabinet?" *The Economist*, November 2, 1991; Stephen Engleberg, "Economic Tonic Braces Poland, But Ills Remain," *New York Times*, October 25, 1991; Gabrielle Glaser, "Walesa Picks Economic Foe as Premier," *New York Times*, December 6, 1991.

[28]Marlise Simons, "A Sign of Bad Times in Yugoslavia: Trade War Between Two Republics," *New York Times*, January 28, 1990; Stephen Engelberg, "Feuds Crippling Yugoslav Economy," *New York Times*, April 20, 1991; "Business in Eastern Europe," *The Economist*, September 21, 1991, 9; Collins and Rodrik, *Eastern. . .* , 17–18.

[29]"Business in Eastern Europe," *The Economist*, September 21, 1991, 5, 9.

investment. But the experience of incorporation into West Germany has also had devastating effects on the present economy. Industrial production has fallen by 50 percent, far more than in Poland, and unemployment may reach one-half of the work force. The reason for this is that East German goods simply could not compete in quality or price with those from the West. Further complicating matters has been an increase in wages, reducing competitiveness even more. For the combined Germany, a large trade surplus has been wiped out and replaced by a small deficit, and rising inflation led the Bundesbank to raise interest rates to the highest levels since the 1940s. In the long run, the success of the old East Germany is dependent on its capacity to develop industries based on its comparative advantage in Germany and in Europe. This may require replacing much of this area's capital stock and rebuilding its infrastructure. At the end of 1991, the combination of government investment ($83 billion in 1991) and private investment had produced some cause for optimism in the east.[30]

A key element of the integration of Eastern Europe into the world economy is its ability to develop new and successful patterns of foreign trade. Although autarchy was a key element in the original view of a command economy in the 1920s and 1930s, it became a less accurate description of affairs beginning in the 1960s. The Council for Mutual Economic Assistance (CMEA) was established in the 1940s to facilitate trade within the Soviet bloc in Eastern Europe. By 1987, as much as one-fifth to one-third of production in Poland and Hungary was for export. But this was heavily concentrated within the bloc, with exports to other Eastern European countries or the Soviet Union accounting for 40 percent to 80 percent of total exports.[31] This also means that even before the reforms of 1990–1991, some trade with the West was taking place. Trade within CMEA was defined primarily by implicit Soviet subsidies resulting from Soviet sales of raw materials (mostly oil) at below world market prices and the purchase of manufactured goods from Eastern Europe that could not meet world standards. This arrangement has already changed to the detriment of Eastern Europe.[32]

The most likely trade partners in the future are those where precommunist trade was concentrated: in Western Europe and among each other. This scenario raises serious questions about the willingness of the European Community to open its markets in areas where it has traditionally seen the need for protection, namely agriculture and low technology manufactures. But resistance to this process of a shifting division of labor could bring reform

---

[30]Bruce Stokes, "Germany's Trauma," *National Journal*, May 4, 1991, 1040–1043; Ferdinand Protzman, "A Cost of German Unity," *New York Times*, June 12, 1991; Stephen Kinzer, "East Germans, Nurtured by Bonn, Take Heart and Begin to Prosper," *New York Times*, September 29, 1991.

[31]Percentages for 1988 are given in Collins and Rodrik, *Eastern. . .* , 30; trade totals for 1987 are given in Williamson, *The Economic. . .* , 5.

[32]John Pinder, *The European Community and Eastern Europe*, London: Pinter, 1991, 92.

in Eastern Europe to a halt. Some form of multilateral trade negotiations will be needed to facilitate these new trade patterns.

Privatization

We have concentrated on the process of freeing domestic markets, prices, and foreign trade. But this will lead to economic growth only if there are entrepreneurs with control over productive assets who can respond to price signals with output. Perhaps the most difficult barrier to effective economic change in Eastern Europe and the former Soviet Union is the fact that command economies concentrated control of economic resources in the state. For markets to work, these assets must be in the hands of persons who are capable of effectively organizing production and competing with domestic and foreign firms.

This means that state-owned firms must be transferred to private control, a complicated and difficult process. The collapse of the central planning authority in many of these countries means that effective control of many firms has passed from the government to the workers and managers of those firms. Very often, this has resulted in simply stealing the firm's assets by groups who lack the incentives or knowledge to make them into profitable enterprises. Beyond this, privatizing state businesses is blocked by the lack of private capital and the absence of institutions for organizing the capital that does exist. There are no substantial stock markets or commercial banks in most of Eastern Europe. Also missing is an effective system of accounting to give some sense of the assets, profits, and losses of these entities. One important difference between Eastern Europe and the CIS comes in who is permitted to own and manage the new private firms. In the CIS former Communist managers and even ministers have played a key role in redesigning the old state firms. Governments in Eastern Europe have shied away from this arrangement, leaving them to try to create a new managerial and ownership class.[33] Perhaps the only solution there is to establish some procedure for giving the assets to the population at large and letting natural entrepreneurialism and markets take over. This is the plan in Czechoslovakia, where each citizen can invest about one week's pay (equal to approximately $35) for coupons that can be exchanged for stock in the state enterprise of their choice. But this giveaway strategy is an enormous risk, given the lack of business experience and the fact that the plan will produce no managerial changes and little new capital.[34]

---

[33] Knecht, "From Soviet. . . ," 25–26.

[34] Again, the discussion in "Business in Eastern Europe," *The Economist*, September 21, 1991, 10–20, is very helpful. Also see, "Czechs by the Millions Are Investing $35 in a State Bargain," *New York Times*, January 21, 1992.

This discussion of privatization helps to highlight the problem of the sequence of reforms. Given the organic quality of the needed changes in prices, ownership, trade, and institutions, any effort to define a precise set of stages is hopeless and even dangerous. Furthermore, these nations have already started into the process, most frequently attacking the area of prices first. Nevertheless, there are significant issues associated with deciding what to do when. If privatization cannot occur without an efficient banking system, should the government create this first? But if profitable private firms don't exist for banks to lend to, what is the mechanism for developing a viable system of private banking? In general terms, the problem confronting Eastern Europe involves creating an entire economic system, when each of the parts can only function properly as all the other parts come into place. This is equivalent to requiring that everything be done at once or nothing be done at all.[35]

Aid From Capitalist States?

Much has also been made of the role that might be played by the capitalist world in promoting and assisting change in Eastern Europe and the former Soviet Union. However, we should be somewhat restrained in our expectations of the likely scale of this help and its probable impact. The two main paths for aid are trade and money. Because of the scale of needs and the contradictory interests of Western societies, neither path should be seen as a central element in supporting or easing the pain of change.

Some of the relatively easy decisions have already been made. All six East European countries are now members of GATT, the IMF, and the World Bank. Several former Soviet republics, including Russia, are to be admitted to the IMF and World Bank. This opens the door to technical help and aid. In addition, one-half of Poland's government-to-government debt of $33 billion was written off in March 1991. Both Bulgaria's and Hungary's debts are substantial but are owed to private banks. Some form of Western help in rescheduling these debts may occur.[36] In late 1991, members of the G–7 agreed to postpone the annual principal payment of $6 billion in the foreign debt of the former Soviet Union. The total of this debt may be as high as $70 billion. The deferment averted imminent default and was conditioned on the former republics assuming the debt of the former Soviet Union.[37]

---

[35] An excellent elaboration of the issues involved in the sequencing problem can be found in "Business in Eastern Europe," *The Economist*, September 21, 1991, 5–6.

[36] Pinder, *The European. . .* , 93.

[37] Serge Schmemann, "Creditors to Let Soviets Postpone Paying Principal," *New York Times*, November 22, 1991.

But any realistic measure of possible Western aid pales when we consider the capital requirements needed to bring Eastern Europe and the CIS up to the same income and productivity levels as their Western neighbors. The capital needs of this area are immense due mainly to the poor quality of much of the capital stock accumulated under communism. One estimate of the requirements for a ten-year transition to raise income and productivity levels to the standards of Western Europe is more than $1.5 trillion dollars per year.[38] An optimistic estimate of the likely amounts of net capital transfers from official Western sources and private banks to both the CIS and Eastern Europe (excluding Germany) is $30 billion per year.[39] Clearly, the source of the largest proportion of capital must be from domestic savings. There is also some doubt as to whether aid will help or hurt the process of establishing free markets. Aid might be used to shore up the existing system or simply be siphoned off into corruption. Conversely, outside support may be essential to stabilize the ruble and other currencies. These uncertainties and the formidable scale of the capital requirements may have contributed to the vague state of aid plans from the West.[40]

Pessimistic conclusions about the process of change must be tempered by the fact that the interests of the West in a successful transition from Communism to market economies are very large. High incomes in Eastern Europe and the CIS create natural markets for the goods of the capitalist West. At the same time, failure generates not only a bad market but millions of immigrants and political instability. Probably the most important act for the West would be to throw open its markets to the goods of these post-communist states. The availability of a giant market would make it much easier to attract private capital for modernization. But such an arrangement is very unlikely for two reasons. First, this could drain capital from the West to the East at undesirable levels. Second, it would require that Western states accept the political consequences of displacing many of their workers and businesses who could not compete with the new imports. Indeed, there is already considerable evidence of reluctance to take these steps.[41]

---

[38]Collins and Rodrik, *Eastern.* . . , 76–79.
[39]Collins and Rodrik, *Eastern.* . . , 83–89.
[40]Thomas L. Friedman, "Ex-Soviet Lands to Get Swift Aid," *New York Times*, January 24, 1992. Estimates of actual aid include $45 billion to Eastern Europe and $80 billion to the former Soviet Union from 1989 to 1991. The overwhelming role of Germany must be noted. For example, $46 billion of the $80 billion to the former Soviet Union came from Germany, much of it designed to facilitate Soviet acceptance of reunification. See *Orlando Sentinel*, January 23, 1992, A–3; and Paul Montgomery, "Aid to Eastern Europe Estimated at $45 Billion," *New York Times*, November 12, 1991. The role of private investment has been much smaller. For this and indications of problems in German investment in Eastern Europe, see Stephen Engelberg, "Eager if Uneasy, East Europe Accepts German Investments," and Ferdinand Protzman, "Germany Curbs Trade Aid for Former Soviet States," both in *New York Times*, January 23, 1992.
[41]This paragraph relies on Pinder, *The European.* . . , 3, 17; and "Business in Eastern Europe," *The Economist*, September 21, 1991, 6.

PROSPECTS FOR THE FUTURE

■ Predicting the course of events for post-communist states is an adventure for the foolhardy and naive. There are many variables that could redirect events in ways we cannot now foresee. At best, offering a short catalogue of circumstances that may shape the direction of change seems the wisest path.

In the past, neither reform nor revolutionary change have persisted for very long without prompting a backlash or reaction that can stop or even reverse course. This is certainly a possibility in all post-communist states, especially when we imagine a beleaguered population beset by the traumas of economic dislocation turning to more conservative groups who promise relief. Even if these societies successfully traverse the initial downturn and begin the process of growth, significant economic reverses can be expected. In the best of circumstances, growth is an uneven process. And given the fragility of these societies and their dependence on external markets and capital, major problems should come as no surprise.

A second dimension of uncertainty involves the fact that the development of post-communist societies comes at a critical juncture for the world economy. The European Community is on the verge of its own transformation into a single market with strengthened processes of centralized decision. The United States is militarily strong but economically weak. Remember, the United States is the largest debtor country in the world, with an enormous budget deficit of its own.[42] And Japan remains uncertain about its role in Asia and in global affairs. Given fear of Japan in Europe and Japan's own interests in Asia and the United States, a major role in this process seems unlikely. The diversity of the positions of the main actors in the world economy raises the question of whether they can cooperate with each other to deal effectively with the wrenching process of change in Eastern Europe. Although the rich nations in the world economy cannot solve these problems, their actions can affect the character and pace of events.

Finally, there is the relationship of security and economic growth. Economic instability and dislocation frequently contribute to problems of military security. Remember that World War I, World War II, and the Cold War all began over Eastern Europe. Events in Yugoslavia and the Soviet Union have already produced military confrontation and bloodshed. The main questions involve whether economic development can occur in the absence of a sense of physical security among the populations and elites of the area and whether security systems can be developed to cope with the military consequences of economic difficulties. Peace in Europe over the past forty years is a result of a complex mixture of bipolarity, U.S. commitment and involvement, and

---

[42]Indeed, some might say that the advice offered to states in Eastern Europe and the former Soviet Union applies to the United States as well.

a variety of international institutions. Uncertainties abound about the future, but most thinking suggests that without a major commitment from the most powerful capitalist states, insecurity, disorder, and war may prevail in and among post-communist states.[43]

ANNOTATED BIBLIOGRAPHY

Susan M. Collins and Dani Rodrik, *Eastern Europe and the Soviet Union in the World Economy*, Washington: Institute for International Economics, 1991.
An extraordinarily rich source of information and analysis.

Padma Desai, *Perestroika in Perspective*, Princeton: Princeton University Press, 1989.
An analysis of the economic dimensions of reform.

Charles Gati, *The Bloc That Failed*, Bloomington: Indiana University Press, 1990.
A very detailed study of political relations after 1985.

Bartlomiej Kaminski, *The Collapse of State Socialism*, Princeton: Princeton University Press, 1991.
The best theoretical analysis of the internal flaws of the command economy.

Michael Mandelbaum, ed. *The Rise of Nations in the Soviet Union*, New York: Council on Foreign Relations Press, 1991.
A useful collection of essays focusing on U.S. policy alternatives.

Alec Nove, *An Economic History of the U.S.S.R.*, New York: Penguin, 1989.
A classic source.

John Pinder, *The European Community and Eastern Europe*, London: Pinter Publishers, 1991.
An indispensable source.

Graham Smith, ed. *The Nationalities Question in the Soviet Union*, London: Longman, 1990.
A detailed look at each former republic.

---

[43]For a thorough discussion of these issues, see John Mearsheimer, "Back to the Future: Instability in Europe After the Cold War," *International Security*, 15.1, Summer 1990, 5–56; Jack Snyder, "Averting Anarchy in the New Europe," *International Security*, 14.4, Spring 1990, 5–41; and Stephen Van Evera, "Primed For Peace: Europe After the Cold War," *International Security*, 15.3, Winter 1990/91, 7–57.

CHAPTER 8

RICH AND POOR STATES
IN THE WORLD ECONOMY

During the first forty years of the post-World War II era, world politics largely revolved around the ideological chasm between the East and the West. With the waning of the Cold War, however, coming decades seem likely to bring growing attention to the development gap between the North and the South. This disparity takes the form of astonishing contrasts between the life prospects of the average citizen of the world's poor countries, whose population approaches four billion, and the typical resident of the rich countries, which are home to roughly eight hundred million people.[1]

The present level of international social and economic inequality is historically unprecedented. Before this century living standards had never diverged so widely across different countries and regions of the world. The moral and political issues raised by this inequitable distribution of resources take on

---

[1]Scholars, journalists and politicians have invented many labels to distinguish the richer and poorer countries of the world from one another. Some use the terms North and South, since most of the wealthier countries of the world are located in the northern latitudes while the poorer countries tend to find themselves south of the equator. The term Third World orginated in an effort to distinguish the world's poor countries from the industrialized capitalist countries, called the First World, and the industrialized communist countries, called the Second World. Southern countries are sometimes referred to as developing, less developed, or underdeveloped to contrast them with the advanced industrialized or developed countries. In general, these labels attempt to distinguish between relatively high-income countries which have undergone extensive industrialization and lower-income countries which remain at the earlier stages of industrialization. The latter countries often also share in common the experience of colonization. None of these labels are terribly precise. Some countries are difficult to classify. This is not surprising, since development is a continuum, not an either-or proposition. Moreover, the use of these terms to place large numbers of states in broad categories often misleadingly implies a unity and commonality among them which does not exist in reality. Nevertheless, in deference to common usage, we shall employ these terms interchangeably throughout the text.

added urgency when one considers the persistence of absolute poverty and hunger, runaway population growth, and the prospects of ecological disaster in many of today's poorer countries. Most disturbingly, despite some improvement in Southern living standards and the rapid economic growth of a handful of developing countries, the divide between rich and poor appears stubbornly resistant to amelioration.

This development gap poses moral, political, and economic challenges for the relatively wealthy countries of the North. While the rhetorical fireworks of the seventies have since dimmed, Third World countries continue to press the North to agree to reforms in the international economic order which might help spur Southern development. Failure to reach agreement between North and South on some issues, such as Third World debt, could have far reaching consequences for Northern economies. Other issues of great concern to the North, such as illegal immigration, the destruction of the world's rain forests, and the drug trade, can be traced indirectly to continuing Third World poverty. Inequality and economic deprivation can also contribute to the outbreak of violence and war, both within and among countries. Finally, conflicts between North and South, as well as among Southern countries themselves, over the control of important resources, such as oil and strategic minerals, are likely to persist.

To cope more readily with the serious consequences which the development gap holds for both rich and poor countries, we need to understand the political economy of North-South relations. This chapter and the four that follow will provide the background necessary to understand the nature of these relations by focusing on two related issues. The first of these concerns North-South bargaining over the distribution of gains from the economic ties between them. The development gap has rendered North-South economic relations more conflictual than the links among Northern countries. There is far less agreement between North and South over the basic rules and norms that should structure the world economic system. As a result, relations have rested less upon shared values than upon the exercise of political and economic power. We will examine the ways in which North-South bargaining has been influenced by asymmetries in power and the efforts of Third World states to offset the enormous power advantages of the North.

The second major focus addresses the struggle of Third World governments to devise workable strategies of development in the international system. In particular, countries have varied in the degree to which they are willing to open their economies to trade and investment with the North. We argue that such choices are heavily influenced by the particular political and economic circumstances, both domestically and internationally, faced by given Third World states.

The debate over appropriate strategies of development is, however, partly driven by disagreements over the origins and continuing sources of the development gap between North and South. Why did the North develop first? Can the South succeed by following the pattern established by the North?

Or do the differing international conditions faced by Third World countries today dictate an altogether different path (or paths) to development? Do extensive economic ties with the North help or hinder Third World development efforts? These are some of the questions this chapter seeks to explore by examining alternative theoretical perspectives on the development gap. Prior to doing so, however, it may be instructive to investigate the dimensions of the economic inequalities between North and South.

MEASURING THE DEVELOPMENT GAP

■ Northerners often find it tempting to adopt a fatalistic attitude toward the enormous development gap between North and South, based on the assumption that such disparities have always existed and therefore always will. Yet Latin America, Africa, and Asia each served as the home of civilizations that once rivaled or surpassed European society in science and technology, culture, and economic productivity. In fact, the present concentration of global wealth and income is of quite recent origin.

It has been estimated, for instance, that per capita GDP in what we now refer to as the North exceeded that of the South by only 50 percent in the mid-nineteenth century. Table 8.1, based upon data calculated by Paul Bairoch, shows just how recently it has been that Northern development began to outrace that in the South. In 1830, what is now the Third World accounted for over 60 percent of world manufacturing production as compared with 34 percent for Europe as a whole. Matters changed rapidly over the next thirty years, however, as the industrial revolution allowed Europe's share to rise to over 53 percent, while the Third World's share declined to just under 37 percent.

TABLE 8.1

Relative Shares of World Manufacturing Output: 1750–1900

	1750	1800	1830	1860	1880	1900
Europe	23.2	28.1	34.2	53.2	61.3	62.0
United States	0.1	0.8	2.4	7.2	14.7	23.6
Japan	3.8	3.5	2.8	2.6	2.4	2.4
Third World	73.0	67.7	60.5	36.6	20.9	11.0

SOURCE: Adapted from Paul Bairoch, "International Industrialization Levels from 1750 to 1980," *Journal of European Economic History*, 11, 1982, 296.

The North continued to expand its lead through the remainder of the nineteenth century and well into the twentieth century. In contemporary times, the social and economic contrasts between North and South have become truly stark. In 1989, the average per capita GNP in the 95 countries the World Bank classifies as low- and middle-income came to $800. At $19,090, the corresponding figure for the nineteen high-income countries belonging to the Organization for Economic Cooperation and Development (OECD) was more than twenty-three times larger.[2] Between 1965 and 1989, per capita GNP grew at an average annual rate of 2.5 percent in less developed countries, equaling the growth rate of the developed countries.[3] This comparison is, however, somewhat misleading because the South's growth rate was built upon such a low base. Expressed in absolute terms, the gap between North and South appears to be growing larger, not smaller. The growth in real per capita income in less developed nations between 1950 and 1980 amounted to $81 compared with an improvement of $5,807 for the North.[4]

The gap shows up as well in more direct measures of social and physical well-being. In 1989, the typical Northerner could expect to live seventy-six years, thirteen years longer than the average Southerner. The average Third World citizen must make do on a diet consisting of more than one-quarter fewer calories than the average Northerner consumes daily.[5] In 1990, the World Bank estimated that 950 million of the world's 5.2 billion people suffered from chronic malnutrition.[6] The overwhelming majority of the hungry are to be found in the South. In 1984, Northern countries averaged one physician for every 450 persons. The corresponding figure for the South was one doctor for every 4,990 people (in Sub-Saharan Africa, the ratio is 1:26,640). While eight infants out of every 1,000 born in the North die within their first year of life, the corresponding figure for the South is 65. Yet, despite this high infant mortality rate, the South's population growth rate is over three times that of the North. These rapidly growing populations place difficult strains on the environment, lead to overcrowding in large cities, and force economies and agricultural systems to race to provide adequate jobs and food. While 99 percent of Northern citizens meet minimal standards of literacy, only an estimated 60 percent of Southerners can read and write at a basic

---

[2]World Bank, *World Development Report, 1991*, New York: Oxford University Press, 1991, Table 1, 205. These figures exclude six non-OECD members which the World Bank includes in its high-income category: Israel, Saudi Arabia, Singapore, Hong Kong, Kuwait, and the United Arab Emirates. The figures given for North and South will continue to reflect the classification scheme used above, where the South is equated with the Bank's low- and middle-income countries while the North is treated as co-extensive with the countries of the OECD.

[3]*World Development Report, 1991*, Table 1, 205.

[4]Based upon 1980 dollars. See Mitchell A. Seligson, "The Dual Gaps: An Overview of Theory and Research," in Mitchell Seligman, ed. *The Gap Between Rich and Poor: Contending Perspectives on the Political Economy of Development*, Boulder: Westview Press, 1984.

[5]*World Development Report, 1991*, Tables 1 and 28.

[6]Robin Broad, John Cavanaugh, and Walden Bello, "Development: The Market Is Not Enough," *Foreign Policy*, Winter, 1990–91, 145.

level. In the North, secondary school enrollment amounts to 95 percent of total secondary school age youths. The figure for the South is only 42 percent. Finally, while 77 percent of Northerners live in cities, the same is true for only 42 percent of Southerners.[7]

These aggregate figures hide the fact that the South's meager resources are not shared equally by the members of those societies. Glaring gaps exist within Third World societies between rich and poor. In fact, inequities in income, wealth, and landholding are typically much more pronounced in the South than in the North.[8]

The structure of Southern economies and their relationship to the global economy differ markedly from the North. Forty-seven percent of Southern merchandise exports consist of fuels, minerals, metals, and other primary commodities, with the rest comprised of manufactured goods. Though Asian countries tend to count a high percentage of manufactured goods among their exports, Africa still relies upon primary commodities for 89 percent of its exports, while such goods account for two-thirds of Latin American exports. Only 19 percent of Northern exports, by contrast, consist of primary commodities as opposed to manufactured goods.[9]

Agriculture plays a larger role in Third World economies, where it accounts for 19 percent of total GDP on average, than in the North, where agriculture comprises only 3 percent of total production.[10] The terms of trade deteriorated for the South throughout the decade of the eighties. In other words, the average prices of Southern exports fell relative to the average prices of the goods the South imported. The same quantity of Southern exports, which could buy $100 worth of Northern goods in 1980, could only buy eighty-nine dollars worth of the same products in 1988.[11] The Third World debt crisis severely hampered the Third World's ability to import additional goods over the past decade. After rising at an annual rate of 5.0 percent between 1965 and 1980, Third World imports grew by only 1.4 percent per year from 1980 to 1989.[12]

CONTENDING PERSPECTIVES ON DEVELOPMENT

■ Scholars disagree over both the sources of the development gap and the likelihood that it can be narrowed in the future. There is also extensive debate

---

[7] All data from *World Development Report, 1991*, Tables 1, 28, 29, and 31.

[8] See Montek S. Ahluwalia, "Income Inequality: Some Dimensions of the Problem," in Mitchell Seligman, ed. *The Gap Between Rich and Poor: Contending Perspectives on the Political Economy of Development*, Boulder: Westview Press, 1984, 14–21.

[9] All data from *World Development Report, 1991*, Table 16.

[10] *World Development Report, 1990*, Table 3.

[11] *World Development Report, 1990*, Table 14.

[12] All data from *World Development Report, 1991*, Table 14.

over whether or not the South benefits from its extensive economic ties with the North. These disagreements revolve around much more than how to interpret the available factual data. Fundamentally, they stem from differing assumptions about the nature of the development process itself. Here we identify and compare two contrasting bodies of thought related to the problems of Third World development and North-South political economy.

These two theories, labeled respectively modernization and dependency, are primarily scholarly in nature. As such, they provide a necessary conceptual introduction to some of the issues and debates that we will examine in a more substantive and concrete way in later chapters. Ultimately, this necessarily abstract discussion will provide us with the tools needed to sort through the complex and messy realities of North-South political economy.

Yet, it is worth noting that these ideas have found their way from the sanctuaries of academia to the stormy citadels of the political world. In debates between representatives of the North and the South in the United Nations and elsewhere, arguments drawn from these two perspectives are often featured in the political rhetoric of the respective sides. Northern spokespersons often appeal, implicitly, to modernization theory, which emphasizes the benefits to the South of openness to trade and investment from the North. Third World representatives, on the other hand, regularly invoke dependency theory as a basis for demanding the reform of an exploitative world economic system. Aside from their merits as explanations for the development gap, therefore, the differing perspectives represented by the modernization and the dependency theories are worth examining for the insights they provide into the intellectual bases of political debates between North and South.

Modernization Theory

Modernization theory views the obstacles to Third World development through the prism of the North's own development experience. The North grew rich, according to this account, not by exploiting the South, but by discovering the secrets of sustained economic growth. The cultural values and social, political, and economic institutions that provided the keys to Northern development are embodied in the notion of modernity. The modernization of Europe involved the gradual shedding of traditional ways of organizing society. While little of this process was planned, simultaneous trends in a number of different spheres of social life converged to create the basis for dynamic economic growth and industrialization.

What are the principle elements of modernity? The list of traits provided by different authors varies enormously.[13] But among the most commonly

---

[13] A partial list of works in the modernization tradition would include: Alex Inkeles and David H. Smith, *Becoming Modern: Individual Change in Six Development Countries*, Cambridge: Harvard

cited are secularization (or the declining centrality of religion in social and cultural life), urbanization, the rise of science and technology, increased social mobility, a system of social rewards based upon merit rather than inherited status, a tolerance for social innovation and intellectual diversity, the limitation of controls placed by political authorities on social and economic life (i.e., the emergence of a "private" sphere), the ascendance of rule by law, and the development of an extensive division of labor within society. All of these traits complement the development of modern market-based economies where economic decision-making is decentralized among large numbers of producers, consumers, and laborers and relatively free of direct control by political or religious authorities.

Traditional societies are dominated by religious authority, revolve around rural life, lack the capacity to generate scientific and technological discoveries, suffer from rigid social structures allowing little mobility, distribute social rewards based upon inherited status rather than merit, discourage innovation and new ideas, place few controls on the arbitrary exercise of political authority, and feature little social differentiation. The economies of traditional societies often rest upon either subsistence agriculture, where extended families produce only for their own needs, or feudal or semifeudal landholding arrangements, where relatively small numbers of large landowners live off of the surplus produced by an indentured peasantry.

The most critical element in the transition from a traditional society to a modern one, from the standpoint of economic development, is the emergence of a system of rewards for innovation. The society must not only come to expect and welcome change and to embrace the notion of progress, but also willingly tolerate the inequalities which result from allowing individuals to reap handsome private returns for innovations that have high social value. For this to be possible, the state must devise means of organizing and protecting private property. By property, we refer not just to material possessions but also to the propriety which innovators must have over their own original ideas if others are not to profit from them instead. Although the state must protect property rights, it must at the same time allow economic decisions to be made in at least partial autonomy from political oversight and intervention. This is necessary because innovation is most likely if decision-making

University Press, 1974; David McClelland, *The Achieving Society*, Princeton: Van Nostrand Co., 1961; Henri Avjac, "Cultures and Growth," in Christopher Saunders, ed. *The Political Economy of New and Old Industrial Countries*, London: Butterworths, 1981; Kalman Silvert, "The Politics of Social and Economic Change in Latin America," in Howard Wiarda, ed. *Politics and Social Change in Latin America: The Distinct Tradition*, Amherst: University of Massachusetts Press, 1974; Myron Weiner, ed. *Modernization: The Dynamics of Growth*, New York: Basic Books, 1966; Cyril Black, *The Dynamics of Modernization*, New York: Harper and Row, 1966; Gabriel Almond and James S. Coleman, *The Politics of Developing Areas*, Princeton: Princeton University Press, 1960; and Daniel Lerner, *The Passing of Traditional Society*, New York: Free Press of Glencoe, 1958. For a critique of the modernization school, see Alajandro Portes, "On the Sociology of National Development: Theories and Issues," *American Journal of Sociology*, July, 1976.

is decentralized through competitive market arrangements that encourage and reward new ideas while punishing inefficiency and stagnation. As this discussion suggests, the development of capitalist institutions lies at the heart of modernization, although the rise of capitalism in the North would not have been possible without the simultaneous transformations already mentioned in the noneconomic spheres of society.

Modernization theorists suggest that before sustained and self-generating economic growth becomes possible in the South, Third World societies must undergo the same transition from traditionalism to modernity previously experienced by the North. The path to development thus lies through emulation of the North. The principle obstacle to modernization arises from the persistence of traditional cultural values and institutions in the South that are incompatible with economic growth and industrialization.

Adherents to this school of thought disagree over just how likely it is that Third World societies will progress smoothly toward modernity. Perhaps the majority believe that modernization of the Third World is an inevitable process. The agents of progress, in this view, are many. They include the modernizing political elites (often Northern educated) to be found in many Third World countries. Multinational corporations serve as transmitters of modern skills and values while also providing close-up examples of modern forms of economic organization. Exposure to international trade in general offers Southern societies with incentives to embrace reform and change if they are to compete effectively. The penetration of Third World societies by European or U.S. culture through books, films, advertising, consumer products, and the media also helps to assimilate Southerners to modern values and beliefs.

North-South economic interdependence is to be valued, according to modernization theorists, not simply for the mutual gains which routinely flow from market transactions but for the beneficial impact such ties have in helping to erode and undermine the traditional social values and structures that hold back development. Over time, both external and internal pressures will tend to shrink the traditional sector of the economy and society while the growth of the modern sector proceeds apace. Evidence of these trends at work, according to modernization theorists, can be found in growing urbanization, the development of a wage labor force, and broadened educational opportunities.

A minority of modernization theorists accept the distinction between traditionalism and modernity but question the assumption that Southern societies will necessarily modernize over time, leading eventually to a convergence between the social and economic structures of North and South. These authors instead see traditionalism as deeply embedded in the cultures and institutions of many Third World countries. Change may come slowly and not necessarily in the direction of a European inspired ideal of modernity. Others who question the inevitability of modernization and convergence between North and South go further to suggest that economic development may well be possible in societies that embrace some elements of modernity but not others. There may be, in other words, multiple paths of development.

Modernization theory has been criticized on a number of grounds. It has been pointed out, for instance, that the concept of traditionalism is quite nebulous. In practice, the traditional label has been applied to virtually any social practices and institutions that are not modern, or in other words, not characteristic of present day European and North American societies. To bundle all of the many varied and diverse Third World cultures that do not meet the criteria for modernity under the label "traditional" perhaps serves to obscure more than to illuminate.

Some also charge that modernization theory springs from an ethnocentric viewpoint. Certainly, it is not difficult to deduce that most modernization theorists consider modernity good and traditionalism bad. This obviously reflects a Euro-centric bias. Whatever the merits of Northern societies, they are certainly not above reproach, and Southerners who embrace modernity in a general way may well hope to avoid some of the less appealing aspects of Northern societies even while seeking to match Northern living standards. Moreover, modernization theorists may be too dismissive of traditional societies, ignoring the possibility that they might contain redeeming traits worth preserving.

Some point out that modernization theory incorrectly assumes that the obstacles to Third World development lie solely in the persistence of the traditional sector of the society. This ignores the possibility that the modern sector itself may be subject to contradictions and distortions that slow growth. Moreover, the movement from traditionalism to modernity is likely to be anything but smooth. Modernization in Europe proceeded in fits and starts, and the process often generated enormous dislocations such as war, revolution, unemployment, mass immigration, and class conflict. There is little reason to expect modernization to be any less disruptive as it transforms Third World societies.

Modernization theorists are quite sanguine about the benefits of North-South economic exchange for Southern development. Whether or not it is true in general that links with the North spur modernization, most authors in this tradition ignore the potential conflicts of interest between North and South. This is apparent in their tendency to downplay the North's potential economic power over the South. As we will discuss, the South's dependence upon the North offers the latter with political leverage that can be used to capture a disproportionate share of the benefits flowing from North-South economic exchange.

Despite these criticisms, modernization theory offers important insights into the development experience of the North. It would be surprising indeed, despite the changed context, if these insights did not hold useful lessons for those seeking to promote Southern development. Perhaps the most important of these is that capitalism, as a distinctive way of organizing economic relationships within a society, is a powerful mechanism for producing wealth.

The development of capitalism, in turn, is dependent upon the evolution of supportive social, political, and cultural institutions in the noneconomic spheres of society. Whether these innovations can be successfully transplanted to a society from without or whether they must evolve indigenously is a crucial question in assessing the prospects for capitalist-led development in the Third World. This is, in fact, the central question raised by dependency theory, our second perspective on Third World development.

Dependency Theory

Dependency theorists reject modernization theory's optimistic prediction that Third World states that imitate the cultural attitudes, institutions, and policies of the North can follow the same path toward development previously trod by present-day rich countries.[14] They point out that the international context facing developing societies today is vastly different from that which confronted the early industrializers. Capitalism developed largely indigenously in Europe and the first wave of industrializers faced no competition from already-developed rivals. Moreover, industrialization in Europe was helped along by the access that conquest provided Europeans to the raw materials and cheap labor of colonized lands.

Present-day developing countries face an entirely different set of international realities. Third World efforts to industrialize must cope with the formidable competition provided by the already well-established manufacturing capacities of the North. Moreover, the infrastructure needed to support scientific and technological innovation is overwhelmingly located in the North. In general, capitalism was introduced to Southern societies from the outside on terms largely set by, and favorable to, Northern governments, merchants, and investors. Southern economies remain heavily dependent upon external trade with the North, and Northern multinational corporations often dominate the most dynamic industries in many Third World countries.

---

[14]Among the major works in the dependency school are Theotonio Dos Santos, "The Structure of Dependence," in K. T. Fann and Donald Hodges, eds. *Readings in U.S. Imperialism*, Boston: Porter Sargent Publisher, 1971; Fernando Henrique Cardoso and Enzo Falleto, *Dependency and Development in Latin America*, Berkeley: University of California Press, 1979; Fernando Henrique Cardoso, "The Consumption of Dependency Theory in the United States," *Latin American Research Review*, 12, no. 3, 1977; Susanne Bodenheimer, "Dependency and Imperialism", *Politics and Society*, May, 1970; Samir Amin, *Accumulation on a World Scale*, New York: Monthly Review Press, 1974; Andre Gunder Frank, *Capitalism and Underdevelopment in Latin America*, New York: Monthly Review Press, 1967; Andre Gunder Frank, *Latin America: Underdevelopment or Revolution*, New York: Monthly Review Press, 1969; C. Furtado, *Development and Underdevelopment*, Berkeley: University of California Press, 1964; A. Emmanuel, *Unequal Exchange*, London: New Left Books, 1972; Paul Baran, *The Political Economy of Growth*, New York: Monthly Review Press, 1957; and Immanuel Wallerstein, *The Modern World-System: Capitalist Agriculture and the Origins of the European World-Economy in the Sixteenth Century*, New York: Academic Press, 1976.

Dependencies theorists contend that these differences (and others) between early and late developers mean that the development experiences of the North hold little relevance for assessing the present-day prospects for Southern development. These distinctions are considered so important, in fact, that dependency theory locates the primary obstacles to Third World development in the international system rather than the domestic political, cultural, and social characteristics of particular states. In other words, the international system, rather than the nation-state, is viewed as the appropriate unit of analysis.

Capitalism is the most important defining feature of the contemporary international system, according to dependency theorists. Capitalism is a distinct set of economic relations defined by the private ownership of property, wage labor, and market exchange. The capitalist world system, which some dependency theorists believe has existed since the sixteenth century[15], involves two sets of exploitative relationships. Within particular firms, the owners of capital exploit workers by profiting from their labor. The second relationship of exploitation, and the more relevant from our standpoint, exists between core and peripheral states in the world economy. Capitalism does not develop evenly. Instead, it tends to concentrate development in certain areas, called the core, which are characterized by advanced industrialization, rapid technological development, and high wage rates and living standards. Peripheral areas, which constitute the geographic bulk of the world economy, instead feature limited industrialization, little technological innovation, and relatively low wages and living standards.

The development of core countries is linked to the underdevelopment of the peripheral countries. The workings of the capitalist world system tend to perpetuate and reinforce economic inequalities among countries. As two prominent advocates of dependency put it: "Both underdevelopment and development are aspects of the same phenomenon, both are historically simultaneous, both are linked functionally and, therefore, interact and condition each other mutually."[16]

Third World countries were drawn into the capitalist world economy through colonialism as well as the expansion of European trade and investment. European countries used their political domination to create and enforce a division of labor which reserved the most dynamic segments of the world economy for themselves. North-South trade was built around the movement

---

[15]For information concerning the origins of the capitalist world system, see Immanuel Wallerstein, *The Modern World-System: Capitalist Agriculture and the Origins of the European World-Economy in the Sixteenth Century*, New York: Academic Press, 1976.

[16]Quoted in J. Samuel Valenzuela and Arturo Valenzuela, "Modernization and Dependency: Alternative Perspectives in the Study of Latin American Underdevelopment," in Heraldo Munoz, ed. *From Dependency to Development: Strategies to Overcome Underdevelopment and Inequality*, Boulder: Westview Press, 1981, 25. Translated from Osvaldo Sunkel and Pedro Paz, *El subdesarrollo latinoamericano y la teoria del desarrollo*, Mexico, 1970, 6.

of manufactured goods from North to South and the transfer of primary products, including minerals, raw materials, and agricultural goods, from South to North. Moreover, while Northern countries traded extensively with one another, Southern countries traded almost exclusively with the North. Colonialism left the economies of Southern countries geared more toward the needs of Northern markets than the domestic needs of their own societies. This set of economic relationships, dependency writers point out, outlived colonialism itself.

This position of Southern subordination to, and dependence upon, the North is captured in Theotonio dos Santos' widely cited definition of dependency: "Dependency is a situation in which a certain number of countries have their economy conditioned by the development and expansion of another. . . placing the dependent country in a backward position exploited by the dominant country."[17]

Dependency theorists offer a number of mechanisms by which dependency hampers Southern development. Some cite unequal exchange as the primary means by which Northern societies extract surplus wealth from the South. The prices of the primary goods exported by the South, it is argued, tend to decline over time relative to the prices of the manufactured goods Southern societies must import from the North. A country that finds itself in this situation, where, over time, a given quantity of the country's exports can purchase less and less of the imports it desires, is said to be suffering from declining terms of trade.

Northern multinational corporations are also viewed as instruments of exploitation. Foreign firms bring inappropriate technology, use their mobility and transnational links to evade taxes and regulations, drive out local competitors, manipulate Southern governments, refuse to hire and train top management drawn from the host country, and repatriate their profits rather than invest them locally.

Dependency theory asserts that these forms of Northern exploitation, along with others such as foreign aid, commercial bank lending, and the influence of multilateral lending agencies, work to hinder Southern industrialization and development.

Dependency theorists differ over how severe and universal the constraints that dependence places on Third World development are. Some, especially among the early writers, argued that dependence allowed little latitude for development and was likely to continue to produce growing immiserization and poverty among most Southerners. The principal beneficiaries of dependence in the South would consist of a "compradore" class of elites who benefited

---

[17]Quoted in Valenzuela and Valenzuela, "Modernization and Dependency," 25–26. Also see Theotonio Dos Santos, "The Structure of Dependence," in K. T. Fann and Donald Hodges, eds. *Readings in U.S. Imperialism*, Boston: Porter Sargent Publisher, 1971.

from their privileged ties with the North, whether they be political or economic, and who acted as the local agents of imperialism.

Some dependency authors concede that dependency is not incompatible with economic growth and development, even including a degree of industrialization. Moreover, some countries are likely to progress further than others. These authors nevertheless maintain that dependence constrains development in most Southern countries, rendering economic growth and industrialization slower and less substantial than might otherwise be the case. They also generally argue that the overall relative position of the periphery in comparison with the core is unlikely to improve even where absolute gains are made.

A third set of authors argue that while dependency is sometimes compatible with vigorous economic growth, it nevertheless produces a myriad of undesirable "distortions" that are peculiar to dependent Southern societies and economies. Among these are growing income inequality, wasteful consumption, cultural degradation, and political repression. The main concern of these authors is not with whether "development" is occurring, but rather with the type of development produced under conditions of dependence.

Dependency theorists differ widely over the appropriate remedy for Third World dependence upon the North. Some favor inwardly directed development strategies that emphasize production for the domestic market. This would imply a curtailment of economic ties with the North through high protectionist barriers designed to nurture domestic industry and the strict regulation of foreign investment.

Others advocate some form of collective bargaining strategy, whereby Southern states pool their political and economic resources to press for reforms in the international economic order, much as trade unions attempt to ameliorate capitalist exploitation of workers. This can take the form of resource cartels, such as OPEC, which are designed to reverse the declining terms of trade, or broad coalitions that demand Northern assent to various specific reforms such as the lowering of Northern protectionist barriers to Southern manufactured goods, commodity stabilization plans, or mandatory codes of conduct for multinational corporations. Those who advocate this strategy often stress the importance of improving economic ties, including the development of regional common markets, among Southern countries as a means of lessening dependence upon the North.

Finally, some dependency theorists argue that Third World states can only escape dependence upon the capitalist world system through socialist revolution and reconstruction. Such a strategy would involve the elimination of private capital and the development of nonexploitative links with other like-minded countries.

In short, while modernization theory asserts that Southern economic ties with the North are desirable because they transfer needed technology and skills, foster efficiency through competition, and break down cultural and institutional barriers to development, dependency theory views Northern economic and political penetration of the South as exploitative, producing a transfer of resources from the poor to the rich.

In order to evaluate dependency theory, we must distinguish between two lines of argument, each of which can be found, together or separately, in the writings of different authors. The first strain of dependency theory has primarily to do with economics. The concern here is with the way in which Third World states have been incorporated into the world capitalist system and the effects this process has had on their prospects for development. The second focuses on politics. In particular, this aspect of dependency theory explores the asymmetries in power and interdependence that influence bargaining between North and South over the rules of the international economic system. While both the economic and political dimensions of dependency theory derive from the same body of thought, each deserves separate treatment in any effort to assess the strengths and weaknesses of the dependency approach to Third World development and North-South relations.[18]

The economic dimension of dependency theory revolves around the suggestion that dependent capitalism, introduced to the South via Northern colonialism, trade, and investment, differs from the home-grown variety. The dependence of Third World economies on trade and investment with the North and their subordinate position in the international division of labor constrains the prospects for Southern development and leads to imbalances and distortions.

Critics of dependency theory have pointed to several difficulties with these claims.[19] One of these is that many of the features that are associated with dependency, such as penetration by multinational corporations and heavy reliance on external trade and technology, are also characteristic of many developed countries. Canada, for instance, is more dependent upon direct foreign investment than India. Moreover, as any reader of Dickens can surmise, the extreme social and economic inequalities that are painful features of most developing countries today were not unknown to the European

---

[18]Our discussion of these two strains in dependency theory draws upon a similar distinction made in James Caparaso and Behrouz Zare, "An Interpretation and Evaluation of Dependency Theory," in Heraldo Munoz, ed. *From Dependency to Development: Strategies to Overcome Underdevelopment and Inequality*, Boulder: Westview Press, 1981, 44–45.

[19]For critical reviews of dependency theory, some more sympathetic than others, see David Ray, "The Dependency Model of Latin American Underdevelopment: Three Basic Fallacies," *Journal of Interamerican Studies and World Affairs*, February, 1973; Sanjaya Lall, "Is Dependence a Useful Concept in Analyzing Underdevelopment?," *World Development*, November, 1975; Richard Fagen, "Studying Latin American Politics: Some Implications of a Dependencia Approach," *Latin American Research Review*, Summer, 1977; Raymond Duvall, "Dependence and Dependencia Theory: Notes Toward Precision of Concept and Argument," *International Organization*, Winter, 1978; Tony Smith, "The Underdevelopment of the Development Literature: The Case of Dependency Theory," *World Politics*, January, 1979; and Bill Warren, "Imperialism and Capitalist Industrialization," *New Left Review*, September-October, 1973. For an effort to subject dependency propositions to empirical testing, see Vincent Mahler, *Dependency Approaches to International Political Economy: A Cross-National Study*, New York: Columbia University Press, 1980.

societies of one hundred and fifty years ago. This suggests that some of the inequities and distortions which have been attributed to external dependence may instead be characteristic of the early stages of capitalist development more generally.

Dependency writers might respond that the nature of North-North trade differs substantially from North-South trade. Northern countries trade principally in manufactured goods with one another. Southern trade with the North, by contrast, rests to a much larger degree upon the exchange of raw materials for manufactured goods. If, as dependency theorists assert, the latter form of trade is subject to deteriorating terms of trade for the kinds of goods which Third World countries typically export, then this division of labor works to the disadvantage of the South.

Yet, while recent years have indeed witnessed a deterioration in the South's terms of trade with the North, studies that have examined longer time periods provide little support for the unequal exchange thesis. The prices of primary goods, such as raw materials and agricultural goods, do tend to fluctuate more widely than the prices of manufactured goods, a pattern which leads to cycles of feast or famine for countries which depend upon only a few primary products for the bulk of their exports. The empirical evidence, however, shows no long-term tendency for the prices of primary goods to fall relative to manufactured goods over the course of the twentieth century. Even if trends in the terms of trade did favor manufactured goods, however, the implications of this would be complicated by the fact that some core countries, such as the United States, depend upon primary goods for a substantial portion of their exports, while some developing countries, especially in East Asia, have become substantial exporters of manufactured goods.

As we will discuss in a later chapter, multinational corporations often hold superior bargaining positions vis-à-vis Third World host states. This allows them to extract considerable benefits from their Third World operations and to escape some forms of regulation. Yet, this does not establish that direct foreign investment stymies Third World development. The economic benefits that multinational corporations bring Third World societies vary depending upon the nature of the investment. Manufacturing investments likely offer the host state more than extractive investments, such as mining or agricultural production. Yet the package of assets foreign firms bring to the country, including capital, technology, managerial expertise, and global marketing networks, often cannot be matched by local firms, whether private or state-owned. In any case, the ability of Third World countries to maximize the benefits of direct foreign investment while minimizing the negatives varies across countries and over time.

Perhaps dependency theory's greatest shortcoming is that it has trouble explaining the enormous diversity of Third World development experiences. While many Third World countries remain locked in poverty and show few signs of narrowing the gap with the North, a growing handful of countries have displayed impressive economic dynamism. Located primarily in East

Asia, these so-called newly industrializing countries (NICs), have grown at rates far exceeding those in the North. As we will discuss more thoroughly in the next chapter, they have also developed diversified economies that rest increasingly upon the production and trade of manufactured goods. Some have even become the originators of new technology.

Moreover, these countries have succeeded not by asserting greater autonomy from the North, but by integrating themselves ever more thoroughly into the international economic system. While the strategies pursued by these countries do not necessarily suggest a blueprint for success by other Southern nations, it does seem clear that the nature of the international economic system does not preclude the possibility of development for all Third World countries. Indeed, since the external constraints faced by the NICs did not differ radically from those facing many other Southern states, these cases of success should shift our attention toward those internal or domestic characteristics that can account for such different outcomes. This requires close attention to factors that are not typically included in dependency analysis.

The other strain of dependency theory emphasizes the disparities in political power between North and South. The most obvious power advantage possessed by the North lies in its preponderance of military resources over the South. Since economic conflicts are rarely resolved through the use of coercion, however, North-South bargaining is more directly influenced by other forms of power.

Northern leverage depends principally upon asymmetries in the relations of economic interdependence between North and South. Simply put, asymmetrical interdependence exists where two countries each depend upon trade, investment and other economic ties with one another, but one country is significantly more dependent upon the relationship than the other. If the relationship were for some reason suddenly cut asunder, in this case, the more dependent trade partner would be hurt far more than the less dependent partner. The less dependent country can therefore play upon the weakness and vulnerability of the more dependent country as a source of power or leverage.

A hypothetical case may help to clarify this point. Let us imagine that two countries, which we will refer to as A and B, engage in trade with one another. For country A, its trade with country B constitutes only a small share of its overall trade with all countries and a much smaller proportion of its total national income. Were trade between A and B to be curtailed, country A would be only marginally hurt and could probably substitute for the losses by expanding its trade with alternative partners. Country B, however, is much smaller and less well-developed than country A. Trade with A constitutes a large portion of country B's overall trade and a significant increment of its national income. The loss of trade with country A would be devastating to country B's economy. Moreover, as a less developed nation dependent upon a narrow range of exports, country B might find it difficult to locate alternative buyers for its goods. This, in extreme form, is a relationship of asymmetrical interdependence. Country B's vulnerability to a rupture in trade provides country A with a source of power over B. Should political or commercial conflicts arise between the two countries, country A can reliably compel concessions from country B by threatening to withhold trade.

Dependency theorists point out that this hypothetical case conforms rather closely to the actual realities of economic ties between many Northern states and many Southern states. As a result, it is the North's interests that dominate in bargaining between the two.[20]

Dependency theorists are on much firmer ground with this line of argument than in their critique of dependent capitalism. Southern dependence upon the North may not pose an insuperable obstacle to development, but it does clearly give rise to disparities in power and influence both in relations between particular states and in collective negotiations over the rules and institutions of the international economic order.

Before we embrace these conclusions, however, several caveats are in order. It should be noted that the recognition that power flows from asymmetrical interdependence is not unique to dependency theory. Indeed, the concept of asymmetrical interdependence can, with appropriate modifications, be applied to the analysis of power in many different spheres of social, political, and economic life. Moreover, asymmetries exist not just between North and South but also among Northern countries themselves, although the resulting disparities in power are unlikely to be as wide in the latter instances as in the former. Finally, power relationships among states are not static. OPEC, for instance, managed to turn the tables on the North during the seventies when it took advantage of the industrial world's enormous dependence on a particularly crucial resource.

CONCLUSIONS

■ What seems clear from our overview of modernization and dependency theory is that neither provides an entirely adequate, overall understanding of the problems facing Southern countries as they attempt to close the development gap with the North. Modernization theory ignores some of the less appealing aspects of economic development under capitalism. It is also vague on some key theoretical points, such as the concept of traditionalism. Moreover, modernization theory overlooks the importance of power disparities between the North and the South. Dependency theory has weaknesses as well, especially in its tendency to exaggerate the constraints that the international system places on development. The concept of dependence is vague,

---

[20]For a seminal discussion of how asymmetries in economic dependence can provide one party with potential power over another, see Albert Hirshman, *National Power and the Structure of Foreign Trade*, Berkeley: University of California Press, 1969.

and the links between it and underdevelopment are tenuous. Dependency theory also provides us with few means for understanding why some Third World countries are rapidly developing while others are falling further behind. These shortcomings in the two principle alternative perspectives on development are perhaps a measure of the limits to our knowledge about the complex process of economic development.

Nevertheless, both modernization and dependency theory offer useful insights. Modernization theory provides a convincing account of the factors which contributed to the development of the North, and it points to a number of present-day obstacles to development in the cultures and institutions of Southern societies. It also makes a strong case for the proposition that the spread of capitalism and the incorporation of Third World states into the international economic system provide an overall positive contribution to Southern economic development. Dependency theory, on the other hand, reminds us that great power disparities flow from Southern dependence upon the North.

In general, we suggest that modernization theory is closer to the mark in contending that the gains to the South from North-South economic ties outweigh the losses. Indeed, as one might expect from market exchanges, both North and South tend to benefit. Yet this does not imply that both sides benefit equally. The gains from mutual trade and investment may accrue to both North and South, yet not in equal proportions. As dependency writers point out, market relations are not free from the exercise of power. Asymmetrical interdependence provides the North with leverage over the South. The use of this leverage can, as we will see in later chapters, allow the North to bend the rules of the game in its favor to ensure that the benefits of North-South economic relations flow disproportionately its way. These insights, drawn from both modernization and dependency theory, will structure much of the discussion that follows. The South has been attracted toward greater involvement with the world economy by the promise of economic gain and accelerated modernization through exchange with the North. Yet, it has also been repelled due to the dangers posed by overreliance upon the North and the potential this dependence holds for exploitation.

While modernization and dependency remain the principle general perspectives on development and North-South political economy, recent years have brought a shift in the terms of debate. New questions are being raised. Increasingly, scholars are turning to comparative studies that ask why countries facing similar international circumstances pursue differing development strategies. These policy choices, in turn, are seen as critical to economic outcomes.

Neither dependency nor modernization theory is well adapted to answering these sorts of questions. Dependency theory's emphasis on external constraints rules out domestically generated variation across countries. Modernization theory does look at domestic factors but emphasizes broad social and cultural traits that change slowly and are only loosely connected to specific policy choices. The newer literature, by contrast, pays close attention to the roles that political coalitions, as well as bureaucratic, institutional, and political structures, play in determining which development path a particular state is likely to choose. These sorts of factors are used to help explain, for instance, why the large countries of Latin America, including Brazil and Mexico, have generally pursued inward-looking development strategies stressing autonomy while a number of successful East Asian countries, such as South Korea and Taiwan, have opted for outward-looking strategies based upon export expansion. We will explore the issues raised by this recent literature at length in the following chapter.[21]

ANNOTATED BIBLIOGRAPHY

Cyril Black, *The Dynamics of Modernization*, New York: Harper & Row, 1966.
A widely cited statement of modernization theory.

Fernando Henrique Cardoso and Enzo Falleto, *Dependency and Development in Latin America*, Berkeley: University of California Press, 1979.
A classic study of Latin American political and economic development from a dependency perspective. Cardoso and Felleto offer a less determinististic and more historical and contextual approach to the study of dependency than many of the earlier authors in this tradition.

Vincent Mahler, *Dependency Approaches to International Political Economy: A Cross-National Study*, New York: Columbia University Press, 1980.
An attempt to subject dependency theory to empirical testing.

Alajandro Portes, "On the Sociology of National Development: Theories and Issues," *American Journal of Sociology*, July, 1976.
A critique of modernization theory.

Tony Smith, "The Underdevelopment of the Development Literature: The Case of Dependency Theory," *World Politics*, January, 1979.
A critique of dependency theory from a liberal perspective.

J. Samuel Valenzuela and Arturo Valenzuela, "Modernization and Dependency: Alternative Perspectives in the Study of Latin American Underdevelopment," in Heraldo Munoz, ed. *From Dependency to Development: Strategies to Overcome Underdevelopment and Inequality*, Boulder: Westview Press, 1981. Perhaps the best and most concise comparison of the modernization and dependency perspectives.

---

[21]Two recent examples of research in this vein are Stephan Haggard, *Pathways from the Periphery: The Politics of Growth in the Newly Industrialized Countries*, Ithaca: Cornell University Press, 1990; and Sylvia Maxfield, *Governing Capital: International Finance and Mexican Politics*, Ithaca: Cornell University Press, 1990.

Bill Warren, "Imperialism and Capitalist Industrialization," *New Left Review*, September-October, 1973.

A critique of dependency theory from a Marxist perspective.

World Bank, *World Development Report, 1991*, New York: Oxford University Press, 1991.

Issued annually, these reports contain a wealth of information on all aspects of Southern economies. Each report focuses upon a different theme related to Third World development. In addition to the tables, charts, and boxes scattered throughout the text, an appendix titled "World Development Indicators" is provided at the end of each volume. This section contains comprehensive social and economic data on each country displayed in thirty or more tables.

CHAPTER 9

Strategies of Southern Trade and Development

T hird World development strategies have varied across nations and over time. Some countries have enjoyed enormous success, while many have stumbled along the path to a better life for their citizens. Various models of economic growth and industrialization have shifted in and out of fashion. This chapter examines the diverse ways in which Southern states have managed the process of development and their nations' ties to the international economy. We distinguish between national and collective strategies for overcoming underdevelopment and closing the gap between North and South. National strategies involve policies designed to spur growth in a particular country. Collective strategies revolve around the coordinated efforts of multiple Third World countries to enhance their bargaining power vis-à-vis the North and to shift the rules of the international economic order to the South's advantage.

National Strategies of Trade and Industrialization

■ Development strategies in the Third World have followed a rough historical progression. Under colonialism, Third World economies were forcibly oriented toward trade patterns dictated by the colonial powers. The colonized lands provided raw materials and agricultural commodities to the imperial center, which, in turn, sold consumer and industrial goods to the colonies.

For the most part, this arrangement precluded the possibility of industrialization in the South. Indeed, the colonial powers intentionally discouraged the development of manufacturing industries that might compete with their own. The British, for instance, dismantled thriving textile and handicraft industries in India when they arrived. The legacies of colonialism made it difficult for Southern countries to break free of this pattern even after the colonists departed. The colonial powers built infrastructures designed to service the colonial trading system. Roads and railways, for instance, linked mines or plantations with ports, bypassing population centers in the interior of the country. While natives were often incorporated into the colonial bureaucracy, they were given few opportunities to learn entrepreneurial skills. Vast agricultural regions were converted from the production of staple foods for domestic consumption to cash crops designed for export. Without a domestic manufacturing capability of their own, the former colonies remained dependent on the revenues earned from these exports in order to finance consumer good imports. Many countries, in Africa, for instance, remain entrenched in the colonial trading pattern, reliant upon the export of a narrow range of agricultural goods or raw materials.[1]

Beginning in the 1930s, however, a number of countries, especially in Latin America, began to develop a substantial manufacturing sector based upon a strategy known as import substitution industrialization (ISI). This strategy was forced upon Latin American countries during the thirties and early forties when the Great Depression first eroded traditional export markets while World War II later interrupted the flow of consumer goods from the North. Initially out of necessity and then, after World War II, as a matter of conscious choice, Latin American countries began to seek greater self-sufficiency and domestic industrialization.

The difficulty in pursuing such a course, once the war had ended, was that Southern firms were generally too small and inexperienced to withstand direct competition from Northern exporters. In an effort to nurture these infant industries and substitute domestic production for previously imported goods, Third World governments raised protectionist barriers to stymie foreign competition. The first industries to be offered protection were producers of consumer goods, since the technical barriers as well as the capital requirements to this sort of production were lower. Due to the lack of experienced entrepreneurs, these firms were often created and owned by the state. Besides tariff protection, the new firms were offered other forms of assistance, including subsidized financing and preferential access to foreign exchange with which to purchase imported inputs. Where domestic industry lacked the knowledge or capital to engage in certain types of production, Northern multinational corporations were encouraged to jump protectionist barriers and to serve local markets through domestic production rather than exports.

---

[1] For a brief discussion of colonialism, see Paul Harrison, *Inside the Third World*, 2nd. ed., New York: Penguin Books, 32–46.

Other policies were also associated with ISI. Local currencies were kept overvalued. This cheapened the price of imported inputs such as oil, raw materials, and capital goods for ISI industries. Wage rates were allowed to rise and social spending increased so as to encourage the growth of a domestic market for the consumer goods produced by ISI industries. Although the export of cash crops remained necessary in order to secure the foreign exchange needed for imported industrial inputs, the agricultural sector was generally squeezed. Investment was shifted from agriculture to industry and surplus rural labor was channeled toward urban areas.

ISI produced impressive growth and industrialization during the fifties in much of Latin America and elsewhere.[2] Yet by the sixties, ISI began to run out of steam due to contradictions inherent to the strategy. Once the potential for further growth in the consumer goods sector slackened, governments began to pursue the "deepening" of ISI by encouraging the development of manufacturing capabilities in basic and intermediate industries such as steel and capital goods. For the most part, these investments involved larger scale commitments of capital and more sophisticated technologies than had been the case in the consumer goods industries. This required foreign borrowing or massive government spending. Moreover, since the domestic market for such goods remained small in many countries, new factories could not operate at efficient economies of scale, leading to high prices and large government subsidies.

These were not the only problems encountered by countries pursuing ISI. The justification for protecting the initial ISI industries from foreign competition was that they needed a breathing spell until they attained sufficient size and experience to compete successfully on their own. In fact, many firms became dependent on protectionism and lobbied hard against lifting barriers. With little effective competition, moreover, these firms had few incentives to maximize efficiency or to carry out innovation. They were also free to charge monopoly prices.

Financial difficulties also characterized the late stages of ISI. Government subsidies to industry and high social spending led to large budget deficits. Foreign borrowing, the repatriated profits of multinational corporations, and the discouragement of exports due to overvalued currencies also led to external deficits and a growing debt, despite the substitution of domestically produced goods for imports. Growing wage levels, large budget deficits, and the high prices associated with inefficient and monopolistic ISI industries created severe inflationary pressures.

Brazil's experience provides a useful illustration of these trends. Brazil's ISI strategy, spectacularly successful at generating economic growth during

---

[2]For a discussion of Latin America's experience with ISI, see Robert Alexander, "Import Substitution in Latin America in Retrospect," in James L. Dietz and Dilmus D. James, eds. *Progress Toward Development in Latin America: From Prebisch to Technological Autonomy*, Boulder: Lynne Rienner, 1991, and other essays in the same volume.

the sixties and seventies, was derailed in the 1980s. ISI succeeded in producing a diverse industrial structure in Brazil. Growth in GNP averaged 9 percent per year from 1965 to 1980. Yet much of this expansion was fueled by massive foreign borrowing. This accumulation of debt harmed Brazil's creditworthiness and led to a sharp contraction of foreign bank lending to the country in the 1980s. Brazilian industry also became increasingly inefficient as it remained sheltered from international competition and was nursed along with government subsidies. Before March 1990, imports were simply prohibited in 1,000 categories of goods while quotas restricted many other sorts of imports. Tariffs averaged 40 percent, and the central bank strictly controlled access to foreign exchange. Imports represented only 5 percent of Brazilian GNP in 1989, compared with 28 percent for South Korea and 33 percent for Taiwan. The eighties witnessed the failure of Brazil's ISI strategy. Per capita income stagnated, while inflation averaged 260 percent per year.[3] Brazil's experience was not atypical. Much of Latin America has been subject to similar patterns.

Among development experts, ISI is now largely in disrepute. Although ISI may once have played a necessary role in jumpstarting the process of industrialization in Latin America and elsewhere, many observers have concluded that the rigidities and inefficiencies that ISI policies produce have more recently served to hinder growth and development. The past decade or so has brought great interest in an alternative path to development often referred to as export-led industrialization (ELI). This strategy entails an emphasis on the growth of manufacturing production aimed at the international market, in contrast with ISI, which focused on producing for the domestic market. ELI is rooted in theories of international trade which emphasize that countries are best off specializing in those goods where they possess a comparative advantage, while opening their economies to the import of goods that can be produced more cheaply elsewhere. While the goal of ISI was to develop a well-rounded and relatively self-sufficient industrial economy, the goal of ELI is to exploit a country's particular advantages by finding a narrower, but profitable, niche in the world economy.

The most successful examples of export-led industrialization can be found in East Asia. The "Four Tigers" — South Korea, Taiwan, Singapore and Hong Kong — have sustained astonishingly high rates of economic growth over the last several decades and stand poised to join the ranks of the world's most highly developed nations.

A statistical portrait of these four nations underscores their economic dynamism.[4] Over the past four decades, Taiwan has averaged real GNP growth

---

[3]"Brazil's Economy: The Right Stuff," *The Economist*, June 9, 1990.

[4]Data on Taiwan and South Korea in the next four paragraphs are taken from "The Economies of South Korea and Singapore," *The Economist*, February 23, 1991; "Korean GNP Up a Brisk 9 percent," *New York Times*, April 1, 1991; Sheryl WuDunn, "Taiwan Sets Course for Modernity,"

of 8.7 percent per year. By 1989, per capita income had climbed to $7,500. Life expectancy in Taiwan jumped from fifty-nine years in 1952 to seventy-four in 1988. Forty-five percent of young Taiwanese go on to gain some higher education. In 1988–89, one-third of all college students were pursuing degrees in engineering, while 10 percent of the workforce as a whole has had some engineering training. In 1988, Taiwan had an unemployment rate of 1 percent. The last time unemployment exceeded 2 percent was 1964.

South Korea's real GNP growth rate averaged 8.4 percent per year between 1961 and 1990. After a serious slump in the early eighties, South Korea's economy rebounded sharply to achieve annual growth rates averaging 12 percent from 1986 through 1988. At the close of 1990, a year when the economy grew more than 9 percent, South Korea's average per capita income had risen to $5,569. South Korean life expectancy reached seventy years in 1988, up from fifty-eight in 1965. Thirty-seven percent of Korean students go on to higher education after graduating high school, and unemployment levels have ranged between 2 percent and 4 percent over the past twenty years.

In much of Latin America, economic development has been accompanied by extreme and growing inequalities in income and wealth. Data from 1980 show that in Brazil, for instance, the top 10 percent of the population accounted for 50.9 percent of the national income, while the earnings of the bottom half amounted to only 12.6 percent.[5] This unfortunate pattern has been avoided among the East Asian newly industrializing countries (NICs). In Taiwan, for example, growth has generally brought greater, not less, equity. The combined income of the top 10 percent of Taiwanese households amounted to fifteen times the bottom 20 percent in the early fifties. By 1980, this ratio had fallen to 4.2:1 (below that of many Northern countries, including the United States, Sweden, and Japan). While inequality worsened slightly during the eighties, Taiwan remains one of the most economically egalitarian societies in the world.

Both Taiwan and South Korea have based their strategies of development on rapid export growth and international specialization. South Korea is the world's tenth largest trading nation, and trade equals 60 percent of Korean GDP. After years of large trade surpluses, Taiwan had accumulated $72 billion in official foreign exchange reserves by 1991, the largest of any nation in the world. For South Korea, Taiwan, Hong Kong, and Singapore, their combined rate of annual export growth averaged 16 percent over the past thirty years.

Des Moines Register, October 27, 1991; "South Korea," *The Economist*, August 18, 1990; Damon Darlin, "Taiwan, Long Noted for Cheap Imitations, Becomes an Innovator," *Wall St. Journal*, June 5, 1990; "Taming the Little Dragons," *The Economist*, July 14, 1990; "South Korea," *The Economist*, May 21, 1988; and "Taiwan and Korea: Two Paths to Prosperity," *The Economist*, July 14, 1990.

[5]Francis Hagopian and Scott Mainwaring, "Democracy in Brazil: Problems and Prospects," *World Policy Journal*, Summer, 1987, 490.

Singapore, a small city-state with a population of 2.7 million, has been equally successful, with growth averaging 9 percent in recent years. Singapore's per capita income now exceeds those of Spain and Ireland. A consulting group known as the Business Environment Risk Information Corporation, has rated Singapore's work force the best in the world, an important factor in explaining the large waves of foreign direct investment Singapore has succeeded in attracting.[6] A center of Asian finance and commerce, Hong Kong's per capita GNP matches that of Singapore.[7]

A group of export oriented states in Southeast Asia has begun to follow the path forged by the Four Tigers (and before them, by Japan). While world export growth averaged 13 percent from 1987 through 1989, Indonesian exports grew by an average of 15 percent, Malaysia's exports jumped 23 percent per year, and Thailand achieved stunning annual export growth of 31 percent. During the same period, the Thai economy grew by 10 percent per year.[8]

Success has brought new challenges for the East Asian NICs. South Korean wage levels doubled from 1987 to 1990 in the wake of that country's transition to democratic rule, though wage growth has slowed more recently. Wages rose by 40 percent in Taiwan between 1986 and 1990. As a result of higher labor costs, both countries face increasing competition from the fast-growing, lower-wage countries of Southeast Asia. Taiwan's trade surplus has narrowed in recent years, while South Korea's large surpluses of the mid-to-late eighties have given way to renewed trade deficits.[9]

Each of the Four Tigers has responded by encouraging the growth of high-technology manufacturing and information-based service industries. Seeking to become a high-tech innovator rather than an imitator, Taiwan doubled private and public spending on research and development from 1985 to 1990. Taiwan's many small manufacturing firms, which are highly efficient but lack the capacity to engage in large-scale research or investment projects, have begun to forge new links with bigger Japanese and American firms. In 1991, for instance, a recently formed state firm called the Taiwan Aerospace Corporation offered to purchase 40 percent of McDonnell Douglas, an American aerospace firm, for $2 billion. The Taiwanese government hoped to shift some production to Taiwan while gaining access to advanced aerospace technology. While, as of early 1992, objections by some political figures in Washington D.C. threatened to scuttle this deal, the size and audaciousness of Taiwan's bid spoke volumes about that country's new financial clout as well

---

[6]See "Business in Singapore: A Snappy Little Dragon," *The Economist*, June 9, 1990.

[7]Hong Kong's future remains cloudy. Presently a British colony, Hong Kong will revert to the control of mainland China in 1997. Although China has pledged to respect Hong Kong's autonomy in many respects, many Hong Kong residents and business firms fear Chinese interference in the island's traditionally laissez-faire economy.

[8]"Southeast Asia's Economies: Sitting Pretty," *The Economist*, September 8, 1990.

[9]"The Economies of South Korea and Singapore," *The Economist*, February 23, 1991.

as its ambitious strategies for nurturing technologically sophisticated and capital-intensive industries.[10]

Taiwanese firms are also moving their low-wage production to surrounding countries. China, Indonesia, Malaysia, and Thailand received a combined $5 billion in Taiwanese investment capital in 1988 and 1989. Taiwan's government recently announced a massive six-year project designed to upgrade the country's infrastructure, with planned investments totaling $300 billion.[11]

South Korea and Taiwan have also begun to reduce the state's role in directing economic growth and to shift away from mercantilist trade policies. Between 1986 and 1990, average tariff levels fell from 28 percent to 10 percent in Taiwan and from 24 percent to 13 percent in South Korea. The South Korean government is engaged in efforts to loosen restrictions on foreign investment, raise social welfare spending at home, increase the availability of credit to small businesses in an effort to curb industrial concentration, and has allowed the Korean currency, the won, to appreciate against the dollar and other foreign currencies.[12]

The East Asian NICs share some important commonalties which help to explain their success.[13] South Korea and Taiwan each received large sums of aid from the United States during the 1950s, a factor which helped jumpstart the drive toward industrialization. Each carried out extensive land reform in the early post–World War II period. These steps broke the political and economic power of conservative landholding elites while establishing the necessary conditions for relatively egalitarian growth patterns. Organized labor has been politically weak in both countries. Each was ruled, over much of the post-war era, by strong, centralized authoritarian states which governed largely autonomous of control by particular social groups.

South Korea and Taiwan passed through relatively brief phases of import substitution industrialization before switching to export-led strategies in the early sixties. Each developed powerful economic ministries staffed by skilled

---

[10]Sheryl WuDunn, "McDonnell's Rich Taiwanese Backer," *New York Times*, December, 2, 1991.

[11]"Taiwan and Korea: Two Paths to Prosperity," *The Economist*, July 14, 1990; Damon Darlin, "Taiwan, Long Noted for Cheap Imitations, Becomes an Innovator," *Wall Street Journal*, June 5, 1990; and Sheryl WuDunn, "Taiwan Sets Course for Modernity," *Des Moines Register*, October 27, 1991.

[12]"Taming the Litte Dragons," *The Economist*, July 14, 1990 and "Korea's Anti-Mercantilists," *The Economist*, June 11, 1988.

[13]For discussions of the East Asian development model and the political conditions that underlay it, see Stephan Haggard, *Pathways from the Periphery: The Politics of Growth in the Newly Industrializing Countries*, Ithaca: Cornell University Press, 1990; a special issue of *International Studies Notes*, Winter, 1990, on the East Asian development model; various essays in Frederic C. Deyo, ed. *The Political Economy of the New Asian Industrialism*, Ithaca: Cornell University Press, 1987; Bela Balassa, *The Newly Industrializing Countries in the World Economy*, New York: Pergamon Press, 1981; Leroy Jones and Il Sakong, *Government, Business, and Entrepreneurship in Economic Development: The Korean Case*, Cambridge: Harvard University Press, 1980; and David Yoffie, *Power and Protectionism: Strategies of the Newly Industrializing Countries*, New York: Columbia University Press, 1983.

technocrats who have used tax incentives, subsidies, credit, and regulatory policies to promote favored industries. State industrial policies have sought to push development along a path of increasing technological sophistication. Both South Korea and Taiwan have encouraged high rates of domestic savings and investment while carefully screening direct foreign investment.

Singapore and Hong Kong began their paths to prosperity as regional financial and marketing centers before broadening their economies to encourage manufacturing growth and exports. Like South Korea and Taiwan, each have nondemocratic political systems, skilled bureaucracies, and weak labor unions.

Some interesting differences distinguish the East Asian NICs from one another. South Korea, the most statist of the four, has relied heavily upon large industrial conglomerates, both state-owned and private, whose growth has been fueled by cheap credit and heavy borrowing. Sales of the top four South Korean industrial groups equaled one-half of the country's total GNP in 1989. South Korea has also accumulated a substantial foreign debt, although its creditworthiness is considered far stronger than Latin American countries with similar debt loads.

Taiwan's economy, by contrast, rests upon a collection of many small equity-based companies. Unlike South Korea, Taiwan has avoided extensive foreign borrowing. Hong Kong is alone among the four East Asian NICs in relying almost solely upon market mechanisms rather than aggressive state intervention to steer economic growth and development. Unlike South Korea or Taiwan, Singapore has depended heavily upon foreign direct investment to stimulate growth, even to the point of favoring foreign firms over local firms.

The World Bank and other development agencies have held up the success of the East Asian NICs as examples to be copied by other Third World nations. Indeed, dozens of countries have begun to pursue export-led strategies of development.

India is one such recent convert from ISI to ELI. For decades, India has been among the most devoted practitioners of an inward-looking strategy of development. The state controlled and directed strategic sectors of the economy; foreign investment was strictly limited and highly regulated; import substitution policies were designed to protect and nurture domestic industrialization; and India's currency, the rupee, was purposefully overvalued.

After traveling to Asia and expressing admiration for South Korea's model of development, however, newly appointed Finance Minister Mohammed Singh announced a dramatic shift in economic strategy in the summer of 1991. This turnabout was prompted by India's worsening financial straits, including persistent balance of payments deficits, dwindling foreign reserves, and a burdensome foreign debt which had risen from $20.5 billion in 1980 to $72 billion by 1991. India's predicament was exacerbated by a precipitous decline in previously significant levels of Soviet foreign aid as well as the shrinkage of Soviet demand for Indian goods.

Following Singh's initiative, the Indian government pledged to devalue the rupee, eliminate the state budget deficit, cut subsidies to public firms while closing those which were particularly unprofitable, remove restrictions which discourage foreign investment, and reduce many barriers to imported goods. The World Bank and the IMF quickly rewarded India's shift from ISI toward a more liberal economic strategy by granting extensive new credits designed to relieve the immediate financial strains plaguing the country. Domestic reactions were more mixed, with many groups and individuals expressing worry and dismay that the new policies would produce increased unemployment and hardship among those reliant upon state support.[14]

A similar wave of reforms has swept Latin America in recent years, with countries such as Mexico, Brazil, Argentina, and Peru abandoning the ISI strategies of previous decades in favor of more liberal, open, and export-oriented economies. The recent experience of the Southeast Asian countries suggests that some of the nations seeking to emulate the Four Tigers will succeed. Yet, it is far from certain that the East Asian model of industrialization can be generalized to large numbers of Third World countries.

For one thing, the liberal version of ELI now being urged upon Third World countries by the World Bank and many development experts differs in subtle but important ways from the more mercantilistic strategy pursued by the East Asian NICs in the early stages of their economic takeoff. In South Korea and Taiwan, industrialization involved a heavy dose of state economic management and intervention. In this respect, East Asia and Latin Amercian shared much in common. They differed, however, in whether industrial production was directed toward the domestic market or external markets. Contemporary advocates of ELI have typically embraced the export orientation of the East Asian countries while ignoring or rejecting the heavy state economic role that was characteristic of such nations until recent years. Whether the liberal version of ELI now being pursued by many Third World countries can match the accomplishments produced through the more mercantilist strategies adopted by the early export-oriented industrializing countries is an interesting but as yet still untested question.

It is also important to note that the successes of South Korea and Taiwan seem to be associated with a number of characteristics peculiar to the historical development of these societies. These factors include the rule of strong authoritarian governments, the development of skilled bureaucracies, the weakness of the landowning class, and low levels of labor mobilization. Each also enjoyed favored relations with the United States, bringing considerable economic aid as well as military protection during the early stages of their industrialization drives.

The issue of historical timing also deserves attention. The East Asian NICs adopted ELI at a time when most other Third World countries were

---

[14]See Bernard Weintraub, "Economic Crisis Forcing Once Self-Reliant India to Seek Aid," *New York Times*, June 29, 1991; Bernard Weintraub, "India Is Now in a New Ballgame," *New York Times*, July 8, 1991; "Indian Economy: Pepsi Generation," *The Economist*, June 9, 1990; and "India's Plan is Backed," *New York Times*, September 23, 1991.

pursuing inward-looking strategies. Northern markets were growing at a brisk pace, while trade barriers were falling rapidly. Conditions were ripe for the success of a strategy built around the targeting of Northern markets with manufacturing goods built by low-wage workers. In today's climate, by contrast, many Third World nations are competing to service the same Northern markets, growth in Northern demand is sluggish, and Northern protectionism against Southern goods has risen.

Many Third World countries may find it difficult or impossible to duplicate the supportive domestic and international conditions that launched the East Asian nations along their path to prosperity. The challenge such countries face is to find ways of adapting an export-oriented strategy to their own unique circumstances.[15]

Those who seek to emulate countries such as South Korea and Taiwan must also reckon with the less appealing consequences of rapid industrialization in East Asia. In South Korea, for instance, growth has brought staggering levels of industrial pollution. In one highly publicized incident, a large chemical leak on March 14, 1991 contaminated a major reservoir which provided drinking water to nearby communities. Hundreds, perhaps thousands, of people became violently ill after drinking the sullied tap water. This episode led to an emotional debate among South Koreans over the environmental costs of development.[16] Although South Korea and Taiwan have recently moved tentatively toward democracy, the East Asian NICs have traditionally featured repressive authoritarian regimes which squelched political opposition and severely limited the rights of labor.

COLLECTIVE STRATEGIES OF DEVELOPMENT

■ Some Third World countries have sought development not through industrialization and diversification of their economies but instead by attempting to turn the tables of traditional colonial trade patterns against the North. During the seventies, there existed great interest in the potential of resource cartels to enhance Southern wealth. The aim of this strategy was to exploit the North's dependence upon various Southern raw material or agricultural exports. Although no single Third World country controlled a sufficient market share to manipulate world prices for the commodities it exported, the major Southern producers acting collectively might successfully coordinate production and pricing decisions so as to maximize their joint revenues.

Although, for reasons we will discuss later, most such efforts failed, this strategy produced one spectacular success story: the Organization of Petroleum

---

[15]For an argument that the success of the East Asian NICs cannot be duplicated by other Third World countries, see Robin Broad and John Cavanaugh, "No More NICs," *Foreign Policy*, Fall, 1988.
[16]David Sanger, "Chemical Leak in Korea Brings Forth a New Era," *New York Times*, May, 1991.

Exporting Countries (OPEC). The history of how the oil exporting states gained control over their petroleum resources from Northern oil companies and accumulated enormous riches during the seventies and early eighties is a fascinating one. Yet, this Third World success story is not unblemished. OPEC has been plagued by serious internal divisions, some resulting in war and violence, while, over the last decade, the oil exporting nations have witnessed a humbling fall in oil prices and revenues.

Prior to the 1970s, relations between the oil exporting countries and the major Northern oil companies worked decidedly to the advantage of the latter. Seven large oil firms (sometimes called the Seven Sisters) came to dominate the world oil market. These included five U.S. firms (Esso, Mobil, Standard of California, Gulf, and Texaco), one British (British Petroleum), and one Anglo-Dutch (Shell). A French company, CFP, later became a major player as well. These large firms pioneered the global search for new oil reserves, striking major finds in most of the present day OPEC countries during the period from World War I through the early fifties.[17]

The oil-producing countries initially found themselves almost entirely dependent upon the seven major firms for the development of their oil resources. None had the skills, technology, or marketing networks necessary to exploit their oil riches without outside help. Relations between oil-producing states and firms revolved around the concession system. Contracts negotiated between these parties gave particular firms or groups of firms the exclusive right to explore for oil in an agreed-upon territorial area within the country. Whatever oil was found belonged to the firm, which controlled all exploration, production, refining, and marketing decisions and activities. In return for these rights, Northern oil companies agreed to turn over a share of their revenues to the producing state in the form of taxes or royalties. This system gave the seven major firms control over production and pricing, although producing states sometimes attempted to influence such decisions.

Challenges to these arrangements were met with resistance, not only from the oil firms themselves, but also from Northern governments who saw the major oil companies as agents of the national interest and key guarantors of the Northern access to a critical resource. In the early fifties, for instance, the seven major oil firms organized a boycott of Iranian oil after the nation's prime minister, Mohammed Mossadegh, ordered the nationalization of assets belonging to the Anglo-Iranian oil company. When the boycott failed to lead to a reversal of the nationalization decision, the United States helped to organize a coup d'etat which toppled Mossadegh and returned Mohammed Reza Pahlavi to his previous position as Shah.

---

[17]For readable accounts concerning the relationship between the major oil firms and producing countries, consult Anthony Sampson, *The Seven Sisters: The Great Oil Companies and the World They Created*, rev. ed., London: Coronet, 1988; Daniel Yergin, *The Prize*, New York: Simon and Schuster, 1991; and John Blair, *The Control of Oil*, New York: Pantheon, 1976.

As time went on, the major oil-producing states increasingly chafed under the traditional arrangements. Each found it difficult, however, to bring about fundamental change acting on its own. The oil companies adopted a united stand in negotiating with host countries and played oil producers off against one another.

In 1960, at the initiative of Venezuela, five major oil-producing countries (the other four were Iran, Iraq, Saudi Arabia, and Kuwait) attempted to improve their collective bargaining position by forming the Organization of Petroleum Exporting Countries (OPEC).[18] The immediate precipitating factor was the decision by the major oil firms to lower prices in the face of a global glut of petroleum. Their revenues threatened, the oil-producing countries denounced the price cut and set out to gain greater control over the production and pricing of oil.

OPEC achieved relatively little of major significance during its first decade of existence. Beneath the surface, however, several trends were setting the stage for a revolution in the world of oil. Northern oil consumption rose at a rapid rate during the sixties. At the same time, the growth of U.S. oil production began to slow and, by the early seventies, had reached a plateau. The juxtaposition of these two trends led to a tightening of world oil supplies, especially after the United States began importing increasing amounts of foreign oil to compensate for the stagnation of domestic production.

Other important factors contributed to OPEC's fortunes as well. A growing number of independent oil companies began to challenge the seven major firms for access to foreign oil reserves. These newcomers were often willing to strike bargains more favorable to the oil-producing countries, undermining the unity of the major oil firms. The oil-producing countries themselves came to acquire increasing skill and competence in matters relating to oil, thus enhancing their confidence that they could manage their own industries with less reliance upon Northern firms. Also, OPEC absorbed a number of new members over the course of the sixties, including Libya, Indonesia, Algeria, Qatar, Nigeria, and Abu Dhabi. By 1970, OPEC members accounted for 90 percent of world oil exports.[19] Finally, the emergence of radical nationalist regimes, such as Libya, upset old arrangements between traditional rulers and the firms while increasing the aggressiveness of oil-producing states in their efforts to revise the old order.

With these elements in place, the dominant position of the major oil companies quickly eroded, and events conspired to magnify OPECs power over world oil markets. In 1970, Libya compelled Occidental Petroleum, an independent oil company, to raise the price of its Libyan produced crude oil.

---

[18]On the origins and evolution of OPEC, see Ian Skeets, *OPEC: Twenty Five Years of Prices and Politics*, Cambridge: Cambridge University Press, 1988.

[19]Robert Mortimer, *The Third World Coalition in International Politics*, 2nd ed., Boulder: Westview Press, 1984, 44.

OPEC moved quickly to exploit Libya's triumph. At an unprecedented meeting in Caracas during February, 1971, twenty-three oil firms acceded to OPEC demands for an across-the-board price increase. The next two years brought further OPEC-dictated price rises along with the beginning of a widespread movement on the part of oil-producing states to nationalize all or part of oil company assets within their nations.

In the midst of the October, 1973 Arab-Israeli war, the Arab members of OPEC cut production by 5 percent and announced an embargo on deliveries of oil to Western supporters of Israel. In an already tight oil market, these actions led to a quadrupling of oil prices to almost twelve dollars a barrel the following December. These high prices were sustained over the next five years, although inflation eroded the real value of OPEC oil revenues. The OPEC revolution triggered an economic recession in the North while generating a massive transfer of wealth from oil-importing countries to the oil-exporting states. The United States largely failed in its efforts to organize a counter cartel of oil-importing countries, although modest levels of cooperation among the principal Northern countries were institutionalized through the creation of the International Energy Agency.

OPEC once again engineered a massive hike in oil prices in 1979, after the onset of the Iraq-Iran war removed 5 percent of world oil supplies from the market. The price of oil tripled to roughly thirty-five dollars per barrel. Once again, the drain of more expensive oil, combined this time with tight monetary policies in the United States designed to reduce inflation, tipped much of the world economy into a major economic downturn.

Many Third World countries drew inspiration from OPEC's success during the seventies, despite the fact that Southern oil import bills rose along with those of the North. Countries that relied heavily upon natural resource exports viewed OPEC as a model for their own development efforts. Producers of bauxite, copper, tin, coffee, bananas, and other Third World commodities formed associations similar to OPEC in hopes of managing supply and driving up both prices and revenues. These ventures enjoyed little success. Beginning in the late seventies and early eighties, slowing demand in the North led instead to declining prices for many Southern raw material and agricultural exports. OPEC's exceptional success stemmed from the critical role of oil in Northern economies, the concentration of vast oil reserves in a relatively small group of Southern oil-producing countries, and, most importantly, the fact that market forces worked in OPEC's favor during the seventies.

OPEC's achievements also invigorated Third World efforts to negotiate a New International Economic Order (NIEO) with the North.[20] Beginning in

---

[20]On the negotiations surrounding the NIEO, see Robert Mortimer, *The Third World Coalition in International Politics*, 2nd ed., Boulder: Westview Press, 1984; Jeffrey Hart, *The New International Economic Order*, New York: St. Martin's Press, 1983; Stephen Krasner, *Structural Conflict: The Third World Against Global Liberalism*, Berkeley: University of California Press, 1985; Jagdish Bhagwati and John Gerard Ruggie, eds. *Power, Passions and Purpose*, Cambridge: MIT Press, 1984.

the sixties, Southern countries worked collectively through the United Nations and informal coordinating mechanisms such as the Group of 77 to hammer out a set of common demands for the reform of North-South relations.[21] The NIEO called for a variety of changes in the rules of the existing global economy: coordinated efforts to raise and stabilize commodity prices, the lowering of Northern barriers to Southern manufactured exports, increased Northern aid and financial assistance to the South, greater Third World voting power in institutions such as the International Monetary Fund and the World Bank, a global code of conduct for multinational corporations, debt relief, and greater Southern access to Northern technology. The Third World coalition counted upon OPEC's demonstrated power, along with its own unity, to provide the South with sufficient leverage to extract Northern concessions.

Indeed, fears that a stalemate in North-South bargaining might prompt desperate Southern responses harmful to the world economy prompted some prominent Northern commentators to embrace a strategy of compromise. Others in the North argued that wealthy countries shared an interest in reforms that might spur Southern growth and stimulate greater North-South trade.[22] For its part, OPEC endorsed Third World demands, pushed for the North to expand negotiations with the South, and increased its own aid to Southern countries harmed by rising oil prices.

While the South's leverage proved sufficient to force the North into a series of global bargaining rounds over the NIEO proposals during the seventies and early eighties, it remained inadequate to bring about real change. Northern countries, particularly the United States, rejected the bulk of Third World demands. Northern leaders perceived the redistributive aspects of the NIEO as contrary to their own nations' interests. Moreover, Northern spokespersons argued that many NIEO provisions would hamper global economic growth by intefering with market mechanisms.[23] Ultimately, negotiations failed also because the South, as well as some in the North, had overestimated the Third World's true power. Southern nations often warned that the North's failure to accept reform would lead to radical Third World responses, such as the proliferation of resource cartels, debt repudiation, nationalization of multinational corporate assets, and political upheaval. In fact, however, few of these consequences followed from the failure of the NIEO negotiations. The underlying reality was that the South remained more dependent upon the North than vice versa. A serious break in economic relations between the

---

[21]Despite its title, the Group of 77 eventually grew to include over 120 Third World countries.

[22]For statements of this viewpoint, see Independent Commission on International Development Issues, *North-South: A Programme for Survival*, Cambridge: MIT Press, 1980; and The Brandt Commission, *Common Crisis, North-South: Cooperation for World Recovery*, Cambridge: MIT Press, 1983.

[23]For a critical assessment of the NIEO, see Robert Tucker, *The Inequality of Nations*, New York: Basic Books, 1977.

two would hurt the South far more than the North. Southern power thus proved a chimera.

The 1980s were a difficult decade for OPEC. The high oil prices of the late seventies and early eighties stimulated successful conservation measures in the North, fuel switching to alternative sources of energy, and increased production from non-OPEC sources. Due to investments in energy efficiency, the amount of oil OECD countries needed to produce an extra dollar of GNP fell by 45 percent between 1973 and 1988. This contributed to a 20 percent drop in OECD oil consumption between 1979 and 1988. At the same time, the production of oil from non-OPEC sources, such as Mexico, the North Sea, and Alaska, grew by 20 percent from 1979 to 1986. Northern countries also began to diversify their sources of supply and build up strategic stockpiles of oil in an attempt to rob OPEC of its power to control the oil market. Thus, OPEC countries lost market share and became marginal producers — serving only that portion of world demand left unsatisfied after non-OPEC sources of supply had been exhausted.[24]

OPEC responded to these challenges by attempting to limit production in an effort to bolster prices. Each member country was allotted a production quota to insure that overall OPEC production did not breach agreed-upon ceilings. In practice, OPEC remained too divided to sustain this sort of cooperation. As prices softened, many countries attempted to sustain falling revenues by producing more oil than called for by their allotments. At first, Saudi Arabia compensated for this overproduction by reducing the rate of its own oil extraction and sales while attempting to persuade other OPEC producers to honor their quota agreements. The Saudis served, in other words, as a swing producer. By 1986, however, Saudi Arabia's market share and revenues had fallen precipitously and jawboning had failed to curb widespread cheating within OPEC. At that point, the Saudis chose to discipline other OPEC members and recapture lost market share by dramatically increasing their own oil production. This flood of oil onto world markets sent prices spiraling downward, falling, by early 1988, to between twelve and thirteen dollars per barrel. In real terms (discounting for inflation), the price of oil now stood below the levels experienced prior to the price hikes of the early seventies. The economic effects on OPEC were disastrous: between 1979 and 1988, per capita income fell by 27 percent among OPEC countries taken together, while imports shrank by half.[25]

By some indicators, OPEC would appear well-positioned to reassert dominance over world oil markets in the decade ahead. During the late eighties and early nineties, oil prices fell too low to sustain expensive oil exploration projects or to spur additional investments in energy conservation. In the

---

[24] All data in this paragraph from "The Cartel that Fell Out of the Driver's Seat," *The Economist*, February 4, 1989.

[25] "The Cartel that Fell. . . ."

United States, virtually all gains in energy efficiency took place prior to 1986. By some measures, such as the fuel efficiency of new cars, progress toward greater energy efficiency has been reversed. Production by non-OPEC sources is unlikely to grow in future years. United States oil production fell by 9 percent per year from 1985 to 1988, while imports rose from 27 percent of American oil consumption in 1985 to 42 percent in 1990. The major oil companies cut expenditures on oil exploration by one-third between 1985 and 1988. Declining investment and growing domestic demand sharply cut Mexican oil exports in the last decade. British and Norwegian production will decline in future years as the North Sea fields are exhausted. Falling investment levels, backward technology, and political instability have recently brought about a precipitous decline in oil production in the former Soviet Union. Due to declining production and rising demand, some OPEC oil exporters, such as Qatar, Gabon, Nigeria, and Ecuador, are likely to produce only enough oil for their own consumption by the turn of the century. Thus, the balance of power within OPEC seems likely to shift even more decisively in favor of the Persian Gulf states that possess enormous oil reserves. In 1990, five Gulf states accounted for two-thirds of the world's proven oil reserves. OPEC as a whole possessed 76 percent of global reserves, a figure that is expected to rise to 80 percent by the year 2000.[26]

Yet, while OPEC's share of world oil production and sales seems destined to rise, this factor alone is unlikely to return OPEC to its glory days of the seventies and early eighties when the organization engineered the massive transfer of wealth from oil-consuming countries to its member states through dramatic price hikes. Not only are prices expected to remain soft over the next decade, but OPEC's ability to control overproduction by its own member states is in doubt.

Most observers predict that world demand for oil will grow only sluggishly during the 1990s and beyond. Economic growth is projected to proceed at a modest pace in the mature economies of the major oil importing countries. What growth occurs is unlikely to be associated with rising levels of energy consumption. As in recent decades, the share of energy-intensive, heavy-manufacturing industries in the overall economies of Northern countries will continue to dwindle, while the shift toward industries requiring relatively low inputs of energy, such as services and high technology, continues apace.

Perhaps most importantly, ecological concerns about global warming are likely to spur efforts to reduce dependence upon fossil fuels. Carbon dioxide, a major product of burning hydrocarbons such as oil or coal, has been found

---

[26]The information in this paragraph has been taken from Mathew Wald, "Gulf Victory: An Energy Defeat?," *New York Times*, June 18, 1991; Saleh Billo, "Six OPEC Nations Have 70.5% of World's Proven Oil Reserves," *Oil and Gas Journal*, February 5, 1990; and "The Cartel That Fell. . . ."

to play a major role in exacerbating the greenhouse effect. Most Northern nations, with the notable exception of the United States, have pledged to stabilize or reduce carbon dioxide emissions over the next decade. Both conservation and fuel switching will be relied upon to achieve these goals. There remains great potential for conservation through the production of more energy-efficient cars (including the growing use of electric-powered automobiles), appliances, homes, and factories. Environmental considerations (along with security concerns about overreliance on foreign oil in the wake of the Persian Gulf war), have already renewed interest in renewable and nonfossil energy sources, including nuclear, solar, wind, hydroelectric, biomass, and geothermal as well as natural gas, a relatively clean-burning hydrocarbon.

Thus, while OPEC's share of the world oil market may indeed rise, overall energy demand is likely to grow only slowly, while oil use may actually fall as it fills a declining proportion of total energy needs. Oil prices are unlikely to rise in this climate. In contrast with the eighties, however, when declining oil prices removed incentives for additional investments in conservation or alternative energy development, Northern governments will be inclined to mandate continued progress in these areas through the use of tax and regulatory policies.

OPEC's economic power is also threatened by serious internal division among member states. As they often have in the past, these deep fractures may well hamper future efforts to coordinate production and pricing policies, both prerequisites to maximizing the cartel's overall revenues. The most obvious divisions are political. There exist deep ideological and political differences between the conservative monarchical regimes of the Persian Gulf region, the radical Arab nationalist governments of Libya and Iraq, and the fundamentalist Islamic republic of Iran, a non-Arab country.

The past decade has brought two instances of armed conflict among OPEC members, both involving Iraq. In each case, Iraqi aggression was partly motivated by considerations related to oil. The Iraqi invasion of Iran in 1980 was stimulated by Iraq's desire to gain exclusive control over a strategic waterway which lies astride the Iraqi-Iranian border. Lacking an adequate port along its short Persian Gulf coastline, Iraq sought a secure means by which it could off-load greater quantities of oil into tankers bound for Northern markets through the Gulf. Iraq's violent attempt to solve this problem touched off an inconclusive eight-year war that claimed one million lives.

Oil also played a key role in Iraq's ill-fated decision to invade Kuwait in the summer of 1990. In the wake of its deadly war with Iran, Iraq faced huge reconstruction costs as well as an enormous foreign debt. Since the country exported little else aside from oil, Iraq's hopes for economic revival rested almost exclusively on its ability to obtain higher oil revenues. Kuwaiti behavior presented a serious obstacle to this goal. In the first half of 1990, Kuwait consistently produced more oil than called for by its OPEC allotted quota. The failure of Kuwait and several other OPEC members to observe agreed-upon limitations on their oil production frustrated Iraqi efforts to engineer a hike in the world price for oil. Kuwait also angered Iraq by refusing to compromise over a dispute in which Iraq charged that Kuwait pumped more than its fair share of oil from a major field straddling the border between Iraq and Kuwait. Finally, Kuwait refused to forgive the $10 billion debt Iraq accumulated from loans used to finance its war with Iran.[27]

The conflict between Iraq and Kuwait over production and pricing policies reflects broader and more enduring divisions among OPEC producers. OPEC has long been split between price "hawks" and "doves". The former countries consistently push for higher oil prices while the latter lobby for price moderation. With some exceptions, the doves, which include OPEC's most important member, Saudi Arabia, among their ranks, have generally won out in recent years.

The countries that favor higher prices share one or more of the following characteristics:

(1) dwindling oil reserves that are likely to be exhausted in the near- to medium-term future at historical levels of production,

(2) large and growing populations, and

(3) relatively modest levels of investment in the wealthy oil-consuming countries of the North.

These nations seek to maximize short-term revenues from a rapidly depleting resource while satisfying the demands for industrialization and a higher standard of living from large numbers of still relatively poor citizens.

OPEC members with abundant reserves, small populations, and extensive investments in the North have very different interests. For these countries, high prices would stimulate oil exploration, conservation, and fuel switching in the oil-consuming countries and thereby reduce the demand for oil in future decades. With small populations, there exists a less urgent need to maximize present income. Moreover, as an increasing share of these nations' revenues come from returns on foreign investment, they must worry that high oil prices might damage Northern economies and interrupt the flow of repatriated profits from abroad.

This division within OPEC overlaps with another: the split between integrated and nonintegrated producers. Several OPEC countries, including Venezuela; Saudi Arabia; Kuwait; and, to a lesser extent, Nigeria, have begun to aggressively integrate their oil production with the ownership of downstream operations, such as refining and retail sales, located in oil-consuming

---

[27]For more on the political divisions within the Arab world, as well as the factors which led to Iraq's invasion of Kuwait, see Yahya Sadowski, "Revolution, Reform or Regression? Arab Political Options in the 1990 Gulf Crisis," *The Brookings Review*, Winter, 1990/91; Geraldine Brooks and Tony Horwitz, "Brotherly Hate: Gulf Crisis Underscores Historical Divisions in the Arab 'Family'," *Wall Street Journal*, August 13, 1990; and "The Middle East: New Frictions, New Alignments," *Great Decisions*, New York: Foreign Policy Association, 1991.

countries. Integrated producers not only desire the revenues from these downstream investments but also seek to lock up outlets for the sale of their own crude oil, thus reducing future uncertainties over foreign demand.

Nonintegrated OPEC producers, such as Iran, Iraq, and Libya, that lack these downstream connections face the risk that they may become marginal producers in the future. In other words, these countries would service only that portion of demand left over after the integrated producers have disposed of their output through refineries and marketing networks abroad. Integrated producers can use their control of downstream operations to assure steady, predictable levels of production and sales, while nonintegrated producers are likely to find themselves unable to locate buyers for all of their output should supply exceed demand.[28]

The aftermath of the Gulf War has left Saudi Arabia in a position of dominance within OPEC. Among the price hawks, Iraq has been defeated in war while Iran is eager to curry Saudi favor. Saudi Arabia vastly increased its oil output during the war in an effort to compensate for lost Iraqi and Kuwaiti production. Since the war's conclusion, Saudi leaders have been eager to maintain these high levels of production and the corresponding market share. In September 1991, the Saudis compelled other OPEC countries to agree to raise the official overall ceiling on OPEC production while rejecting proposals that Saudi exports be reduced in order to bolster oil prices. Saudi leaders appear to look forward to a long period of price moderation and stability in world oil markets as well as closer cooperation with oil importing countries.[29]

CONCLUSIONS

■ As is evident from this overview, Third World states have pursued a variety of development paths. It should also be clear that no single model or strategy of development is appropriate for all countries or all times. Progress toward economic prosperity is dependent upon the right fit or mix among three sets of factors:

(1) the internal economic, political, and cultural attributes of a given country,

(2) the opportunities and constraints provided by the international political economy, and

(3) the policy choices made by governing elites.

---

[28]Bob Williams, "OPEC Ventures Downstream: Industry Threat or Stability Aid?," *Oil and Gas Journal*, May 16, 1988.
[29]Youssef M. Ibrahim, "Oil Output is Raised by OPEC," *New York Times*, September 26, 1991.

Analysts are often led astray by focusing on the latter of these three, the choice of development strategy, in isolation from the first two. Yet policies which lack domestic political support or are poorly tailored to a country's specific mix of economic resources are unlikely to succeed. Similarly, the continuing evolution of the international economic system means that policies which are feasible and desirable during one period may become less so as time goes on.

The notion that policy success is dependent upon supportive domestic and international conditions is reinforced by the evidence reviewed in this chapter. Among major Latin American countries, the shift to ISI was prompted by the disruptions in international trade produced by the Great Depression and World War II. These policies were sustained after the war by the rise of nationalist political movements at home. The initial stage of ISI proved successful until its growth potential was exhausted due to the limited domestic market for consumer goods. The deepening phase of ISI was accompanied by the emergence of authoritarian governments and growing international indebtedness. The internal contradictions of ISI, combined with unfavorable international economic conditions during the late seventies and early eighties, set the stage for a lost decade of economic stagnation in Latin America. The harsh realities of the eighties prompted the abandonment of ISI in many countries by the end of the decade and initiated a trend toward more liberal economic strategies with still uncertain consequences.

The East Asian NICs passed through brief ISI stages before shifting to ELI strategies in the early sixties. Domestic and international conditions proved favorable to the success of such policies. Rising wage levels in the North made it possible for the first wave of export-led industrializers to target Northern markets for labor-intensive goods. The growing openness of the world economy combined with rapid economic expansion in the North also offered a congenial environment for ELI. Domestically, the East Asian countries featured strong, autonomous states free of serious challenges from either organized labor or landed elites. Technocratic bureaucracies were given the power to orchestrate state intervention so as to upgrade the levels of technology and skills in the economy and to target capital toward promising export industries. International and domestic factors thus supported a strategy of ELI. Whether other countries now attempting to emulate the success of the East Asian NICs will enjoy similar supportive internal and external conditions remains to be seen.

For decades, the oil-producing countries proved unable to fully exploit the economic potential of their vast petroleum reserves. Domestically, these countries lacked the skills, capital, and political will necessary to curb their dependence upon the major international oil companies. Internationally, the lack of coordination among producing countries, the glut of oil on world markets, and the political influence of Northern consuming countries all weighed against the efforts of producing countries to boost oil revenues.

These circumstances began to change in the sixties, leading to OPECs spectacular successes of the seventies. Shifting market conditions, combined with
disunity among oil producers during the eighties, partially eroded the gains
made during the seventies.

This suggests that it can be misleading to think of Third World development in terms of "models" that can be evaluated in the abstract and adopted
or abandoned at will by given states. Instead, development strategies evolve
historically, and their success or failure must be considered in light of the
particular circumstances facing specific countries. It is not policy alone, but
the fit between an overall strategy of development and the domestic, as well
as international, factors confronting public and private decision-makers which
determines the path of economic development.

ANNOTATED BIBLIOGRAPHY

Robert Alexander, "Import Substitution in Latin America in Retrospect," in
    James L. Dietz and Dilmus D. James, eds. *Progress Toward Development in
    Latin America: From Prebisch to Technological Autonomy*, Boulder: Lynne
    Rienner, 1991.
    Provides a historical overview and evaluation of Latin America's experi-
    ence with import substitution industrialization.

Robin Broad and John Cavanaugh, "No More NICs," *Foreign Policy*, Fall, 1988.
    The authors argue that the success of the export-oriented industrializers
    of East Asia will not be easily duplicated by other Third World countries.
    They outline an alternative path of development.

Frederic C. Deyo, ed. *The Political Economy of the New Asian Industrialism*,
    Ithaca: Cornell University Press, 1987.
    An excellent collection of essays on the political factors underlying the
    economic strategies of the East Asian newly industrializing countries.

Stephan Haggard, *Pathways from the Periphery: The Politics of Growth in the
    Newly Industrializing Countries*, Ithaca: Cornell University Press, 1990.
    An informative and provocative comparison of the development strategies
    pursued by the newly industrializing countries of East Asia and Latin
    America. Haggard emphasizes the role of external crises, state-society rela-
    tions, and development ideas in determining the policy choices made by
    state officials, as well as their consequences.

Robert Mortimer, *The Third World Coalition in International Politics*, Boulder:
    Westview Press, 1984.
    A comprehensive and detailed history of the rise and fall of the Third
    World's quest for a New International Economic Order.

Daniel Yergin, *The Prize*, New York: Simon and Schuster, 1991.
  This is a classic study of the politics and economics of oil. Written by a noted historian and energy analyst, this especially well-written and accessible treatment makes for fascinating reading. Contains an extensive discussion of OPEC.

C H A P T E R   10

FOREIGN AID AND
THIRD WORLD DEVELOPMENT

Conceived of a marriage between idealism and self interest, the world heralded the birth of foreign aid almost half a century ago. Great things were expected of aid, not least of which was the conquest of world poverty. At present, however, foreign aid has settled into a beleaguered middle age, marked by unfulfilled dreams and scaled-down expectations. Sapped of their youthful spirit, many aid agencies find themselves engaged in a lonely battle to defend their very existence against legions of critics.

The high hopes that once surrounded foreign aid stemmed from its early accomplishments. Seeking to kickstart a slumping world economy and contain the spread of communism and Soviet influence, the United States poured 2.5 percent of its GNP into the reconstruction of Western Europe between 1947 and 1951.[1] Dubbed the Marshall Plan, U.S. assistance proved critical in hastening Western European recovery from the devastation of World War II.

Motivated by humanitarian impulses as well as pragmatic economic and security interests, the United States sought to replicate this success by expanding foreign aid to the developing world during the fifties. The Point Four program, established in 1951 to provide technical assistance, was followed by the creation of the Development Loan Fund (a precursor of the present-day Agency for International Development), extending concessional financing for development projects and programs in Third World countries.

Meanwhile, the International Bank for Reconstruction and Development (IBRD), or World Bank, also began to shift its emphasis from European reconstruction to Third World development. A World Bank affiliate called the

---

[1]World Bank, *World Development Report, 1985*, New York: Oxford University Press, 1985, p. 94.

International Development Agency (IDA), which provided long-term, interest-free loans to finance development in the world's poorest countries, was created in 1960. The specialized agencies of the United Nations, such as the Food and Agricultural Organization and the World Health Organization, also grew in number and size during the fifties and sixties.[2]

Alongside the expansion of these multilateral agencies came the establishment of aid organizations in the developed nations of Western Europe and elsewhere. Over the next twenty years, the bilateral assistance programs of these donors grew much faster than that of the United States. Whereas the United States accounted for 60 percent of the bilateral assistance provided by all member countries of the Development Assistance Council (DAC) at the time of the organization's founding in 1961, the U.S. contribution dropped to less than 30 percent of the total by 1977.[3] The seventies also brought tremendous growth in the foreign assistance provided by a number of newly wealthy OPEC countries. During the eighties, Japan rapidly expanded its foreign assistance, surpassing the United States to become the world's largest aid donor by the end of the decade.[4] By 1988, official development assistance to the South had grown to over $51 billion.[5] An immense network of organizations and bureaucracies had evolved to administer this large flow of funds. Many of the world's poorest nations had become inextricably dependent upon outside aid.

Yet, faith in aid has diminished even while the flow of assistance has increased. Early hopes that the success of the Marshall Plan could be duplicated in the Third World were soon dashed by the realization that Southern countries lacked not only capital and financing, but also a myriad of other necessary prerequisites to development, including economic infrastructure, skilled and educated populations, competent bureaucracies, stable governments, and experienced entrepreneurs. A greater appreciation of the enormous challenges of Third World development dictated a more modest and reserved set of expectations toward foreign aid.

Yet, this was not the only source of disappointment. Critics increasingly questioned the purposes, philosophy, and methods of those who dispensed and received development assistance. Some charge that aid is a tool for serving the political and economic interests of donor countries. Moreover, aid props up repressive Third World governments, worsens inequality, and

---

[2]On the United Nations agencies, see Douglas Williams, *The Specialized Agencies and the United Nations: The System in Crisis,* London: C. Hurst & Co., 1987.

[3]The DAC is an affiliate of the Organization for Economic Cooperation and Development, or OECD, which includes most major donor countries. *World Development Report, 1985,* 1985, 94.

[4]Anthony Rowley, "Flush with Funds," *Far Eastern Economic Review,* Dec. 29, 1988, 52; and "Foreign Aid: Stingy Sam," *The Economist,* March 25, 1989, 26.

[5]World Bank, *World Development Report, 1990,* New York: Oxford University Press, 1990, 127.

destroys the environment.[6] Others attack aid as a needless and costly subsidy that sustains bloated Third World bureaucracies and discourages recipient governments from carrying out needed policy reforms or supporting private sector growth.[7] Both left and right condemn the inefficiency and corruption that too often plague foreign aid.

Disillusionment toward foreign aid is also widespread among average citizens in both the North and the South. A survey conducted in 1986 found that 54 percent of U.S. citizens favored U.S. economic assistance to the Third World in principle, while 39 percent were opposed. Humanitarian concerns were the most often cited reasons for supporting foreign aid. Yet, a series of ten polls conducted between 1973 and 1984 found that between 66 percent and 75 percent of Americans thought that the U.S. spent too much on foreign aid, while only 3 percent to 5 percent believed too little was being spent. In 1986, 85 percent considered the U.S. aid bureaucracy wasteful; 88 percent believed that foreign governments misused aid; and 75 percent thought aid created dependence.[8]

Systematic data on Third World attitudes toward foreign aid are scarce, but anecdotal evidence of frustration abounds. Popular movements have arisen to protest the social dislocations and environmental destruction that have accompanied huge aid-funded projects in Brazil, India, and Indonesia. Widespread resentment over the suspected misuse and theft of aid funds played a role in the political upheavals that forced Ferdinand Marcos from power in the Philippines. The unpopular policy reforms demanded of major debtor countries in recent years by bilateral and multilateral donors as a condition for further funding have prompted rioting in various countries. In a small, but perhaps symbolic, incident which occurred in 1985, Haitian peasants waved machetes in an attempt to fend off U.S. helicopters attempting to deliver food aid. These farmers acted out of fear that cheap foreign food would depress prices and undermine their livelihood.[9]

These critical responses to the growth of foreign aid are not surprising. Indeed, the emotionally charged debate over aid may flow inevitably from the fundamental nature of foreign assistance. Aid's very existence can be traced to the persistent gap between rich and poor in the world economy.

---

[6]For two examples among many, see Theresa Hayter and Catherine Watson, *Aid: Rhetoric and Reality*, London: Pluto Press, 1985; and Frances Moore Lappe, Joseph Collins and David Kenley, *Aid as Obstacle: Twenty Questions About Our Foreign Aid and the Hungry*, San Francisco: Institute for Food and Development Policy, 1981.

[7]See, for instance, P.T. Bauer, *Reality and Rhetoric: Studies in the Economics of Development*, Cambridge: Harvard University Press, 1984, especially chapters 3 and 4, 38–72; and Nick Eberstadt, "The Perversion of Foreign Aid," *Commentary*, June, 1985.

[8]All data from Christine Contee, *What Americans Think: Views on Development and U.S.–Third World Relations*, Interaction and Overseas Development Council, 1987, 23–25, 29, and 31.

[9]Lloyd Timberlake, "The Politics of Food Aid," in Edward Goldsmith and Nicholas Hildyard, eds. *Earth Report: Monitoring the Battle for Our Environment*, Mitchell Brazley, 1988, 24.

From a Third World standpoint, aid is often viewed as a poor substitute for structural reforms in the international economic order, which might more directly reduce this inequality between the haves and have-nots of the world. Moreover, stark contrasts inevitably arise between the humanitarian declarations used to justify aid and the political as well as economic motives that govern the allocation of assistance. This clash between rhetoric and reality leaves aid-givers vulnerable to charges of hypocrisy. Finally, while aid may, on the whole, make a modest contribution to Third World development and poverty reduction, it also fosters dependence. The relationship between donor and recipient, never an equal one, is almost certain to provoke resentment and provide opportunities for manipulation.[10]

The remainder of this chapter examines various controversies surrounding the relationship between aid and development. After a brief discussion of the different types and strategies of aid giving, we explore the effectiveness of foreign assistance in spurring economic growth, reducing poverty, and enhancing environmental sustainability in the Third World.

TYPES OF AID

■ From where does aid originate? How is it administered? The advanced industrialized nations of the North account for most of the aid provided to Third World countries.[11] Yet Northern donors vary greatly in the proportion of their national incomes devoted to foreign aid. The Nordic countries, including Norway and Sweden, are among the most generous. Although the U.S. aid program is large in absolute terms, the American contribution ranks next to last among twenty major donor countries when measured as a percentage of GNP. In 1988, DAC countries devoted slightly less than four-tenths of 1 percent of their combined annual GNP to foreign aid.

Aid is dispensed through both bilateral and multilateral agencies. Each major donor country runs its own bilateral aid program, which provides money, food, and technical advice directly to individual recipient nations. The principal organization responsible for U.S. foreign aid, for instance, is the Agency for International Development. In addition, a number of multilateral agencies, including the World Bank; the three major regional development banks in Latin America, Africa, and Asia; and the specialized agencies of the United Nations, provide development assistance funded through member contributions and other means. Bilateral aid accounts for almost two-thirds

---

[10]For a general discussion of the tensions between aid givers and recipients, see the chapter entitled "Donors, Recipients and the Aid Giving Process" in Jeffrey Pressman, *Federal Programs and City Politics*, Berkeley: University of California Press, 1975.

[11]Foreign aid takes many different forms. Some are beyond the scope of this chapter. We give little attention, for instance, to foreign military aid or to assistance provided by private voluntary organizations. Our focus is on official economic assistance.

of overall foreign assistance, with multilateral programs making up 22 percent. The remaining 14 percent is funneled through nongovernmental organizations that raise many of their funds privately.[12]

TABLE 10.1

Aid As a Percentage of GNP, 1988

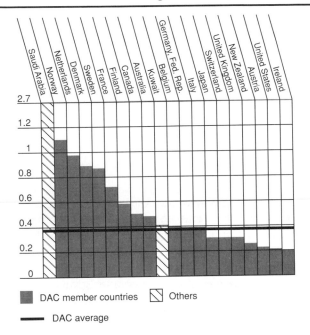

DAC member countries · Others

DAC average

SOURCE: Organization for Economic Cooperation and Development 1989. Taken from World Bank, *World Development Report, 1990*, Oxford: Oxford University Press, 1990, Box figure 8.4, 129.

THE RATIONALE FOR AID

■ The rationale for aid rests upon its presumed superiority, in some respects, over private financial flows as an instrument for furthering Third World development. The World Bank cites the advantages foreign assistance offers in promoting both efficiency and equity.[13]

---

[12]*World Development Report, 1990*, 128. We should note that substantial portions of the budgets of "private" aid groups are funded with government money as well.

[13]See *World Development Report, 1985*, 99–100.

Official aid, according to the World Bank, finances certain types of projects that promise large social and economic returns but, nevertheless, seldom attract the interest of private capital. These include investments in health, education, agricultural research, and basic infrastructure. Many such projects pay off only over thirty- to forty-year periods, a time frame longer than most private investors are willing to accommodate. Moreover, some types of technical assistance and policy advice provided by official aid institutions are simply unavailable through private sources. Aid's principal role in development is to complement, rather than substitute for, the private sector. The desired result is a more well-rounded and efficient pattern of economic growth. Aid is also justified on equity grounds. Because most aid is provided on concessional terms, poorer countries gain access to resources that they would otherwise find unaffordable. Similarly, without the subsidies made possible by concessional assistance, the poor within recipient countries would be unable to pay the full costs for the services they receive.

STRATEGIES OF FOREIGN ASSISTANCE

■ The basic strategies and philosophies of development underlying foreign aid have shifted markedly over time. We can distinguish between three major approaches. A top-down model, pursued most vigorously during the fifties and sixties, sought to stimulate Third World development through the provision of infrastructure and technical advice. The seventies brought a more egalitarian "bottom-up" strategy, designed to combine "growth with equity" through investment in the poor. During the eighties, attention shifted to the strengthening of market mechanisms. New conditions placed on aid encouraged governments to remove barriers to trade and foreign investment, encourage private sector growth, and adopt more orthodox economic policies.[14]

Early approaches to foreign aid were consistent with the theories of modernization then in vogue. Development was equated with industrialization and the expansion of the largely urban-based "modern" sectors of Third World economies at the expense of the "traditional" rural sectors. Most lending went to state-owned infrastructural projects, including such items as dams, roads, electrical grids, communications networks, and port facilities. The inadequacy of infrastructural development was considered a critical bottleneck

---

[14]For useful overviews of the history of foreign aid and the shifting strategies of assistance, see Robert Packenham, *Liberal America and the Third World: Political Development Ideas in Foreign Aid and Social Science*, Princeton: Princeton University Press, 1973; *World Development Report, 1985*, 94–99; Robert Wood, *From Marshall Plan to Debt Crisis: Foreign Aid and Development Choices in the World Economy*, Berkeley: University of California Press, 1986; Stephen Hellinger, Douglas Hellinger and Fred M. O'Regan, *Aid for Just Development: Report on the Future of Foreign Assistance*, Boulder: Lynne Rienner Publishers, 1988, 13–32; and Brice Nissen, "Building the World Bank," in Steven Wasserman, *The Trojan Horse: A Radical Look at Foreign Aid*, Berkeley: Ramparts Press, 1974.

to Third World growth and industrialization. Once this constraint had been overcome, economic growth would proceed according to the comparative advantage of various Third World countries.

This strategy relied heavily upon the creation of conditions likely to attract foreign investment. Multinational corporations would be enticed by cheap labor, abundant raw materials, and a growing Third World consumer market. Technical advice played a key role in providing state bureaucrats and local entrepreneurs with the skills and knowledge needed to manage a modern economy.

Agriculture took a backseat to industry, and the rural population was viewed primarily as an enormous reserve of potential wage labor, to be tapped gradually over time according to the expanding demands of the modern sector. Nevertheless, traditional agricultural exports were counted upon to generate foreign exchange that, in turn, could be put toward the importation of needed capital goods. Thus subsistence farmers producing basic food staples for their own consumption were encouraged to switch to specialized commodities that could be marketed abroad.

Although this strategy succeeded in stimulating industrialization in many countries, it became apparent, by the late sixties, that the benefits of modernization were not trickling down to the poor majority as its proponents had hoped and had promised. In some countries, such as Brazil, income inequality worsened considerably, and the bottom 40 percent to 60 percent ended up both relatively and absolutely worse off than before.

These considerations led to a rethinking of traditional wisdom during the seventies. Under the leadership of Robert McNamara (1968–81), the World Bank, working particularly through its "soft" loan affiliate, the International Development Agency, began to focus more directly on eliminating the sources of Third World poverty.[15] This orientation was often referred to under the label of "growth with equity." Around the same time, the U.S. Congress passed "New Directions" legislation designed to refocus the work of the Agency for International Development (AID) toward the needs of the poor majority. The Foreign Assistance Act of 1973 directed that AID place greatest emphasis on "countries and activities which effectively involve the poor in development. . . ."[16] Many European countries followed suit.[17]

Concerns about equity were not the only ones driving this new attention to the plight of the poor. It was expected that poor people, if given the proper

---

[15]For an examination of the World Bank policies toward the poor during the McNamara years, see Robert L. Ayres, *Banking on the Poor: The World Bank and World Poverty*, Cambridge: MIT Press, 1983.

[16]Hellinger, Hellinger, and O'Regan, *Aid for Just Development*, 22. Also on the impact of the "New Directions" legislation, see Robert L. Curry, "The Basic Needs Strategy, the Congressional Mandate, and U.S. Foreign Aid Policy," *Journal of Economic Issues*, December, 1989.

[17]See Steven Arnold, *Implementing Development Assistance: European Approaches to Basic Needs*, Boulder: Westview Press, 1982.

training and resources, could become productive contributors to development rather than drags upon it. This belief undergirded the two principal components of the new growth with equity strategy. The first was an emphasis on satisfying the basic needs of poor rural and urban dwellers. Proponents of this approach argued that the poor cannot become economically productive as long as they are afflicted by illness, malnutrition, illiteracy, inadequate shelter, and the lack of access to clean water supplies. Without these basic needs, the poor become locked in a continuing cycle of poverty, unable to earn a livelihood or to improve their economic circumstances.[18]

The second component of the strategy followed from the first. Once the poor were secure in their basic needs, they required new opportunities to begin providing for themselves and contributing to the remainder of society. The role of aid was to fund expanded education programs, agricultural extension schemes, rural cooperatives, small business development, and other projects designed to enhance the economic productivity of the poor.

Aid officials who embraced this growth with equity strategy rejected calls for more far-reaching efforts to redistribute wealth and income. The emphasis remained on growth. New-style investments were expected to produce economic returns as high or higher than more traditional projects.[19] Greater equity would emerge as a by-product of this strategy, however, as the retargeting of investment priorities allowed the poor to lay claim to larger increments of future growth.

This bottom-up approach to development drew criticism from a number of different directions. Some argued that, despite rhetoric about investing in human resources, the new lending programs did little more than subsidize consumption by the poor. Such "welfare" programs only created dependence, without providing the poor with the means to provide for themselves.

Others suggested that the aid community's new emphasis on aiding the poor amounted to less than met the eye. As the accompanying table shows, poverty-oriented lending by the World Bank increased from 5 percent to 30 percent of total disbursements during the seventies. Yet, this left 70 percent of the Bank's funds devoted to traditional projects. Moreover, some critics charged that much of the money allocated for the poor actually benefited those who were already relatively well-off in Third World societies, either because elites found ways of siphoning off aid for their own uses or because aid agencies used too sweeping a definition of who counted as poor.

---

[18]For a discussion of basic needs, see Paul Streeten and Chahid Javed Burki, "Basic Needs: Some Issues," *World Development*, Vol. 6, No. 3, 1978.

[19]A study by the Overseas Development Council, based upon World Bank data through the early eighties, suggests that poverty-oriented World Bank projects performed better than nonpoverty projects along a variety of economic criteria, including overall return on investment. Moreover, repayment rates were as high for poverty projects as for nonpoverty projects. Education directed at the poor offered the highest gains. See Sheldon Annis, "The Shifting Grounds of Poverty Lending at the World Bank," in Richard Feinberg, ed. *Between Two Worlds: The World Bank's Next Decade*, New Brunswick: Transaction Books, 1986.

TABLE 10.2

World Bank Classification of
Its Sector Lending by Poverty Focus
(Percentage of Total, Three-Year Averages)

SECTOR	FISCAL YEARS			
	1968–70	1971–73	1976–78	1979–81
Directly poverty-oriented				
Rural development	3.2	7.6	16.5	15.3
Education (primary and nonformal)	0.2	0.8	1.4	1.6
Population, health, nutrition	_____	0.7	0.6	0.3
Small-scale industry	_____	0.2	1.7	1.7
Urbanization	_____	1.3	2.6	3.4
Water supply/sewerage	1.6	4.7	4.6	6.7
Subtotal	5.0	15.3	27.4	29.5
Other				
Agriculture	16.1	13.3	15.8	13.4
Energy (power)	24.6	14.9	13.8	15.0
Energy (oil, gas, coal)	0.3	0.9	0.9	3.5
Industry (incl. DFCs)	15.7	16.4	16.5	13.5
Transportation	27.5	21.9	15.9	13.5
All other	10.9	16.3	9.6	11.6
Total	100.0	100.0	100.0	100.0

SOURCE: World Bank *Focus on Poverty* (Washington, 1983), 6. Taken from Robert E. Wood, *From Marshall Plan to Debt Crisis*, Berkeley: University of California Press, 1986, Table 24, 216.

In any case, enthusiasm for the new focus on poverty waned with the replacement of McNamara as head of the World Bank and the election of Ronald Reagan as president in the United States. Both the World Bank and AID shifted priorities during the eighties.[20] Previous approaches to foreign aid, it was argued, placed too little emphasis on the encouragement of free

[20]For discussions of these changing priorities at the World Bank and AID during the eighties, see Clive Crook, "The World Bank," *The Economist*, September 27, 1986; John Sewell and Christine Contee, "U.S. Foreign Aid in the 1980s: Reordering Priorities," in John Sewell, Richard Feinberg, and V. Kallab, eds. *U.S. Foreign Policy and the Third World*, New Brunswick: Transaction Books, 1985; Christopher Madison, "Exporting Reaganomics — The President Wants to Do Things Differently at AID", *National Journal*, May 5, 1982; Christine Contee, "U.S. Foreign Aid in the 1980s," *Policy Focus* (published by the Overseas Development Council), No. 4, 1985; Joel Johnson, "Foreign Aid: The Reagan Legacy", *Policy Focus* (published by the Overseas Development Council), No. 2, 1988.

markets and private enterprise. The centerpiece of the new strategy designed to correct this oversight became known as "policy dialogue."

The World Bank began to expand program and structural adjustment lending. These loans were not tied to specific projects, as in the past, but instead provided budgetary or balance of payments support. To qualify for such loans, however, governments were required to agree to policy reforms designed to reduce the state's role in the economy. These policy adjustments included the privatization of state-owned enterprises, decreased social welfare subsidies, trimmer government budget deficits, lower trade barriers, and the elimination of regulations that discouraged foreign investment. These demands were justified on the grounds that heavy state intervention stifled economic growth and that aid provided leverage to correct such impediments to development.[21]

Alongside this emphasis on policy dialogue came a renewed effort to strengthen the roles of foreign investment and the private sector in Third World economies. The World Bank expanded funding for the International Finance Corporation, which, unlike other branches of the Bank, made equity investments in partnership with private firms. Likewise, during the Reagan Administration, a new entity known as the Bureau for Private Enterprise was created within AID with much the same mission.[22]

Aside from the merits of any one approach, these frequent shifts in the assumptions and strategies favored by the aid community deserve further comment. The movement from one approach to another is less the result of steadily accumulating knowledge and insight into the process of development than a function of shifting political winds in the North. The top-down approach of the fifties and sixties must be understood in the context of the Cold War. The United States and its allies hoped that the emphasis on infrastructure would provide quick, tangible evidence of Western largess, strengthen friendly governments, and, by stimulating rapid growth, inoculate Third World societies against the appeals of socialism. The poverty-oriented focus of the seventies reflected the liberal political climate of that era. In particular, the Vietnam War brought home for many the dangers of supporting narrowly based Third World elites without attention to the needs of the poor majority. Finally, the emphasis on markets and private enterprise during the eighties stemmed from the conservative philosophy of newly elected Northern leaders such as Ronald Reagan and Margaret Thatcher.

What difference does it make which approach to development is embraced by the aid community? Most obviously, the assumptions underlying foreign assistance affect project selection and design as well as the allocation of funds. Yet far more significant is the broader influence these ideas exert

---

[21]For a report on one such effort to link aid with policy reform, see John Felton, "Egypt: Aid Payments Used to Spur More Economic Reforms," *Congressional Quarterly*, August 26, 1989.
[22]See Madison, "Exporting Reaganomics. . . ."

over the policies of the recipient countries themselves. The World Bank is one of the key sources of data and analysis on development issues. Its reports, publications, and activities are widely followed and play a pivotal role in debates among experts and government officials. As we have seen, the Bank, along with other institutions, such as AID and the IMF, actively seeks to shape the economic policies of Third World states. Changes in approach and philosophy at the largest aid agencies thus ripple through the entire Third World, altering, in both approach and emphasis, the development choices made by Southern governments.

This has been particularly true during the last decade, when the World Bank and other agencies have sought to expand and strengthen the scope of policy dialogue with recipient nations. Thus World Bank president Barber Conable's remark, in February 1990, about changing strategies of development in the Third World could be read as a measure of the Bank's success in gaining acceptance for ideas it aggressively sponsored in recent years: "If I were to characterize the past decade, the most remarkable thing was the generation of a global consensus that market forces and economic efficiency were the best way to achieve the kind of growth which is the best antidote to poverty."[23]

THE EFFECTIVENESS OF AID

■ Does aid work? Has it contributed to efficient and equitable Third World development? Measuring the effectiveness of aid is a challenging task. It is difficult, for instance, to know what might have happened in the absence of aid. Moreover, success can be defined in different ways, depending upon whether one chooses to emphasize overall economic growth, poverty reduction, equity, or environmental impact. In addition, many factors besides aid affect a country's economic performance. Singling out aid's contribution is therefore tricky at best.[24]

Clearly, however, success stories are available, whether we are speaking of projects that have brought real benefits to targeted recipients or nations that have used aid as a tool for stimulating overall development. One study covering a ten-year period examined the economic rate of return for 504 World Bank projects where results could be estimated. On average, these investments brought a return of 18 percent, quite healthy by any standard.[25]

---

[23]Robin Broad, John Cavanaugh, and Walden Bello, "Development: The Market is Not Enough," *Foreign Policy*, Winter, 1990-91, 144. Broad, Cavanaugh, and Bello offer a critique of the overwhelming emphasis on markets in the approach described by Conable.

[24]For a detailed survey that attempts to assess aid's effectiveness, see Robert Cassen and Associates, *Does Aid Work?*, Oxford: Clarendon Press, 1986.

[25]*World Development Report, 1985*, 103.

The World Bank also points to South Korea and Indonesia as countries where aid played a major role during the formative stages of development to both spur growth and reduce poverty.

Yet many countries, such as Tanzania, the Sudan, Zaire, Mozambique, Niger, Togo, Zambia, and Haiti, have been, and remain, heavily dependent on external aid but show disappointing economic results. The difference between success or failure, the World Bank argues, has to do with a country's willingness to pursue sound, market-oriented policies. Aid works within a conducive policy setting but cannot compensate for the deleterious effects of poor economic decision making.[26]

Yet, aid's critics suggest that foreign aid itself possesses inherent shortcomings stemming from the structure of the aid process as well as the priorities and motives of the donors. We take up seven of these criticisms in the sections that follow.

Poverty and the Misallocation of Aid

Perhaps the most widely accepted rationale for foreign aid lies in its potential for reducing Third World poverty. Indeed, as we have seen, public support for aid rests principally upon its purported humanitarian purposes, yet aid's success in ameliorating poverty is far from proven. After a quarter-century of aid flows, the World Bank estimates that one-third of the Third World's population, or 1.1 billion people, continue to live in absolute poverty (defined as annual income below \$370).[27] Indeed, in a report reviewing the history of foreign aid between 1969 and 1985, the DAC concluded that "the most troubling shortcoming of development aid has been its limited measurable contribution to the reduction — as distinguished from the relief — of extreme poverty, especially in the rural areas of both middle-income and poor countries."[28]

Part of the explanation for aid's disappointing record in attacking poverty is that political and economic considerations have influenced the allocation of foreign assistance. Substantial amounts of aid do not go to the countries which are most in need. To be sure, aid accounts for a significant portion of the income and investment in some of the world's poorest countries (see Table 10.4). Yet in 1988, 41 percent of aid was distributed to middle- and high-income countries.[29] As Table 10.3 suggests, aid receipts per capita bear little relation to average income. Indeed, Israel, a relatively wealthy country,

---

[26] For the World Bank's views on aid's effectiveness, see *World Development Report, 1985*, 101–105; and *World Development Report, 1990*, 128–33.

[27] *World Development Report, 1990*, 1.

[28] *World Development Report, 1990*, 127.

[29] *World Development Report, 1990*, 127.

received more than twice as much aid per capita as the next highest nation on the list.

TABLE 10.3

Per Capita Aid Receipts, 1988

COUNTRY	AID RECEIPTS PER CAPITA	GNP PER CAPITA
Israel	282.07	8,650
Jordan	108.95	1,500
Gambia, The	102.63	200
Senegal	78.85	650
Zambia	63.73	290
Egypt	29.91	660
Nepal	22.05	180
Ethiopia	21.05	120
Syrian Arab Republic	16.34	1,680
Bangladesh	14.62	170
Pakistan	13.32	350
Myanmar	11.22	. . .a
Indonesia	9.34	440
India	2.58	340
China	1.84	330
Nigeria	1.09	290

a. GNP per capita estimated at less than $500.

Source: Organization for Economic Cooperation and Development 1990 and World Bank data. Taken from *World Bank, World Development Report, 1990,* Oxford: Oxford University Press, 1990, Table 8.3, 128.

The diversion of aid from poorer to relatively better-off Third World countries stems principally from the political and economic interests of donor countries. The influence of nondevelopmental considerations on aid allocation decisions is most pronounced in the case of the United States. In 1986, according to the World Bank, development assistance to low-income countries accounted for only 8 percent of the overall U.S. aid budget.[30] One study found that among seventeen donor countries, the United States ranked last in the degree to which it allocated aid according to the poverty-related needs of recipient countries.[31]

---

[30]*World Development Report, 1990*, 127–28.

[31]Mark McGillivray, "The Allocation of Aid among Developing Countries: A Multi-Donor Analysis Using a Per Capita Aid Index," *World Development*, Vol. 17, No. 4, 1989, 565.

TABLE 10.4

The Relative Importance of Aid in Selected Developing Countries, 1987

COUNTRY	TOTAL AID RECEIPTS AS A PERCENTAGE OF GNP	AID RECEIPTS FROM DAC COUNTRIES AS A PERCENTAGE OF EXPORTS TO OECD MARKETS
Guinea-Bissau	89.3	956.0
Gambia, The	55.6	89.1
Mozambique	51.7	509.2
Chad	28.3	332.2
Malawi	23.6	61.0
Zambia	22.5	53.0
Tanzania	17.0	270.4
Lesotho	15.6	1,041.7
Bangladesh	9.4	105.9
Benin	7.9	108.5
Sierra Leone	7.6	26.4
Kenya	7.5	60.3
Myanmar	3.6	261.6
Pakistan	2.7	18.2
Indonesia	1.9	7.7
India	0.7	11.8
China	0.5	3.9

SOURCE: Organisation for Economic Co-operation and Development 1990. Taken from *World Bank, World Development Report, 1990*, Oxford: Oxford University Press, 1990, Table 8.2, 127.

A substantial portion of U.S. aid is channeled through the Economic Support Fund (ESF) which is administered by AID. ESF aid is explicitly intended to reward friendly countries and to promote political stability in areas considered important to U.S. interests. A substantial portion of ESF assistance goes to Israel and Egypt as a reward for their willingness to enter into the Camp David Accords. Other countries, such as the Philippines, have received ESF funds as compensation for their willingness to allow U.S. military bases on their soil. Although some ESF aid goes to fund development projects, most provides general balance of payments support or finances commodity imports. After rising during the early eighties, ESF funding declined later in the decade, although it still accounted for 37 percent of U.S. economic aid in 1988.[32]

---

[32]Calculated from figures given in Johnson, "Foreign Aid: The Reagan Legacy," 3.

The Ironies of Food Aid

Food aid is among the most widely misunderstood forms of foreign assistance.[33] Sending food to hungry Southerners is popularly viewed in the North as a particularly humanitarian act. In fact, however, food aid often does more harm than good.

The least controversial form of food aid is emergency assistance designed to compensate for shortfalls during times of drought and famine. Under these circumstances, outside food can save hundreds of thousands or even millions of lives. The need for such assistance has grown, rather than lessened, over time, particularly in the case of many African countries that have experienced repeated food shortages over the last two decades. In early 1991, the United Nations estimated that 27 million people in 25 African countries would require emergency food relief totaling 3.9 million tons. These requirements were the highest ever forecast by international relief experts.[34]

Yet, in practice, emergency food efforts have been plagued by problems. Famine is rarely the result of natural factors alone. It is often exacerbated by government policies that discourage food production, the failure to set aside adequate food reserves during good years, slowness on the part of the government and outside donors in reacting to signs of impending shortages, and the dislocations caused by war or political instability. These essentially political sources of hunger not only serve to heighten the probability of famine but also hinder efforts to assist the hungry once outside help is needed. Conflicts between the local government and international relief agencies are common. Government authorities are often slow to acknowledge the prospect of famine for fear of shouldering the political blame for the country's desperate condition. Moreover, the distribution of food and medical supplies is fraught with political implications in severely divided societies. This often gives rise to intense bargaining between local governments and outside donors over the control of distribution activities.

These complexities are illustrated in the case of the recent famine in the Sudan. In 1990, Sudanese authorities repeatedly denied the prospect of food shortages despite increasingly urgent warnings of impending famine by outside observers and international relief agencies. The Sudanese government refused to request special assistance, effectively limiting donor access to the hungry. Moreover, aid personnel already working in the southern part of the country, where government troops were engaged in the suppression of an ethnic revolt, were forced to leave after authorities accused them of assisting

---

[33]For a brief survey and evaluation of various forms of food aid, see *World Development Report, 1990*, 135.

[34]Paul Lewis, "Sudan Will Allow New Famine Relief," *New York Times*, March 19, 1991.

the rebels.[35] This disturbing case is not unique. Almost identical events disrupted famine relief efforts in Ethiopia during 1984 and 1985.[36]

Emergency aid often arrives too late or fails to reach those in greatest need. The European Community pledged food assistance in 1984 when much of Sub-Saharan Africa faced famine conditions. Yet, actual food deliveries did not begin until 400 days later. The slow response of the international community as well as that of local governments prompted many African farmers to abandon their land and migrate to enormous famine camps. Many who survived failed to return to their farms in time to sow new crops once the rains returned.[37]

Once aid began arriving in 1985, the huge quantities of food overwhelmed port, storage, and transportation facilities. Only 75 percent of the food delivered to Ethiopia was distributed, while the figure for the Sudan was 64 percent. Moreover, food aid failed to end when the famine finally lifted. Aid continued to pour into Kenya after returning rains allowed a record harvest in 1985. The overabundance of food flooded markets, depressed prices and lowered rural incomes.[38]

A more ironic case of misdirected food aid occurred in the wake of the 1976 earthquake in Guatemala. Large quantities of food were delivered despite the fact that agricultural production remained unaffected by the quake and no food shortages existed.[39]

Despite the problems that surround emergency food programs, virtually all observers agree that such relief efforts are both necessary and useful. Yet, emergency assistance accounted for only 5 percent of all food aid in 1985.[40] The remainder is divided between project and program aid, both of which are the subject of controversy.

Project aid, which accounted for 25 percent of all food assistance in 1985, targets food toward specific purposes and populations. Examples include "food for work" schemes such as the enormous World Food Program project in Ethiopia where thousands of rural dwellers are given food in exchange for

---

[35]"African Famine: Yet Again," *The Economist*, January 5, 1991, 33; and Alyson Pytte, "Congress Is Using Aid as a Lever to Protest Rights Abuses" and "Somalia and the Sudan: Two Countries Plagued by Poverty, Famine and War," *Congressional Quarterly*, May 13, 1989, 1132–35. In March of 1991, Sudanese officials finally decided to make a formal appeal for emergency food aid and allow relief workers freer access to the country. Lewis, "Sudan Will Allow New Famine Relief."

[36]See the epilogue to William Shawcross, *The Quality of Mercy: Cambodia, Holocaust and Modern Conscience*, New York: Simon and Schuster, 1985.

[37]Timberlake, "The Politics of Food Aid," 24.

[38]Timberlake, "The Politics of Food Aid," 23–24.

[39]Timberlake, "The Politics of Food Aid," 24. For extended treatments of emergency and disaster assistance programs, see Randolph Kent, *Anatomy of Disaster Relief: The International Network in Action*, London: Pinter Publishers, 1987; and Lynn H. Stephens and Stephen J. Green, eds. *Disaster Assistance: Appraisal, Reform and New Approaches*, New York: New York University Press, 1979. For a readable and interesting case study of international famine relief operations in Cambodia during the early eighties, see Shawcross, *The Quality of Mercy*.

[40]Timberlake, "The Politics of Food Aid," 22.

work. In this case, recipients planted trees and terraced slopes in an effort to improve soil conservation. A different form of project aid provides supplemental food for populations considered at risk. Although useful in many instances, project aid may simply substitute for, rather than supplement, government social service assistance. Moreover, some projects go awry. One study of a child nutrition program found that the children's health actually improved after the project ended. While aid was available, mothers fed their children only the free grain and butterfat available through the program. Afterwards, they reverted to a more balanced diet, including locally available fruits and vegetables.[41]

Program aid made up 70 percent of all food aid in 1985. Food is simply provided free or sold at subsidized prices to governments to do with what they please. Governments generally resell the food within their own country, using the resulting revenue for other purposes. The motives behind this form of food assistance have less to do with altruism than with the political and economic interests of donor countries. Sir William Ryrie, former head of the British Overseas Development Administration has observed that the bulk of food aid "is frankly more a means of disposing of European agricultural surpluses than of helping the poor."[42] The same, of course, is true of the $1.5 billion United States Food for Peace program.[43]

Food aid is often distributed to friendly countries as a political reward. Owen Cylke, former acting director of the U.S. Food for Peace program, has commented that "it's used as a slush fund of the State Department to meet political requirements around the world."[44] In 1983, six of the top ten recipients of U.S. food aid were net food exporters. Egypt, a U.S. ally, received 20 percent of all cereal aid to the Third World in 1985–86 and 50 percent of all such aid to Africa. This was despite the fact that Egypt's average caloric intake is 28 percent higher than necessary for a healthy diet. Because Egypt subsidizes food sales, bread is cheaper than chicken feed and is often fed to livestock. Patterns such as these prompted one World Bank study to conclude that "the distribution, quantity and nature of food aid sometimes bears little relation to dietary deficiency."[45]

The influx of cheap, subsidized, Northern food into poor Third World countries can encourage dependence and vulnerability. Insecure governments prefer to keep food prices low so as to appease politically active urban populations. However, this practice denies rural farmers adequate revenue, thus discouraging agricultural investment and production as well as

---

[41]Timberlake, "The Politics of Food Aid," 24–26.

[42]Timberlake, "The Politics of Food Aid," 27.

[43]Martha Ann Overland, "Lawmakers Seek to Remove Politics from Foreign Aid," *Des Moines Register*, July 22, 1990.

[44]Overland, "Lawmakers Seek to Remove Politics from Foreign Aid."

[45]Timberlake, "The Politics of Food Aid," 27–28. Also see Overland, "Lawmakers Seek to Remove Politics from Foreign Aid."

perpetuating rural poverty. The result is that cities swell with rural immigrants, while the country becomes vulnerable should food aid levels fall due
to poor harvests and dwindling surpluses in the North.[46] Food aid is therefore often resisted by rural residents who make up the majority of the population in many Third World countries. Indonesian officials recently appealed
to the U.S. ambassador to stop the shipments of 700,000 tons of U.S. grain
after local farmers protested that they would be forced out of business due
to the influx of aid.[47]

The deficiencies of the U.S. food aid program have recently prompted
Congress to begin considering reforms that would direct food toward countries that are truly experiencing significant nutritional deficiencies. Such a
measure, if enacted, would address some, though not all, of the criticisms
that have been leveled at food aid.[48]

Growth versus the Environment

Over the past decade, aid agencies have experienced enormous pressure from
groups in both the North and the South to give greater attention to the
environmental, social, and cultural impacts of the projects they sponsor. The
World Bank, in particular, has come under attack for a series of controversial
projects that critics charge have brought devastating consequences to the
environment and local inhabitants. Although the Bank has taken steps to
revise its lending practices, many environmental groups remain skeptical
about its commitment to reform.[49]

The environmental and social costs associated with the Bank's emphasis
on economic growth are plainly evident in the case of the Super Thermal
Power Plant and coal mine in India's Singrauli region. Funded by an $850
million World Bank loan, the project led to the forcible resettlement, with
little compensation, of 23,000 local inhabitants. Ash from the coal-fired plant
has polluted neighboring cropland and a nearby reservoir, leading to the
growing incidence of tuberculosis and malaria among local residents. The
World Bank and Indian authorities have, moreover, been slow to provide
assistance to resettled villagers.[50]

A migration project in Indonesia, financed by a $1 billion Bank loan, has
led to the resettlement of 3 million poor people from Java and Bali to outlying

---

[46]Timberlake, "The Politics of Food Aid," 29.

[47]Overland, "Lawmakers Seek to Remove Politics from Foreign Aid."

[48]Overland, "Lawmakers Seek to Remove Politics from Foreign Aid."

[49]For a discussion of bargaining between environmental advocacy groups and the World Bank,
see Pat Aufderheide and Bruce Rich, "Environmental Reform and the Multilateral Banks,"
World Policy Journal, Spring, 1988.

[50]See Art Levine, "Bankrolling Debacles?," *US News and World Report*, Sept. 25, 1989, 43–44,
and Graham Hancock, *Lords of Poverty: The Power, Prestige and Corruption of the International Aid
Business*, New York: The Atlantic Monthly Press, 1989, 130–31.

islands. Authorities hoped to relieve overcrowding and provide peasants with small plots of new farmland. Millions of acres of tropical rain forest have been cleared to make room for new settlers. The land of traditional local inhabitants has also been seized, leading to violent confrontations with the Indonesian army. Yet, only one-half of the new farms have succeeded, due largely to poor soils that are unsuitable for agriculture. Many settlers have begun migrating back to the cities in search of work.[51]

A World Bank funded colonization scheme in Brazil known as "Polonoroeste" has brought similar results. Hundreds of thousands of poor peasants have poured into the Rondonia and Mato Grosso provinces of the Amazon region along a highway constructed with World Bank financing. Huge tracts of virgin rain forest have been cleared and indigenous Indian populations displaced. Yet, due to the leaching of minerals from the soil caused by heavy rains, most farms prove productive for only a few years. Many resettled peasants have responded by burning and clearing additional forest acreage. In 1987, it was estimated that the Amazon basin as a whole was afflicted by 6,000 forest fires, the great majority man-made.[52]

In May 1987, World Bank president Barber Conable conceded the Bank's poor environmental record and promised a better performance in the future: "If the World Bank has been part of the problem in the past, it can and will be a strong force in finding solutions in the future."[53] The Bank subsequently created a new environmental division staffed by sixty specialists. Some pending projects, including dams in India and Brazil, have been rejected on environmental or social grounds. New projects that exclusively address environmental problems have been approved, and environmental concerns have played a larger role in the planning of traditional projects. The World Bank now claims that nearly one-half of all Bank projects have environmental concerns built into them.[54]

Nevertheless, critics argue that the Bank's conversion has been less than complete. Peggy Hillward, director of forestry research for Probe International, for instance, charges that the World Bank is sponsoring "the same old projects with a few trees planted around the edges."[55] A Congressionally mandated report issued in June 1990 by the United States Agency for International Development cited twenty-seven Bank projects that posed

---

[51]See Levine, "Bankrolling Debacles?," 46–47, and Hancock, *Lords of Poverty*, 133–38.

[52]Hancock, *Lords of Poverty*, 131–33.

[53]Pat Aufderheide and Bruce Rich, "Environmental Reform and the Multilateral Banks," *World Policy Journal*, Spring, 1988, 301.

[54]On the Bank's reforms, see Philip Shabecoff, "World Bank Stressing Environmental Issues," *New York Times*, Sept. 24, 1990; Jeremy Warford and Zeinab Partow, "Evolution of the World Bank's Environmental Policy", *Finance and Development*, Dec. 1989, 5–9; and Bruce Rich, "The Emperor's New Clothes: The World Bank and Environmental Reform," *World Policy Journal*, Spring, 1990.

[55]Shabecoff, "World Bank Stressing Environmental Issues."

environmental or social dangers.[56] As of January 1990, an estimated 1.5 million people had been forcibly displaced by ongoing Bank projects, and proposed plans threatened to displace a similar number.[57]

Bank funding for the Sardar Sarovar dam project in north-central India has continued, for instance, despite the Indian government's five year refusal to prepare required environmental studies and the absence of a resettlement plan for 90,000 peasants who would be displaced by the dam's huge reservoir. In addition, 94,000 acres of forest and agricultural land will be submerged by water. In September 1989, opposition among local inhabitants led 60,000 people to gather near the dam site in protest.[58]

The serious environmental and social costs associated with some forms of development are not easily accommodated within the traditional models of economic growth embraced by most aid agencies. For this reason, the World Bank and other development organizations have begun to experiment with new models that include measures of ecological and resource depletion alongside long accepted yardsticks of development.[59] These innovative measurements can reveal the hidden trade-offs underlying development. This new thinking about sustainable growth must be incorporated into project selection and design, however, before it will produce any widespread practical effect. This seems unlikely to occur until the incentives that prompted planners to give priority to growth over the environment in the first place are directly addressed. These include the necessity of finding jobs and creating a decent standard of living for poor and rapidly growing Third World populations.

The Overreliance on Outside Experts

Development agencies have been criticized for relying too heavily on foreign experts in the design and implementation of aid projects while failing to take advantage of local talent or to consult with the poor about the plans that affect their lives. These tendencies often lead to poorly designed projects and feed resentment among recipients. Even worthwhile projects may wither over time if local people are not given the training, incentives, or responsibility necessary to sustain them.

The proclivity of aid agencies to manage aid projects through the use of imported expertise is pervasive. It has been estimated that at least 150,000 foreign-aid workers and consultants are employed in the Third World at any

---

[56]Levine, "Bankrolling Debacles?," 43.

[57]Rich, "The Emperor's New Clothes," 313.

[58]See Rich, "The Emperor's New Clothes," 304 and 314–15; Art Levine, "Bankrolling Debacles?," 47; and Hancock, *Lords of Poverty*, 142–43.

[59]For a brief discussion of these issues, see James Robertson and Andre Carothers, "The New Economics: Accounting for a Healthy Planet," *Greenpeace*, January/February, 1989. On how these ideas have crept into World Bank thinking, see Warford and Partow, "Evolution of the. . . ."

given time. The expense of keeping expatriate personnel in the field is considerable — $100,000 or more per year for each employee — and usually much greater than that associated with the use of local labor.[60]

Not all of these foreign experts originate from the North. Many multilateral agencies, such as the United Nations Development Program, hire substantial numbers of Third World personnel. Yet these employees are often assigned to foreign postings. Only 10 percent of United Nations professionals, for instance, work in their home country.[61] Paul Streeten, a consultant to the World Bank, notes that "a mediocre Indian, who might be useful within his competence in India, is recruited by the UN to work in Sierra Leone at ten times the salary he would earn at home, on a job for which his is ill-qualified, while a Sierra Leonean advises India."[62]

Foreign aid workers are often clustered in separate project units, outside of the recipient country's normal bureaucratic structure. This inhibits the accumulation of skills and learning experiences on the part of local officials and leaves aid projects without a strong constituency inside the regular bureaucracy. As a result, projects are often abandoned once outside aid is terminated.[63]

The work of this vast legion of aid emissaries is seldom effectively coordinated by various donor agencies. Some countries suffer from "aid overload." The proliferation of aid projects from a multitude of donors simply overwhelms the capacity of the local bureaucracy to cope. In one recent year, for instance, Burkina Faso was visited by 350 separate aid missions. Project duplication is common and little standardization in equipment or design takes place. Donors provided Kenya, for instance, with eighteen different varieties of water pumps for the country's rural water-supply system.[64]

Nor are the intended beneficiaries of aid typically given significant roles in designing or implementing aid projects. A study completed in 1988 by the World Bank's Operations Evaluations Department candidly concluded that "the principles guiding beneficiary participation in Bank-financed projects have been quite abstract and of limited operational impact. Beneficiaries were not assigned a role in the decision-making process, nor was their technical knowledge sought prior to designing project components."[65]

The consequences of failing to consult local knowledge can be devastating to project success. Two examples may help to illustrate this point. AID experts relied upon a local irrigation canal to provide water to a fish farm project in

---

[60]Hancock, *Lords of Poverty*, 115.

[61]Hancock, *Lords of Poverty*, 117.

[62]Hancock, *Lords of Poverty*, 115.

[63]*World Development Report, 1990*, 132.

[64]Cassen, *Does Aid Work?*, 221, 223.

[65]Hancock, *Lords of Poverty*, 125–26. For more on this problem, see Hellinger, Hellinger and, O'Regan, *Aid for Just Development*.

Mali. Yet, it was later discovered that the canal carried water for only five months out of the year. To prevent the fish pond from going dry during the remainder of the year, an expensive diesel powered pump was installed to bring water from a source over two kilometers away. Moreover, fish food had to be imported since no suitable local source could be found. Absurdly, the costs of capital and inputs to the farm mushroomed to an estimated $4,000 per kilo of fish. In a second such experiment, this time in the southern African nation of Malawi, a fish farm was located next to a bird sanctuary, providing the nearby population of fish-eating fowl with a tasty diet. The mistakes associated with these projects, and others like them, might have been avoided had local expertise been tapped in the first place.[66]

The Costs of Tied Aid

The common Northern practice of "tying" bilateral aid to the purchase of exports from the donor country substantially reduces the real value of such assistance to Third World countries. The purpose of tied aid is to allow manufacturers in the donor's own country to capture a larger share of the sales stimulated by foreign aid. Tied aid also promotes future orders for donor country exporters. Once an aid recipient installs machinery or equipment purchased from a particular supplier, it is likely to go back to that same firm for parts, supplies, and replacements. Thus tied aid generates a stream of business.

When aid is tied in this way, however, recipient countries are forbidden to shop around for the least expensive or most appropriate equipment. On average, tying aid reduces its value by roughly 20 percent.[67] Moreover, Northern firms that benefit from tied aid serve as vested interests, lobbying for aid projects requiring heavy Northern inputs, whether or not these projects are the most appropriate from the recipient's point of view.

Japan, France, and Germany each tie much of their bilateral aid. Of the $1.4 billion in bilateral aid Germany provided in 1986, 86 percent returned to the country through the purchase of German products.[68] Similarly, 80 percent of Japanese aid went to pay for Japanese exports. Overall, two-thirds of the bilateral aid provided by major donor countries is tied. Tied aid finances an estimated one-third of the $25-$30 billion in annual capital goods exports worldwide.[69]

---

[66]Both cases are discussed in Hancock, *Lords of Poverty*, 123–24.

[67]C.J. Jepma, "The Impact of Untying Aid of the European Community Countries," *World Development*, Vol. 16, No. 7, 1988, 804.

[68]"Playing the Aid Game," *World Press Review*, Feb. 1989, 51.

[69]Clyde Farnsworth, "US Will Tie Aid to Exports in Bid to Curb the Practice," *New York Times*, May 14, 1990.

The United States ties less of its aid than other countries. In fact, the United States has tried to persuade other donors to end or reduce the practice. Recently, however, the Bush Administration created a new tied aid fund. Its purpose is to pressure other donors into negotiations while, in the meantime, providing a competitive advantage for American exporters.[70]

The Preference for Bigness

Some of the most persistent criticisms of aid have to do with the size and type of projects that donors typically sponsor.[71] Aid agencies tend to prefer large-scale, capital-intensive investments that require a sizable import component over smaller, labor-intensive projects relying principally upon locally produced inputs. Thus, in competition for the same funds, a single expensive infrastructure project, such as a dam, road, or port facility, will often win out over multiple smaller and less costly projects, such as rural health clinics or agricultural extension programs. These biases in project lending tend to skew development toward the modern urban sector of the economy to the detriment of the poorer rural areas and often contribute to an overdependence on imports.

The sources of this behavior stem from various bureaucratic needs of the aid agencies themselves. Most foreign assistance programs, for instance, finance only the foreign currency component of the projects they sponsor. This encourages recipient nations to maximize the proportion of total project costs that depend upon imported goods and favors reliance upon foreign suppliers over local firms. Future orders of parts and replacement equipment are likely to go to these same foreign companies as well. Another consequence is that projects relying heavily on "hardware," such as imported capital equipment, are favored over those involving heavy labor costs that must be paid in local currency.

The preference for "bigness" is also related to bureaucratic factors. Aid agencies are under enormous pressure to "move money." Success is defined less in terms of the quality of projects or their contributions to development or poverty alleviation than in the total amount of funds dispersed. Within the agency, a good administrator is viewed as one who can lend the most money at the least cost in terms of bureaucratic overhead. Large projects are most efficient in this regard. The paperwork and man-hours required to initiate and review the progress of a small project are scarcely less than those needed to administer a large project. An overworked bureaucrat who seeks to impress his/her superiors with his/her productivity will thus find the oversight responsibilities associated with a single large loan far more manageable

---

[70]Farnsworth, "US Will Tie Aid. . . ."

[71]The discussion that follows in this section is drawn principally from Judith Tendler, *Inside Foreign Aid*, Baltimore: Johns Hopkins University Press, 1975.

and rewarding than those that accompany many small loans. These incentives to think big become even more intense when the quantity of funds available to lend suddenly rises faster than the agency's work force, as in 1988 when donors approved a $75 billion jump in World Bank capital, almost doubling the Bank's resources.

This syndrome is reinforced in the case of bilateral agencies that must spend their aid allocations within a given time period or lose access to the funds altogether. Moreover, if funding for a particular year is not fully dispersed, legislative overseers may conclude that future aid appropriations can be safely cut. These external funding constraints typically lead to an end-of-the-fiscal-year frenzy to spend all remaining funds. Under these circumstances, even marginal projects may be considered more favorably than before, particularly if they promise to move money quickly.

Recipient Country Corruption

Corruption, entrenched inequality, and the insensitivity of elites to the plight of the poor in many Third World countries seriously hamper even sincere efforts on the part of outside agencies to reach those in need. According to Volkmar Kohler, West German secretary for development, "We have to work with elites who have no interest in seeing the poorer classes in their societies advance."[72] Unrepresentative political regimes are many times plagued by officially sanctioned corruption. One World Bank staffer has admitted that Third World governments often demand financial kickbacks from firms involved in aid projects: "We know that it happens all the time. Its how business is done in those countries."[73] For these reasons, democracy is increasingly viewed by many economists as a prerequisite to equitable development. A recent United Nations study rated countries according to their achievements in "human development." It noted that twenty of the twenty-five nations scoring lowest on the human development scale were African dictatorships.[74] Donor countries have begun to take such considerations into greater account when allocating aid budgets. In 1991, several Western governments canceled or scaled back assistance programs to Kenya in the wake of revelations that large amounts of aid money were regularly lost to government sanctioned corruption.[75] Canada and Great Britain recently declared that their foreign aid would, in the future, be conditioned on the recipient country's respect for human rights.[76]

---

[72]"Playing the Aid Game," 51.

[73]Levine, "Bankrolling Debacles?," 44.

[74]Paul Lewis, "Poorest Countries Seek Increases in Aid," *New York Times*, July 3, 1990.

[75]Jane Perlez, "Citing Corruption in Kenya, Western Nations Cancel Aid," *New York Times*, October 21, 1991.

[76]"Summit Leaders Link Human Rights to Foreign Aid," *Des Moines Register*, October 17, 1991.

THE FUTURE OF FOREIGN AID

■ The prospect of significant future increases in Northern aid to the South seems slight. After rising during the early eighties, U.S. foreign aid has declined since then. Even those congressmen sympathetic to U.S. foreign assistance programs concede that serious budget constraints make aid a likely target for spending cuts.[77]

The lessening of Cold War tensions between East and West and the fall of Communist regimes in Eastern Europe seem likely to have profound effects on aid flows to the South as well. During the Cold War, the United States. and the Soviet Union used aid as an inducement in their competition for Third World allies. With the waning of this rivalry, the United States will see less need to use aid as a tool for countering Soviet influence, while Third World countries will no longer find it as easy to win assistance by appealing to Cold War fears. The breakup of the Soviet Union and the economic turmoil that has plagued its successor states has virtually eliminated the flow of aid to former Soviet allies, such as Cuba and Vietnam.

Moreover, Third World countries have expressed alarm at the prospect that new and existing aid funds will be diverted to Eastern Europe.[78] Although referring to private capital flows, World Bank president Barber Conable, nevertheless, did little to quiet these fears with his recent remark that developing nations "must work harder to attract investment or money will go to Eastern Europe."[79] Indeed, the World Bank plans to extend $5 billion in loans to Eastern European nations over a three-year period stretching from 1990 through 1992. One-half of this money will go to support free-market reforms in Poland. In addition, the newly created European Bank for Reconstruction and Development, capitalized at $12 billion by Western governments, is designed to provide financing for Eastern European development with a focus on the promotion of private enterprise.[80]

The decline in aid from other sources may be partially offset by the rapid growth of Japanese assistance to Third World countries. Japan's share of the official development assistance provided by all members of the Development Assistance Council rose from 2 percent in 1962 to 18 percent in 1987. Japan is now the world's largest provider of foreign aid, and its spending levels seem likely to rise still further in the near future.

While recipient countries may welcome Japan's growing commitment to foreign aid, they have less reason to cheer the conditions attached to such

---

[77]David Obey and Carol Lancaster, "Funding Foreign Aid," *Foreign Policy*, Summer, 1988.

[78]Paul Lewis, "Poorest Countries Seek Increases in Aid," *New York Times*, July 3, 1990.

[79]"Conable Advice to Third World," *New York Times*, June 14, 1990.

[80]Pamela Fessler, "Eastern Europe: Republicans Scramble to Meet Democrat's Aid Challenge," *Congressional Quarterly*, February 10, 1990; and John Granford, "Aid Plan for Eastern Europe," *Congressional Quarterly*, February 24, 1990.

funds. Three-quarters of Japan's assistance is directed to countries in Asia and Oceania, where Japanese trade and investment levels are also high. Comparatively little finds its way to Africa or Latin America. Moreover, Japanese aid to the world's least developed countries carries hard terms and contains a greater proportion of loans (versus grants) than is true for other aid donors. As we have seen, Japan ties a high proportion of its aid to the purchase of Japanese goods. Finally, a relatively large share of Japanese funds go toward infrastructural projects that bring few immediate benefits to the poor.[81]

CONCLUSIONS

■ This chapter has struck a largely pessimistic note regarding the effectiveness of aid in promoting development and alleviating poverty in the Third World. Such a conclusion does not imply that all aid is bad or useless. Indeed, as we have also emphasized, aid comes in many shapes and forms. Not surprisingly, aid can claim many successes alongside its failures. Most projects probably have mixed effects, with costs and benefits spread unevenly across the affected population. Overall, aid may well provide measurable, and sometimes significant, economic benefits in many Third World countries. Indeed, it would be puzzling if the billions of dollars in aid that flow to the Third World each year did not have some positive impact.

Yet aid has surely failed to perform up to the hopes of its early proponents or, perhaps, even to the standards of its more modest defenders within the aid community today. We have surveyed a variety of specific criticisms that have been directed at aid. Three broader, more general points take us to the roots of aid's shortcomings.

The contribution foreign aid can make to Southern development is limited in part by the modest size of aid flows. In 1988, foreign assistance from all sources amounted to 1.3 percent of overall Third World GNP, or a little less than $9 for each Southerner.[82] To bring the limited contributions of aid into even clearer perspective, it has been estimated that the total value of Northern aid is far exceeded by the costs to the Third World of Northern protectionism against Southern exports.[83] While aid totals in the tens of billions of dollars may appear impressive, they seem less so when placed in the context of overall Third World needs. Moreover, as noted above, present aid levels seem unlikely to significantly increase in the foreseeable future.

Another fundamental source of aid's limited success has to do with the poor state of our knowledge about the process of economic development.

---

[81]For data on Japanese aid, see Rowley, "Flush with Funds" and Anthony Rowley, "On Toyko's Terms," *Far Eastern Economic Review*, March 9, 1989, 78.
[82]*World Development Report, 1990*, Table 20, 217.
[83]"Foreign Aid: Stingy Sam," 26.

What seems clear is that there are many potential routes to development rather than a single model that can be successfully applied under all circumstances. This rather messy reality, however, only makes it more difficult to fashion aid strategies appropriate to each country. Changing academic and political fashions have combined with the inherent complexity of the development problem to produce a series of wrenching shifts in the strategies and philosophies embraced by the aid community. This inconsistency itself has detracted from aid's effectiveness.

Yet, the most important constraints on aid are political. Why does aid often fail to reach the poor or to benefit them more directly? The fundamental answer is rather simple: the crucial decisions regarding aid are made by governments, over the heads of the poor themselves. While aid is certainly not free of humanitarian motives and purposes, these often take a back seat to other concerns, including the pursuit of political power.

Donor governments use aid to reward friends and woo neutrals, to exercise leverage over the internal and external policies of recipients, to strengthen threatened allies, to pry open foreign markets, and to enhance the donor country's image at home and abroad. From the standpoint of the recipient government, aid provides resources that help bolster the political power and legitimacy of the existing leadership. Political elites in these nations often use aid to reward supporters, while denying resources to opponents, and sometimes indulge in direct corruption. Aid also encourages certain patterns of development that benefit different elements of society unevenly, perhaps, for instance, strengthening the modern, urban sector at the expense of the traditional, rural sector.

Seeing aid in terms of its effects on the political power of both donor and recipient governments helps us to understand why Third World political elites sometimes express ambivalent attitudes toward external assistance. While aid may strengthen political leaders in relation to their domestic rivals, it also places them and their countries in a position of dependence upon aid donors. And dependence, of course, means increased vulnerability and the greater potential for external manipulation. This same aspect of the relationship makes the continuation of aid attractive to donor country leaders, even when foreign aid is unpopular among taxpayers and when evidence of its success in promoting development is ambiguous.

Given the political stakes associated with aid, the poor's lack of participation in the aid process is hardly accidental. Indeed, were aid to be reformed to focus more directly and effectively on the poor and to provide them with substantial input and control, aid would undoubtedly lose much of the appeal it presently holds for political elites in both donor and recipient nations. Ironically, taking the "politics" out of foreign aid might simply undercut the motivation for governments to go on spending and receiving foreign aid, leading to a massive contraction of such programs. This likelihood merely underscores the close association between politics and economics in North-South relations.

ANNOTATED BIBLIOGRAPHY

Robert L. Ayres, *Banking on the Poor: The World Bank and World Poverty*, Cambridge: MIT Press, 1983.
A detailed examination of the World Bank's poverty lending programs during the 1970s.

P.T. Bauer, *Reality and Rhetoric: Studies in the Economics of Development*, Cambridge: Harvard University Press, 1984.
Chapters three and four present a conservative critique of foreign aid.

Robert Cassen and Associates, *Does Aid Work?*, Oxford: Clarendon Press, 1986.
A detailed, thorough, and balanced effort to measure the contributions of foreign aid to Third World development and poverty reduction.

Graham Hancock, *Lords of Poverty: The Power, Prestige and Corruption of the International Aid Business*, New York: The Atlantic Monthly Press, 1989.
A biting critique of foreign aid written by a journalist with extensive experience in the Third World. Criticizes the hypocrisy and ineffectiveness of the foreign aid bureaucracy.

Theresa Hayter and Catherine Watson, *Aid: Rhetoric and Reality*, London: Pluto Press, 1985.
A radical critique of foreign aid.

Stephen Hellinger, Douglas Hellinger, and Fred M. O'Regan, *Aid for Just Development: Report on the Future of Foreign Assistance*, Boulder: Lynne Rienner Publishers, 1988.
Presents proposals for reforming foreign aid.

Judith Tendler, *Inside Foreign Aid*, Baltimore: Johns Hopkins University Press, 1975.
Although dated, Tendler's book continues to offer important insights into how bureaucratic factors influence and hamper the performance of foreign aid agencies.

Robert Wood, *From Marshall Plan to Debt Crisis: Foreign Aid and Development Choices in the World Economy*, Berkeley: University of California Press, 1986.
A theoretical and empirical examination of the post–World War II foreign aid system. Links foreign aid and the debt crisis with an approach drawing upon both dependency theory and regime analysis.

CHAPTER 11

MULTINATIONAL CORPORATIONS IN THE THIRD WORLD

T he growth and expansion of the multinational corporation (MNC) is one of the most revolutionary, as well as controversial, phenomena in the development of the world economy during this century. MNCs are business firms that own or control production in more than one country. In practice, the largest MNCs orchestrate an ensemble of investments scattered across dozens of countries. Tied together by a vast communications web, these firms match various corporate functions, such as research and development, production, and marketing, with locales around the globe featuring the right mix of necessary ingredients, whether these be the skills and wage rates of local labor, the tax and regulatory policies of governments, the availability of needed infrastructure, or the supply of natural resources. The sheer size of many MNCs, combined with their economic efficiency and international mobility, not only provides such firms with a key place in the world economy, but also endows them with considerable political power and influence.

In 1980, as few as 350 MNCs, controlling 25,000 affiliates, accounted for a full 28 percent of all the goods and services produced in the capitalist world.[1] The yearly sales of the largest MNCs dwarf the annual GNPs of a vast majority of Third World countries (see Table 11.1).

The large-scale movement of modern direct foreign investment (DFI) to the Third World dates from the turn of the century. The earliest MNCs to invest in the developing countries focused on agricultural goods and the extraction of raw materials. The demands of rapidly growing Northern

---

[1]Rhys Jenkins, *Transnational Corporations and Uneven Development: The Internationalization of Capital and the Third World*, New York: Methuen, 1987, 8.

industries as well as the rising affluence of European and North American consumers created a healthy market for Southern resources and cash crops. Very little Northern investment in the South flowed into manufacturing at this stage. In 1914, for instance, mining, oil, and agriculture accounted for 70 percent of all U.S. DFI located in developing countries, while manufacturing amounted to only 3 percent.[2]

TABLE 11.1

One Hundred Fifty of the Largest Countries and Industrial Corporations
(Ranked by Annual GDP and Sales in Millions of Dollars, 1988)

1	UNITED STATES	$4,847,310	34	INT. BUSINESS MACHINE	$59,681
2	JAPAN	2,843,710			
3	GERMANY, FED. REP.	1,201,820	35	THAILAND	57,950
4	FRANCE	949,440	36	ALGERIA	51,900
5	ITALY	828,850	37	TOYOTA MOTORS	50,789
6	UNITED KINGDOM	702,370	38	GENERAL ELECTRIC	49,414
7	CANADA	435,860	39	MOBIL	48,198
8	CHINA	372,320	40	BRITISH PETROLEUM	46,174
9	SPAIN	340,320	41	IRI	45,521
10	BRAZIL	323,610	42	ISRAEL	44,960
11	AUSTRALIA	245,950	43	HONG KONG	44,830
12	INDIA	237,930	44	DAIMLER-BENZ	41,817
13	NETHERLANDS	228,280	45	PORTUGAL	41,700
14	SWITZERLAND	184,830	46	HITACHI	41,330
15	MEXICO	176,700	47	GREECE	40,900
16	KOREA, REP. OF	171,310	48	NEW ZEALAND	39,800
17	SWEDEN	159,880	49	PHILIPPINES	39,210
18	BELGIUM	153,810	50	COLUMBIA	39,070
19	AUSTRIA	127,200	51	CHRYSLER	35,472
20	GENERAL MOTORS	121,085	52	MALAYSIA	34,680
21	FORD MOTORS	92,445	53	EGYPT ARAB REP.	34,330
22	FINLAND	91,690	54	SIEMENS	34,129
23	NORWAY	91,050	55	PAKISTAN	34,050
24	DENMARK	90,530	56	FIAT	34,039
25	INDONESIA	83,220	57	MATSUSHITA ELECTRIC IND.	33,922
26	EXXON	79,557			
27	ARGENTINA	79,440	58	VOLKSWAGEN	33,696
28	SOUTH AFRICA	78,970	59	TEXACO	33,544
29	ROYAL DUTCH SHELL GROUP	78,381	60	E.I. DUPONT DE NEMOURS	32,514
30	SAUDI ARABIA	72,620	61	UNILEVER	30,488
31	TURKEY	64,360	62	NIGERIA	29,370
32	VENEZUELA	63,750	63	NISSAN MOTORS	29,097
33	YUGOSLAVIA	61,710	64	PHILIP'S	28,370

[2]Jenkins, *Transnational Corporations and Uneven Development*, 5.

65	HUNGARY	$28,000	110	MCDONNELL DOUGLAS	$15,072
66	NESTLE	27,803	111	SYRIAN ARAB REP.	14,950
67	SAMSUNG	27,386	112	PETROBRAS	14,806
68	ENAULT	27,109	113	FUJITSU	14,797
69	PHILIP MORRIS	25,860	114	MITSUBISHI MOTORS	14,183
70	IRELAND	27,820	115	BAT INDUSTRIES	14,066
71	PERU	25,670	116	TOTAL	13,986
72	TOSHIBA	25,440	117	MITSUBISHI HEAVY IND.	13,398
73	ENI	25,226	118	USINOR	13,247
74	CHEVRON	25,196	119	PEMEX	13,060
75	BASF	24,960	120	PEPSICO	13,007
76	SINGAPORE	23,880	121	CAMEROON	12,900
77	UNITED ARAB EMIRATES	23,850	121	NIPPON OIL	12,773
78	HOECHST	23,308	122	THOMSON	12,566
79	PEUGEOT	23,249	123	WESTINGHOUSE-	12,499
80	BAYER	23,025		ELECTRIC	
81	HONDA MOTORS	22,236	124	KUWAIT PETROLEUM	12,078
82	CHILE	22,080	125	CIBA-GEIGU	12,059
83	CGE	21,487	126	ELECTROLUX	12,055
84	ELF AQUITAINE	21,175	127	ROCKWELL	11,946
85	AMOCO	21,150		INTERNATIONAL	
86	IMPERIAL CHEMICAL IND.	20,839	128	ALLIED-SIGNAL	11,909
87	KUWAIT	19,970	129	BMW	11,762
88	BANGLADESH	19,320	130	RUHRKOHLE	11,749
89	NEC	19,626	131	MANNESMANN	11,619
90	OCCIDENTAL	19,417	132	DIGITAL EQUIPMENT	11,475
	PETROLEUM		133	PHILLIPS PETROLEUM	11,304
91	PROCTER & GAMBLE	19,336	134	SUDAN	11,240
92	PERRUZZI FINAZIARIA	18,311	135	RHONE-POULENC	10,971
93	UNITED TECHNOLOGIES	18,087	136	GOODYEAR TIRE &	10,810
94	ATLANTIC RICHFIELD	17,626		RUBBER	
95	ASEA BROWN BOYERI	17,562	137	LOCKHEED	10,667
96	DAEWOO	17,251	138	MINNESOTA	10,581
97	NIPPON STEEL	17,108		MINING & MFG.	
98	EASTMAN KODAK	17,034	139	CATERPILLAR	10,435
99	BOEING	16,962	140	SARA LEE	10,423
100	RJR NABISCO	16,956	141	ECUADOR	10,320
101	MITSUBISHI ELECTRIC	16,857	142	SONY	10,133
102	THYSSEN	16,796	143	BRITISH AEROSPACE	10,044
103	DOW CHEMICAL	16,682	144	WEYERHAEUSER	10,004
104	XEROX	16,441	145	ADAM OPEL	9,935
105	USX	15,792	146	UNISYS	9,902
106	VOLVO	15,752	147	HANSON	9,900
107	ROBERT BOSCH	15,746	148	PETROFINA	9,898
108	TENNECO	15,707	149	SAINT-GOBAIN	9,886
109	MAZDA MOTORS	15,150	150	INDIAN OIL	9,853

Source: World Bank, *World Development Report, 1990,* Oxford: Oxford University Press, 1990, Table 3, 182–83; *Fortune,* July 31, 1989, 282–283.

The composition of DFI in the Third World began to change during the interwar period. U.S. firms, in particular, established growing numbers of manufacturing subsidiaries in Latin America. By 1939, Latin America was the home of 200 foreign-owned manufacturing operations, two-thirds of the total for all developing countries.[3] Yet, foreign investment in Third World manufacturing did not really take off until after World War II. Today, the subsidiaries of Northern-owned MNCs account for substantial shares of invested capital, employment, and output in the manufacturing sectors of most Third World countries (See Table 11.2 and Figure 11.1). Their dominance is greatest in the most technologically advanced types of products and manufacturing processes.

TABLE 11.2

Share of Manufacturing Industry Controlled by Foreign Firms in Selected Third World Countries

COUNTRY	YEAR	FOREIGN SHARE %	BASIS OF CALCULATION
Latin America:			
Argentina	1972	31	Production
Brazil	1977	44	Sales
Central America	1971	31	Production
Chile	1978	25	Sales
Colombia	1974	43	Production
Ecuador	1971–3	66	Assets of public corporation
Mexico	1970	35	Production
Peru	1974	32	Production
Venezuela	1975	36	Value added
Trinidad and Tobago	1968	40	Employment
Africa:			
Ghana	1974	50	Sales
Kenya	1976	30–35	Employment
Nigeria	1968	70	Assets
Zaïre	1974	30–35	Employment
Asia:			
Hong Kong	1971	11	Employment
India	1975	13	Sales
Iran	1975	10–15	Employment
Malaysia	1978	44	Value added
Philippines	1970	7	Employment
Singapore	1978	83	Output
South Korea	1975	11	Sales
Thailand	1970	9	Employment

Source: Rhys Jenkins, *Transnational Corporations and Uneven Development*, New York: Methuen, 1987, Table 1.2, 10.

---

[3]Jenkins, *Transnational Corporations and Uneven Development*, 5–6.

FIGURE 11.1

Transnational Corporations

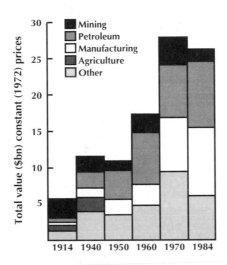

Nevertheless, despite growth in the absolute levels of foreign investment in the South, DFI has expanded even more quickly in the North. MNCs have increasingly preferred to invest the bulk of their resources in already-developed countries. On the eve of World War I, DFI located in the developing countries accounted for 60 percent of the total worldwide. By the early sixties, the Third World share of DFI had fallen to one-third. This proportion fell further to roughly one-quarter in the mid-eighties.[4] Over one-half of all U.S. DFI is located in only five developed countries (Great Britain, Canada, Germany, Switzerland, and the Netherlands).[5]

The relative significance of DFI to Third World economies has also declined. MNC investment in the South grew from an annual average of $2.6 billion during 1967-69 to $12.8 billion in 1979-81. Largely due to rising levels of commercial bank lending, however, the share of DFI in overall private financial flows to the Third World declined from over 50 percent in 1970 to 20 percent in 1985. Indeed, levels of new foreign investment fell absolutely during the early eighties, dropping to an annual average of roughly $10 billion. A modest turnaround began in 1986 as the flow of DFI to developing countries increased to $12.5 billion. During the same year, DFI once again

---

[4]Jenkins, *Transnational Corporations and Uneven Development*, 5 and 13.
[5]John R. O'Neal, "Foreign Investment in Less Developed Regions," *Political Science Quarterly*, vol. 103, no. 1, 1988, 137–38.

accounted for almost 50 percent of private financial flows. This was largely due, however, to a collapse in bank lending to the Third World.[6]

As Table 11.3 reveals, only eight countries accounted for over one-half of the total stock of DFI in all of the developing world as of 1983. Foreign investment has tended to flow disproportionately to relatively prosperous Third World countries that have succeeded in developing diversified industrial structures.

TABLE 11.3

Stock of Direct Foreign Investment in Less Developed Countries by Major Host Countries, 1976 and 1983

	1967		1983	
	bn $	%	bn $	%
Brazil	3.7	11.3	24.6	17.5
Mexico	1.8	5.5	13.6	9.7
Singapore	0.2	0.6	7.9	5.6
Indonesia	0.2	0.6	6.8	4.9
Malaysia	0.7	2.1	6.2	4.4
Argentina	1.8	5.5	5.8	4.1
Venezuela	3.5	10.6	4.3	3.1
Hong Kong	0.3	0.9	4.2	3.0
Eight countries	12.2	37.2	73.4	52.4
TOTAL LDCs	32.8	100.0	140.0*	100.0

*Estimate.

SOURCE: Rhys Jenkins, *Transnational Corporations and Uneven Development*, New York: Methuen, 1987, Table 1.4, 14.

MOTIVES FOR FOREIGN DIRECT INVESTMENT IN THE THIRD WORLD

■ Northern firms have a variety of motives for investing in Third World countries. Some seek access to Southern resources. Extractive industries, such

---

[6]Gerald Pollio and Charles H. Riemenschneider, "The Coming Third World Investment Revival," *Harvard Business Review*, March/April, 1988, 114; and Stephen Krasner, *Structural Conflict: The Third World Against Global Liberalism*, Berkeley: University of California Press, 1985.

as mining, oil, or timber, are attracted by the presence of raw materials or mineral deposits. Many Southern countries, by virtue of their climate or geography, are particularly well suited to the production of cash crops desired in the North, such as sugar, coffee, cocoa, or tropical fruits. Northern agribusiness firms invest in the production, processing, and packaging of such agricultural commodities in the South.

Manufacturing firms have greater freedom over where they locate their investments than do natural resource producers. The former often have a choice between servicing foreign markets through export or foreign investment. Decisions to invest in the Third World are influenced both by competitive pressures in particular industries and by the incentives created by government policies. One school of thought, known as product life-cycle theory, suggests that firms that gain a monopoly position as a result of successful innovation will move abroad in search of new markets or lower costs as a means of preserving higher than normal profits once imitation has begun to erode their initial advantage over rivals at home.[7]

Most manufacturing DFI in the Third World produces commodities aimed at the local market. This sort of investment is most common in the larger, more prosperous Southern countries that have sizable and therefore attractive consumer bases. MNCs may decide to produce in such countries rather than export in order to better adjust to local tastes or to take advantage of lower labor or capital costs.

Often, however, the decision to invest abroad is prompted by the necessity of jumping protectionist barriers in order to gain access to Third World markets. Southern governments may erect tariffs or other sorts of barriers precisely in order to discourage imports while encouraging local production of the protected goods. The aim of this strategy, often referred to as import substitution, is to spur industrialization. Many MNCs have discovered ways to benefit from such policies. A single large factory can service the entire local demand for a given product in many Third World countries. Thus, the first foreign firm to gain entry can profit handsomely. Freed from competition due to the umbrella of protection and the limited size of the domestic market, the local subsidiary can establish an effective monopoly, allowing it to charge higher prices and earn greater than normal profits. This very fact has engendered local resentment toward foreign firms.

A final attraction of investing in the Third World, for some firms, is to escape environmental regulations or higher taxes in their home country. As we will see, operations transplanted abroad for these reasons are particularly controversial.

---

[7] For elaboration, see Charles Kindleberger, "The Monopolistic Theory of Direct Foreign Investment" and Raymond Vernon, "The Product Cycle Model," both in George Modelski, ed. *Transnational Corporations and World Order: Readings in International Political Economy,* San Franciso: W.H. Freeman & Co., 1979.

THE BENEFITS OF DIRECT FOREIGN INVESTMENT TO THIRD WORLD HOST COUNTRIES

■ Our primary concern in this chapter is with the impact of direct foreign investment on the Third World and the relationship between MNCs and host countries. Considerable debate surrounds these topics. Defenders of MNCs argue that DFI stimulates economic growth and development. MNCs augment scarce local resources and bring with them a package of assets which can seldom be matched by indigenous firms. Elements of this package include:

Capital — Many Third World countries are characterized by low rates of domestic savings. As a result, their economies are dependent upon external capital flows to finance new investment. DFI offers one means by which scarce local capital can be supplemented. To be sure, MNCs demand a price for injecting fresh capital into the host country's economy. Specifically, foreign investors prefer to repatriate a large portion of the profits they earn abroad. Yet, the terms of DFI often compare favorably with those accompanying other sources of external financing. Commercial loans from Northern banks, for instance, carry interest charges that must be paid regardless of whether the local investment they finance proves profitable. In contrast, while MNCs share in the benefits from DFI, they also bear much of the risk. If one of its Third World subsidiaries loses money, an MNC will find that there are no profits to repatriate. Indeed, the headquarters of the firm may well choose to inject new capital into the failing subsidiary in an attempt to turn the operation around and salvage its initial investment. DFI also offers certain advantages over foreign aid. While foreign assistance may be provided on favorable financial terms, it often carries political strings attached, whether implicit or explicit. This is seldom the case for DFI.

Technology — While some Third World countries have managed to establish impressively modern manufacturing sectors, the vast majority of the new technology created worldwide still originates in the laboratories and universities of the North. MNCs provide one mechanism by which Northern technology is transferred to the Third World. MNCs tend to invest in the most technologically advanced sectors of Third World economies, supplying goods and services that are beyond the technological capacity of local firms to produce efficiently. MNCs also aid in technological diffusion through means such as licensing technology to other firms or passing along knowledge, skills, and techniques to local partners through joint ventures.

Management Expertise — The Third World subsidiaries of MNCs often organize production more efficiently than local firms due to superior management skills and techniques. MNCs possess great experience in managing large scale enterprises. Branch plant managers can draw upon the vast storehouse of information and expertise contained within the corporation as a whole. Knowledge of modern management methods is spread through the training of indigenous personnel, whose representation in the ranks of management typically grows at the expense of expatriates the longer the MNC subsidiary is in place.

Marketing Networks — Even where local firms can match MNCs in price and product quality, they may lack easy access to the extensive foreign marketing networks available to Northern firms. MNCs often possess long-standing relationships with, or even control over, Northern wholesale and retail outlets, enjoy greater information about market demand and consumer tastes, and command larger advertising resources.

The Costs of Direct Foreign Investment to Third World Host Countries

■ Critics argue that the economic and political costs of DFI often outweigh the benefits.[8] Many of these criticisms center around differences between foreign and domestic firms and the ways they each do business.

MNCs are accused of earning excessive profits in Third World countries, made possible by their oligopoly position in local economies.[9] The largest proportion of these profits are repatriated to shareholders in the firm's country of origin rather than reinvested locally. According to some studies, MNCs also overcharge for technology transfer to their own subsidiaries and rely

---

[8]For critical treatments of MNC operations in the Third World, see Richard Barnet and Ronald Muller, *Global Reach: The Power of the Multinational Corporations*, New York: Simon and Schuster, 1974; Volker Bornschier and Christopher Chase-Dunn, *Transnational Corporations and Underdevelopment*, New York: Praeger, 1985; John Cavanaugh and Frederick Clairmonte, *The Transnational Economy: Transnational Corporations and Global Markets*, Washington: Institute for Policy Studies, 1982; Stephen Hymer, "The Multinational Corporation and the Law of Uneven Development," in Jagdish Bhagwati, *Economics and World Order*, New York: Macmillan Publishers, 1972; Richard Newfarmer, "Multinational and Marketplace Magics in the 1980s," in Jeffry Frieden and David Lake, eds. *International Political Economy: Perspectives on Global Power and Wealth*, New York: St. Martin's Press, 1991; Osvaldo Sunkel, "Big Business and 'Dependencia' " and Johan Galtung, "A Structural Theory of Imperialism," both in Modelski, *Transnational Corporations*.

[9]Business concentration is especially high in many extractive sectors. Data from the seventies indicate that three MNCs shared 70 percent of the world production, marketing, and distribution of bananas. Six firms controlled 70 percent of world aluminum production capacity. Fewer than ten corporations dominated the global production and processing of the following commodities: copper, iron ore, lead, nickel, tin, tobacco, and zinc. Garrett Fitzgerald, *Unequal Partners*, New York: United Nations, 1979, 11–12.

more heavily upon imported parts and machinery than domestic firms. Each of these practices tends to reflect negatively in the host country's balance of payments position.

Critics contend that MNCs often borrow from the already scarce supply of local capital rather than bring new investment funds into the country. Because of their size and resources, foreign firms typically receive preferential terms from local banks when borrowing money, as compared with local firms. Another criticism is that MNCs discourage local entrepreneurship by often entering a country through the acquisition of an existing Third World firm or using superior resources to drive native competitors out of business.

Third World governments particularly object to a common MNC practice known as "transfer pricing." MNCs resort to this technique in an attempt to lower their overall tax burden or evade restrictions on the repatriation of profits. Transfer pricing is essentially an accounting practice applied to intrafirm trade. Different branches or subsidiaries of the same firm, located in different countries, often exchange goods. A U.S. based manufacturer, for instance, might produce parts in a factory located in Texas but ship these parts to a plant in Mexico for assembly. In turn, the assembled product is transported back to the United States for final sale. The price that the home firm charges the Mexican subsidiary for the parts or that the subsidiary charges the home firm for the assembled product is essentially arbitrary since these transactions take place within the same company and are not exposed to market forces. If, let us say, Mexico imposes a higher tax on corporate profits than does the United States, then the MNC can lower its overall tax bill by overpricing the parts shipped to Mexico while underpricing the assembled products that are "sold" back to the home firm in the United States. By manipulating the prices on intrafirm trade in this way, the Mexican subsidiary will show little profit on its books, thus avoiding the high Mexican tax rate, while the profit of the home firm will be artificially boosted — allowing it to be taxed at the low U.S. rate. This sort of practice is hard to detect because it is difficult to know what the products might have sold for in arm's-length transactions among independent firms. Since most Third World countries tax the profits of foreign corporations at relatively high rates, they are often targets of transfer pricing schemes and suffer a loss of potential tax revenue as a result.

Some forms of DFI represent attempts to export pollution from Northern countries, where environmental enforcement is stringent, or to exploit reserves of cheap labor. Mexico, for instance, is host to 1800 U.S. owned product assembly plants located along the border. Called *maquiladoras*, some of these factories relocated to Mexico in order to take advantage of lax Mexican environmental laws and to break free of stricter regulations in the United States. A study by the American National Toxic Campaign found that of twenty-three such factories sampled, seventeen were responsible for significant toxic waste discharges. Much of Southern California's furniture industry has moved across the border to escape severe air pollution controls on solvent emissions.

Mexico has recently taken steps to tighten its environmental laws and crack down on polluters, but its enforcement mechanisms remain inadequate. In addition to the environmental problems associated with *maquiladoras*, critics point out that the jobs created through these factories are extremely low-paying and that work conditions as well as health and safety standards are far below those in the United States.[10]

DFI also carries political risks. MNCs may appeal to their home government to exert pressure on a host state when disputes arise. The Hickenlooper Amendment, passed by the U.S. Congress in 1962, requires that aid be denied to countries that nationalize the assets of U.S. corporations without prompt and adequate compensation. The law has been applied, or its use threatened, on several occasions. More dramatically, the United States, through the use of CIA covert operations and economic pressure, took part in the overthrow of governments in Iran (1953), Guatemala (1954), and Chile (1973) after the assets of foreign firms from the United States and other Northern countries were nationalized. Although other factors influenced these decisions as well, the desire of U.S. officials to defend U.S. corporate interests abroad played an important role in all three instances.

A BARGAINING FRAMEWORK FOR ANALYZING MNC–HOST-COUNTRY RELATIONS

■ Are MNCs a boon or a burden to Third World host countries? The answer is more complex than either of the two perspectives outlined above would suggest. Whether or not the benefits of DFI outweigh the costs depends substantially upon the balance of bargaining power between the firm and the host state. This bargaining relationship determines whether a state will have the capacity to control the activities of foreign investors and thus limit negative impacts. In this section, we first review the various types of regulation Third World states have attempted to impose upon MNCs in the past. We then examine the sources of bargaining power available to each party.

Regulating MNC Behavior

During the seventies, in particular, Third World states adopted a variety of regulations designed to control and channel the activities of MNCs. Many countries exclude foreign investment in certain crucial sectors of the economy such as public utilities, mining, steel, retailing, insurance, and banking. In

---

[10]See William Burke, "The Toxic Price of Free Trade in Mexico," *In These Times*, May 22–29, 1991; and Robert Reinhold, "Mexico Says It Won't Harbor U.S. Companies Fouling Air," *New York Times*, April 18, 1991.

some cases, foreign investors are required to form joint ventures providing majority control to local partners. A number of Latin American countries limit profit repatriation and technology payments by foreign-owned subsidiaries. Requirements that a stated percentage of production must be exported are common. Some countries require that indigenous labor be hired into middle and upper-level management positions. Several countries have placed limits on MNC access to local capital markets in an effort to encourage greater contributions of external financing for new investments. Finally, attempts have been made to encourage MNC subsidiaries to carry out local research and development.[11]

These controls have been imposed most successfully by the larger, more prosperous Third World countries, which are in a relatively strong position to bargain over the terms of DFI. In addition to the risk that demanding regulations will simply scare away foreign investors, smaller, less developed countries have a more difficult time enforcing investment rules.

Indeed, impressively strict regulations designed to enhance local control often have surprisingly little effect on MNC operations in practice.[12] Consider the common stipulation that MNCs must enter into joint ventures providing majority ownership to local partners. Compliance with this regulation is often achieved through fictitious means. A foreign firm will simply lend to the local partner the capital needed to acquire majority ownership. Or the original equity investment in the project is held artificially low so as to make it possible for the local partner to come up with the required money. The enterprise then funds its operations through debt rather than equity, often borrowing funds from the parent company of the foreign partner. These sorts of nominal shareholding arrangments create the illusion, without the reality, of a large local stake in the enterprise.

Even where local partners legitimately put up the majority of capital to fund a project, they seldom exercise real control. The MNC typically provides raw materials, equipment, spare parts, financing, technology, managerial skills, and marketing services. Since the keys to the success of the enterprise lie with the foreign partner, so does effective control over how it is run. Foreign control may in fact be formalized in basic agreements concluded at the outset of the venture which reserve key functions to the MNC.

---

[11] For general discussions of Third World efforts to regulate DFI, see Jenkins, *Transnational Corporations and Uneven Development*; Krasner, *Structural Conflict*; Robert Cohen and Jeffry Frieden, "The Impact of Multinational Corporations on Developing Nations" and Robert Kurdle, "The Several Faces of the Multinational Corporation: Political Reaction and Policy Response," both in Kendall Stiles and Tsuneo Akaha, eds. *International Political Economy: A Reader*, New York: Harper Collins, 1991; and Francisco Orrago Vicuna, "The Control of Multinational Corporations," in Modelski, *Transnational Corporations*.

[12] The material in this and the next two paragraphs rely upon Franklin B. Weinstein, "Underdevelopment and Efforts to Control Multinational Corporations," in Modelski, *Transnational Corporations*.

Many countries attempt to ensure that MNCs hire, train, and promote local workers into management positions or require that a certain proportion of the final product consist of locally produced parts. Yet the first restriction is often waived when foreign subsidiaries attest that people with the requisite skills and experience are not available locally. In some cases, local managers are hired but given little responsibility. Local content rules can be circumvented by using creative accounting to inflate the value of the portion of the overall product accounted for by local inputs.

The Andean Pact represents one attempt to overcome the poor bargaining position of small countries. In December 1970, Bolivia, Columbia, Chile, Ecuador, and Peru (Venezuela was added in 1973 while Chile abandoned the group in 1976) announced Decision 24, an agreement on the "Common Treatment for Foreign Capital, Trademarks, Patents, Licensing Agreement, and Royalties." This agreement imposed a common set of new regulations on MNCs operating in Pact countries. These included the exclusion of DFI from certain economic sectors, limits on profit repatriation and access to local lending, a phased-in reduction of foreign ownership in MNC affiliates to a maximum of 49 percent, and controls on technology transfer and royalty payments. The impact of these measures has been mixed. Technology payments were renegotiated downward after implementation of the Pact, and local participation in MNC operations increased. Due to incomplete data, however, the effect of Decision 24 on flows of new DFI is difficult to judge with precision. Investments by U.S. MNCs in Pact countries continued to increase during the late seventies, but at a slower pace than in the rest of Latin America. The influx of German capital, on the other hand, was apparently unaffected.[13]

The difficulty with national, or even regional, controls is that MNCs can reallocate their investment flows toward countries that offer less interference. Thus, many Third World countries have long called for a strict, binding global code of conduct for MNCs.[14] Northern countries, however, have resisted these demands. Instead, in 1976, the OECD sponsored a weaker, voluntary code that lacked Third World approval.[15] In the late eighties, negotiations over international regulation of MNC activities resumed under the auspices of the United Nations Center on Transnational Corporations. To

---

[13]Jenkins, *Transnational Corporations and Uneven Development*, 173–75; Robert Cohen and Jeffry Frieden, "The Impact of Multinational Corporations on Developing Nations," 169; R.N. Gwynne, "Multinational Corporations and the Triple Alliance in Latin America," in C.J. Dixon, D. Drakakis-Smith, and H.D. Watts, *Multinational Corporations and the Third World*, London: Croom Helm, 1986, 128.

[14]See United Nations, "Resolution Establishing the Commission on Transnational Corporations and Charter of the Economic Rights and Duties of States," in Modelski, *Transnational Corporations*.

[15]OECD, "Declaration on International Investment and Multinational Enterprises and Guidelines for Multinational Enterprises," in Modelski, *Transnational Corporations*.

date, however, no agreement has been reached due to familiar differences between North and South on this issue.[16]

The Determinants of Relative Bargaining Power

MNCs and Third World states are engaged in an interdependent relationship. Each party wants something from the other. The principal concern of the firm is to maximize profits. To accomplish this, it must gain access to the resources, markets, or cheap labor of the Third World country where an investment opportunity presents itself. The goals of the host state are more diverse. Third World political leaders are attracted to the jobs, skills, output, and technology that MNCs have to offer.

While the goals and interests of the two parties are potentially compatible, the firm's desire to maximize profits may, as we have seen, lead it to engage in practices that reduce the benefits accruing to the host country. Third World states are therefore often inclined to regulate and control MNC behavior so as to maximize the host country's share of benefits from the investment.

The host state's ability to successfully set the terms under which foreign investors do business in the country is constrained by its relative bargaining power. The state's principal bargaining advantage is its capacity to control access to the country and to exert legal control over foreign business operations once an investment has been made. The MNC, however, is far from helpless. Its power derives both from the package of assets it has to offer the host country and from its mobility. If the host state drives too hard a bargain, imposing regulations so onerous as to substantially erode the profit-making potential of foreign owned subsidiaries, MNCs may take their business elsewhere or, less drastically, simply devise ways of evading regulations.

The balance of bargaining power between foreign firms and host states may vary according to: (1) the characteristics of the host country, (2) the characteristics of the investment, (3) changes in the international economic environment.[17] We review each of these factors in the following sections.

Characteristics of the Host Country: Host countries possessing characteristics which render them attractive to foreign investors are likely to find themselves in a relatively strong bargaining position. The more lucrative the investment,

---

[16]Jenkins, *Transnational Corporations and Uneven Development*, 171–72; Cohen and Frieden, "The Impact of Multinational Corporations on Developing Nations," 169.

[17]This section relies heavily throughout on Theodore Moran, "Multinational Corporations and Dependency: A Dialogue for Dependentistas and Non-Dependentistas," *International Organization*, Winter, 1978. Also see Franklin Weinstein, "Underdevelopment and Efforts to Control Multinational Corporations," in Modelski, *Transnational Corporations*.

the more likely it is to be made in spite of heavy host state regulation. Thus, Third World countries with large domestic markets, skilled and disciplined work forces, bountiful natural resources, and well-developed infrastructures can afford to drive hard bargains with foreign firms who, presumably, will be eager to gain access to the country and its many economic opportunities.

The host country's position is also strengthened to the extent that it has available alternatives to foreign investment. If, for instance, the country already possesses a strong industrial structure, whether public or private, or is able to accumulate capital locally due to a high domestic savings rate, then its dependence on DFI is lessened. The price the host state can demand of foreign investors for the right of entry is likely to go up.

Finally, states with large, sophisticated, and honest bureaucracies will be in a better position to bargain on an equal basis with highly skilled MNC negotiators. They will also possess a greater capacity to gather critical information, monitor MNC behavior, and enforce relevant laws and regulations.

Some Third World countries, such as Brazil, Mexico, and South Korea, possess many, though not all, of these characteristics. Yet, most Southern countries lack, in varying degrees, a considerable number of the crucial characteristics which might place them in a favorable bargaining position with foreign firms.

Characteristics of the Investment: The bargaining relationship between governments and firms may vary across different investment projects within the same country. Some types of industry are more easily regulated than others. Bargaining leverage shifts to the host state where projects involve well-known and slowly changing technologies. In such cases, it is well within the capacity of state or locally owned private firms to manage the production facility in question or to establish competing projects. Low-technology foreign investment is therefore often subject to heavy regulation, intense local competition, or even outright nationalization.

Investment projects resting upon more sophisticated or rapidly changing technology are less vulnerable to state demands. In these cases, the local skills and knowledge needed to manage the project or to create competitive local alternatives may not exist. Moreover, the success of such ventures depends upon continuous infusions of new technology from the home firm. This increases the host state's dependence upon a foreign firm and places the latter in a strong bargaining position.

Much the same logic applies with respect to the foreign marketing requirements associated with production for export. Products marketed through complex networks, especially where the latter are controlled by the multinationals themselves, may require the cooperation of foreign firms if they are to be exported successfully. Where products can be more readily sold abroad by state or locally owned private firms, then it is easier for Third World governments to escape dependence on foreign capital and to assert control over local production.

Capital-intensive projects typically require large fixed investments in factories and machinery. Once these are in place, the foreign firm is hostage to state control due to high sunk costs. Only continued production and sales will possibly allow the firm to recoup its sizable initial outlay. Where fixed investment is low, however, a firm can more easily close up shop and relocate to a different country should state demands prove intolerable. Thus, the size of the initial investment influences relative bargaining power.

Related to this point is the fact that potential foreign investors have greater bargaining power before a project is established than after. Knowing that the host state may be eager for additional investment, the firm will seek explicit pledges of favorable treatment prior to committing to a project. MNCs often attempt to play countries off against one another in an effort to strike the best and most reliable deal. Once the project is in place, however, the firm's threat to relocate becomes less credible, and further concessions will be difficult to obtain. Indeed, Third World states often seek to alter the original bargain in their own favor.

In general, Third World bargaining power has been greatest with respect to mining and raw materials investments. These projects typically involve well-known and slowly changing technologies, simple marketing requirements, and high fixed investments. Owing to these factors, many foreign-owned extractive operations were nationalized by Third World governments during the seventies.

MNCs usually have greater leverage in manufacturing industries, especially those involving sophisticated and changeable technologies, complex foreign marketing requirements, and low fixed investments. Indeed, it is just such industrial sectors in which the concentration of MNC ownership is highest in the Third World.

Changes in the International Economic Environment: The balance of bargaining power between states and firms can vary over time due to a changing international economic climate. During the seventies, for instance, external conditions tended to strengthen Third World states relative to MNCs. Growing competition among MNCs made it easier for governments to play firms off against one another in an attempt achieve a more favorable bargain. In particular, previously dominant U.S. firms now faced growing competition from European and Japanese MNCs. The U.S. share of DFI among thirteen OECD member countries declined from 60 percent between 1961 and 1967 to 30 percent from 1971 to 1979. Moreover, European and Japanese firms often proved more tolerant of state regulation than U.S. corporations.[18]

Another international economic factor that favored Third World states during the seventies was the growing availability of commercial bank lending.

---

[18]Stephen Krasner, *Structural Conflict: The Third World Against Global Liberalism*, Berkeley: University of California Press, 1985.

This provided an alternative source of capital and lessened Third World dependence upon DFI. Able to do without MNCs more easily, developing country governments tightened regulations and funneled borrowed funds into state owned corporations that sometimes served as direct competitors to existing foreign firms.

Finally, the seventies were a time of relative growth and prosperity for many Third World countries. Manufacturing exports expanded rapidly. Moreover, world prices for raw material commodities were high during the first half of the decade. The wave of Third World nationalizations of foreign investments in extractive industries was largely prompted by host-state efforts to ensure that the benefits of these soaring prices would be captured locally rather than carried abroad in the repatriated profits of MNCs.[19]

These favorable conditions changed rapidly during the eighties. A Northern recession led to declines in both Southern manufacturing exports as well as commodity prices. This, combined with higher oil prices and rising interest rates, led to a financial squeeze that culminated in the Third World debt crisis. As many countries teetered on the brink of insolvency, Northern banks drastically contracted their lending operations in the Third World.

Suddenly, many Third World countries came to view increased flows of DFI as one of the few available options that might allow them to sustain economic growth while simultaneously digging their way out from under a mountain of debt. Yet, just when it was most needed, flows of DFI to the South entered a period of absolute decline. This was prompted in part by the dire economic circumstances in most Third World countries, but it was also a result of the strict regulations and controls many MNCs confronted in developing nations.

Facing an unfavorable international economic environment and chastened by declining investment flows, their weakened bargaining position led most Third World states to loosen controls on foreign investment as the eighties progressed. Mexico entirely revamped its foreign investment codes, removing many of the restrictions imposed during the seventies. Venezuela has done the same and has recently decided to invite back many of the same international oil companies whose assets it nationalized in 1976 to help with the exploitation of the Orinco Belt.[20] Many developing nations, especially in Asia, now offer special incentives to MNCs willing to set up assembly operations in so-called "export processing zones." Governments seek to attract export-oriented production by offering tax, tariff, and regulatory concessions to foreign firms that agree to establish factories in these special areas.[21] Other common elements of deregulation include guarantees of unrestricted profit

---

[19]Pollio and Riemenschneider, "The Coming Third World Investment Revival."

[20]John McClean, "Venezuela Reverses Economic Course," *Chicago Tribune*, May 27, 1991.

[21]Joseph Grunwald and Kenneth Flamm, *The Global Factory: Foreign Assembly in International Trade*, Washington: Brookings, 1985.

repatriation, tax breaks, special electrical rates, the removal of export and local input requirements, and streamlined approval procedures.

These relaxed controls and new incentives have had only limited success so far in attracting large amounts of new investment. Moreover, Third World countries now face new competition from Eastern Europe for foreign investment, especially in the area of low-wage manufacturing. As of early 1990, foreign investors had already signed 3,300 joint ventures with Eastern European firms.[22]

This bargaining framework approach to understanding the relationship between host states and foreign firms offers considerable advantages over treatments that exaggerate either the virtues or the villainy of MNCs in the Third World. Southern states can potentially influence the balance between the costs and benefits of DFI by setting the terms under which the subsidiaries of MNCs must operate. Whether a given government can do so effectively without discouraging desired flows of investment depends upon the relative bargaining strengths of the state and the firm. This, in turn, varies across countries and industries as well as over time.

A bargaining approach does, however, contain one major drawback. This sort of analysis is based upon the assumption that state managers in developing societies are motivated only by the desire to serve the national interests of their own country. The primary goal of the political leadership is to maximize the economic welfare of the society as a whole through the bargains they strike with foreign investors. In some cases, however, this is an unrealistic assumption. Some observers argue that while political elites in Third World countries may sometimes possess the capability to bargain effectively with foreign corporations, they often lack the political will to do so.

This is most obviously the case where MNCs use their considerable resources to win favors through bribery and corruption. In one example, five nations banded together in 1974 to form the Union of Banana Exporting Countries. Each government agreed to place an export tax on banana exports. One of the affected corporations, United Brands, paid a $1.25 million bribe to the Honduran Minister of Economics. In return, the Honduran government partially reneged on its agreement with other banana-exporting countries by cutting its export tax from fifty cents to twenty-five, a move that would have saved United Brands from $6 to $7 million yearly. In this case, United Brands' efforts backfired. Unlike most such episodes, news of the deal leaked to the public and the Honduran government was overthrown.[23]

Corruption is not the only threat to host-state autonomy. Some Third World elites maintain power in part through close military, economic, and

---

[22]Richard Lapper, "Dressed for Designer Deals," *South*, March, 1990, 13.

[23]Not long afterwards, the chairman of United Brands committed suicide by leaping from the forty-fourth floor of a New York skyscraper. Paul Harrison, *Inside the Third World*, Middlesex, England: Penguin Books, 1981, 349.

political relationships with the home governments of local MNC affiliates. Vigorous efforts to control MNC activities may threaten to sour these relationships. It is also possible that political motives may prompt some Third World leaders to adopt an overly restrictive stance toward MNCs, purposely discouraging investments that could bring considerable benefits to the country. This might be the case, for instance, where the legitimacy of a government rests upon its nationalist appeal. Under these circumstances, MNCs may provide convenient scapegoats, perhaps diverting attention from government responsibility for other pressing national problems. Finally, some Third World governments may be divided on the question of foreign investment and thus unable to adopt any consistent bargaining position.

These considerations suggest the need for caution in applying a bargaining analysis to host-state–MNC relations. Nevertheless, considerable evidence suggests that host states have in fact proven eager, in most instances, to strike better deals with MNCs when their bargaining position so allows. The extremes of cooptation or destructive defiance appear the exceptions rather than the rule.

RECENT TRENDS IN MNC–HOST-COUNTRY RELATIONS

■ Several important trends are reshaping the nature of foreign investment in the Third World. The geographic locus of investment flows has shifted from Latin America and the Middle East to Asia. Two long-term shifts in the sectoral orientation of MNC activities in the Third World are also continuing. Manufacturing investments are increasingly favored over those in the extractive industries while, within the manufacturing sector, export-oriented production is growing faster than production for the domestic markets of the Southern host countries. Finally, the terms of MNC entry into Third World countries are changing dramatically, with foreign firms increasingly shedding the risks of outright ownership in favor of more limited and indirect forms of involvement in the Third World.

The redirection of direct foreign investment toward East and Southeast Asia is both a response to, and partial source of, the rapid economic growth rates experienced in recent years by many countries of the region, including South Korea, Singapore, Taiwan, Hong Kong, Thailand, Malaysia, and Indonesia. By contrast, many other parts of the Third World (including Latin America, a traditional destination for many foreign investors) remain mired in the economic doldrums that began in the eighties, rendering them unattractive to foreign investors.

The emphasis on Asia also reflects the growing foreign role of Japanese corporations, the most active foreign investors in the region. The internationalization of Japanese firms has stemmed in part from their accumulation of vast financial resources as a result of Japan's export successes. These firms have also been prompted to search for low-cost manufacturing sites abroad as a way of compensating for rising Japanese wage levels. Between 1985 and 1989, the flow of Japanese capital, including DFI, to other Asian economies grew sixfold in dollar terms. Japanese firms have focused on countries with well-educated and disciplined work forces. These include Thailand, where one new Japanese factory was opened for each work day in 1989, and Malaysia, which received $25 billion in DFI, most from Japanese investors, over the six years ending in 1991.[24]

The shift in the sectors targeted by foreign investors from extractive industries to manufacturing and from production for domestic consumption to exports is illustrated by data on U.S. MNC affiliates located in the Third World. Between 1950 and 1984, the share of U.S. Third World DFI located in extractive industries fell from over one-half to less than 40 percent while the proportion accounted for by manufacturing rose from 15 percent to 37 percent.[25] The share of exports in the total sales of U.S. MNC subsidiaries in the South grew from 8.4 percent in 1966 to 18.1 percent in 1977 and has continued to rise.[26]

Perhaps the most important trend in Third World host-country–MNC relations during the recent years has been the development of new, more flexible forms of investment.[27] Traditionally, foreign investment entered the Third World in the form of a tightly integrated package under the ownership and control of the MNC. Elements of this package included capital, technology, managerial expertise, and marketing. Foreign investors typically resisted pressures from the host country to break up this package by allowing greater local control over various elements. Third World governments often responded by attempting to steer the behavior of foreign firms through the imposition of external legal and regulatory controls.

Out of these conflicting perspectives emerged a set of arrangements that satisfied neither party. Third World governments argued that foreign control over all aspects of investment concentrated too much economic power in foreign hands, especially in critical sectors; limited the spin-off of skills, technology, and other benefits to the rest of the local economy; and led to abuses such as those surveyed earlier in this chapter. MNCs, for their part, became increasingly frustrated by government regulations that raised costs, cut profits, and hemmed in their autonomy. The result was a standoff: governments resorted to more extreme measures of control, such as outright nationalization, while MNCs increasingly steered clear of new commitments in the Third World.

---

[24]See "Asia's Emerging Standard-Bearer," *The Economist*, July 21, 1990; and David Sanger, "Power of the Yen Winning Asia," *New York Times*, December 5, 1991.

[25]Jenkins, *Transnational Corporations and Uneven Development*, 7.

[26]United Nations Centre on Transnational Corporations, *Transnational Corporations and International Trade: Selected Issues*, New York: United Nations, 1985, 6.

[27]This discussion relies upon Lapper, "Dressed for Designed Deals," and Pollio and Riemenschneider, "The Coming Third World Investment Revival."

In recent years, however, each side has begun to abandon previously rigid positions and to seek out more cooperative arrangements designed to reconcile conflicting interests. As we have seen, Third World governments have begun to dismantle the unwieldy system of regulatory controls that served to discourage new foreign investment. MNCs, meanwhile, have begun to abandon the insistence on formal ownership and control over all phases of investment, thus removing one of the concerns which prompted Third World governments to impose onerous controls in the first place.

While the older forms of MNC investment in the Third World continue to persist, a host of new ventures involve foreign firms as limited partners in projects often initiated and largely controlled by Third World businesses or governments. Typically, foreign firms provide only those elements of the overall project that local participants lack the means to provide for themselves. The once monolithic packaging of capital, technology, management, and marketing has given way to a new division of labor in which local and foreign partners perform different functions, depending upon the particular strengths they bring to the project.

These partnerships take many forms. In joint ventures, local and foreign firms team up to provide capital and management while dividing up profits. Or, Third World firms may subcontract to provide components of a larger product or carry out assembly operations for a foreign firm. In some cases, foreign firms provide the missing ingredients for a project that is predominantly controlled by Third World partners. For instance, a foreign firm may, in return for a fee, license technology to a Third World firm to be used in the production or design of a particular product. Foreign firms may also provide managers for a project that is locally owned. Turnkey contracts call for foreign firms to construct factories that are then turned over to a Third World firm for operation. Product-in-hand contracts are like turnkey contracts, except that the foreign partner also trains local managers in how to operate the plant. Finally, some Third World businesses act as franchisees, putting up the capital or paying royalties and providing management while the franchiser provides technology and trademarks along with direction in how the operation is to be run.

Malaysia's effort to develop a domestic automobile industry provides one example of the new flexibility in MNC–host-country relations. The government forged a partnership with the Japanese firm Mitsubishi to produce a small economy car called the Proton. In return for one-third ownership, Mitsubishi provided the necessary design, technology, and machinery. When difficulties plagued the plant after it opened under Malaysian management, Mitsubishi was called in to provide managerial expertise as well. The operation has become profitable and has begun to generate exports on top of healthy domestic sales.[28]

---

[28]"New Car for Malaysia, New Influence for Japan," *New York Times*, March 6, 1991.

These new arrangements satisfy many Third World concerns about foreign involvement in their economies. Much greater control is vested in local parties. This limits the potential for MNC abuses while contributing to the local accumulation of skills, knowledge, and experience. Third World governments, which often take a direct role in such ventures, gain greater say over which projects are initiated and how they are run, thus lessening the need for indirect controls and regulations. At the same time, some of the benefits foreign investment can provide are preserved, such as access to skills and technology unavailable locally. Another benefit is less obvious. Many of the Northern firms involved in such deals are small to medium-sized businesses and have little prior experience in Third World markets. Their growing presence opens new channels for foreign investment in the Third World and presents established MNCs with greater competition. Overall, this improves the bargaining climate for Third World countries in their relations with foreign capital.

These new "designer deals" do, however, hold potential drawbacks for the Third World. By gaining greater control, Third World governments and private firms also shoulder higher risks. Where their role is lessened, MNCs give up responsibility for assessing the wisdom of investment decisions. If a project fails, the losses are felt much more directly in the Third World itself and much less in the bottom line of MNC spreadsheets. A related problem is that these arrangements provide only limited infusions of foreign capital into Third World host countries. Capital, a precious commodity in most Third World countries, must be raised locally or borrowed from abroad.

This shift of responsibility, risk, and uncertainty to the Third World partners is precisely what makes the new forms of involvement attractive to many MNCs. Often, they profit by providing services under contract without the necessity of putting their own capital at risk. The lower profile of these new investment forms also removes the political spotlight from foreign business involvement in the Third World, lessening the prospect of populist and nationalist agitation against their presence.

CONCLUSIONS

■ Many MNCs make handsome profits on their Third World operations. Southern countries often benefit from the capital and know-how that accompany such investments. The potential for mutual gain has indeed perpetuated the ongoing relationship between Northern firms and Southern host governments. Yet, while each party is, in varying degrees, dependent upon the other, the interests, purposes, and perspectives of MNCs and Third World states diverge in some essential respects. These differences have given rise to a history of conflict. The "rules of the game" governing foreign investment in various Third World countries have shifted greatly over time, often in response to changes in relative bargaining power. Efforts to devise a lasting and mutually acceptable framework for MNC–Third World relations have generally produced disappointing results.

The fundamental source of MNC–Third World conflict stems from the varying attributes of the two parties. MNCs are economic entities that seek to maximize profits on a global scale. Though, in practice, DFI may contribute to the development of a host country's economy, this is, from the firm's perspective, an incidental result, not the primary purpose of the investment. Changes in corporate practice that might maximize the benefits to a host country appeal to corporate executives only if they also happen to make sense in terms of overall profitability, a circumstance that is probably rare.

Third World states are political entities bounded by territorial borders. The principal concerns of Southern leaders are to promote economic development while also reducing their country's vulnerability to foreign manipulation. From the Third World perspective, MNCs represent both opportunity and threat. DFI brings economic assets that are scarce in most Third World countries. Yet, in the absence of effective regulation, these assets are subject to foreign control. Decisions made outside the country's borders ultimately determine both the economic and political effects of DFI.

MNCs would prefer a world without borders. Yet, they must operate in a system of sovereign states. MNCs cannot escape the realities of fragmented political authority in the international system, but they can and do attempt to minimize the interference of national regulation on their global operations by translating their mobility, knowledge, and resources into bargaining power.

Short of outright nationalization, host states cannot alter the global or transnational character of the MNC. They can, however, use their legal and territorial control to impose regulations designed to ensure that DFI takes place on terms that further national development goals. Their ability to do so, without disrupting the stream of foreign investment, depends upon the stringency of the regulatory regime the state seeks to impose as well as its relative bargaining power.

The tensions between Northern MNCs and Southern host states may wax or wane over time. The outcomes of bargaining between them may vary as well. But the fundamental character of their relationship is likely to persist. Conflicting interests and desires will continue to weigh against the mutual dependence of firms and states upon one another, ensuring a stormy marriage between the two.

ANNOTATED BILIOGRAPHY

Volker Bornschier and Christopher Chase-Dunn, *Transnational Corporations and Underdevelopment*, New York: Praeger, 1985.
A conceptual analysis of international capital flows employing world systems theory, a school of thought that is closely related to the dependency perspective.

Rhys Jenkins, *Transnational Corporations and Uneven Development: The Internationalization of Capital and the Third World*, New York: Methuen, 1987.
A comprehensive treatment of MNCs in the Third World written from a dependency perspective. Contains a wealth of data, history, and theoretical analysis.

Richard Lapper, "Dressed for Designer Deals," *South*, March, 1990.
Offers a brief overview of recent innovations in MNC–host-country relations.

George Modelski, ed. *Transnational Corporations and World Order: Readings in International Political Economy*, San Francisco: W. H. Freeman & Co., 1979.
Although dated, this reader contains a number of classic theoretical works on the politics and economics of foreign direct investment.

Theodore Moran, "Multinational Corporations and Dependency: A Dialogue for Dependentistas and Non-Dependentistas," *International Organization*, Winter, 1978.
A seminal source on the bargaining approach to analyzing MNC–host-country relations.

CHAPTER 12

THE POLITICS OF
THIRD WORLD DEBT

W hen Mexican finance minister Jesus Silva Herzog stepped from his plane as he arrived in Washington, D.C., on August 13, 1982, for urgent meetings with Federal Reserve Board chairman Paul Volker and other U.S. officials, he strode into a new era in the life of his country and, indeed, of much of the Third World. Prior to Silva Herzog's trip, Mexico had experienced years of breakneck economic growth financed, for the most part, by Northern banks. Over the previous six years, in particular, Mexican president Jose Lopez Portillo, a proud, aristocratic man of extravagant tastes, had driven his country down a seemingly endless path of growing prosperity built upon modern industry and recently discovered oil riches. He bet his place in history on the unlimited potential of Mexico's economic future.

The purpose of Silva Herzog's Northern pilgrimage was to acknowledge the failure of Lopez Portillo's gamble.[1] In the biggest financial crisis of its history, Mexico stood on the verge of bankruptcy, unable to make payments due on its enormous international debt or to convince bankers to supply sufficient new credits to keep up the fiction of Mexico's solvency. Virtually overnight, the hopes and dreams of millions of Mexicans for a better way of life were punctured. The Mexican peso, already battered by a 100 percent inflation rate, lost much of its value. Businesses found themselves unable to borrow urgently needed funds. All too accurate rumors spread that the

---

[1]For additional details on Silva Herzog's trip and the ensuing negotiations, see Robert Bennett, "Mexico Seeking Postponement of Part of Its Debt," *New York Times*, August 20, 1982; Robert Bennett, "Bankers Pressured to Assist Mexico," *New York Times*, August 21, 1982; and Alan Riding, "Jesus Silva Herzog: Survivor," *New York Times*, August 21, 1982.

government would soon raise prices on basic foodstuffs, drastically cut all kinds of spending, and eliminate many thousands of jobs.

The crisis forced Mexico to set aside its jealous independence and plead for help from its colossal neighbor to the North. This successful bid for U.S. assistance was, however, only the beginning. Silva Herzog next approached the IMF and Mexico's major creditors hoping to obtain new funds while postponing and restructuring payments on Mexico's old debts. Northern bankers agreed only on the humbling condition that Mexico submit to IMF supervision of its economic policies. Since that time, Mexico has lost much of its national autonomy on economic matters. The policies of its government have been largely dictated from abroad while its citizens have paid dearly in an effort to honor the country's foreign debt.

Mexico's story differs from those of other Third World debtor countries only in the details. The Mexican crisis of 1982 ushered in a period during which many nations experienced the same sequence of near bankruptcy, rescue, and economic austerity. The debt crisis was indeed the principal cause of a stunning change in trajectory for much of the South, from healthy rates of economic growth during much of the sixties and seventies to stagnation in the eighties. This chapter seeks to uncover the dynamics of the debt crisis. We begin by inventorying the dimensions and costs of Third World debt. Next, we introduce the principal actors in this continuing drama. In the heart of the chapter, we outline the origins and evolution of the debt crisis up to the present, including a discussion of recent policies. Finally, we examine the bargaining process between North and South over the debt issue.

THE COSTS OF THIRD WORLD DEBT

■ Hovering menacingly over much of the Third World, a dark cloud of debt has dimmed prospects for Southern economic growth and development for over a decade now. In 1970, Third World debt to Northern banks and governments as well as multilateral lending institutions, such as the IMF and the World Bank, totaled $70 billion. By 1979, this sum had risen to $400 billion. A decade later, in 1989, Southerners owed Northerners more than $1.3 trillion. This latter figure was 25 percent greater, after adjusting for inflation, than in 1982 and represented roughly 50 percent of total Southern GNP.[2]

The burden of paying the stream of principal and interest due each year on this enormous debt has imposed severe costs on people throughout the

---

[2]Edward R. Fried and Philip H. Trezise, *Third World Debt: The Next Phase*, Washington: Brookings, 1989, 5. This figure includes only medium and long-term debt. Third World countries owe many additional billions of dollars in short-term debt.

Third World. Partly in response to Northern pressure, numerous Third World governments have adopted belt-tightening measures as a means of coping with the debt crisis. These austerity plans are designed to generate foreign exchange by reducing the demand for imported goods while directing a larger share of domestic production toward exports. Surplus export earnings may then be devoted to debt repayment. Because they squeeze domestic consumption in order to free the resources needed to satisfy the debt burden, these measures invariably produce economic hardship. As Jamaica's former prime minister Michael Manley observed in 1980, officials in debtor countries often face a cruel choice between "using your last foreign exchange to pay off Citibank and Chase Manhattan or buying food and medicines for your people."[3]

Between 1980 and 1985, for instance, two-thirds of Third World countries experienced negative or negligible economic growth rates.[4] The gross domestic product of sub-Saharan Africa (already the poorest region of the world) fell by an average of 1 percent per year from 1974 to 1984.[5] This fall is a symptom of what former World Bank president A.W. Clausen has called "the worst economic crisis any region has faced since World War Two."[6] The real incomes of Mexican workers declined by 40 percent between 1980 and 1988, while, similarly, average real wages dropped 38 percent in Venezuela from 1983 to 1989. Per capita GNP in Latin American as a whole, which had risen by 40 percent during the seventies, fell by 7 percent in the eighties.[7]

No less shocking than these economic statistics are the social consequences of the debt crisis. From 1980 to 1984, government spending on health care fell in fourteen Latin American countries while education outlays declined in ten.[8] Other areas of the Third World, particularly Africa, have been hit even harder. In its 1989 *State of the World's Children* survey, UNICEF focused on what it refered to as "children in debt." Its findings, as the following summary suggests, are disturbing:

> [I]n the thirty-seven poorest countries (most of which are in Africa), per capita spending on health has fallen by half over the last few years, and on education by a quarter. Malnutrition is rising in Burundi, Gambia, Guinea-

---

[3]Quoted in Michael Moffitt, *The World's Money: International Banking from Bretton Woods to the Brink of Insolvency*, New York: Simon and Schuster, 1983, 127.

[4]Robin Broad and John Cavanaugh, "How to Approach Third World Debt," *New York Times*, March 3, 1988.

[5]Chandra Hardy, "Africa's Debt Burden," *Policy Focus* (ODC), no. 5, 1985.

[6]Quoted in Kari Polanyi Levitt, "Linkage and Vulnerability: The 'Debt Crisis' in Latin America and Africa," in Bonnie Campbell, ed. *Political Dimensions of the Debt Crisis*, New York: St. Martin's Press, 1989, 15.

[7]For data on changes in Latin income levels, see Tom Wicker, "The Real Danger of Debt," *New York Times*, December 2, 1988; Alan Riding, "Rumblings in Venezuela," *New York Times*, March 7, 1989; and Clyde Farnsworth, "U.S. Falls Short on Its Third World Debt Plan," *New York Times*, January 9, 1990.

[8]"Latin American Debt: Living on Borrowed Time?," *Great Decisions, '89*, New York: Foreign Policy Association, 1989, 30.

Bussau, Niger, Nigeria, and other African countries. Some 350,000 more African children died last year due to reduced health budgets, deteriorating sanitation, and the lack of foreign exchange to import even basic medicines.[9]

Although not solely responsible for these gloomy developments, the debt crisis has been an important contributor to each.[10]

The political costs of the debt crisis have proven almost as threatening for some Third World governments. Economic hardship has heightened the risks of political instability. This is particularly true in Latin America. Many countries in the region abandoned authoritarian regimes in favor of democratic governments during the 1980s. Yet, the viability of these fledgling democracies is placed in jeopardy by the burden of external debt. Latin American expert Douglas Payne has remarked that "democracy is beginning to be identified more with hardship than with freedom."[11]

Though events have yet to confirm the more dire predictions of political upheaval, troubling signs of unrest abound. In 1989, "IMF riots," so called because they followed announcements of new government austerity policies demanded by the IMF in return for new loans, broke out in a number of Latin American countries. These incidents of unrest left fourteen dead in Argentina, 200 dead in the Dominican Republic, and resulted in 300 fatalities in Venezuela, not to mention the many injured and the millions of dollars in losses from supermarket looting and vandalism. Although Venezuela's economy rebounded vigorously in 1991, much of this growth bypassed the poor, leading to renewed unrest. In early 1992, the government's perceived weakness and ineffectiveness prompted an attempted coup d'etat led by disaffected segments of the military. Although loyal military units put down this grab at power, the government's political popularity remains perilously low.

Wrenching economic reforms launched by Brazil during 1990, designed in part to prepare the country for renewed debt negotiations, led to severe economic recession and immense political and social turmoil. In June of that year, an estimated 1.5 million workers participated in 330 separate strikes in protest of spreading unemployment and a declining standard of living. Striking workers at a Ford plant demolished cars and computers, while a peasant organization announced a "massive and radical offensive" of land occupations.[12] The story is similar in many parts of Africa. Urban insurrection in Sudan following the introduction of IMF reforms in 1985 toppled the government of Gaafar al-Nimeiry, while similar policies have led to rioting in Nigeria, Tunisia, and Morocco.[13]

---

[9]Ernest Harsch, "After Adjustment," *Africa Report*, May/June, 1989, 47.

[10]Also see Fran Hosken, "Austerity's Human Toll," *The Humanist*, January/February, 1989.

[11]George de Lama, "Latin World Teeters on Edge of an Abyss," *Chicago Tribune*, June 4, 1989.

[12]James Brooke, "Brazil's Costly Trip to a Free Market," *New York Times*, August 6, 1990; de Lama, "Latin World Teeters on Edge of an Abyss." Also see Riding, "Rumblings in Venezuela."

[13]Harsch, "After Adjustment," 48.

The costs of the debt crisis are not limited to the South. Some groups in the United States and other Northern countries have also paid a heavy price. In an effort to reduce the outflow of foreign exchange, the four largest Latin American countries reduced their imports by one-third to one-half between 1981 and 1986.[14] As a result, the U.S. trade balance with Latin America dropped from a small surplus in 1980 to an $18 billion deficit in 1985.[15] U.S. exports to the region fell from $42 billion in 1981 to $30 billion in 1988, costing an estimated one million jobs in U.S. export industries.[16] The economies of towns and cities on the U.S. side of the border with Mexico were so devastated by the loss of cross-border business after the Mexican financial crisis of 1982 that then California governor Edmund Brown, Jr. requested that Federal economic disaster relief funds be sent to the area.[17]

The enormous costs to all concerned have recently brought movement in negotiations between North and South over methods for coping with the debt problem. Announced in the spring of 1989, the so-called Brady Plan, named after its sponsor, U.S. Secretary of the Treasury Nicholas Brady, signaled the North's newfound willingness to embrace limited debt forgiveness as a response to the burdens of the most heavily indebted countries. Northern governments have also offered debt relief to the poorest debtor nations, especially those in Africa.

In other respects as well, the debt crisis has eased somewhat. At its height, many feared that if one or more of the largest debtor countries defaulted on their international obligations, proving either unable or unwilling to continue payments on their debts, the entire world banking system could be threatened. After all, the world's largest banks were heavily exposed in Third World lending. In 1981, the nine largest U.S. banks held Third World debt equal to 246 percent of their primary capital.[18] Since the international banking system is so closely intertwined, the failure of several large banks might have set off a chain reaction of bank failures that could have swiftly spread beyond the ability of governmental authorities to control. A collapse of global credit institutions could have choked off economic activity worldwide.

---

[14]Clyde Farnsworth, "Debts of Latins Making Trade Links Tortuous," *New York Times*, Dec. 26, 1987.

[15]Broad and Cavanaugh, "How to Approach Third World Debt."

[16]"Latin American Debt: Living on Borrowed Time?," 27. Southern countries increasingly turned to barter, or, as they are officially called, countertrade deals during the eighties. By swapping goods directly with foreign firms rather than paying with cash or credit, Southern governments or businesses attempted to maintain trade levels with a minumum commitment of scarce foreign exchange. Reported countertrade deals involving developing countries grew from 18 in 1980 to 304 in 1985. See Klaus Netter and Anh Nga Tran-Nguyen, "LDCs' Countertrade in the 1980's: Practices, Policies and Outlook," *The Courier*, July/August, 1989, 80; and Farnsworth, "Debts of Latins Making Trade Links Tortuous."

[17]Wayne King, "Peso's Turmoil Shakes Economies of Cities on Mexican–U.S. Border," *New York Times*, August 22, 1982.

[18]Harold Lever and Christopher Huhne, *Debt and Danger*, Boston: Atlantic Monthly Press, 1985, 18.

However plausible it once may have been, this worst-case scenario now seems unlikely. Over the past several years, Northern banks have lowered their exposure to Third World debt by selling off loans, diversifying their portfolios, and setting aside financial reserves against the possibility of Third World losses. As a result, Federal Deposit Insurance Corporation chairman William Seidman assured Congress in early 1989 that no U.S. bank would be rendered insolvent even if the six largest Third World debtor countries defaulted on all of their bank debts.[19]

Nevertheless, the problem of Third World debt will remain a serious one for some time to come, whatever policies are chosen. What roles do different actors play in the debt saga? How did the debt crisis begin and in which directions has it evolved? These are questions to which we now turn.

ACTORS

■ The drama of Third World debt involves many actors. The following discussion describes the roles of the principal ones.

Debtor Countries

Although most Third World countries carry some degree of foreign debt, not all find the burdens of repayment unbearable. Forty-five percent of medium and long-term Third World debt is accounted for by fifty countries that are generally in a sound position to manage their debt service burdens. For this group as a whole, interest payments amount to 7 percent of export earnings, on average. Commercial banks hold about 40 percent of this debt while Northern governments and multilateral lending agencies account for the rest.[20]

The debt crisis is far more serious for the poor and vulnerable countries of sub-Saharan Africa that together account for 5 percent of total Third World debt. Very little of African debt is owed to commercial banks for the simple reason that the banks have traditionally considered the mostly poverty-stricken countries of the region poor credit risks. Over 90 percent of African debt is therefore accounted for by loans from Northern governments or multilateral lending agencies.[21] While small as a proportion of the Third

---

[19]James Galbraith, "Its Time to Settle the Debt," *In These Times*, June 7–20, 1989, 16.

[20]All data cited in this section is for 1989, unless otherwise indicated. Fried and Trezise, *Third World Debt*, 5–6.

[21]Maurice Williams, "Should the IMF Withdraw from Africa?," *Policy Focus*, (ODC), no. 1, 1987.

World total, the debt burden of African countries has been severe in relation to their ability to pay. Scheduled payments of interest and principal have hovered around a high 50 percent of the region's export earnings.[22] As a result, many African countries have fallen behind on their debt repayments in recent years.[23]

In recognition of these stark realities, Northern governments have begun to forgive, reschedule, or reduce the interest payments on the debts of many African countries on the condition that they agreed to follow economic adjustment programs designed by the IMF or the World Bank.[24]

At the heart of the debt crisis are fifteen heavily indebted Third World countries who together owe $480 billion in medium- and long-term debt, or 38 percent of the total for the South as a whole. Latin American countries, led by Brazil, Mexico, and Argentina, account for 80 percent of the debt held by the countries in this category. Other Latin American countries included among the fifteen largest debtors are Bolivia, Chile, Columbia, Ecuador, Peru, Uruguay, and Venezuela. The remaining countries on the list are the Ivory Coast, Morocco, Nigeria, the Philippines, and Yugoslavia.[25]

Northern banks are heavily exposed among these countries, holding 64 percent of their combined debt. The remainder is split roughly equally between multilateral lending agencies and Northern governments. Interest payments average 25 percent of these countries' export earnings and 4 percent of their GNP. In 1988, per capita consumption for the group as a whole stood 5 percent below 1980 levels.[26]

Although a variety of Third World entities hold Northern loans, the public or state sector accounted for the bulk of Southern borrowing during the seventies. Governments often relied upon foreign funds to finance their budget deficits. State-owned industrial firms or public utilities also borrowed heavily from abroad. PEMEX, Mexico's publicly owned oil company, alone borrowed $15 billion from external sources in 1981.[27] Governments often funneled foreign loans into national development banks, which then relent the money to private firms. When governments did not borrow money directly, they nevertheless commonly provided guarantees for loans undertaken

---

[22]Hardy, "Africa's Debt Burden" and Williams, "Should the IMF Withdraw from Africa?"

[23]In 1980, when the total external debt of sub-Saharan Africa was $54 billion, debt payments in arrears, or past due, amounted to $600 million. By 1987, total debt had risen to $126.5 billion while payments in arrears had skyrocketed to $18 billion. Joshua Greene, "The Debt Problem of Sub-Saharan Africa," *Finance and Development*, June, 1989, 9.

[24]Peter Kilborn, "Bush Acts to Ease Africa Debt," *New York Times*, July 7, 1989; and Steven Greenhouse, "Third World Tells IMF the Poverty Has Increased," *New York Times*, Sept. 29, 1988.

[25]Fried and Trezise, *Third World Debt*, 5–6.

[26]Fried and Trezise, *Third World Debt*, 5–6.

[27]The Debt Crisis Network, *From Debt to Development: Alternatives to the International Debt Crisis*, Washington: Institute for Policy Studies, 1985, 26.

directly by private corporations or banks.[28] Less noticed than Third World governments and private businesses, the local subsidiaries of Northern multinational corporations have also been major borrowers, accounting in 1983 for roughly $100 billion of overall Third World debt.[29]

The Banks

Most commercial lending to Third World countries is organized through bank syndicates. Many banks working together contribute, in varying proportions, to large "syndicated" loan packages to a given Third World country. The big banks that put up the largest amount of money negotiate with borrower countries on behalf of all of the other banks. These deals often involve an enormous number of banks. Six hundred banks were party to negotiations over rescheduling agreements with Mexico in 1983, while similar negotiations with Brazil during the same year involved 560 banks.[30] Yet, while many banks have some stake in the debt crisis, Third World lending is overwhelmingly concentrated with a very few large banks. In the mid-1980s, nine large institutions together accounted for 63 percent of all Third World lending by U.S. banks.[31]

Northern Governments

Northern governments are major creditors to the Third World through their foreign aid programs. Much Northern aid is given in the form of loans rather than outright grants, although usually at less than market interest rates. The major Northern creditor governments hammer out common strategies in their negotiations over debt issues with Third World countries through an informal consultative arrangement known as the "Paris Club."

Northern governments play other roles in the debt crisis as well. They provide capital to the International Monetary Fund and the World Bank and control the policies of those organizations through their preponderance of

---

[28]The mix of borrowing by public or private actors varied from country to country. In Brazil, and to a lesser extent Mexico and Venezuela, most of the debt was contracted by public sector entities. In Chile, private firms accounted for most of the borrowing, while Argentina was a mixed case. See Jeffry Frieden, "Winners and Losers in the Debt Crisis: The Political Implications," in Barabara Stallings and Robert Kaufman, eds. *Debt and Democracy in Latin America*, Boulder: Westview Press, 1989, 26–28; and Jeff Frieden, "Third World Indebted Industrialization: International Finance and State Capitalism in Mexico, Brazil, Algeria and South Korea," *International Organization*, Summer, 1981.

[29]The Debt Crisis Network, *From Debt to Development*, 24.

[30]Vinod K. Aggarwal, *International Debt Threat: Bargaining Among Creditors and Debtors in the 1980s*, Policy Papers in International Affairs, no. 29, Berkeley: University of California Press, 1987, 16.

[31]Lever and Huhne, *Debt and Danger*, 17.

voting power. Government authorities in the North regulate the behavior of banks falling under their jurisdiction. Northern governments have provided temporary financing designed to help debtor countries avoid default. And, finally, the United States in particular has intervened in the relationship between debtor countries and their creditors with comprehensive proposals for managing the debt problem.

Multilateral Lending Agencies

The International Monetary Fund is the multilateral lending agency most directly involved in the debt crisis, although, as we discuss below, the role of the World Bank has grown in recent years. The principal purpose of the IMF is to lend money to countries experiencing shortfalls in their current accounts. Fund loans must be repaid within one to three years. Member countries gain the right to borrow foreign exchange from the Fund by contributing a combination of the country's own currency and gold to the Fund's reserves. Each member's contribution is roughly proportional to the size of its economy.

Beyond certain credit limits (which vary according to the country's original contribution), however, Fund authorities may set conditions on additional borrowing. Before lending large amounts to a member country, in other words, the IMF extracts promises from the government that it will undertake various policy reforms that the Fund believes are necessary to correct existing current account deficits and earn the foreign exchange needed to repay loans issued by the Fund. The terms of IMF policy reform packages are generally based upon the assumption that countries that run large deficits or borrow heavily abroad are living beyond their means by consuming more than they produce. Fund supported "stabilization programs," as they are commonly known, are designed to reduce domestic consumption and consequently lower the country's demand for imported goods and foreign loans.

The specific package of policy reforms sponsored by the IMF varies, but typically includes a number of the following measures: abolish or liberalize foreign exchange and import controls; reduce growth in the domestic money supply and raise interest rates; increase taxes and reduce government spending; abolish food, fuel, and transportation subsidies; cut government wages and seek wage restraint from labor unions; dismantle price controls; privatize publicly owned firms; reduce restrictions on foreign investment; and depreciate the currency.

The economic hardship these policies typically produce make them politically unpopular. The IMF's ability to compel governments to pursue these reforms stems less from the size of the loans the Fund itself has to offer (which are typically only a portion of the country's overall needs), than from the fact that Northern banks will not extend new credits or reschedule old debts with a country that has not reached an agreement with the IMF. A debtor country's international credit standing, in other words, rests upon its ability to obtain an IMF seal of approval. An accord with the IMF signals to private lenders that, in the Fund's view, a debtor country is pursuing the appropriate course necessary to correct past and present financial imbalances.

The World Bank has played an increasingly important role alongside the IMF in managing the Third World debt crisis. While the Bank once focused overwhelmingly on "project" lending, whereby loans were tied to specific investments such as a hydroelectric dam or a new road, more recently the Bank has shifted a large portion of its resources toward "structural adjustment" loans. This latter type of lending links balance of payments financing to reforms in broad sectors of the economy. The sorts of reforms supported by the Bank are similar to those sponsored by the IMF; indeed, the two institutions often coordinate the advice they give client countries.[32]

THE ORIGINS AND EVOLUTION OF THE THIRD WORLD DEBT CRISIS

■ The fundamental origin of the debt crisis lies in the dependence of many Third World countries on external capital rather than internal savings to finance economic growth. During the fifties and sixties, outside capital flowed to the Third World principally through Northern aid and direct foreign investment. Beginning in the late sixties, these sources declined in relative importance as commercial banks stepped up their lending to Third World countries. This shift is captured in the following statistics: while official development assistance from the North dropped from 58 percent of total Third World financial receipts in 1960 to 30 percent in 1978, the share accounted for by bank lending rose from 2 percent to 33 percent during the same period. Real private bank lending to the Third World grew by 144 percent from 1970 to 1973.[33]

This change in the composition of financial flows from North to South was perhaps as important as the dramatic increase in the total volume of

---

[32]The growing role of the World Bank in debt management has sometimes led to frictions between it and the IMF. Some IMF officials are said to resent World Bank intrusions on traditional IMF turf. In September, 1988, for instance, the World Bank announced that it planned to loan $1.2 billion to Argentina. This was the first time that the World Bank had approved lending to a debtor country without first demanding that the receipient obtain IMF approval for its economic reform plans. High officials at the IMF were reportedly angered that the Fund was not consulted. Steven Greenhouse, "Japan Is Seeking Larger Role in World's Financial System and Debt Crisis," *New York Times*, September 27, 1988.

[33]Esmail Hosseinzadeh, "The Crisis of Third World Debt: Is There a Way Out?," Roger Oden, ed. *Proceedings of the Fifteen Annual Third World Conference*, Chicago: TWCF Publications, 1991, 27.

such flows in contributing to financial crisis in the Third World. From the recipient's standpoint, foreign aid and direct foreign investment each offer advantages over bank borrowing. Foreign aid normally includes a concessionary element, sometimes taking the form of outright grants. Even when assistance must be paid back, aid funds come with little or no interest attached. As for direct foreign investment, the physical assets transferred to a host country through foreign investment are unlikely to be dismantled and removed. Direct foreign investment often produces a transfer of skills and technology as well. While a stream of profits from the investment may leave the country, this will occur only so long as the investment is productive and generating output, wages, and tax payments locally. If the investment goes sour, the outward flow of profits ceases and the costs of coping with a bad business decision are shared between the multinational and the host nation.

The terms on which commercial bank loans enter a Third World country are more strenuous. Unlike foreign aid, all commercial bank lending must be repaid at market interest rates. By contrast with direct foreign investment, the principal and interest on these loans fall due on a regular basis regardless of whether or not the investment financed by the loan is generating revenue.[34] Indeed, the cost of the debt may rise for reasons beyond the control of the debtor. Two-thirds of the Third World loans issued from 1973 to 1983 carried variable rather than fixed interest rates, meaning that Southern debt payments rise or fall with changes in Northern interest rates.[35] Commercial borrowing places much of the risk on the borrower.

The demanding and inflexible terms of commercial bank lending thus played a role in the origins of the Third World debt crisis. This raises an obvious question: Why were the risks that accompanied the explosion of bank lending to the South so clearly underestimated by both the banks and the Third World borrowers?

Despite its rigorous conditions, bank lending is, of course, a common feature of modern economic life. There is no inherent reason why borrowing money from a bank should lead to economic ruin. Indeed, large corporations routinely borrow from banks to finance expansion plans. The key to assessing the riskiness of any given loan is to ask whether the productive activities financed by the loan are likely to generate revenues sufficient to allow the borrower to pay back the principal, with interest, over an agreed upon time period. If so, then both lender and borrower will be well served by the transaction. If not, then the results are likely to be less happy.

---

[34]For a comparison of bank borrowing and direct foreign investment, see Hosseinzadeh, "The Crisis of Third World Debt."

[35]Sarah Bartlett, "A Vicious Circle Keeps Latin America in Debt," *New York Times*, Jan. 15, 1989. It was estimated in 1988 that every point rise in the rate of interest charged on Third World debt cost Southern debtors $3.5 billion annually. See Steven Greenhouse, "Third World Tells IMF that Poverty Has Increased," *New York Times*, September 29, 1988.

The Misplaced Optimism of the Seventies

The debt crisis of the eighties was built upon the misplaced optimism of the seventies. Banks lent money to Third World countries based upon hopes that the ambitious development schemes espoused by government planners would fuel rapid Southern growth and export expansion. This faith, shared by bankers and Third World borrowers alike, was eventually shattered when it became clear that too few of the funds borrowed from the North found their way into projects capable of paying for themselves.

There were several reasons why bankers took such imprudent risks. The first is a lack of historical memory. Latin American debt crises were common in the nineteenth and early twentieth centuries. Prior to the current crisis, the most recent such episode occurred in the 1930s when many Latin American countries defaulted on their outstanding loans. Few bankers, unfortunately, took serious note of such cautionary precedents.[36]

Why, though, did Northern banks suddenly rediscover the Third World in the seventies? Many found themselves awash with loanable funds early in the decade but experienced great difficulty attracting creditworthy borrowers in the North. With no place else to turn, the banks sent the surplus South.

These surplus funds came from two sources. During the sixties and early seventies, the United States routinely ran balance of payments deficits. Many of these dollars remained overseas, finding their way into dollar-denominated accounts at banks abroad. Since the bulk of these dollars ended up in European banks or in the subsidiaries of American banks located overseas, they came to be referred to as Eurodollars.

This accumulation of overseas dollars expanded dramatically when OPEC nations, finding themselves with far more money than they could possibly spend after the quadrupling of oil prices in 1973, also began to make huge deposits of their largely dollar-denominated oil revenues in Western banks. These developments allowed the Eurodollar market to grow from $315 billion in 1973 to $2 trillion in 1982.[37] For the banks to profit from these new deposits, of course, they had to find customers willing to borrow the funds they contained.

Yet, partly as a consequence of the OPEC engineered oil price rise, most Northern nations slipped into economic recession during 1975. Businesses cut back plans for expansion and consumers put off big-ticket purchases. With money to lend and few prospects in the North, banks began to look South.

---

[36]On the historical precedents for the international debt crisis of the 1980s, see Barry Eichengreen and Peter Lindert, eds. *The International Debt Crisis in Historical Perspective*, Cambridge: MIT Press, 1989; Albert Fishlow, "The Debt Crisis in Historical Perspective," in Miles Kahler, ed. *The Politics of International Debt*, Ithaca: Cornell University Press, 1985; and John Makin, *The Global Debt Crisis: America's Growing Involvement*, New York: Basic Books, 1984, 36–53.

[37]The Debt Crisis Network, *From Debt to Development*, 25.

There they discovered many eager customers. The newly industrializing countries of the Third World, particularly those in Latin America, found themselves amidst an explosion of manufacturing production and exports. To sustain this growth, Third World countries needed financing to pay for increasingly expensive oil imports as well as the purchase of imported capital goods, such as the machinery used in newly built Southern factories. Rapid Third World growth was fueled not only by increased manufacturing exports but also by the strong prices most Third World commodities fetched on world markets early in the decade. Commodity prices rose by 13 percent in 1972 and a further 53 percent in 1973.[38] Overall, the Third World's share of world exports increased from 18 percent to 28 percent during the seventies.[39]

Normally reserved bankers expressed an almost giddy sense of elation at the growth and promise of the profitable new markets of the South. Some portrayed commercial lending as a magical cure for underdevelopment. Foreign debt was seen as a badge of honor and success, not shame, for Third World countries. This bravado is reflected in the comments of G. A. Costanzo, then vice president at Citibank, on Mexico's economic prospects: "Mexico . . . is in a particularly favorable position as it enters the 1980s . . . Mexico's external debt may surpass that of Brazil during this decade, reflecting not an uncontrolled deficit but the recognition of unparalleled investment opportunities."[40]

Southern borrowers shared this optimism. From their perspective, moreover, Northern loans looked like bargains. Due to high inflation levels, real interest rates were remarkably low, while the dollar's weakness made dollar-denominated loans seem cheap.

Alongside these economic motivations, Third World governments welcomed bank financing for political reasons as well. Nationalist sentiment ran strong in many countries. Seeking to harness these passions to their own benefit, many Third World politicians directed nationalist agitation toward multinational corporations, the most obvious and intrusive forms of Northern penetration in Southern societies. Moreover, Southern governments chafed against the superior bargaining power many MNCs derived from their mobility.

Particularly in Latin America, therefore, governments sought to create alternatives to the MNCs by buttressing state-owned firms. A strong publicly owned sector of the economy strengthened the hand of Southern governments in bargaining with MNCs while also providing political leaders with greater direct control over the economy and a means of asserting their nationalist credentials. Since reducing dependence upon MNCs required access to alternative sources of capital, Third World governments looked to Northern

---

[38]Lever and Huhne, *Debt and Danger*, 36.

[39]Andre Gunder Frank, "Can the Debt Bomb Be Defused?" *World Policy Journal*, Spring, 1985, 729.

[40]William Greider, *Secrets of the Temple*, New York: Simon and Schuster, 1987, 434.

banks who, in a relatively low-profile and unobtrusive manner, provided funds subject to the direct control of state bureaucrats and politicians.[41]

For a variety of reasons, therefore, both Northern lenders and Southern borrowers were well motivated to deepen their relationships with one another, and favorable conditions made international lending seem a good bet for all concerned. The eagerness of the banks to cash in on this huge and profitable new market was, moreover, relatively unrestrained by normally cautious Northern government bank regulators. Eurodollar funds were largely beyond the reach of government regulations designed to limit risky lending behavior. U.S. dollars deposited overseas escaped the jurisdiction of U.S. banking officials, while European bank regulations applied only to local European currencies, not to foreign currency denominated accounts. This lack of normal oversight contributed to overlending.[42]

Northern banks found overseas lending quite profitable for a time. Earnings from the foreign operations of the seven biggest U.S. banks climbed from 22 percent of total profits in 1970 to 60 percent in 1982. Many bankers waved aside the concerns of those who questioned whether the large buildup of foreign debt by still-poor Third World societies was sustainable. Citibank chief Walter Wriston, whose bank epitomized the frenetic climate of international banking in the seventies, predicted that "this fear that banks have reached a limit will turn out to be wrong tomorrow, as it always has in the past."[43]

The Bottom Falls Out:
The Fickleness of the World Economy

Yet, the economic conditions that nurtured the growth of Third World borrowing during much of the seventies shifted dramatically as the decade drew to a close. After several years of relative stability in oil markets, OPEC managed to engineer a trebling of world oil prices in 1979. The oil bill of oil-importing Third World countries leapt from $7 billion in 1973 to almost $100 billion in 1981.[44] This proved a bitter pill to swallow for the newly industrializing countries of the Third World, whose appetite for additional oil was rising just as prices rocketed skyward.

Far more devastating in the long run, however, was the North's reaction to OPEC's price hike. In the United States, the Federal Reserve clamped down on the U.S. money supply in an effort to wring inflation from the

---

[41]Frieden, "Third World Indebted Industrialization."

[42]See Miles Kahler, "Politics and International Debt: Explaining the Crisis," in Kahler, ed. *The Politics of International Debt*; and Mary Williamson, "Banking Regulation and Debt: A Policy of Flexible Response," *Policy Focus*, Overseas Development Council policy paper no. 1, 1988.

[43]Greider, *Secrets of the Temple*, 433.

[44]Moffitt, *The World's Money*, 100.

economy. This had several undesirable effects from the standpoint of Third World borrowers. Interest rates climbed to an average of 15.5 percent during the 1979 to 1982 period. This meant higher payments on most commercial bank loans to the Third World. The U.S. economy, along with those of other Northern countries, entered the worst economic downturn since the Great Depression. Global growth averaged only 1.1 percent from 1979 to 1982 and world trade actually shrunk. Slow growth hurt Southern exports to the North. Commodity prices fell by one-fourth between 1980 and 1982 as demand slackened.[45] Southern manufacturing exports were dampened not only by the economic slowdown itself, but also by increased Northern protectionism as economic hardship in the North pushed governments to attempt to save jobs in industries threatened by Southern imports.[46] The dollar, strengthened by high interest rates in the United States, rose to record highs, forcing Third World governments to expend more in their local currency to obtain the dollars necessary to pay back the banks.

Peter Nunnenkamp has estimated that external factors (such as those mentioned above) over which Third World governments had little or no control accounted for $570 billion in new debt accumulation between 1974 and 1981.[47] By 1982, debt payments consumed 70 percent of the export revenues of the twenty-one largest non-oil-exporting debtors, up from 36 percent in 1973, and the overall current account balance for all non-oil-exporting Third World countries reached a deficit of $97 billion.[48]

Southern Mismanagement, Capital Flight, and Corruption

Unfavorable international developments were not the only forces working to transform Third World debt from a problem into a crisis. Internal factors such as poor policy choices and capital flight served to further aggravate matters.[49]

---

[45]Lever and Huhne, *Debt and Danger*, 38.

[46]By 1988, the cost to the Third World in lost export revenues due to Northern protectionism amounted to twice the value of Northern aid to the South. Greenhouse, "Third World Tells IMF that Poverty Has Increased."

[47]Hosseinzadeh, "The Crisis of Third World Debt: Is There a Way Out?" 9.

[48]The Debt Crisis Network, *From Debt to Development*, 32. Moffitt, *The World's Money*, 101.

[49]Corruption also played a role in the worsening of the debt problems of some countries. Funds ostensibly borrowed to finance development often found their way into the pockets of Third World government officials or businessmen. Ferdinand Marcos is said to have stolen and funneled into overseas investments $10 billion during his long reign in office. This compares with a Philippine foreign debt of $26 billion at the time Marcos stepped down in 1986. Similarly, it has been charged that $3–$4 billion of Zaire's $5 billion external debt was diverted by President Mobutu Sese Seko for his own uses. See Graham Hancock, *Lords of Poverty*, New York: Atlantic Monthly Press, 1989, 175–79. For a general discussion of mismanagement and corruption as sources of the debt crisis, see George B. N. Ayettey, "The Real Foreign Debt Problem," *The Wall Street Journal*, April 8, 1986, 28.

Many Third World governments, particularly in Latin America, supported artificially high exchange rates during the late seventies and early eighties in an effort to control inflation without recession.[50] Overvalued currencies badly hurt exports, encouraged import growth, and led to large trade deficits that were covered by further borrowing from abroad.[51]

As conditions worsened, it became clear that these overvalued currency rates could not be sustained and that severe currency depreciation lurked just around the corner. Holders of liquid assets in these countries feared that the value of their cash holdings might take a nosedive. In response, the wealthy began converting their assets into dollars in massive amounts and sent the proceeds abroad. As further incentive for this so-called capital flight, interest rates in many Third World countries were held artificially low by legal ceilings even as rising inflation rendered the real rate of return on savings accounts negative. Just the opposite was true in the United States, of course, where monetary policies were at the same time producing skyrocketing real interest rates.

This combination of factors led to a hemorrhaging of foreign exchange toward the North. For the years 1976 to 1984, the World Bank estimated that Mexico experienced $54 billion in capital flight (57 percent of Mexican external debt), that Argentina saw an outflow of $28 billion (60 percent of external debt), and that $35 billion fled Venezuela (a sum greater than Venezuela's entire external debt).[52] In 1985, IMF estimates put total Third World capital flight at $200 billion; a figure which, by 1989, would rise to $340 billion for the fifteen largest debtors alone.[53]

With high interest rates, a buoyant stock market, and a stable political system, the United States attracted roughly one-half of all Latin American flight capital. Between 1977 and 1985, deposits by Mexican investors in U.S. banks increased 570 percent; for Argentinians, the increase in deposits was 450 percent; and Peruvian deposits rose 750 percent.[54]

Capital flight exacted a steep price from Third World debtors. During the years 1983 and 1984, Northern banks accepted more money in deposits from Southern sources than they dispersed to Third World countries in new loans. Capital flight took a toll on foreign exchange reserves, domestic investment, and tax revenues in Third World countries. Mexico lost an estimated $3.2 billion in taxes between 1977 and 1984 due to capital flight.[55]

---

[50]Remember, high exchange rates tend to reduce the price of imports, which then act to keep other domestic prices from rising.

[51]Rudiger Dornbusch, "The Latin American Debt Problem: Anatomy and Solutions," in Stallings and Kaufman, eds. *Debt and Democracy in Latin America*, 8.

[52]"Latin American Debt: Living on Borrowed Time?" 28.

[53]Hosseinzadeh, "The Crisis of Third World Debt: Is There a Way Out?" 9; and Mike McNamee and Jeffrey Ryser, "Can This Flight Be Grounded?" *Businessweek*, April 10, 1989.

[54]Frank Riely, "Third World Capital Flight: Who Gains? Who Loses?," *Policy Focus*, Overseas Development Council, no. 5, 1986.

[55]Riely, "Third World Capital Flight: Who Gains? Who Loses?"

Staggered by these blows, Third World governments attempted to maintain the momentum of growth by continuing to borrow. The banks, once again flush with deposits from OPEC nations, proved willing to accommodate Third World demands for additional funds; however, they began to exact higher spreads, premiums tacked onto base interest rate levels, as compensation for the greater riskiness of the new loans.[56] Ominously, however, most of the new lending during this period went not to finance promising development projects but instead to allow debtors to make payments on past debts. This expedient succeeded in staving off default for a time. Meanwhile, bankers and Third World governments hoped that the newly unfavorable world economic climate would change again for the better and allow the resumption of Third World growth.

The World Holds Its Breath: The Mexican Crisis

These hopes proved illusory. The bubble of false optimism burst in August 1982 when Mexican officials announced that their country, then the world's second largest debtor, lacked the funds to cover scheduled loan payments and stood on the verge of involuntary default. Ironically, given the role of the 1979 OPEC oil price hike in worsening the indebtedness of so many Third World countries, the first large debtor to approach default was a major oil exporter. In addition to the external circumstances mentioned above, such as higher interest rates and Northern recession, the Mexican predicament was exacerbated by unrealistic government economic policies.

The Mexican economy grew at the explosive rate of 8.1 percent per year between 1978 and 1981. This growth curve was clearly unsustainable in the face of an unfavorable international economic climate. Most significantly, oil prices began to slide during the early eighties, causing a $6 billion drop in Mexican oil revenues in 1981 as compared with oil revenues in 1980.[57] Yet, officials attempted to maintain a feverish pace of economic growth through massive government spending. By 1982, the government budget deficit, largely financed by foreign borrowing, reached a stupendous 16.3 percent of Mexican GNP. Seeking to quickly exploit large, newly discovered oil deposits, Mexico also borrowed heavily to finance the import of capital equipment for expansion of the oil industry. Lastly, Mexican officials maintained an overvalued exchange rate, thereby encouraging imports and discouraging exports.[58]

---

[56]By pushing interest payments still higher, these added premiums worsened matters by increasing the burden placed on the many debtor countries already experiencing difficulties in servicing their loans. The Debt Crisis Network, *From Debt to Development*, 33, and Moffitt, *The World's Money*, 110.

[57]Robert Bennett, "Mexico Seeking Postponement of Part of Its Debt," *New York Times*, August 20, 1982.

[58]Lever and Huhne, *Debt and Danger*, 40–41.

Mexico's day of reckoning arrived when Northern banks balked at providing enough additional financing to cover the large payments falling due on old debts plus the continuing demand for new funds needed to pay for the excess of imports over exports. The prospect of Mexican default set off alarm bells in Northern governmental and banking circles as the stark realization finally sunk in that the stability of the entire Northern financial system stood in jeopardy. Mexico owed the Bank of America and Citibank roughly $3 billion each.[59] Citibank's Mexican exposure equaled two-thirds of its net corporate assets.[60] A long-term interruption of Mexican debt payments could have spelled disaster for a number of the largest U.S. banks.

At this point, the U.S. government, abandoning its previously aloof stance toward Third World debt, stepped in to provide emergency short-term financing designed to keep Mexico solvent until a longer-term solution could be found. As part of the deal, the United States also made an immediate $1 billion advance payment for discounted Mexican oil and provided Mexico with $1 billion in credits toward the purchase of surplus U.S. grain. Mexico subsequently entered into negotiations with the IMF and its private bank creditors, during which debt payments were suspended for 120 days. Ultimately, the IMF provided almost $4 billion, and the banks $5 billion, in new financing while payments on almost $19 billion in old debt were stretched out over a longer time period. In return, Mexico agreed to follow a stabilization plan designed by IMF officials, which, among other things, required the government to close its budget deficit and devalue the peso.[61]

The most difficult phase of the negotiations revolved around the bankers' reluctance to loan new money to Mexico. Additional money was needed in order to finance necessary imports, complete ongoing investment projects, and roll over old debt. Without new funds, Mexican default seemed assured. Collectively, of course, the Northern banks all had an interest in avoiding this outcome. Yet, individually, many bankers feared that Mexico would never pay its debts in full and none wished to throw good money after bad. The Mexican deal almost came apart because many banks, especially the smaller ones, wished to benefit from a successful conclusion to the negotiations without, however, putting up new money of their own. If enough banks had maintained this attitude, of course, a successful deal would have proven impossible.

Drawing upon powers it had never previously exercised, the IMF provided the solution by compelling banks into involuntary lending. IMF officials, supported by the United States, threatened to withdraw their portion of the loan package, as well as their oversight of Mexican reforms, unless

---

[59] Alan Riding, "Mexican Outlook: Banks Are Wary," *New York Times*, August 17, 1982.

[60] "Latin American Debt: Living on Borrowed Time?" 28.

[61] For a chronology of the Mexican debt rescheduling negotiations, see Aggarwal, *International Debt Threat*, 66–67.

each bank contributed new funds proportionate to its previous stake in Mexico.[62] This succeeded in persuading the banks to follow the IMF's lead in the short run, but it failed to resolve the longer-term problem of the bank's newfound reluctance to provide even prudent amounts of new lending to Third World debtors.

The IMF Takes Charge

The IMF quickly assumed a role at the center of the debt crisis as more debtor countries experienced problems similar to Mexico's. During the seventies, the IMF typically found itself drawn into negotiations with a few troubled debtors each year. In the wake of Mexico's troubles, dozens of countries on the verge of default, seeking to secure new loans and renegotiate the terms of old ones, approached the IMF and the banks. By 1983, the IMF had conditional lending programs in forty-seven countries.[63]

The IMF's cure for the problems of Third World debtors flowed from its diagnosis of the illness. Michel Camdessus, executive director of the IMF, attributed the debt crisis to "the criminal conduct" of "politicians who neglect to take care of urgent problems and prefer to wait for a miracle."[64] Having identified the cause of the debt crisis as economic mismanagement by debtor country governments, the IMF, supported by Northern governments and banks, placed the burden of adjusting to the crisis on the debtor countries themselves. Third World officials were expected to adopt correct economic policies, such as those previously discussed, and their citizens, having earlier lived beyond their means, would now have to swallow the medicine of austerity, no matter how unpleasant its taste.

In its deal with Mexico, for instance, the IMF demanded that subsidies on basic foodstuffs be reduced and that wages be restrained. As a result, authorities raised the prices of corn tortillas by 40 percent and bread by 100 percent. Wages were allowed to grow by only one-third the inflation rate.[65]

The IMF prescription for Third World debtors generally led to substantial improvement in debtor country trade balances, but, as the statistics cited at the beginning of this chapter attest, the price was frightening in lost economic growth and deteriorating social conditions. As a result, the IMF's remedy for Third World debt problems came under severe criticism.

Many of these criticisms had to do with the economic soundness of the Fund's policy prescriptions. One study found that low-income countries that followed Fund programs during the seventies performed no better by a

---

[62]Robert Bennett, "Bankers Pressured to Assist Mexico," *New York Times*, August 21, 1982.

[63]"Latin American Debt: Living on Borrowed Time?" 29.

[64]James Brooke, "Zaire Dispute with IMF Centers on Capital Flows," *New York Times*, September 29, 1988.

[65]"Latin American Debt: Living on Borrowed Time?" 29.

variety of economic measures than countries not under the Fund's guidance.[66] Another survey conducted by the IMF itself found that Fund-sponsored programs in sub-Saharan African countries met preestablished targets for growth, inflation, and trade in only a minority of cases.[67]

Some critics maintained that the IMF focused too exclusively on reducing Third World imports by dampening demand while neglecting supply-side measures that might stimulate debtor country exports. Domestic investment levels slumped during the eighties in most Third World countries, declining, for instance, by 25 percent in Latin America between 1980 and 1988.[68] Among the fifteen most heavily indebted countries, domestic investment plummeted from an average of 24 percent of GNP during the years from 1971 to 1981 to 18 percent for the 1982–1987 period.[69] With insufficient investment in export industries, Third World countries found themselves limited in their ability to increase their export capacity or to enhance the efficiency and competitiveness of their products.

The effectiveness of another IMF tool, currency devaluation, has been a subject of controversy as well.[70] One undesirable consequence of devaluing a nation's currency is higher domestic inflation as the prices of imported goods rise. Moreover, devaluation can produce effects contrary to its intended purposes. Some imported goods, such as oil, are so necessary that the increased prices caused by devaluation lead to only small declines in import volumes.[71] In such cases, the net effect of devaluation is to widen, rather than narrow, the nation's trade deficit. Much the same is true with regard to export industries that rely heavily upon imported inputs, such as raw materials, parts, or capital goods. Part of the advantage devaluation offers such industries by allowing them to sell their products more cheaply abroad is taken away by the higher costs these same firms incur due to domestic inflation and more expensive imported inputs — both also consequences of devaluation.[72]

---

[66]John Loxley, *The IMF and the Poorest Countries*, Ottawa: North-South Institute, 1984.

[67]Cited in John Loxley, "IMF and World Bank Conditionality and Sub-Saharan Africa," in Peter Lawrence, ed. *World Recession and the Food Crisis in Africa*, London: James Currey, 1986, 96.

[68]Greenhouse, "Third World Tells IMF that Poverty Has Increased."

[69]Eduardo Borensztein, "The Effect of External Debt on Investment," *Finance and Development*, September 1989, 17.

[70]For a critique of the effectiveness of devaluation, see "When Devaluation Breeds Contempt," *The Economist*, November 24, 1990, 71.

[71]Technically, economists refer to the demand for such products as price inelastic: a change in price produces a relatively small shift in the volume of sales.

[72]IMF policies have also had unintended effects on South-South trade. Though the great majority of Southern exports are targeted toward Northern markets, the seventies witnessed considerable growth in trade among Southern countries. This encouraging trend reversed itself in the eighties due to the fact that so many Southern debtors were simultaneously pursuing IMF-imposed austerity policies and thus cutting back on imported goods from all sources. Especially hurt by this phenomenon was Brazil, 40 percent of whose exports in 1981 went to other less-developed countries such as Argentina, Mexico, Chile, Venezuela, and Nigeria. See "Resurgent Inflation Ruins Brazil's Plan," *New York Times*, August 9, 1982.

The widespread perception that IMF austerity policies often brought political instability also increased the reluctance of some governments to cooperate with the Fund. Perhaps the most feared element of the typical IMF package involves the removal of government subsidies for basic foodstuffs and other necessities, such as fuel oil and public transportation. Price rises in these sensitive areas have provoked unrest in many Third World countries.

This was the case, for instance, when food-price increases prompted large-scale rioting in Egypt during 1977. Over a decade later, memories of that event stiffened the resolve of Egyptian President Hosni Mubarak to resist IMF demands for the wholesale removal of food subsidies. Despite the burden of Egypt's $50 billion foreign debt and moves by some donors to suspend further aid due to Egypt's tardiness in making debt repayments, negotiations between the Egyptian government and the Fund remained deadlocked over this issue after three years of talks. Although Mubarak made some concessions toward IMF demands, he also took care to cast himself as a defender of the nation's poor at home, publicly referring to the IMF as "a quack doctor" and "the Fund of Misery."[73]

Smoke and Mirrors:
The Baker Plan

By 1985, the flaws in the case-by-case strategy devised during the initial phase of the debt crisis were evident even to policymakers in Washington, who, since the Mexican bailout of 1982, had adopted a relatively passive stance toward the debt problems of the Third World. The signs of failure were numerous. Mexico once again found itself approaching default, and another debt rescheduling agreement was required to pull it back from the brink. Interest rates were on the rise, and most major debtor countries remained mired in the economic doldrums despite the return of steady, if unspectacular, economic growth in the North. Northern exports to the South also remained depressed.

U.S. policymakers feared that Southern debtor governments, alarmed by political instability, might begin to explore radical solutions if the painful adjustments they had undertaken failed to bring either economic growth or renewed access to international credit markets. This concern prompted the United States to announce a new initiative called the Baker Plan, after the U.S. treasury secretary, James Baker.

The purpose of the Baker Plan was to revive growth among a group of fifteen indebted Third World countries while also enhancing these countries' long-term capacity to service their debts. Baker argued that austerity alone failed to provide the new investment needed for continued growth, especially

---

[73] Alan Cowell, "In Egypt, Two Penny Loaf is Family Heartbreak," *New York Times*, July 8, 1990.

in the crucial export industries, and only worsened the problem of capital flight. The Baker Plan's answer to this problem was three-pronged:

1. While debtor countries were still asked to restrain domestic demand, Baker favored greater emphasis on supply-side measures designed to stimulate export growth.

2. Commercial banks were urged to provide additional new lending to finance investments in Southern export industries.

3. The United States supported expanded lending by the IMF and the World Bank.

While many Third World debtors welcomed Baker's shift in emphasis from austerity to growth, they remained disappointed with the Plan's rejection of debt reduction, the failure of the U.S. government to offer new resources of its own, and Baker's vagueness about just how he proposed to persuade bankers to voluntarily expand their Third World lending.

Experience over the next several years bore out the Third World's pessimism and exposed the faulty assumptions upon which the Baker Plan was based. Baker's plea to the banks that they supply some $7 billion in new money (also called net lending, this is equal to net loan disbursements minus repayments of principal on past loans) annually over the next three years fell upon deaf ears. In fact, 1986 and 1987 together brought only $2 billion in new lending while lending actually fell short of repayments by $4 billion in 1988. Adding interest payments to repaid principal, the flow of funds from the South to the North far exceeded new bank lending for all three years. Bank financing was also highly concentrated, with only a few countries having access to funds during this period. A number of nations that had followed strict adjustment policies found themselves unable to gain new credit.[74]

Much the same was true of official credit. Net lending by official creditors amounted to only 87 percent of Southern interest payments in 1986, a figure that fell to 38 percent in 1988.[75] The debt crisis continued to drain funds from the South, making it difficult, if not impossible, for Southern countries to make the investments needed to spur additional growth.

It is doubtful, however, that the Baker Plan could have fully succeeded even had the banks proven more cooperative. Northern economies continued to experience sluggish rates of economic growth during the eighties as compared with the sixties or seventies. Global prices for most Southern commodities remained dismally low. In early 1985, for instance, world sugar prices hovered around five to six cents per pound, while production costs in the

---

[74]Fried and Trezise, *Third World Debt*, 4.

[75]Ishrat Husain, "Recent Experience with the Debt Strategy," *Finance and Development*, September, 1989, 14. Also see Paul Lewis, "3rd-World Funds: Wrong Way Flow," *New York Times*, February 11, 1988.

Philippines averaged between twelve and fourteen cents per pound.[76] By 1990, coffee prices had fallen one-third and cocoa prices two-thirds from 1979 levels.[77] Nor is it clear whether Northern markets were ready to absorb large increases in Southern manufactured exports. Under these conditions, it is quite possible that increased bank lending to the South may have increased the Third World debt bill without proportionately enhancing the debtor countries' ability to pay.

Facing Reality:
The Banks Take Cover

In 1987 and 1988, the behavior of Northern banks began to reflect the uncertainties that surrounded the repayment of Third World debt. Partly due to increased pressure from government bank regulators, banks began to make large additions to their loan loss reserves. These are funds designed to cushion a bank's reported profits should debtors default on their existing loans to the bank. Implicitly acknowledging that not all of the money they had lent to Third World countries was likely to be repaid, virtually all of the large American banks involved in Third World lending followed the lead of Citibank, which set aside $3 billion against potential losses in May 1987.[78] In the short term, shifting funds into their loan loss reserves took a substantial toll on bank profits. Yet, paradoxically, these moves also strengthened the bank's hands in bargaining with debtor countries. With larger reserves on hand, banks were less vulnerable to the threats of debtor country default and could afford to drive a harder bargain in negotiations over debt rescheduling.

Seeking to reduce their overall exposure to Third World debt, the banks also began to diversify their loan portfolios. This led to the development of a so-called "secondary market" for Third World debt. Losing confidence that debtor countries would ever repay their debts in full, many banks became willing to sell their Third World loans to other banks or investors at less than the loan's face value. A bank fearful of future Mexican default, for instance, might sell a $1 million Mexican loan to another investor for only $700,000. Even though the bank will take a loss when it sells the loan, it does so in the expectation that the loss would be greater still if it held onto the loan only to see the debtor country default. The "discount" offered on loans traded in the secondary market reflects the judgments of both buyers and sellers about the likelihood that the debt will be repaid. A very risky loan, one where the chances of full or partial default seem high, will typically carry a steep discount.

---

[76] The Debt Crisis Network, *From Debt to Development*, 9.
[77] Steven Greenhouse, "Oil Shock Squeezing Third World," *New York Times*, August 18, 1990.
[78] Jaclyn Fierman, "Fast Bucks in Latin Loan Swaps," *Fortune*, August 3, 1987.

A number of big banks turned to the secondary market in 1988 as a means of reducing their exposure to Third World debt. Citicorp sold off $1.2 billion in loans; Chase Manhattan sold off $1 billion; and Manufacturer's Hanover sold off $656 million.[79] Most of these transactions did nothing to reduce the obligations of the debtor countries. After a sale, the debtor still owed the full amount of the original loan, only now to a new creditor.

In some instances, however, the willingness of banks to sell risky loans on the secondary market worked to the benefit of Third World countries. Where countries possessed sufficient foreign exchange on hand, debtor nations sometimes simply purchased their own debts at a discounted price. Bolivia, for instance, reduced a $650 million debt to $300 million in 1988 through this means.[80] The principal constraint on more such cash buy-backs lies in the scarcity of foreign exchange for most Third World countries.

Southern countries also extinguished some of their debt through so-called debt-for-equity swaps. A typical version of this arrangement might work like this: A bank sells its Mexican loans to a Northern electronics company for seventy cents on each dollar. The electronics company then exchanges the debt with the Mexican central bank in return for pesos at a rate equivalent to perhaps eighty cents on each dollar of the original face value on the loan. The firm invests these pesos in constructing a new assembly plant in Mexico.

Notice how the benefits are distributed among the partners in this deal. While the bank takes a loss, it also rids itself of a risky loan and improves the quality of its portfolio. The electronics company profits by purchasing the loan at 70 percent while later selling it at 80 percent of its face value. It also, of course, ends up with the pesos it needs to make the assembly plant investment. The Mexican government erases some of its debt at a 20 percent discount without the use of precious foreign exchange. In place of foreign bank debt, the country now has an equity investment that, while owned by a foreign firm, produces employment, taxes, and products locally.[81]

Despite these benefits, debt-for-equity swaps are limited in their potential to solve the Third World debt crisis. There are, for instance, only so many Third World investment opportunities that might lure foreign firms into such deals, even with the attraction of subsidies. Indeed, some fear that the incentives offered to multinational firms through debt-for-equity swaps do little more than shift foreign investment from one country to another without adding to aggregate investment in the Third World as a whole. Another problem is that the printing of additional local currency needed to buy back

---

[79]Merril Collett, "Brady's Debt Plan is Short on Principle," *In These Times*, April 12–18, 1989, 2.

[80]Peter Kilborn, "Debt Reduction: Ways to Do It," *New York Times*, April 6, 1989.

[81]New rules issued by the Federal Reserve in 1987 made it possible for banks to increase their equity investment in nonfinancial companies from 20 percent to 100 percent. This made it easier for banks to swap debt for equity among themselves, without the need for the participation of multinational corporations. Pamela Sherrid, "The Brave New World of Swaps," *U.S. News and World Report*, August 31, 1987, 41.

the debt can swell the money supply and lead to inflation.[82] For these reasons and others, some of the enthusiasm that accompanied the expansion of debt-for-equity swaps in 1988 diminished thereafter.[83]

Debt-for-debt swaps provided a final mechanism for translating secondary market discounts into debt reduction for Third World countries. In these transactions, old unguaranteed loans are swapped at a discount for new securities carrying some form of partial or full guarantee of repayment. In a deal fashioned by Morgan Guarantee, for instance, Mexico exchanged $3.6 billion in old debt for $2.5 billion in new securities for a total debt reduction of $1.1 billion. Banks who participated in the deal were willing to trade the old loans for the new loans at a discount because the principal (though not the interest) on the new bonds was backed by U.S. government guaranteed securities. Although the new bonds were worth less than the old, the bankers were assured repayment in full on the newer securities.[84]

Altogether, cash buy-backs, debt-for-equity swaps, and debt-for-debt deals eliminated $25 billion in Third World debt from 1985 through 1988.[85] While this might seem a rather modest figure when compared with the overall size of the Third World debt burden, these transactions helped to ease acceptance of an important principle: that Third World countries should benefit from the lowered values that the secondary market placed on Third World debt. This principle is at least partially embraced by the Brady Plan, the most important Northern initiative toward solving the debt crisis to emerge thus far.

Inching Toward the Inevitable: The Brady Plan

Although named after U.S. Treasury Secretary Nicholas Brady and presented as an American initiative in the spring of 1989, the Brady Plan largely followed proposals earlier developed by Japanese officials.[86] In a significant departure from the Baker Plan, the Brady Plan included the first U.S. acknowledgment that debt reduction and forgiveness would have to comprise a part of any successful scheme for coping with the Third World debt crisis.

---

[82]Fierman, "Fast Bucks in Latin Loan Swaps."

[83]The past few years have also brought the emergence of so-called debt-for-nature swaps, which work similarly to debt-for-equity swaps. In the first of a number of such deals, a group called Conservation International acted through Citibank to purchase $650,000 in Bolivian debt at fifteen cents on the dollar for $100,000 in 1987. The group then forgave the debt in return for Bolivia's agreement to protect four million acres of forest and grassland in the Beni River region of the country. John Walsh, "Bolivia Swaps Debt for Conservation," *Science*, August 7, 1987, 596–97.

[84]Kilborn, "Debt Reduction: Ways to Do It."

[85]Kilborn, "Debt Reduction: Ways to Do It"; and Robert Bennett, "Lesson on Mexican Debt," *New York Times*, March 1, 1988.

[86]See Steven Weisman, "Japan Takes a Leading Role in the Third World Debt Crisis," *New York Times*, April 17, 1989.

The Brady Plan aimed at reducing Third World debt to private creditors. Brady originally set a goal of $70 billion in debt forgiveness for fifteen heavily indebted countries to be achieved over several years. This would constitute roughly a 20 percent reduction in outstanding bank debt.

The heart of the Brady Plan consists of a set of incentives designed to induce banks to forgive part of the debt owed them. Banks are offered the opportunity to exchange their old loans for new bonds carrying either a reduced principal or lower interest rates. The attraction of the new bonds, despite their discount, is that, unlike the old loans, they include guarantees of repayment secured by special funds set aside for the purpose. The new bonds thus carry a much lower risk of default than the old debt. As with the Baker Plan, only nations agreeing to adopt IMF-sponsored policy reforms are eligible for participation in Brady Plan deals.

The special funds set aside as security for the new bonds are financed through new loans issued by the IMF, the World Bank, and Northern governments, especially Japan. Banks reluctant to provide interest or principal reduction are offered the option of lending new money. All private creditors are expected to accept one of these three forms of sacrifice (or a combination of them) in degrees proportional to their stake in the country's debt. Banks that initially refuse are likely to experience considerable pressure to participate from other banks and Northern governments.[87]

Mexico was the first country to reach an agreement with its bank creditors under the Brady Plan. The negotiations proved complex and arduous. Although the broad outlines were accepted in July, 1989, the precise details of an agreement were not worked out until the following February. Roughly equal numbers of banks chose to reduce the principal on their loans by 35 percent or to accept a lower interest rate of 6.25 percent. A relatively small group of banks offered to extend new funds equal to 25 percent of their old loans. Mexico managed to lop $7 billion in principal off its total debt of $95 billion through the deal while also gaining reduced interest payments on a portion of the remainder and $1.5 billion in new lending. Mexico borrowed $5.7 billion, however, from the IMF, the World Bank, and Japan to finance the collateral fund set up to guarantee interest payments for a period of eighteen months. Overall, Mexico reduced its yearly debt service burden by roughly 10 to 20 percent. Similar deals have lately been reached with Venezuela, Costa Rica, the Philippines, Argentina, and Uruguay. As of the spring of 1992, Brazil stood on the verge of an agreement and negotiations with several other countries continued.[88]

---

[87]For descriptions of the Brady Plan's provisions, see Clyde Farnsworth, "World Bank and IMF Approve Plan to Cut Debt of Poorer Lands," *New York Times*, April 5, 1989; and Shafigul Islam, "Going Beyond the Brady Plan," *Challenge*, July–August, 1989, 39–45.

[88]On the Mexican deal, see Sarah Bartlett, "Reservations Expressed About Mexican Debt Accord," *New York Times*, July 27, 1989; and Larry Rohter, "Pact Is Signed to Cut Mexico's Debt," *New York Times*, February 5, 1990. On the deals involving Venezuela, Uruguay, Argentina, and Brazil, see Jonathan Fuerbringer, "Venezuela Agrees to Debt Proposal," *New York Times*,

In late June, 1990, President Bush announced an extension of the Brady Plan to cover official as well as private credit. Bush offered to begin negotiations with Latin American countries, which could lead to reductions totaling $7 billion in the debt they owe the U.S. government. The United States also offered to expand its support for collateral funds designed to guarantee payment on private bank debt and to increase U.S. assistance (contingent upon matching funds from Europe and Japan) in support of policy reforms designed to privatize publicly owned firms or to remove restrictions on direct foreign investment or currency exchange. Bush coupled these announcements with a call for negotiations over the creation of a hemispheric free-trade pact.[89] As of mid–1991, however, official U.S. debt relief had been provided to only one Latin American country, Chile, and then in the modest amount of $16 million. Congressional objections to Bush's plan mainly accounted for the lack of movement.[90]

Is the Brady Plan the solution to the Third World debt crisis? Although many consider the plan a major step forward, some observers regard its prospects with considerable skepticism. Many argue that the degree of debt reduction is insufficient to allow for a return to healthy growth in much of the Third World. After the Mexican deal was signed, the *New York Times* reported that "officials in several Latin American countries" described "Mexico's gains from the agreement as extremely limited and modest." The same officials concluded that "the Brady Plan appears to offer them little hope for a resolution of their own debt crises."[91] Evidence regarding the return of Third World growth is mixed. Growth in per capita GDP in the Third World as a whole fell from 2 percent in 1988 to 1 percent in 1989, and to only .2 percent in 1990. What little growth occured in 1990 took place in East Asia. Latin America and sub-Saharan Africa both experienced declines exceeding 2 percent of per capita GDP.[92] 1991 brought a turnabout in Latin America, where growth averaged 3 percent, and inflation fell substantially, although overall Third World per capita income again fell by .2 percent.[93]

March 21, 1990; Jonathan Fuerbringer, "Uruguay and Banks Reach Accord on Revamping Debt," *New York Times*, October 13, 1990; and Michael Quint, "Banks See Accord on Brazil Debt," *New York Times*, May 1, 1992.

[89] Andrew Rosenthal, "President Announces Plan for More Latin Debt Relief," *New York Times*, June 28, 1990.

[90] Clyde Farnsworth, "U.S. and Chile in Pact to Trim Debt," *New York Times*, June 27, 1991.

[91] Rohter, "Pact Is Signed to Cut Mexico's Debt." For other reactions to the Brady Plan, see Clyde Farnsworth, "Brady Sees Plan Spreading to Other Developing Nations," *New York Times*, February 3, 1990. For the IMF's own more optimistic evaluation of the Mexican deal, see Mohamed A. El-Erian, "Mexico's Commercial Bank Financing Package," *Finance and Development*, September, 1990; Eliot Kalter and Hoe Ee Khor, "Mexico's Experience with Adjustment," *Finance and Development*, September, 1990; and Islam, "Going Beyond the Brady Plan," 39–45.

[92] "Poor Nations' Growth Hurt by Gulf War," *New York Times*, September 23, 1991.

[93] Eugene Robinson, "Latin America Optimistic on Recovery," *New York Times*, January 19, 1992; James Brooke, "Venezuela is Surging Again After Period of Difficulties," *New York Times*, September 16, 1991; and Steven Greenhouse, "Third World Economics Shrink Agains," *New York Times*, April 16, 1992.

One of the Brady Plan's purposes is to lure flight capital, along with direct foreign investment, back to debtor countries and to increase domestic savings through a combination of debt reduction and policy reforms. It is too soon to tell whether these expectations will be borne out, but early indications in the Mexican case are not entirely reassuring. Despite the announced prospects of a debt-reduction agreement, the flow of direct foreign investment into the Mexican economy fell in 1989 from 1988 levels, and Mexican officials have worried that investors might ignore Mexico in their eagerness to take advantage of opportunities in Eastern Europe.[94] In 1989, $3 billion in repatriated Mexican capital was returned, but reports indicate that much of it went into government securities and financial speculation rather than plants and equipment. Moreover, government plans to increase social-welfare spending threatened to eat up some of the gains from external debt reduction.[95] There are, on the other hand, signs that foreign investors again consider Mexico a creditworthy borrower for loans that are tied directly to promising new investment projects. While the recent renewal of borrowing on commercial markets will add to Mexico's total debt, the investments may help spur growth and thereby pay for themselves.[96] Modest levels of economic growth have returned to Mexico, averaging 3 percent per year, and total foreign debt has fallen from 76 percent of Mexico's GNP to 30 percent. Nevertheless, Standard and Poor, a private American debt rating service, recently declared that Mexico's ability to repay long-term foreign debt is "only adequate, with minimal protection likely during unfavorable circumstances."[97]

Another worry, according to some observers, is that Brady Plan deals are accelerating a trend in which bank debt is replaced by debt owed to official creditors, especially multilateral agencies. Of the total debt owed by the fifteen most heavily indebted countries, the share accounted for by the IMF and the multilateral development banks rose from 7 percent in 1982 to 16 percent in 1988 and has since continued to grow.[98] This is a concern in part because the quality of the loan portfolios held by official multilateral creditors has declined. Indeed, arrears on the loans issued by the IMF reached a historic high of $4 billion in 1990, forcing the agency to consider selling some of its gold holdings in order to replenish its liquid reserves.[99] More troubling, from the perspective of Third World countries, is that the bylaws of international lending agencies prevent them from forgiving outstanding

---

[94]Jorge Castaneda, "Mexico's Dismal Debt Deal," *New York Times*, February 25, 1990.

[95]Larry Rohter, "Mexico's Economy: Is It In Peril?" *New York Times*, February 3, 1990.

[96]Louis Uchitelle, "Borrowing is Resumed by Mexico," *New York Times*, September 4, 1990.

[97]"S&P's Concern on Mexico," *New York Times*, November 14, 1991.

[98]Islam, "Going Beyond the Brady Plan," 39–45.

[99]Clyde Farnsworth, "IMF Is Urged to Sell Gold as Hedge Against Bad Loans," *New York Times*, February 1, 1990.

loans. Thus a growing proportion of the remaining Third World debt is non-negotiable.[100]

Finally, some argue that Brady Plan deals undermine the bargaining position of debtor countries in any future negotiations with bank creditors. Because Mexico has set aside a fund that guarantees interest payments for eighteen months, it can no longer use the threat of a default or moratorium as a bargaining tool against the banks.[101]

Ironically, Northern bankers have also expressed serious reservations toward the Brady Plan. The 180-member Institute for International Finance, a banker's lobby based in Washington, D.C., has warned the IMF that "banks need a new rationale to stay in the process" of foreign lending. Martin Feldstein, former chairman of the President's Council of Economic Advisers under Ronald Reagan, has predicted that banks would refuse to lend more money to the Third World unless it was accompanied by government guarantees.[102] One banker complained that "it's hard to justify putting more money at risk, or reducing your exposure so that you can lend more, just because it is a concern to the United States government."[103]

Bankers offer a variety of other objections as well. Many question whether the commitment of public money is sufficient to finance the guarantees that lie beneath the Brady Plan. Some debtors, according to the banks, have the resources to make good on their debts and should not be let off the hook. Providing relief to debtors who have suffered from poor economic management sends the wrong message, say the banks, to those countries who have managed their economies well and faithfully repaid their debts. The IMF's recent willingness to lend money to countries that have not yet cleared their arrears with foreign banks has attracted criticism. Indeed, countries have recently proven less hesitant about falling behind in their debt payments. By the end of 1990, total arrears on payments to Northern banks reached $24 billion, three times the level when the Brady Plan was announced.[104] And, finally, bankers worry about the free-rider problem: the banks which offer debt relief subsidize those who do not. The latter are left with higher-quality loan portfolios without contributing to the resolution of the debt crisis.[105]

Finally, some critics have complained that the Brady Plan pushes the burdens of others' misjudgments onto Northern taxpayers. Not only are taxpayers asked to help fund increases in the lending resources of the IMF and

---

[100]Castaneda, "Mexico's Dismal Debt Deal."

[101]Castaneda, "Mexico's Dismal Debt Deal."

[102]Collett, "Brady's Debt Plan is Short on Principle," 2.

[103]Sarah Bartlett, "US Efforts to Aid Debtor Nations Bring 'Profound Disappointment'," *New York Times*, July 24, 1989.

[104]Jonathan Power, "Debt Crisis is Crushing Nations," *Des Moines Register*, December 23, 1990, 26.

[105]Bartlett, "US Efforts to Aid Debtor Nations Bring 'Profound Disappointment'," and Clyde Farnsworth, "IMF Plan on Lending is Challenged by Banks," *New York Times*, September 18, 1990.

the World Bank, but, in the United States, they must also compensate for the revenues lost when U.S. banks deduct losses on foreign loans from their overall tax liabilities.[106]

Alongside the Brady Plan, which addresses itself to the largest debtor countries, have come a variety of Northern initiatives designed to reduce the burdens of the poorest debtor nations, particularly those in sub-Saharan Africa. At a 1988 summit in Toronto, the major Northern donor countries decided to provide debt relief for low-income countries willing to agree to policy reforms overseen by either the IMF or the World Bank. In 1989, the World Bank created a new Debt Reduction Facility designed to help poor countries repurchase their debt at a discount.[107] While these moves should help the poorest debtor countries in the long run, the short-run benefits have been modest. It has been estimated that if the debt relief promised as of the end of 1989 were to be fully implemented, Africa's debt burden would still be equal to 106 percent of the region's GDP, as compared with 28 percent of GDP in 1980.[108]

What is the future of the Third World debt crisis? Notwithstanding the progress made in improving debtor country trade balances and the recent moves toward debt reduction and forgiveness, the problem is that Third World debt remains far from resolved. The rise of oil prices that accompanied the approach of the 1991 Gulf War hurt oil-importing debtor countries badly for a time, although the subsequent price fall following Iraq's defeat placed limits on the extent of economic damage.[109] While lower interest rates have benefitted debtor countries in recent years, the lengthy U.S. recession of 1990–1992 also depressed Third World export earnings. What seems clear is that although the debt problem is more manageable now than it was only a few years ago, Third World debtors remain quite vulnerable to unfavorable external shocks.

---

[106]Albert Fishlow, "Coming to Terms with the Latin Debt," *New York Times*, January 4, 1988.

[107]Stanley Fischer and Ishrat Hussain, "Managing the Debt Crisis in the 1990's," *Finance and Development*, June, 1990, 25–26.

[108]"Forgive, Don't Forget," *The Economist*, December 23, 1989, 67. While softening its stance on some issues, moreover, the North has hardened its position on others. The United States and other Northern nations recently agreed to increase the lending resources of the IMF by 50 percent. At the same time, however, the Bush Administration persuaded other countries to go along with stiff new sanctions aimed at debtor countries that have fallen behind in their payments to the Fund. Countries seriously in arrears will lose their IMF voting rights. Currently, this could affect eleven nations that are more than six months behind in their IMF payments. Clyde Farnsworth, "IMF Panel Votes to Add $60 Billion to Pool for Loans," *New York Times*, May 9, 1990.

[109]For a discussion of effects of the rise of oil prices on Third World countries, see Greenhouse, "Oil Shock Squeezing Third World," and "Developing World Faces Economic Pain from Crisis," *Des Moines Register*, August 23, 1990; Leonard Silk, "Oil Shock's Blow to Rich and Poor," *New York Times*, September 28, 1990; Alan Cowell, "Egypt's Threadbare Economy Worn Further by Gulf Crisis," *New York Times*, September 20, 1990; Clyde Farnsworth, "Brady Urges Aid to Lands Hurt in Crisis," *New York Times*, September 27, 1990; and James Brooke, "Gulf Crisis Has Brazil in a Tailspin," *New York Times*, August 27, 1990.

THE POLITICS OF THIRD WORLD DEBT

■ In the late seventies and the early eighties, many analysts predicted that Third World debt would provide these countries with enormous political leverage over the North, power that the Third World could use to wrest concessions from Northern nations on the reform of the international economic order. The reasoning behind this argument was captured by a well-worn saying: "If you owe the bank a thousand dollars, you have a problem. If you owe the bank a million dollars, the bank has a problem."

In fact, however, it is the North that has gained leverage from the debt crisis. Early on, the nature, origins, and solutions to the debt crisis were defined largely by the North. The burden of adjustment fell upon the Third World in the form of IMF-administered austerity programs. Northern governments, the United States in particular, refused to alter related policies, such as those concerning interest rates or market access, to accommodate debtor country concerns. Nationalistic strategies of development in the South, meanwhile, gave way during the eighties to policies long-favored by the North, such as the lowering of barriers to Northern goods and investments.

More recently, of course, the failure of earlier Northern-sponsored approaches has compelled Northern governments and bank officials to accept the prospect of limited debt reduction. Yet, what remains striking about the debt crisis during the eighties has been the inability of the Third World to wrest greater concessions from the North and the reluctance of Southern officials to contemplate radical strategies for responding to the debt crisis. The final section of this chapter attempts to account for the political balance of power between North and South in bargaining over the debt.

Why Not Repudiation?

The costs of attempting to repay their foreign debt have been high for many Third World countries while the benefits have been few. Why, then, have more countries not simply repudiated their debts, refusing to pay on the grounds that their citizens have sacrificed enough? While no major debtor country has flatly repudiated its foreign debt, several, including Peru, Brazil, and Argentina, have suspended or limited their debt payments for periods of time. These measures are typically intended both to gain breathing space during periods when foreign reserves have run low and as a bargaining tactic designed to force Northern banks to offer concessions in return for resumed debt payments.

Although debt moratoria can provide short-term relief and may bring concessions from creditors, they also involve costs for the debtor country itself. In particular, wayward debtors sacrifice their international creditworthiness, although this constraint has declined in significance in recent years as

Northern banks have cut the flow of long-term lending to even the most diligent debtor countries.

Countries still fear, however, that a defiant stance on debt repayment could result in a loss of access to short-term trade credit. Short-term credits, consisting mostly of loans issued for periods of days or weeks between the time of sale and the actual delivery of traded goods, are heavily relied upon to lubricate the wheels of international commerce. Without them, a nation must face the difficult prospect of conducting its trade with the outside world on a cash-only basis. The denial of trade credits is perhaps the ultimate sanction banks have available for disciplining defiant debtors. Brazil accumulated $6 billion in arrears during its most recent payments moratorium. However, according to John Reed, chairman of Citibank, Brazil also lost access to some $3 billion in normal short-term lending.[110]

Actual debt repudiation might lead to even sterner sanctions, such as legal moves by bank creditors to seize a debtor country's assets abroad in fulfillment of its debt. The risk for any single country that decides to pursue a radical strategy is that it may rupture the entire web of relationships it holds with the international economic community. These calculations make clear the dependence of many, if not most, Third World states on the world economy. This reality is captured in Silva Herzog's recollection of deliberations among Mexican policymakers as they attempted to formulate a strategy for coping with the country's financial crisis in 1982: "We asked ourselves the question what happens if we say, 'No dice. We just won't pay.'? There were some partisans of that. But it didn't make any sense. We're part of the world. We import 30 percent of our food. We just can't say, 'Go to Hell.' "[111]

Bargaining Power and the Debt: Southern Disunity and Northern Unity

If Third World debtors find it difficult to go it alone in defying Northern creditors, then why not pool their leverage through cooperation? The possibility of a debtors' cartel has been a much-discussed topic among bankers, academic observers, and government officials since the early eighties when the idea was first seriously broached. Third World debtors have indeed made sporadic attempts at cooperation in negotiating with the North. Latin American countries have been the most vigorous in their efforts to forge greater unity. Representatives from the region's major nations gathered frequently throughout the eighties to discuss their common debt problems.

These meetings have typically produced declarations calling upon creditor governments and banks to share some of the burden of easing the debt crisis.

---

[110]"Brazil's Plan for Its Debt," *New York Times,* August 20, 1990.
[111]Greider, *Secrets of the Temple,* 484.

Meeting in Ecuador in 1984, Latin American representatives appealed to creditors to "harmonize the requirements of debt servicing with the development needs of each country."[112] In November 1987, eight Latin American presidents meeting in Acapulco, Mexico called for "mechanisms that will allow our countries to benefit from discounts in the value of the respective debts in the market and from the consequent reduction in the servicing of such debts" and the establishment of "interest rate limits, in accordance with procedures decided upon between the parties."[113] This was followed in 1989 by a meeting of the twenty-six nations of the Latin American Economic System (SELA) to continue consultations on a common debt bargaining strategy.[114] Beyond Latin America, UNCTAD, the Third World trade organization, issued a call in September 1988 for commercial banks to forgive 30 percent of the debt owed by the fifteen most heavily indebted countries.[115]

The results of these consultations among debtor countries, however, have seldom progressed beyond verbal expressions of unity. Latin American debtors have rejected the notion of forming a true debtors' cartel. Even lesser forms of cooperation, such as coordinating the timing of debt renegotiations or agreeing on common terms, demands, and objectives in bargaining with the North, have generally eluded debtor countries.

This disunity among debtors stands in contrast with the generally high degree of coordination among banks, Northern governments, and international organizations. It also seems to make little sense given the common position of debtor countries vis-à-vis their Northern creditors. Many frustrated advocates of Southern unity have pointed out that the collective strength of the largest debtor countries, if harnessed together, could be significant. Moreover, the threat of default by a debtors' cartel need not actually be carried out in order to serve its purpose. By simply demonstrating the will, purpose, and organization needed to make such a threat credible, a group of large debtors could conceivably place itself in a position to compel Northern concessions. Yet, no serious movement toward assembling a debtors' cartel has been made.

Why has debtor country cooperation proven so feeble? Part of the reason is that, despite their common interests, debtor countries are also in competition with one another for Northern funds. This rivalry can lead countries to seek the favor of creditors by adopting a more cooperative stance than their neighbors.[116] Governments may be slow to associate themselves with the radical positions sometimes taken by other debtors, on the other hand, for fear that their own creditworthiness will be marred.

---

[112]"Latin Amerian Debt: Living on Borrowed Time?" 31.

[113]Mike Tangeman, "Safety in Numbers: Latin American Looks at Unity to Solve Debt Crisis," *In These Times*, February 3–9, 1988.

[114]Collett, "Brady's Debt Plan is Short on Principle."

[115]Wicker, "The Real Danger of Debt."

[116]Aggarwal, *International Debt Threat*, 31.

This was the case in 1984 when President Raul Alfonsin of Argentina called for debtor-country unity in confronting the IMF and the banks. Instead of rallying around Argentina in its time of need, other Latin American countries sided with Northern creditors and persuaded Argentina to back down from its confrontational stance. Neighboring debtor nations even went so far as to provide Argentina with the short-term financing needed to pay its overdue debt bill.[117] Commenting on this episode, one Mexican Foreign Ministry official pointed out, "We have a lot of incentives to convince the other nations to be cautious. We have suffered a lot to get where we are, and we don't want to see them upset it."[118]

A related obstacle to greater unity has to do with the differing timing of their respective financial crises. When Argentina moved toward a more radical strategy in 1984, as we have seen, it was discouraged by Mexico and Brazil; both of these countries had reached agreements with their creditors and therefore felt less urgency about their debt problems. Peru unilaterally declared that it would devote no more than 10 percent of its export earnings toward debt payments in 1985. Still fearful of damaging their access to international credit, Mexico, Brazil, and Argentina refused Peru their support. Brazil and Argentina had new stabilization programs in place in 1986 when Mexico came close to suspending payments, and, once again, they refused to contemplate a more unified and confrontational course. Much the same was true in 1987, when Brazil declared a moratorium on payments to its private creditors. Mexico, by that time, had initiated a new stabilization plan in cooperation with its creditors, and Argentina was in no mood to rock the boat.[119]

Differences in size also impede cooperation. Small debtor countries have been more supportive of a radical course than larger debtors countries. Large countries receive more favorable treatment by Northern creditors than do small countries, precisely because the big debtors pose a greater threat to the world financial system. Larger debtors also have better prospects of gaining renewed access to international credit markets in the future than their smaller brethren, and thus have more reason to protect their credit-worthiness. For reasons of image and pride, moreover, large and relatively well-developed countries like Brazil and Mexico do not wish to be lumped together with small poverty-stricken countries like Bolivia or Peru.[120] Finally, large debtor countries resent the prospect that small countries would serve as free riders on the efforts of the big countries in any cooperative

---

[117]Richard Feinberg, "Latin American Debt: Renegotiating the Burden," in Richard Feinberg and Ricardo French-Davis, eds. *Development and External Debt in Latin America: Bases for a New Consensus*, Notre Dame: Notre Dame University Press, 1988, 59.

[118]Aggarwal, *International Debt Threat*, 32.

[119]Alan Riding, "Brazil's Reversal of Debt Strategy," *New York Times*, February 22, 1988.

[120]Feinberg, "Latin American Debt: Renegotiating the Burden," 59.

endeavor. Small countries would benefit from any favorable outcomes gained in bargaining with the North alongside large debtors while contributing very little to the success of such a venture.[121]

Indeed, movement toward a debtors' cartel raises the problem of cheating. The North would inevitably seek to split any debtors coalition by offering some countries special incentives to defect. This sort of obstacle has already served to stymie cooperation. Mexican officials, for instance, have at times believed that they could gain a better deal by relying upon their country's special relationship with the United States rather than by joining other debtor countries in a stance of defiance.[122]

Domestic factors also inhibit movement toward a radical strategy. The economic interests of the middle and upper classes in many Southern countries serve to sap governing elites of the will needed to confront the North over the debt issue. The well-to-do in many debtor countries invested substantial portions of their assets abroad during the eighties. With large amounts of money in Northern banks, these individuals have little interest in endorsing methods that might wreak havoc on Northern financial institutions.[123]

Related to this is the presence of many technocrats in the economic ministries of most Third World countries. Often trained in the North, these internationalist-oriented bureaucrats share much of the ideology and outlook of organizations such as the IMF. They may lobby for compliance with IMF or World Bank-sponsored reforms because they are convinced that such policies are conducive to long-term economic growth, regardless of the short-term costs. The outcome of internal battles between these policymakers and their more nationalist-oriented colleagues varies across countries and over time. IMF and World Bank officials sometimes attempt to strengthen their allies in such conflicts so as to smooth acceptance of the policies they advocate. They do so indirectly by training Third World financial and development officials at special schools run by the Fund and the Bank.[124] More directly, one study has documented efforts by World Bank officials to bypass and isolate nationalist bureaucrats, while cooperating with international technocrats, in the development and implementation of a structural adjustment program in the Philippines during the early eighties.[125]

Northern banks also face a number of obstacles to mutual cooperation in their negotiations with debtor countries. Perhaps the largest of these stems from the sheer number of banks whose assent must be gained in any given deal. This is true of even relatively small-scale loans. A 1983 rescheduling

---

[121]Aggarwal, *International Debt Threat*, 52-53.

[122]Feinberg, "Latin American Debt: Renegotiating the Burden," 59.

[123]Feinberg, "Latin American Debt: Renegotiating the Burden," 60.

[124]These are the IMF Institute and The World Bank's Economic Development Institute. Robin Broad, *Unequal Alliance: The World Bank, the International Monetary Fund, and the Philippines*, Berkeley: University of California Press, 1988, 26, 31.

[125]Broad, *Unequal Alliance*

agreement concerning Ecuador's $1.2 billion in overdue loan payments required the participation of over 400 banks.[126]

Coordination among this number of actors would be difficult under most circumstances. But cooperation is rendered more problematic by conflicting interests. Banks involved in international lending differ widely in their size and their proportional exposure to Third World debt. Smaller and less heavily exposed banks are typically more reluctant than larger and more deeply committed banks to lend new money to help troubled debtors keep current on payments stemming from previous loans. Bankers are also divided by national origin. During the early eighties, conflicts arose over the fact that U.S. banks were more heavily involved in lending to Latin America than European banks, while the latter had lent more to Poland and other Eastern European countries than those in the U.S. Banks of different nationality also face varying regulatory requirements from their home governments.[127]

The relationship between banks and Northern governments has at times presented problems as well. Tensions have arisen over the distribution of burdens between the two in coping with the debt crisis. Moreover, while banks are primarily concerned with profits, governments are motivated by broader political concerns, such as the maintenance of political stability or the spread of democracy in debtor countries. The potential for conflict between these outlooks is captured in a statement attributed to a Citicorp vice chairman: "Who knows which political system works? The only test we care about is: Can they pay their bills?"[128]

Over most of the past decade, however, Northern banks have been remarkably successful in maintaining unity among themselves, despite these obstacles, and in securing the cooperation of other actors. The difficulties of sustaining cooperation among large numbers of banks have been eased by the rules and practices of syndicated lending as well as the web of ties that bind banks together. Most syndicated loans agreements, for instance, require two-thirds approval before a debtor can be declared in default. Since voting is weighted according to each bank's share of the total loan, this rule effectively provides the big banks with veto power over such decisions.

Less formally, large banks have developed procedures for monitoring small-bank behavior and pressuring them to cooperate in rescheduling deals. An advisory committee of fourteen major banks carried out the bulk of negotiations with Mexico, for instance, in 1982. Once a deal was reached, each of these banks took responsibility for bringing ten regional banks on board. Each regional bank, in turn, sought to secure the cooperation of ten nearby smaller banks. This arrangement became standard operating procedure in

---

[126]Charles Lipson, "International Debt and International Institutions," in Kahler, ed. *The Politics of International Debt*, fn. 14, 223.

[127]Aggarwal, *International Debt Threat*, 15–21.

[128]Aggarwal, *International Debt Threat*, 38.

subsequent rescheduling negotiations. The major banks, as well as the debtor countries themselves, nudged recalcitrant banks toward cooperation in new lending by threatening to exclude the latter from future syndication deals. Due to their need to protect long-term business relationships with larger banks, small banks often found such threats compelling.[129]

Gaps in private cooperation are often filled in by the actions of public authorities. If pressure from the large banks is insufficient to induce cooperation on the part of a small bank, for instance, the latter might become the subject of informal pressure from Treasury Department or Federal Reserve authorities. The regulatory power that government agencies hold over banks provides authorities with a powerful means of influencing bank behavior.

The large banks have found the IMF and the World Bank generally responsive to their concerns and quite useful in protecting overall bank interests. The reasons for this are simple. Both institutions have weighted voting schemes that give the North far more voting power than the South. The top officials of both institutions are invariably drawn from the North and often have roots in the banking world. The IMF and the Bank also raise funds by issuing securities in Northern financial markets. Finally, both institutions are influenced by prevailing economic doctrines, which are predominantly shaped by Northern intellectuals.

These factors generally incline the IMF toward policies favored by the banks. Indeed, bankers treat the Fund's relationship with Third World countries as an indicator of the latter's creditworthiness. A country unable to resolve its differences with the Fund will likely be snubbed by the banks as well. Banks find it too costly and difficult to develop detailed economic and political data concerning each Third World country. They instead rely upon the expertise and judgment of the Fund. The Fund is also in a much better position to impose, administer, and monitor policy reform programs in troubled debtor countries than are the banks. As a public institution that loans only to member countries, the legitimacy of the Fund's authority is greater than that of a private bank. Moreover, with the Fund in the lead, debtor countries find it more difficult to divide the bank coalition by striking special deals with some creditors but not others. Finally, the Fund sometimes defends the collective interests of all banks by compelling reluctant individual banks to share their part in the burden of new lending.[130]

In general, Northern actors have been far more unified in bargaining over the debt than their Southern counterparts. The resources at their disposal have also been greater. Yet, while still favoring the North, the balance of bargaining power has shifted somewhat in favor of debtor countries during

---

[129]On private cooperation, see Aggarwal, *International Debt Threat*, 21–29; and Charles Lipson, "Bankers' Dilemma: Private Cooperation in Rescheduling Sovereign Debts," *World Politics*, October, 1985.

[130]On the relationship between the Fund and the banks, see Aggarwal, *International Debt Threat*, 35–44.

the past few years. Debtor countries have pursued bolder tactics in their search for concessions from the North. By allowing their new lending to the South to dwindle, the banks have diluted one of the incentives that previously induced a more cooperative stance on the part of debtor countries. Conflicts have intensified, moreover, between the banks and Northern governments. The Brady Plan calls upon banks to make sacrifices not altogether to their liking. It was motivated in part by fears that lack of progress in defusing the debt crisis might lead to political instability in Latin America. This risk was driven home when left-wing candidates came close to winning the presidencies of both Mexico and Brazil. Broader political considerations, along with continuing pressure from U.S. export interests harmed by Latin American austerity, apparently came to partially outweigh U.S. government responsiveness to banker preferences.

CONCLUSIONS

■ The Third World debt crisis dramatically illustrates the politics of assymetrical interdependence. With the stability of many Third World governments and the soundness of the world financial system both at stake, political bargaining quickly displaced market mechanisms as the primary conduit for coping with Third World debt problems. Governments and public agencies assumed major roles, alongside the banks, in crafting responses to the difficulties that have grown from Southern indebtness in the years since the Mexican crisis of 1982. This strongly political dimension of the debt crisis has highlighted the significant role that power relations play in determining the distribution of benefits and burdens from North-South economic links.

The fact that the principal burden of coping with the debt crisis has fallen on Third World countries can be attributed neither to neutral economic processes nor the workings of divine justice. Instead, it is the expected outcome of an international order in which political and economic power are distributed unequally among countries. In this case, the South's dependence upon the North for finance, trade, and technology has provided Northern policymakers and bankers with the leverage needed to impose their own solutions to the debt crisis. To be sure, Third World debtors have at times managed to slow or moderate the pressures for debt repayment, but their ability to deflect such pressures has proven limited. This is due in large part to the fact that it is the South, not the North, that would be harmed the most by the severing of the economic ties that bind the First and the Third Worlds. The weakness that this relationship of assymmetrical interdependence imposes upon the South has only been compounded by the relative lack of unity among debtor countries in their bargaining with the North.

ANNOTATED BIBLIOGRAPHY

Vinod Aggarwal, *International Debt Threat: Bargaining Among Creditors and Debtors in the 1980's*, Policy Papers in International Affairs, no. 79, Berkeley: University of California Press, 1987.
A brief but valuable conceptual treatment of North-South bargaining over solutions to the debt crisis.

Barry Eichengreen and Peter Lindert, eds. *The International Debt Crisis in Historical Perspective*, Cambridge: MIT Press, 1989.
A collection of essays that explore whether previous historical episodes of international debt crises hold lessons for coping with recent Third World indebtedness.

Edward Fried and Philip H. Trezise, *Third World Debt: The Next Phase*, Washington: Brookings, 1989.
Useful for data and policy analysis.

Miles Kahler, ed. *The Politics of International Debt*, Ithaca: Cornell University Press, 1985.
While somewhat dated, this collection features a number of excellent political analyses of the evolution of the Third World debt crisis. Particularly useful as a source for relevant theories and concepts.

CHARTING THE FUTURE:
ECONOMIC INTERDEPENDENCE AND
NATIONAL COMPETITIVENESS

C hange is a pervasive theme in the history of the international political economy. Few essential attributes of the system remain static for long. Our conclusion surveys important trends along two key dimensions of the contemporary world economy and projects them into the future.

We first examine the prospects for successful management of the international economic system. The presence of conflicting interests at both the domestic and international levels precludes the possibility of harmonious economic relations among states. Instead, international economic interdependence rests upon a complex mixture of cooperation and conflict. The balance between the two varies over time, however, depending upon political conditions within and among states.

The volatility of international economic relations is illustrated by the history of the past sixty years. This period can be broken into three distinct eras. The first spanned the decade of the thirties, when competitive impulses overwhelmed cooperative efforts. Under the strains produced by the Great Depression, nations erected stiff protectionist barriers and formed economic blocs in vain efforts to preserve domestic production and employment. These actions led to a painful contraction of world trade and raised political tensions. Attempts to find cooperative solutions to the breakdown of the international economic order produced only limited results, due largely to the weakness of existing international institutions and the absence of any country with the power or willingness to exercise leadership.

The next phase of international economic relations, stretching from 1947 to 1973, brought more serious and fruitful efforts at cooperation. A variety of new institutions and rules were created to help manage and encourage the growth of economic interdependence. Protectionist barriers fell dramatically,

315

and levels of international trade and investment expanded rapidly, especially during the sixties. All of this was made possible by a number of essentially political factors, including U.S. hegemony and leadership, the close security relationships forged among the United States, Western Europe, and Japan during the Cold War, and the lessons political leaders drew from the harsh experiences of the 1930s.

The period since 1973 has brought a more even balance between the cooperative and competitive dimensions of the international political economy. While economic interdependence has continued to expand and deepen, it has done so in an erratic manner. This period has featured two major global recessions, three episodes of oil-supply disruptions, a major bout of inflation during the late seventies, the growth of nontariff barriers and managed trade, the emergence of the Third World debt crisis, and extreme imbalances in trade among the major economic powers. International economic issues have assumed heightened political salience in many countries, and the rules and institutions designed to manage international economic relations have been subject to strains produced by changing economic realities as well as disagreements among the major powers. With unity and common purpose difficult to achieve, political leaders from various states have, nevertheless, found ways of muddling through repeated crises and conflicts, often devising temporary fixes or papering over differences. These expedients have sufficed to avert a plunge into outright economic warfare. Indeed, the world economy has continued to move toward deeper levels of economic interdependence. Yet gaps in the system's management continue to grow, and serious differences in perspective have placed international cooperation under increasing strain.

The first section of this chapter assesses the prospects for successful management of the future international economic order. Will competition spin out of control, leading to mutually destructive conflict, as during the 1930s? Or can the world's nations break free of the indecisiveness and uncertainty of the last two decades and complete the agenda of liberalization begun, but left unfinished, during the fifties and sixties?

In addition to the fate of the international system as a whole, this chapter also examines possible changes in the relative economic fortunes of particular countries and regions. The competitive position of any given nation is influenced by a variety of factors. Institutional change, the unevenness of technological innovation, shifting product cycles, and evolving political and economic strategies each place various countries on different trajectories of rise and decline.

The post–World War II period has witnessed significant shifts of this sort. Over the past four decades, the United States' relative position has eroded, and Japan's position has improved enormously, while Western Europe's experience falls somewhere in between. The economies of Eastern Europe and the Soviet Union failed to keep pace with those of the West during the seventies and eighties, a factor partly responsible for the dramatic political changes that have engulfed those countries in recent years. The Third World has become vastly more diverse. Industrialization surged ahead in many parts of Latin America, especially Mexico and Brazil, during the fifties, sixties, and seventies before slowing to a crawl in the eighties as a result of the debt crisis. Although a handful of OPEC countries achieved instant wealth during the seventies as a result of two steep price rises, the same nations were compelled to adapt to more modest revenues as prices once again fell over the past decade. The clearest Third World success stories are to be found in East Asia, where a number of countries, including South Korea, Taiwan, Singapore, Hong Kong, Malaysia, and Thailand, have achieved astonishing growth rates based upon export-oriented strategies of development. With only a few exceptions, the countries of South Asia and Africa, by contrast, have posted consistently disappointing results and remain mired in poverty.

How will the fortunes of various nations and regions fare over the coming decades? Any predictions of this sort are necessarily speculative. Nevertheless, we can gain insights by considering the strengths and weaknesses that different countries possess as they face future international economic competition.

Cooperation and Competition in the World Economy

■ Predicting the future balance between international economic cooperation and competition is a challenging task. The complexity of the real world along with the imprecision and inconsistency of existing theory serve to cloud the crystal ball of even the most acute observer. Rather than suggest a definitive scenario, then, we instead consider the forces that may reinforce cooperation alongside those that seem to point toward conflict and competition.

Harbingers of Cooperation

The most important reason for expecting the persistence of international economic cooperation in the future stems from the growing dependence of national economies on one another for essential goods, services, and raw materials. This global web of trade and investment has arisen partly from technological advances and economic processes. Improvements in transportation have greatly lowered the cost of moving goods, raw materials, and even people from one part of the globe to another. And the communications revolution has made it possible for large corporations to manage far-flung multinational empires. Firms interested in obtaining the cheapest labor and raw materials or expanding into new markets have exploited these new opportunities for international growth.

These fundamental economic realities provide powerful incentives for policymakers to choose cooperative economic strategies. To be sure, interdependence threatens various values and interests, as we later suggest. As a result, states often seek to manage and regulate the nation's relationship to the world economy. Nevertheless, policymakers are generally acutely aware that the costs of "going it alone" in today's world economy are prohibitively high. Indeed, an increasingly elaborate global division of labor has brought greater prosperity to the world economy as a whole. This trend has largely confirmed a key tenet of economic theory that holds that economic welfare is maximized when nations specialize in those goods that they can produce most efficiently while trading for products that they are poorly suited to produce.

There also exists a widespread understanding that the growth of trade and investment is impossible without a substantial commitment among states to openness, policy coordination, and cooperation in setting the rules and institutions needed to manage the system. The fear that spiraling political conflict could undermine the bases for international economic growth and prosperity inhibits policymakers from resorting to extreme nationalistic strategies or pressing too hard for relative advantage. These shared perceptions do not preclude the possibility of serious differences among nations in the future, but they may set broad limits on the scope and intensity of conflict and competition.

The impact of spreading interdependence on domestic interests and coalitions is less certain but may also weigh in favor of stronger international cooperation. In most countries, economic policymaking is influenced by more than simple calculations of the national good. Political leaders are dependent upon coalitions of particular interests. In the making of foreign economic policy, two sets of groups are usually most important: nationalists, who are harmed by the growth of economic interdependence, and internationalists, who directly engage in, and benefit from, foreign trade and investment.

Rising economic interdependence tends to heighten the political mobilization of both groups and intensifies the conflicts between them. With some important exceptions, however, high levels of trade can be expected to strengthen the power of internationalists, who favor cooperation and openness, at the expense of nationalists.

Nationalist coalitions typically emerge when large numbers of domestic industries begin to experience competition from more efficient foreign producers. The affected firms and workers seek government protection in the form of import restrictions or other sorts of regulations designed to counter the economic advantages possessed by foreign competitors. Such efforts are sometimes rewarded, especially under conditions that tend to strengthen the appeal of nationalism, such as prolonged periods of economic hardship or the persistence of negative trade balances.

Yet, while economic interdependence stimulates nationalist interests to mobilize in the defense of jobs and profits, it also, in the long run, weakens the political clout of nationalists by strengthening the relative economic weight of internationalist interests in the national economy. Even if uncompetitive firms or industries succeed in gaining a degree of state protection, this seldom reverses the shrinking importance of such sectors to the national economy as a whole over time. Internationalist coalitions, on the other hand, tend to include many of the nation's largest, fastest-growing and most competitive firms. As trade and investment grow, the absolute and relative number of firms with a stake in economic openness tends to grow over time as well. The force of internationalist arguments in favor of free trade is also bolstered by two additional factors: such policies not only favor consumers, who benefit from the lower prices and greater selection provided by access to foreign goods, but also draw the strong endorsement of economic theory.

While a host of factors may influence the balance of power between nationalist and internationalist forces across countries and over time within a single country, the future spread of interdependence is likely to enhance the relative political weight of internationalist interests. Over the long term, economic success is a surer route to political influence than is failure.[1]

Optimism about the future potential for economic cooperation also rests upon a recent and rather unexpected trend: the growing convergence among nations around similar liberal economic strategies. This was not the case in the past. Indeed, only North America, Western Europe, and a handful of other countries clearly organized their economies around the precepts of economic liberalism, including the primacy of private capital, the reliance upon market forces, and relative openness to international trade and investment. Much of the Third World pursued a nationalist strategy of development, stressing heavy state intervention and import protectionism. The OPEC countries nationalized foreign oil investments and attempted to manage a resource cartel. The East Asian NICs, following Japan's example, pursued an export-oriented version of mercantilism, using the state to carve out new sources of comparative advantage. The socialist bloc countries built command economies that remained largely isolated from the remainder of the world economy.

Although, as the next section indicates, present trends are complex and somewhat contradictory, a host of recent developments may point toward the global triumph of liberalism. National economic strategies appear to be converging around market-centered models of development, a trend that, if sustained, could smooth the route toward international economic cooperation.

The Third World has retreated from demands for a New International Economic Order in which resources would be allocated according to political

[1]On this point, see Robert Baldwin, "The New Protectionism: A Response to Shifts in National Economic Power," 372–373; and G.K. Helleiner, "Transnational Enterprises and the New Political Economy of U.S. Trade Policy," both in Jeffry A. Frieden and David A. Lake, eds. *International Political Economy: Perspectives on Global Power and Wealth,* New York: St. Martin's Press, 2nd ed., 1991.

rather than market criteria. Nationalist import substitution strategies of development have also lost favor. Instead, country after country has, under the pressures of the debt crisis and poor economic performance, begun to privatize state industries, dismantle subsidies and price controls, lower overvalued currencies, and remove barriers to imports and foreign investment.

The East Asian NICs have also begun to reduce the state's role in steering economic development. The same is true in Japan. As the Japanese economy matures and becomes more internationalized, the role of the MITI and other bureaucracies has receded while barriers to imports and foreign investment have eased.

Most dramatic, of course, has been the movement of Eastern Europe and the republics of the former Soviet Union toward capitalism and reintegration with the world economy. Even socialist countries where communist parties remain strong or dominant, such as China and Vietnam, have begun to introduce market reforms and encourage greater trade, investment, and aid from the West.

The future of these trends is still uncertain. How far will market reforms go in Eastern Europe and the remaining socialist countries? Will liberalization succeed in the countries where it is being attempted for the first time? Will political backlash against the costs of liberalization (higher prices, greater unemployment, increasing inequality, and high levels of economic insecurity) stall or reverse reform in some Third World or Eastern European countries? How will Northern countries react if established industries are threatened by the cheap imports upon which Eastern Europe and many Third World countries are pinning their hopes for economic growth? Does the triumph of liberalization necessarily ensure easier economic cooperation among countries, or will it lead to growing competitive pressures and conflict?

Competition

Despite the many factors favoring cooperation, there also exist powerful forces that could lead to heightened conflict and perhaps serve to undermine the basis for growing global interdependence. Some of these are quite traditional and stem from the tensions between national autonomy and economic interdependence as well as the enduring sources of competitive rivalry among nations. Others are related to more recent trends and developments, such as shifts in relative power and the changing nature of bargaining over trade and other issues.

If it is rare for political leaders to isolate their country from the world economy, it is likewise unusual for a government to permit trade and investment to take place entirely without regulation or restriction. Interdependence brings costs as well as benefits. In managing their nation's economic relationships with the rest of the world, policymakers attempt to balance the benefits of interdependence against the costs.

The most important political cost of interdependence is the erosion of national autonomy. Economic dependence can leave a country vulnerable to manipulation, as even the United States discovered during the seventies when it became dependent upon OPEC oil. In addition, interdependence can greatly complicate the task of economic policy-making as decision makers must now take into account the reactions of foreign firms and governments when choosing among national economic policies and goals. Political leaders may also seek to limit trade and investment with nations that are military rivals for fear that such exchanges might allow the transfer of militarily relevant technologies.

Moreover, while trade between two countries may benefit both, there is no guarantee that they will each prosper equally. Indeed, it is often possible for one nation to gain advantages over other states or to push burdens onto other countries by restricting and regulating trade and investment in various ways. Since the competitive nature of world politics ensures that national leaders are concerned about relative power and position as well as absolute economic gains, growing interdependence is bound to lead to increased struggle for national advantage alongside efforts at cooperation.

These enduring sources of competition and conflict manifest themselves in various forms in the contemporary world economy. The first important source of uncertainty about the future of international cooperation has to do with the consequences of declining U.S. power. The theory of hegemonic stability suggests that periods of openness and growing interdependence are linked to the existence of a hegemonic power willing to exercise leadership by providing collective goods and creating, as well as enforcing, rules of the game. Without this sort of leadership, management of the international economic system becomes complicated by the difficulty of gaining agreement among many competitive and relatively equal states. Sanctions against cheating become less certain as well.

While the United States remains the world's largest single economic power, its relative decline has, nevertheless, allowed the establishment of several competing power centers, each with the capacity to take independent action and to make their wishes felt in bargaining over the future of the global economy. This has rendered the United States less capable of exercising leadership than in the past. Moreover, the United States may also be less willing to champion free trade than it once was. Facing the loss of technological leadership to other advanced industrial nations along with low-wage competition from Third World countries, many U.S. firms and labor unions have begun to press for trade protection. At the same time, Congress has passed legislation designed to press the Executive branch to retaliate more forcefully and speedily against other nations judged guilty of unfair trade practices.

Alongside the decline of U.S. leadership has been the rapid rise of Japan. This shift in relative power has been particularly disruptive. Japan has so far proven unable to fill the leadership vacuum left by U.S. decline. Not only does Japan still lack the power to serve as a genuine hegemon, it also, for historical reasons, lacks both the experience and the willingness needed to accept the political demands of international leadership. Finally, despite recent changes, the Japanese economic model has rested upon a mercantilist rather than a liberal philosophy. Such an approach places only limited emphasis on international cooperation and has led to tensions between Japan and its trading partners.

In combination, the decline of the United States and the rise of Japan have lent momentum to the retreat from globalism and the movement toward regional economic blocs. Within such blocs, international cooperation is high and barriers to trade and investment are partially or wholly removed. Such arrangements, however, may discriminate against imports or investment originating from outside the bloc. The EEC is the most significant manifestation of this trend, but the development of a North American bloc (that one day may come to encompass South America as well) is also well along. An East Asian bloc centered around Japan is less well defined but could tighten if present trends in regional trade, aid, and investment continue.[2]

The formation of regional blocs is essentially a political response to a more competitive international economic environment. There exists a danger that nations may come to see the integration of regional blocs as a hedge against a breakdown in the rules and institutions that manage the global economy. If so, then such behavior could lead to a self-fulfilling prophecy, in which the development of blocs becomes one of the decisive factors in complicating globalist and multilateral solutions to world economic problems.

Another troubling consequence of the shifting competitive positions among states has been the emergence of serious imbalances in the world economy. In particular, Japan (and, until recently, Germany) has run persistently large trade surpluses, while the United States has suffered from large-scale, long-term deficits. These imbalances stem from fundamental economic factors, such as the contrasting savings rates in the United States and Japan, as well as lapses in monetary management and cooperation. The political effect, however, is to raise tensions and galvanize protectionist forces in deficit countries, including the United States.

Until recently, the political consequences of economic competition and rivalry were muted by the close security ties among the advanced capitalist countries. With the waning of the Cold War and the decline of the Soviet threat, this cohesive factor could well begin to weaken. Western Europe and Japan are likely to become less deferential to the United States as they become less dependent upon U.S. military protection. Indeed, it is even possible that the Cold War allies could become military competitors one day in the not-too-

---

[2]See Jeffrey E. Garten, "Trading Blocs and the Evolving World Economy," *Current History*, January, 1989, 15–16, 54–56; Lester Thurow, "America, Europe and Japan: A Time to Dismantle the World Economy?," *The Economist*, November 9, 1985; and Louis Uchitelle, "Blocs Seen Replacing Free Trade," *New York Times*, August 26, 1991.

distant future. Such a development would inevitably have negative effects on economic cooperation.

The future of international economic cooperation is also clouded by the complexity of contemporary bargaining. The early stages of international cooperation in the decades after World War II, such as the Kennedy Round of trade negotiations, focused upon relatively simple goals, like the lowering of tariff barriers. Today, however, the goals are much more ambitious, the scope of the issues addressed is broader, and the intrusiveness of international commitments on the domestic sphere is much greater. Trade negotiators must deal with more varieties of protectionism, many of them less visible and more subtle than tariffs. Bargaining has come to encompass areas excluded from GATT, such as trade in agriculture and services as well as nontraditional concerns, including protections for intellectual property and the rights and obligations of foreign investors. As the Structural Impediments agreements between the United States and Japan and the current U.S.–Mexico free trade negotiations suggest, trade agreements are coming to affect policies once considered purely domestic in nature. Indeed, at issue are fundamental aspects of national economic structure. All of this makes international cooperation more significant and substantial today than in the past. The issues are fundamental and the stakes higher. Yet it also suggests that cooperation at the cutting edge is becoming increasingly complex and politically salient, making agreements more difficult to reach or to implement and honor. In short, the easy part of building an open, liberal international economic order is past, and the hard part remains.

NATIONAL COMPETITIVENESS

■ Whatever the fate of the world economy as a whole, political leaders and citizens care most about the prosperity and security of their own country. A country's economic performance not only determines living standards at home but also affects its power and prestige abroad. For these reasons, nations worry about their relative position in the world economy and draw comparisons with commercial or military rivals. This section surveys the competitive strengths and weaknesses of various countries or regions, discusses some of the principal economic problems faced by each, and projects trends in power and wealth into the coming decades.

The United States

In sheer size, the U.S. economy remains far larger than that of any other single nation. This fact alone guarantees that the United States will remain an influential political and economic power for decades to come. Moreover, the United States brings a number of important strengths to international economic competition, including continued technological leadership in many areas, an enviable system of higher education, ample natural resources, an efficient agricultural sector, and a flexible market-oriented economy. Faced with growing foreign competition, many U.S. manufacturing firms have lowered costs and improved product quality over the past decade. The next decade will bring lower defense-spending burdens, thus freeing resources for the civilian economy. The United States' considerable assets and strengths rule out a calamitous decline and probably ensure a slow but steady absolute rise in living standards in the future.

Nevertheless, the competitive challenges facing the United States are likely to grow over the long term, and its relative position in the global economy may well continue to deteriorate. The United States' large foreign debt guarantees foreign investors a claim on a portion of future U.S. production in the form of repatriated profits for years to come. U.S. technological leadership is slipping rapidly, and U.S. production of scientists and engineers considerably trails that of Germany and Japan on a per capita basis. A number of significant domestic ills, including a low national savings rate, a deteriorating infrastructure, a troubled primary and secondary educational system, and persistent federal budget deficits, continue to retard national economic performance.

The future of U.S. competitiveness will depend upon answers to a number of critical questions: Can a system of government built upon so many checks and balances marshal the political will needed to devise coherent responses to the domestic and international problems outlined? Can U.S. management and labor forge new, more cooperative relationships in the future, making possible real gains in productivity and product quality? Can U.S. corporations develop a longer-term perspective, thus freeing strategic planning from the constraints imposed by concerns about short-term profitability? Will U.S. citizens confront the difficult trade-offs posed by the challenge of retaining U.S. economic competitiveness, such as that between consumption and investment? Is it possible to develop a national consensus around any particular strategy for dealing with international competition?

Western Europe

The outlook for Western Europe is particularly uncertain owing to the many unprecedented changes taking place in the European political and economic order. From an economic standpoint, perhaps the most important of these is the removal of hundreds of barriers to the movement of goods, capital, and labor within the EEC scheduled for 1992. This long-awaited development is expected to produce substantial economic benefits. Transportation and communications costs will decline, while productivity is likely to rise as a result of product standardization, greater economies of scale in production, increased competition, and greater labor mobility. A large amount of foreign capital has already migrated to the region in anticipation of the profits to be had from servicing a larger open market. The size of this unified market is likely to grow in the coming decade as new nations join the EEC, either as full members or in some sort of associated status.

While 1992 will thus give Western Europe a needed boost, it will do less to resolve the underlying structural problems that still plague the European economy. Despite joint efforts and large government assistance, the high-technology sectors of European industry generally lag behind those of the United States and Japan. Europe as a whole continues to suffer from high unemployment and overcapacity in certain industries. Relatively high social-welfare spending levels in many countries serve as an economic burden. European agriculture is relatively inefficient and highly subsidized. The region also depends heavily on imported oil and natural gas, a handicap should energy prices rise in coming years.

The overthrow of Communism in Eastern Europe has mixed implications for the Western half of the continent. A reduced Soviet threat will allow for lower defense-spending levels. Western Europe is likely to benefit as well from greater access to Eastern markets and investment opportunities. In the short run, however, Western economic aid to Eastern Europe has proven expensive. West Europeans also worry that political unrest or ethnic violence could accelerate in much of Eastern Europe. Among other things, this could lead to large-scale migration from East to West, with disruptive social and economic effects on EEC member countries.

Germany, Europe's largest economy, is facing a difficult transition period as it attempts to cope with the economic consequences of reunification. Early efforts to dismantle centralized economic planning in the former East Germany led to virtual economic collapse in that region. The expense of propping up and restructuring the economy of Eastern Germany has led to growing budget deficits, higher taxes, rising interest rates, and a declining trade balance. The full integration of East and West Germany will be enormously expensive and is likely to take a decade or more.

Western Europe faces many serious choices as it attempts to cope with rapid internal change and growing external competition: Should the Community remain open to the world economy, or should it protect embattled economic sectors, particularly those based upon high technology? Should the EEC move toward full monetary integration? If so, how rapidly, and where would control over monetary policy lie? Should the membership of the EEC be expanded? If so, which countries should be allowed in? How fast? Under what terms? How will a larger membership affect the balance of power within the Community or the effectiveness of its decision-making mechanisms? Can Western Europe afford the massive amounts of aid needed to insure the success of market reforms in Eastern Europe? Will growing economic involvement in the East drag Western European nations into the potentially bitter political conflicts of that region?

Eastern Europe

Will the collapse of Communism bring a brighter economic future for Eastern Europe? According to Western economists, market reforms should eventually produce substantial benefits by introducing genuine competition, forcing inefficient producers out of business, and allowing prices to determine production through the mechanisms of supply and demand, but the short-term prospects are less bright. The transition from centrally planned to market economies is filled with pain and confusion. Reforms in Poland and other countries have brought inflation, bankruptcies, unemployment, and falling levels of income and production. The potential for political unrest and public impatience under these circumstances is obvious. This raises questions about whether the region's governments will possess the political stability, legitimacy, and will needed to guide their nations through a difficult and possibly prolonged period of transition.

Western aid and investment may help speed the process of reform and ease the agonies of adjustment. Indeed, significant financial resources and technical assistance have already been provided or pledged. Yet it is uncertain whether the quantities of aid promised so far will be sufficient. Estimates of the costs associated with modernizing the economy of former East Germany have repeatedly risen. Moreover, the obvious priority that German leaders give to this task may reduce their willingness and ability to afford long-term commitments to other countries of Eastern Europe. The United States, meanwhile, is hamstrung from providing large-scale aid by serious budgetary constraints. Japan, on the other hand, has considerable financial resources but is geographically distant from Eastern Europe and has few historical ties to the region.

While Western firms have begun to move into Eastern Europe, some of the initial enthusiasm among investors has cooled. In addition to a still unsettled legal climate and political uncertainty, Western firms have found resistance among Eastern European workers to the discipline and higher productivity expected by their new employers. Existing manufacturing facilities are often outdated and poorly maintained, requiring large-scale investment and modernization. Few local managers possess the knowledge and experience to function effectively in a market environment.

Eastern European leaders speak hopefully about the prospect of one day joining the EEC, but Western European states have strong reasons for moving slowly in this direction. A larger number of members in the Community could well complicate EEC decision-making. This problem appears more serious when one considers the gulf in levels of development between the two halves of Europe and the potential for political instability in the East. Also, since new rules allow for workers to migrate freely across borders within the Community, the addition of poorer Eastern cousins could lead to massive immigration to the West.

Political, social and environmental problems also complicate Eastern Europe's economic future. Serious ethnic cleavages threaten political order in some countries. Severe air and water pollution, legacies of the previous order, pose a serious health threat and will require massive sums to correct.

Finally, there is a larger question about what sort of role Eastern Europe will come to play in the world economy. While many East Europeans look upon the highly technological, service-dominated economies of Western Europe with longing and hope, some have suggested that Latin America might provide a more realistic picture of Eastern Europe's future. Many of the firms migrating to the east are associated with technologically backward smoke-stack industries in search of low labor costs as well as looser environmental regulations. In neither its technological level nor its education and training is Eastern Europe well suited to compete in the information age. Moreover, like Latin America of today, Eastern Europe's large-scale borrowing from the West may lay the seeds of a future debt crisis.

The former Soviet Union faces many of these problems and more. In December of 1991, the Soviet state was officially dismantled and replaced by a loose association called the Commonwealth of Independent States, which included eleven of the former Soviet republics. At the same time, Russia and several of the other former republics initiated a bold program of market re-forms similar to that earlier adopted by Poland. While the member states of the Commonwealth have pledged to cooperate on economic issues, the poten-tial for conflict and disagreement is great. Due to the high interdependence among these new states, the price of potential economic warfare would be high. Even more so than most Eastern Europeans, citizens of the former Soviet Union tend to share a cultural distrust toward entrepreneurial activity and the profit principle in general. This, when combined with the pain that will inevita-bly accompany reform and the insecure legitimacy of the new governments, may produce a popular backlash against economic change. Western aid will have even less impact in the former Soviet Union than in Eastern Europe, if only because the size of the need so far exceeds the funds likely to be provided.

Even assuming the political will to carry through serious reforms, the economies of Russia and the other Commonwealth states are likely to get considerably worse before any substantial improvement is seen. Yet, in the long run, prospects are not quite so dismal. Its sheer size, in population and territory, along with its bountiful natural resources and talented pool of scientific expertise suggest that Russia may eventually enter a stage of recov-ery and emerge as an economic force to be reckoned with as it becomes more deeply involved in international commerce over the coming decades.

Japan

Japan enters the last decade of the twentieth century in an enviable position. Japan's large trade surpluses combined with a high national savings rate provide it with enormous financial clout. The nation's large number of scientists and engineers are pushing Japan toward global technological leadership. Japan is situated in East Asia, the world's most economically dynamic region. Its multinational firms are rapidly integrating the fast-growing economies of other states in the region under Japanese hegemony. Japan's workforce is disciplined, hard-working, and well-educated while Japanese management has often proven itself flexible and innovative. A cooperative relationship ties together government and business in mutually beneficial arrangements. A stable political system along with a skilled and powerful bureaucracy ensure continuity, consistency, and purpose in government policy. Taken together, these elements of the Japanese economic model suggest a potent formula for international competitiveness.

Yet Japan too faces challenges. Some of these, such as the country's high level of dependence upon foreign sources of raw materials, are of long standing. Most, however, derive from more recent changes in Japan's domestic and international position. Its very success, along with the uniqueness of its political and economic systems, has generated charges that Japan does not play fair in international competition. Should strains between Japan and its economic partners continue to grow, Japanese firms could face increasingly severe restrictions on their business activities abroad. Japan must also anticipate growing competition from other East Asian countries, particularly as Japanese wage rates continue to rise. Domestically, Japan's population is aging, raising the prospect of labor shortages combined with a declining savings rate (as retirees draw upon their savings to finance consumption) in the years ahead. As Japan's economy matures, consumers may increasingly rebel against protectionist and collusive practices that drive up prices. Demands for social welfare spending have also increased while the younger generation is less willing than their parents to sacrifice family and leisure time for long hours at the office.

Some of these developments may actually help to soothe Japan's troubled relations with other advanced industrial countries. Continuing social, political and economic changes at home have already served to slow Japan's once-spectacular growth rate while its trade surpluses have likewise begun to narrow. Indeed, Japan is becoming less unique as its political and economic systems move in more liberal and internationalist directions. None of this is meant to suggest, however, that Japan will be anything less than a formidable economic competitor in the coming years. History teaches us that the Japanese system is remarkably adaptable, capable of absorbing lessons from Japan's own experiences, as well as those of others, and turning adversity to the country's own advantage.

The Third World

Some analysts argue that the wave of market-oriented reforms currently sweeping the Third World will place Southern countries on the path toward sustained economic growth. The East Asian NICs are often cited as beacons of the kind of future that could await other nations that follow their example. Yet, these conclusions are not universally shared. Some argue that the successes of the NICs will be difficult to duplicate and that fundamental trends point toward the increasing marginalization of much of the Third World in the decades ahead.

Since World War II, the comparative advantage of most Third World countries has rested upon one of three sets of resources: strategic location, critical raw materials, and cheap labor. All three may well become less central to the functioning of the world economy in the years ahead.[3] A variety of Third World countries benefitted from their perceived military and political importance to one or both superpowers during the Cold War. The United States and the Soviet Union carried their rivalry to the Third World by spreading vast sums of economic and military aid among scores of strategically vital allies. In some cases, these countries were compensated for their willingness to host U.S. or Soviet military bases. In others, the superpowers sought to bolster the allegiance or political stability of countries that sat astride strategic shipping lanes or provided militarily critical resources. Some countries received favor because they were located along the front lines of the U.S.–Soviet rivalry or due to their symbolic value as exemplars of capitalism or socialism.

As the U.S.–Soviet rivalry fades, so will the strategic and political significance of previously favored clients. Foreign aid is likely to decline and will be reallocated according to economic rather than political criteria. Spending for overseas bases will also fall.

Countries that depend upon the bulk export of a few varieties of raw materials will also suffer. In the past, the principal markets for such resources lay in the North. Yet, as Northern economies become less dependent upon manufacturing and more heavily oriented toward services and the production and exchange of information, the demand for imported raw materials will fail to keep pace with overall economic growth. This trend is, in fact, already well established. Today, for instance, Japan uses 60 percent fewer raw materials to produce each unit of economic output than it did in 1973. Another important constraint on the export of Third World resources is the increasing tendency for Northern countries to devise synthetic substitutes for previously imported raw materials. Examples include artificial sweeteners and synthetic rubber.

Some types of industries will continue to shift production to the Third World in search of lower labor costs. But the most dynamic high-technology sectors are likely to remain in the North. For such industries, labor constitutes an increasingly small proportion of total costs. Far more important is access

---

[3]This discussion rests upon Alvin Toffler, "Toffler's Next Shock," *World Monitor*, November, 1990, 34–38, 41–42, 44.

to capital, new knowledge, and a highly skilled work force. Factory managers must have direct and regular contact with Northern based designers and engineers in order to carry out constant modifications in the production process as well as the end product. Economic processes are also increasingly tied to communications networks and technological infrastructures that are lacking in the South.

None of this means that Third World development is at a dead end. It does suggest, however, that Third World countries must forge different paths to development than in the past. It is tempting, under contemporary circumstances, to seek new orthodoxies or universal prescriptions to replace the old. Some point to the export-led strategy pursued by the East Asian NICs as a model for the remainder of the Third World. Such advice must be subjected to careful scrutiny. The development community has, in the past, often been given to faddishness. Witness the fifties, when the now-discredited strategy of ISI was widely hailed as the cure to Third World underdevelopment.

While some countries may well benefit by borrowing selectively from the experiences of the East Asian NICs, the capacity of most to do so is doubtful. There is, in fact, considerable controversy over just which factors are responsible for the success of countries such as South Korea and Taiwan.[4] Moreover, the development strategies devised by these nations grew out of their distinctive political, economic, and cultural institutions. It remains to be seen whether similar strategies can be successfully transplanted to the different institutional soil of other Third World countries. Finally, if a handful of East Asian NICs succeeded in targeting certain vulnerable Northern industries, there is no assurance that dozens of countries could simultaneously accomplish the same feat, particularly if each aims at much the same markets.

Nevertheless, some lessons can be drawn from the experiences of countries such as South Korea and Taiwan. While each of the Asian NICs began their route toward industrialization by developing or attracting low-wage industries, none was content to remain trapped in this particular niche of the world economy. Each sought to upgrade the skills, educational level, and discipline of its work force while also pushing the economy toward higher levels of technological sophistication and autonomy. This allowed these countries to shift upward into more lucrative and dynamic industries, much as Japan had done in earlier decades. This suggests that the surest route to development lies less through cheap labor than through productivity increases that rely upon the application of the new knowledge and the capital accumulated during previous phases of growth.

Unfortunately, these lessons are principally relevant to the already better-off Third World countries. Such a strategy is beyond the realistic means of the poorer Third World countries. The great majority of people in these

---

[4]For summary of the controversy, see Stephan Haggard, "The Newly Industrializing Countries in the International System," *World Politics*, January, 1986.

countries continue to make their living off the land. In such societies, a premature emphasis on modern industry benefits the few at the expense of the many. Scarce resources have often been directed toward showcase industrial projects that end up as white elephants, failing due to poor infrastructural support, inadequate skills and managerial inexperience, or an inability to afford the spare parts and imported energy needed to sustain the project.

The problems of the poorest countries are so serious that quick solutions are unlikely and advice must be offered with a large dose of humility. Nevertheless, it seems clear that the first task for such societies must be to develop a modernized, diversified, and sustainable agricultural sector. There are several keys to successful agrarian development: avoid over concentration of land ownership, allow markets to set realistic prices that provide incentives to producers, make credit and technical information available to small farmers, and encourage environmentally sound and sustainable agricultural methods. As efficiency gains raise rural incomes, it is possible to develop small-scale local industries aimed at providing the tools and implements needed by farmers, as well as a growing supply of consumer goods.

These tasks are, of course, easier said than done. Many Third World countries face harsh climates, unfavorable geography, burgeoning populations, political instability, widespread illiteracy, gross economic and social inequalities, and foreign interference. Though progress is possible, no tidy solutions to these problems are available. What seems clear about the future is that the diversification of the Third World will continue, with some countries experiencing healthy growth and development while others, perhaps the majority, struggle to keep up.

Conclusions

■ The basic themes of this book have revolved around the struggle for power and wealth among nations. Two parallel, yet interacting, structures in the international system shape the pursuit of these goals. Fundamentally, nations seek power as a guarantee of survival in a competitive and anarchic state system characterized by territoriality, legal sovereignty, and self-help. Since there exists no higher authority capable of maintaining order in the international system, states are left to their own devices in seeking ways of promoting their own security. Nations do so primarily through the accumulation of military might, yet a country's military potential rests upon the size and technological sophistication of its economy. The combination of these military and economic resources determines a nation's power, or ability to influence others.

The competitive aspects of the international system largely derive from the fact that power is always relative. More power for one state means less for others. The relative nature of power thus ensures a degree of rivalry. This tendency manifests itself most clearly in arms racing and war, but it also takes the form of economic conflict since political leaders must be concerned that relative economic gains by competing states could one day be translated into greater military might.

Alongside this competitive state system, however, exists the global marketplace, made possible by growing economic interdependence. In this realm, states, as well as firms and individuals, seek wealth for its own sake. States can bring about a higher standard of living for their citizens by encouraging the growth of trade and investment with other countries. While the struggle for relative power engenders conflict, the pursuit of wealth through economic interdependence more often gives rise to cooperation because all can gain simultaneously.

It is the relationship between politics and markets that informs the study of international political economy and gives rise to complex patterns of competition and cooperation among states in the world economy. While much may change in the years ahead, the struggle for both power and wealth is likely to remain a persistent feature of the political and economic relations among states.

GLOSSARY

Absolute Advantage   A situation in international trade where one country is able to produce a good or set of goods at a lower cost than some other country or set of countries. *See also* Comparative Advantage.

Agency for International Development (AID)   A bureaucratic arm of the U.S. State Department charged with dispensing and administering bilateral foreign aid funds.

Andean Pact   An accord signed by five Latin American countries in 1970 in which each pledged to impose common regulations of direct foreign investment. This represented an attempt to increase host-country bargaining power vis-à-vis multinational corporations by limiting the ability of the latter to play small countries off against one another.

Asymmetrical Interdependence   A form of mutual dependence between two parties in which one partner is more dependent upon the relationship than the other. The less dependent party holds potential leverage over the more dependent party.

Autarchy   An economic policy designed to promote an extreme version of economic self-sufficiency. This leads to closing off domestic markets from external trade as well as severely restricting exports. Such a policy frequently is designed to defend the nation against political and ideological imports that accompany trade along with organization of the economy for war.

Baker Plan   Announced in 1985, this American initiative attempted to encourage renewed bank lending to Third World debtors in hopes that these countries could then grow their way out of the debt crisis. Although its immediate objectives were not realized, the Baker Plan represented the first partial step away from the previous reliance on Third World austerity as a solution to the debt problem.

Balance of Payments   An accounting system designed to measure all transactions a nation has with the rest of the world over some period of time. *See also* Current Account; Capital Account.

Basic Needs   A "bottom-up" approach to Third World development designed to enhance the living conditions and earning potential of the poorest segments of Southern societies. This developmental model was popular among aid agencies during the seventies but lost favor in the eighties.

Bilateral Assistance   Foreign economic assistance administered directly by donor country governments.

Brady Plan   Announced in the spring of 1989, the Brady Plan was an American initiative designed to alleviate the problem of Third World debt. The significance of the Brady Plan is that it signaled, for the first time, official Northern recognition that debt reduction should play a role in the management of the debt crisis. The plan provided incentives for Northern banks to forgive a portion of the debt owed them by certain Southern countries.

Bretton Woods   An agreement reached in 1944 at Bretton Woods, New Hampshire, that led to the creation of the postwar international economic order directed by the United States. Centered on the dollar, fixed exchange rates, and the International Monetary Fund, this system ended in 1971.

Capital Account   An item in the balance of payments that measures the investment of resources abroad and in the home country by foreigners. *See also* Direct Foreign Investment; Portfolio Investment.

Central Bank   The government-owned and run bank designed to manage the money supply of the nation. Examples include the Federal Reserve in the United States and the Bundesbank in Germany. In a financial crisis, the central bank provides funds to the system when other lenders (usually private banks) have stopped making loans.

Collective Goods   Goods that meet two strict requirements: consumption by any one person or nation does not reduce the supply of the good and no one can be excluded from consumption. An important issue in the theory of hegemony is the nature and extent to which hegemons provide collective goods to the international system.

Colonial Trade System   A set of trading relationships typical of the colonial era. Colonized countries exchanged raw materials and agricultural commodities for manufactured goods produced by the imperial country. In the postcolonial period, most Third World countries have sought to alter this division of labor between North and South by developing their own industrial capacities.

Command Economy   A system of political economy in most communist states in which decisions about what to produce and about prices for goods are made by central political authorities.

Common Agricultural Policy (CAP)   An important form of protectionism and income support for farmers in the European Community. Arranged in the 1950s and 1960s, CAP provides for funds to maintain high prices for farm products and for tariffs to protect these prices from external competition. *See also* European Community.

Commonwealth of Independent States (CIS)   The successor political organization to the Soviet Union, organized late in 1991. The character, composition, and durability of this organization remains unclear.

Comparative Advantage   A strict definition refers to a situation in which one country may be unable to produce different types of goods more efficiently than another, but it nonetheless produces some goods better than others. This comparative advantage justifies a policy of free trade on economic grounds. A looser usage of the term refers to a country possessing an advantage in producing some goods and a disadvantage in others.

Competitiveness   The capacity of a nation to generate real growth in income for most persons in the country even when its economy is open to trade with the rest of the world.

Complex Interdependence   A theoretical model of international relations that contrasts with traditional models of realism. Complex interdependence posits a world where economic issues are not less important than security issues, where linkages among nations reduce government control over foreign affairs, and where military power is essentially unimportant.

Convertibility   An arrangement in which a government permits the free exchange of its currency for that of other nations. *See also* Exchange Rates.

Cooperation   A situation in which two or more nations bargain over modifying their behavior and/or preferences in order to receive some reciprocal act from each other. The aim of these complementary concessions is coordination of their actions in order to gain some benefit they cannot have alone.

Creditor Nation   This is a measurement of a nation's net foreign position which indicates that it holds more assets abroad than foreigners hold of its assets. *See also* Debtor Nation.

Current Account   This is a summary item in the balance of payments that measures the net of exports and imports of merchandise and services, investment income and payments, and government transactions. *See also* Balance of Payments.

Debt-for-Equity Swaps   This term refers to a set of complex schemes for converting privately held bank debt into equity investments in the Third World. These deals became popular in the late 1980s at a time when Northern banks sought to reduce their exposure to increasingly shaky Third World loans.

Debtor Nation This is a measurement of a nation's net foreign position that indicates that it holds less assets abroad than foreigners hold of its assets. *See also* Creditor Nation.

Debt Service The proportion of export earnings accounted for by the repayment of principal and interest on a nation's foreign debt.

Dependency A theory of development designed to explain the gap between living standards in the North and the South. Beginning with colonialism, Southern development has been constrained by the Third World's dependent or peripheral role in the international economy. North-South economic ties are marked by Northern exploitation of the South. Genuine, self-sustained economic development will require changes in the relationship of Southern countries to the international economic order.

Direct Foreign Investment An investment in a nation by foreigners in which real assets are purchased. These include real estate or plant and equipment assets and involve some effort to manage. *See also* Portfolio Investment.

Dirty Float A system of floating exchange rates in which governments occasionally intervene to prevent unwanted swings in the price of their currency. *See also* Exchange Rates.

Discount Rate The interest rate charged by a nation's central bank to its member banks when they borrow money. The discount rate is a major instrument used by the central bank in controlling interest rates for the economy as a whole and for influencing growth in the money supply. *See also* Central Bank.

Economic and Monetary Union (EMU) A term that refers to the elimination of all barriers to trade in the European Community by the end of 1992 and the development of a single currency later in the decade.

Elasticity A technique for being more precise in stating the relationship between a change in price and resulting changes in demand or supply. When percentage changes in the quantity of demand or supply are greater than percentage changes in price, we speak of an elastic demand (or supply) of a product. When percent changes in demand are less than percent changes in price, this is a case of inelastic demand. For purists, this can be seen in the slope of the demand (or supply) curve.

Eurocurrency (Eurodollar) A development in the 1950s and 1960s in which dollars were deposited in European banks and came to be bought, sold, and borrowed. In the 1970s and 1980s, this expanded to include other currencies.

European Currency Unit (ECU) A weighted average of currencies in the Exchange Rate Mechanism of the European Community used as a benchmark to fix exchange rates among these nations.

European (Economic) Community (EC, EEC) Officially begun in 1958, the European Economic Community established a set of stages for the elimination of tariffs and other barriers to trade. Originally composed of six nations, by 1986 the EEC expanded to twelve members and in 1991 agreed to add six additional members. In 1986, the nations of the EEC committed themselves to a single market by 1992 and to the political arrangements needed to achieve this result. After this decision, the EEC became the known as the European Community. *See also* Common Agricultural Policy; European Currency Unit; Economic and Monetary Union; European Monetary System; Exchange Rate Mechanism.

European Monetary System (EMS) A monetary arrangement created after the breakdown of the Bretton Woods system and designed to maintain a fixed exchange-rate system among some of the countries in the European Community. *See also* European Currency Unit; Exchange Rate Mechanism.

Exchange Rate Mechanism (ERM) The specific means by which a system of fixed exchange rates is maintained in the European Monetary System. Exchange rates are tied to the European Currency Unit (with small room for fluctuation). Governments act to peg interest rates to those in Germany and intervene in foreign exchange markets to maintain the fixed value of their currency. *See also* European Currency Unit; European Monetary System.

Exchange Rates   The price at which one currency can be exchanged for another. The system of exchange can be fixed, with governments acting to keep exchange rates within a certain agreed-on band, or floating (also known as flexible), in which demand and supply in a free market for currencies determine the price or rate of exchange. *See also* Dirty Float.

Export-Led Industrialization (ELI)   Pursued most successfully by a group of East Asian newly industrializing countries, a strategy of Export-Led Industrialization focuses on the production of manufactured goods for export to Northern markets.

Fiscal Policy   This refers to a government's policies on taxing and spending, in particular as these affect the level of economic activity.

Free Trade   A particular international economic system in which barriers to trade have been eliminated. In practice, free trade exists only to a degree since some restrictions on trade across nations have always been present.

Free Trade Agreement   A system of economic cooperation among nations in which tariffs, quotas, and other barriers to trade are removed. Typically, this arrangement does not extend to establishing a common external tariff nor to the development of elaborate institutions for cooperation.

General Agreement on Tariffs and Trade (GATT)   A system of treaties among more than 100 nations establishing rules for the conduct of international trade. Most rules relate to tariffs and quotas, though some arrangements have been made regarding other nontariff barriers. The rules are the result of a series of negotiating sessions that began in the 1940s. *See also* Free Trade; Nontariff Barrier.

Gold Standard   An international monetary system in which gold served as the medium for defining exchange rates. International payments were thereby made in terms of gold and sometimes actually in gold. This system existed from the 1870s to 1914 and briefly after World War I.

Gross Domestic Product/Gross National Product (GDP/GNP)   The total of all goods and services produced by a country over some period of time is GDP. Gross National Product is derived by adding the income of nationals from foreign activity to GDP and subtracting income of foreigners from activity in the country measured.

Hegemony   An international system in which one dominant state takes on the role of organizing and managing the world economic system. This means supplying capital, defining the rules for international trade, promoting political and military security, and having its money operate as a key currency.

Import Substitution Industrialization (ISI)   An inward-directed strategy of industrialization focused on the production of manufactured goods intended for sale in the domestic market. Typically, an ISI strategy provides trade protection or other forms of state assistance to import-substituting firms and industries.

Interdependence   A situation in world affairs in which the linkages among nations makes their fate on certain issues mutually dependent. *See also* Asymmetrical Interdependence.

Interest Rates   Technically, this is the price of borrowing money. There are a vast array of interest rates depending on who is borrowing and the length of time required to pay the money back. *See also* Discount Rate; Prime Rate.

International Monetary Fund (IMF)   An international financial institution funded and governed by member states. Provides financing to countries experiencing balance-of-payments shortfalls. Has played a key role in the Third World debt crisis by conditioning financial assistance upon debtor country policy reforms.

Key Currency   Historically, this is the currency of the international hegemon that comes to be widely accepted as payment for international transactions. This acceptability depends on confidence in the stability of the value of the currency and the reputation for acceptability in payment for goods or debts. In the nineteenth century the British pound and in the mid-twentieth century the U.S. dollar served as key currencies.

Mercantilism   A policy designed to maximize exports while minimizing imports so as to generate the largest possible trade surplus. This was standard practice for nations prior to the mid-nineteenth century.

Ministry of International Trade and Industry (MITI)   This is the unit of the Japanese government most responsible for planning and managing the Japanese economy. Although its powers have diminished since the 1950s, MITI continues to play an important role in encouraging risk-taking and product development by private enterprises in Japan.

Modernization   A theory of development designed to explain the gap between living standards in the North and the South. The North's economic prosperity is attributed to its successful transition from traditional to modern forms of social, political and economic life. The economic backwardness of Southern countries is traced to the persistence of traditional social values and institutions. Southern development is thus dependent upon modernizing domestic reforms.

Monetary Policy   Decisions normally made by a nation's central bank concerning interest rates, the growth of the money supply, and exchange rates. *See also* Discount Rate; Open Market Operations.

Multilateral Assistance   Foreign economic assistance which is channeled from donor countries through international organizations, such as the World Bank or United Nations Special Agencies.

Multinational Corporation (MNC)   A business firm which engages in the production of goods or services in more than one country.

New International Economic Order (NIEO)   A package of proposed reforms in the international economic order sponsored by Third World countries during the 1970s. Largely rejected by the North, these proposals were intended to direct greater economic resources toward the South while also providing Third World countries with a greater role in managing the rules and institutions of the world economy.

Nontariff Barriers   Mechanisms, other than tariffs, used by nations to restrict trade, usually by inhibiting or blocking imports. These can include various kinds of regulations, quotas, or requirements attached to trading with a country that operate as an impediment to trade.

Open-Market Operations   An action of a nation's central bank involving the sale or purchase of government securities in the market. The purpose is to drain funds from the economy — by selling securities, the central bank ends up with more money — or pumping funds into the economy — buying securities results in the central bank exchanging securities for money. This is a key instrument for managing the overall level of the money supply. *See also* Central Bank; Monetary Policy.

Organization of Petroleum Exporting Countries (OPEC)   Formed in 1960, OPEC is a cooperative arrangement among many of the world's major oil exporting countries. Its purpose is to facilitate common agreement among member states on matters relating to oil policy, such as production levels and pricing.

Portfolio Investment   An investment in a nation by foreigners in which debt or stock ownership is involved. The result is a claim on resources, but typically no participation in managing the company or assets is involved.

Privatization   A system for transferring control over government-owned enterprises to private hands. The focus of this effort is in post-Communist states of the Commonwealth of Independent States and Eastern Europe. Some successful transfers of government corporations to private hands took place in Great Britain during the 1980s.

Product Cycle   A term defining a set of stages in the development, production, and sales of a product in which the stages are associated with the comparative advantage of different countries. The creation and development of a product usually take place in advanced industrial countries with large scientific complexes, but once the method of production has matured, manufacture can take place where costs are lowest.

Productivity   Broadly, this is the quantity of output of a good or service measured by the amount of input. For example, the amount of a good one worker can produce in a period of time is a measure of productivity.

Protectionism   A policy of excluding the import of goods and/or services into a nation. Like free trade, this is always a matter of degree since total exclusion is exceedingly rare. *See also* Free Trade.

Regime   A relationship among nations in which there is a convergence of beliefs, expectations, norms, and procedures for making decisions relating to a particular problem or issue in international affairs. A regime is important to the extent that it affects the actions and choices of nations associated with the regime.

Strategic Trade   An international trade policy in which various forms of governmental aid are directed at a specific industry or industries so as to boost their competitive advantages in global markets. The industries selected for targeting typically have substantial positive consequences for the economy or have a cost or market structure that promotes a small number of producers.

Structural Adjustment   In contrast with traditional project loans, which finance particular development investments or activities, the World Bank began shifting part of its lending to structural-adjustment financing in the 1980s. Typically, this newer type of financing provides balance-of-payment support to countries which have committed themselves to Bank-sponsored policy reforms.

Syndication   An arrangement whereby a collection of banks, usually organized by one or a few lead institutions, divide responsibility for financing a major loan package. Syndication was often used in lending to Third World countries during the 1970s. Syndication agreements typically stipulate that agreement among the participating banks is required before any renegotiation of debt arrangements can be implemented.

Tied Aid   A condition attached to foreign economic assistance which requires that the aid extended to a recipient country be spent on goods and/or services produced by firms residing in the donor country.

Transfer Pricing   An accounting practice by which multinational corporations adjust prices on intrafirm trade in order to shift profits from subsidiaries located in high-tax countries to those residing in low-tax countries or to escape restrictions of the repatriation of profits imposed by host-country governments.

World Bank   This term actually refers to a group of related international financial institutions, including the International Bank for Reconstruction and Development (IBRD), the International Development Agency (IDA), and the International Finance Corporation (IFC). Funded largely by capital infusions from Northern governments, these agencies provide financing for Third World development projects or programs.

INDEX